Seed Sown

Notes, Themes and Reflections on the
Sunday Lectionary Readings
Cycles A, B, and C

Seed Sown

Notes, Themes and Reflections on the
Sunday Lectionary Readings
Cycles A, B, and C

Designed for Homilists, Preachers and Study/Sharing Groups

by Jay Cormier

Sheed & Ward

Sheed & Ward™ is a service of The National Catholic Reporter Publishing Company.

ISBN: 1-55612-801-0

Published by: Sheed & Ward
                115 E. Armour Blvd.
                P.O. Box 419492
                Kansas City, MO 64141-6492

To order, call: (800) 333-7373

Clip art in this book is taken from the following Sheed & Ward books:

> *Eye Contact with God Through Pictures,* from the Ade Bethune Collection; pp. 9, 53, 57, 116, 172, 175.
> *Sunday Doorposts I,* Timothy R. Botts; pp. 52, 82.
> *Liturgical Art,* Meinrad Craighead; pp. 16, 40, 43, 62, 99, 104, 117, 120, 122, 158, 168, 170, 193, 198, 201.
> *Sacred Art of Lavrans Nielsen;* pp. 32, 73, 76, 79, 139, 152, 185, 209.
> *Religious Clip Art Book,* Claudia Ortega; pp. 28, 37, 67, 136, 146, 189.

Cover design by Gloria Ortiz.

Jesus spoke to the crowd at length in parables, saying:

"A sower went out to sow.
And as he sowed, some seed fell on the path,
    and the birds came and ate it up.
Some fell on rocky ground,
    where it had little soil.
Some seed fell among thorns,
    and the thorns grew up and choked it.
But some seed fell on rich soil,
    and produced fruit, a hundred or sixty or thirtyfold.

"Hear then the parable of the sower:
The seed sown on the path
    are those who hear the word of the kingdom
        without understanding it,
    and the evil one comes and steals away what was sown.
The seed sown on the rocky ground
    are those who hear the word
        and receive it at once with joy.
    But they have no root and last only for a time.
    When some tribulation or persecution comes
        because of the word,
    they immediately fall away.
The seed sown among the thorns
    are those who hear the word,
    but then worldly anxiety and the lure of riches
        choke the word and it bears no fruit.
But the seed sown on rich soil
    are those who hear the word and understand it,
    who indeed bear fruit
        and yield a hundred or sixty or thirtyfold."

–Matthew 13: 3-5, 7-8, 18-23

The Year of Matthew is dedicated
to the memory of
Father Cyril Schweinberg, C.P.

The Year of Mark is dedicated to
Father Robert Biron

The Year of Luke is dedicated to
Bishop Robert Mulvee

Contents

To the Sower

Welcome to *Seed Sown*.

Seed Sown has been designed to serve as a starting point – *seeds* – for you who have been entrusted with the ministry of preaching and homiletics and who gather together to share and study the Word of God as read and celebrated in the Sunday Scriptures.

The format of the book is simple. Each Sunday section begins with a short commentary on the day's Gospel reading. These notes are designed to set the geographic, cultural and spiritual context for the reading. These notes – briefer and less detailed – focus primarily on the relationship of the First Testament reading and Epistle to the assigned Gospel.

The Gospel notes are followed by a series of themes suggested by the Sunday readings that might serve as starting points for developing homilies, sermons and reflections.

Each section concludes with a series of questions designed to help you and your discussion group discover the connections between your live experiences and the reality of the Christ event in the Gospel. Homilists may find it helpful to reflect on these questions as they think through the preaching process; groups of homilists and preachers might use these questions and notes as a basis for forming homily study groups; and Scripture study and sharing groups could use these materials to explore the Sunday readings in the context of the entire history of salvation, the Church's liturgical cycle and our own faith experience.

Finally, this book comes with a "warning label" of sorts:

> *Seed Sown* is the result of one person's years of writing, researching and preaching the Lectionary cycle. The material here is in no way represented as the last word or the definitive interpretation into the meanings and themes of the Sunday Scriptures. The Word of God is rich in meaning and inspiration; it is the author's hope that this book will help you open the Gospels and readings to discover new and deeper insights into God's presence among us.

And remember: *Seed Sown* is a but a handful of seeds. *You* are the sower.

May the seeds of faith you sow take root and flourish in the hearts of your community!

Lectionary Cycle A
The Year of Matthew

The Proper of the Seasons – Cycle A

Readings: *Matthew 24: 37-44*
Isaiah 2: 1-5
Romans 13: 11-14

Today's Advent **Gospel** is a "wake up" call:

- Noah's flood and the thief are signs that the Lord will return for those who have been faithfully waiting for his return.

- Although Matthew is writing his Gospel for a Christian community who expected Christ's return during their lifetimes, this Gospel can also be read as Jesus teaching us about the reality of our own deaths and being ready at every moment we are given to meet the Lord.

- Jesus calls his Church and Christians of every place and time to be conscientious in the call to be prophets, confronting a "sleeping" world with the risks of losing its soul.

Isaiah is the prophet of the Advent season who proclaims most eloquently and poetically the coming of the "Servant of God," "Emmanuel," who will re-create Israel.

Isaiah preaches to the Jews living in the southern kingdom of Judah eight centuries before Christ. The northern kingdom of Israel had been destroyed by the Assyrians (722 B.C.); the people of Judah are terrified that the same fate will befall them. But Isaiah preaches that God will not abandon them, that a new era of peace, justice and unity – the era of the Messiah – will dawn if only the Israelites "climb the Lord's mountain" and "walk in the light of the Lord." **(first reading)**

Paul's echoes the Advent call to watchfulness (**second reading**). Paul warns us (in his straightforward and intense style) that our pursuit of the "good life" can sidetrack us from the urgent task before us: to prepare for the "new" day of the Lord. Our lives should reflect the light of the Risen One, rather than the dark emptiness of a consumer-oriented lifestyle.

Themes:

Advent: a call to watchfulness.

Advent is a call to watchfulness for the coming of the Lord – the reality of our passing from this life to the life of God. Our time is indeed limited; the moments we are given in this experience of life are precious and few. But God gives us this time that we might come to discover him and know him in the love of others and the goodness of this world as we anticipate the next. Advent is not a season for gloom and despair; it is an invitation to hope, to embrace the light of Christ, to be at peace with one another, to live in joyful expectation of the life of the world to come.

Advent: the first light of Christ.

All three readings contrast the darkness of a world without God with the light of the Lord: "let us walk in the light of the Lord" (Isaiah 2: 5); "the night is far spent, the day draws near" and "put on the armor of light" (Romans 13: 12); "the day your Lord is coming" (Matthew 24: 42).

Light is central to our Christmas observance. The celebration of Christmas, itself, was a "Christianizing" of the ancient Roman feast of *Sol Invinctus* – the Birthday of the New Sun. Sometime in the third century after Christ, the Church adopted the Birthday of the **Sun** to celebrate the Birthday of Jesus, the **Son** of God.

Our Christmas lights illuminate the darkest days of the year: the sun sets in the late afternoon and rises later in the morning; the days of winter are shorter and colder. We already yearn for the warmth of the spring that we know will come. The lights of our Christmas trees, window candles and Yule logs are not only pretty decorations – the lights of Christmas proclaim the dawning of the Christ, the Light of the Father, who illuminates the darkness of injustice and alienation.

Advent: waiting for the Lord.

Life is a constant Advent experience: the world is not as just, not as loving, not as whole as we know it can and should be; we are constantly waiting to become, to discover, to understand, to change, to complete, to fulfill. Hope, struggle, fear, expectation and fulfillment are all part of life's Advent. But the coming of Christ and his presence among us – as *one* of us – give us reason to live in hope: that light will shatter the darkness, that we can be liberated from our fears and prejudices, that we are never alone or abandoned by our merciful Father in heaven. We are not a Christmas people but an *Advent* people living our lives in patient faith and joyful hope for the Lord's coming in our lifetimes.

For reflection:

- How can the busy days ahead of Christmas shopping, decorating, cooking and cleaning, Christmas-card addressing and mailing help you understand the faith dimensions of Advent?

- What stories, remembrances and experiences do you have of *light?* Have you ever experienced a prolonged period of darkness (such as being trapped in an elevator or being without electrical power for a long time) that made you especially grateful for light?

- Do you have any intense experience of *waiting*, of *watching?* What did it teach you about the preciousness of life?

- How have you witnessed that sharp contrast between the darkness of ignorance and the light of knowledge? The darkness of hate and the light of understanding? The darkness of despair and the light of community?

- How is Christmas an "adult" feast?

Readings:

Matthew 3: 1-12
Isaiah 11: 1-10
Romans 15: 4-9

In today's **Gospel**, John the Baptizer makes his appearance this Advent season, preaching a baptism of repentance and conversion of life.

Matthew's details about John's appearance is intended to recall the austere dress of the great prophet Elijah (2 Kings 1: 8). The Jews believed that Elijah would return from heaven to announce the long-awaited restoration of Israel as God's kingdom. For Matthew, this expectation is fulfilled in John the Baptizer. Through the figure of the Baptizer, the evangelist makes the "Old" Testament touch the "New."

Matthew reports that John strikes a responsive chord in the people who have come from throughout the region to hear him at the River Jordan. He has strong words for the Pharisees and Sadducees who step up for his baptism but have no intention of embracing the spirit of conversion and renewal to make their own lives ready for the Messiah who comes.

In proclaiming the Messiah's "baptism in the Holy Spirit and fire," John employs the image of a "winnowing-fan." A winnowing-fan is a flat, wooden, shovel-like tool used to toss grain into the air. The heavier grain fell to the ground while the chaff was blown away. In the same way, John says, the Messiah will come to gather the "remnant" of Israel and destroy the Godless.

Isaiah continues to preach to the people of devastated Judah during the Assyrian crisis (today's **first reading**). God will raise up a new David to lead his people, Isaiah proclaims; but this "shoot from Jesse's stump" will not be the great warrior-king that Israel longs for. In Isaiah's vision, the Messiah, instead, will be "armed" with wisdom and understanding. The Messiah comes not to rebuild the nation but to re-create individual hearts and minds. Rather than bring political and imperial power to Israel, Isaiah's Messiah will bring a new era of peace and justice not just to Israel but to all of the world.

In the **second reading**, from his letter to the Church at Rome, the apostle Paul writes that the era of the Messiah's peace, prophesied by Isaiah, has dawned upon the world. We have been given a new spirit that should enable us to break down the barriers that separate us from one another. If we are faithful to our call as Christians, we will work ceaselessly to build "perfect harmony" among all God's people.

Themes:

Our call to be 'prophets' of the Lord.

Each one of us is called to be a prophet of Christ. The word *prophet* comes from the Greek word meaning "one who proclaims." Not all prophets wear camel skins and eat locusts – there are prophets among us right now who proclaim in their ministries, in their compassion and their kindness, in their courageous commitment to what is right, that Jesus the Messiah has come.

To live our baptisms.

Our baptisms (which, for some of us, took place *so* long ago!) should be a living, thriving reality in our lives. John excoriates those who come to the Jordan to be baptized but have no intention of re-creating their lives in the life of God. In the same way, our baptisms were more than just a "naming ceremony," more than just a symbolic ritual of water poured over our heads. In baptism, we were given new eyes, new minds and new hearts to approach the world. We *live* our baptism as we grow in the "knowledge of the Lord" (Isaiah 11: 9) and as living "wheat" rather than lifeless straw (Matthew 3: 12).

Preparing for Christmas: creating the 'peaceable kingdom.'

On Christmas we will sing the song of the angels over Bethlehem: "Glory to God in the highest. Peace on earth to those on whom his favor rests." But we have a great deal of difficulty in being at peace with one another: progressive against traditionalist, liberal against conservative, social activist against contemplative, rich against poor, labor against management, black against white, Jew against Gentile. Advent is the season for realizing Isaiah's vision of the "peaceable kingdom," for setting the stage for the angels' song: for seeking common ground, for recognizing the humanity we all share and building upon our common interests, values and dreams. The Messiah Jesus comes to reveal to the world that God is Father of all of us, a revelation that should make the distinctions and labels we create to separate one person from another disappear.

For reflection:

- Who are the "prophets" among us now who proclaim the Messiah in our community and our world today?
- What stories in this week's news reflect the sin of intolerance, racism, elitism and discrimination? In what ways has the light of Christ appeared in these situations – or might the light of Christ be brought to illuminate such darkness – to break down the walls of hate existing here?
- Have you seen or witnessed in your own experience the fulfillment of Isaiah's prophecy: the wolf being the guest of the lamb, the leopard resting with the kid, the calf and young lion browsing together, all under the "guidance" of the "child"?

Readings: *Matthew 11: 2-11, Isaiah 35: 1-6, 10, James 5: 7-10*

The picture of John the Baptizer in today's **Gospel** is quite different from last Sunday's thundering, charismatic figure preaching to the crowds along the Jordan. John has been thrown into prison by Herod for publicly denouncing the king's incestuous marriage to Herodias. Left to waste away in prison, John knew that his end was near.

This must have been an anxious time of doubt and despair for John – he had staked his life on proclaiming the coming of the Messiah, and his witness will soon cost him his life. Like any human being, John had to wonder if he had been deluding himself. John and the people of Judaism had been expecting a much different kind of Messiah than the gentle, humble worker of wonders from Nazareth. And so, John sends friends to ask Jesus if he is, in fact, the long-awaited Messiah.

Jesus sends the messengers back to John to report all they have seen Jesus do, fulfilling the prophecies of Isaiah and the prophets of old. While praising John for his faithful witness, Jesus tells his followers that great things will come to all who become prophets of the reign of God.

In today's **first reading**, Isaiah prophesies that the Messiah will come as a *healer*. From our New Testament perspective, our first thoughts are of the miraculous works and healings of Jesus; but Isaiah's prophecy speaks of the Messiah as a *reconciler* who heals the divisions among peoples, who restores the justice and peace of God and who brings men and women back to Lord.

The **second reading** today is one of the few Sunday Lectionary appearances of this obscure letter attributed to James, "the brother of the Lord." This parable on patience might assure the "little people" in the community that their long wait for Christmas will soon be rewarded; but for the "big people" in the congregation, the image of the farmer waiting for the return of spring broadens our view of Advent from the festive anticipation of Jesus' birth to the deeper and sobering anticipation of our imminent re-birth in the Resurrection. We must possess the faith and hope of the farmer: Just as the wheat will grow through the snow because of the farmer's hard work, so will the reign of God be realized in our lives.

Themes:

Advent: the season of hope.

In Charles Dickens' timeless tale, *A Christmas Carol*, Bob Cratchit returns from church with his young crippled son, Tiny Tim. Mother Cratchit asks if Tim behaved himself during the service. His father reports:

"Little Tim was as good as gold. And better. Somehow, he gets thoughtful sitting by himself so much, and thinks the strangest thoughts you ever heard. Little Tim told me that he hoped people saw him in the church, because he was a cripple, and it might be pleasant for them to remember upon Christmas Day who it was who made the lame beggars walk and blind men see."

Tiny Tim emulates Isaiah and John the Baptizer in reminding his neighbors that Christ has come, that there is cause for joy and reason for hope. Sometimes our troubles and doubts overwhelm us, we feel abandoned by God, who seems far, far away from us. But Advent/Christmas is the season of hope: The birth of Christ restores our dreams for "blossoming deserts" and new harvests, for renewed relationships with God and with one another.

Advent: a time for healing and reconciliation.

All three readings today begin with lifeless, depressing pictures that are transformed into life-giving and enriching images: from death to life, from barrenness to harvest, from illness to wholeness. The Christ of Christmas comes to heal the divisions among families and friends, to re-create our world in the mercy and justice of the Messiah, to renew our lives in the joy and hope of the God of unimaginably endless love. Christmas is the time when families and friends gather together to celebrate; it is, therefore, the ideal time for healing the divisions among us, for not only renewing old friendships but for healing broken relationships. We are called to bring such reconciliation to our world through the same love and selflessness taught and lived by Jesus.

Advent: the Messiah's humble, unseen coming.

John's question, *Are you the Messiah?*, confronts us with the apparent silence of God in our secular, amoral society. Like John, we seek a Messiah with decisive answers and vindicating power to overcome the hatred, the intolerance, the selfishness that dooms our earth. But like John, we must come to recognize the Messiah in the humble, merciful, liberating person of Jesus, the healer and reconciler. Selfless love, compassion and forgiveness – revealed in even the smallest and most hidden ways – are the surest sign that the reign of God has come.

For reflection:

- Are there "parched deserts" around us that cry out for life?
- Who are the healers of our age – those who, like Christ, bring sight to the blind, breathe life into the dead and give voice to the silent?
- Have you ever faced a hopeless situation in your life that, somehow, was transformed into joyful promise?
- How can some of our Christmas traditions be opportunities for healing and reconciliation?

Readings:
Matthew 1: 18-24
Isaiah 7: 10-14
Romans 1: 1-7

The last week of Advent shifts our focus from the promise of the Messiah to the fulfillment of that promise in the events surrounding Jesus' birth.

Today's **Gospel** is Matthew's version of Jesus' birth at Bethlehem. This is not Luke's familiar story of a child born in a Bethlehem stable, but that of a young, unmarried woman suddenly finding herself pregnant and her very hurt and confused husband wondering what to do. In Gospel times, marriage was agreed upon by the groom and the bride's parents; but the girl continued to live with her family after the wedding until the husband was able to support her in his home or that of his parents. During that interim period, marital intercourse was not permissible.

Yet Mary is found to be with child. Joseph, an observant but compassionate Jew, does not wish to subject Mary to the full fury of Jewish law, so he plans to divorce her "quietly." But in images reminiscent of the First Testament "annunciations" of Isaac and Samuel, an angel appears to Joseph in a dream and reveals that this child is the fulfillment of Isaiah's prophecy. Because of his complete faith and trust in God's promise, Joseph acknowledges the child and names him "Jesus" ("Savior") and becomes, in the eyes of the Law, the legal father of Jesus. Thus, Jesus, through Joseph, is born a descendent of David.

Matthew's point in his infancy narrative is that Jesus is the Emmanuel promised of old – Isaiah's prophecy has finally been fulfilled in Jesus: the "virgin" has given birth to a son, one who is a descendent of David's house (through Joseph). Jesus is truly *Emmanuel* – God is with us.

Ahaz was king of Judah from 735-715 B.C. Politically naive, the headstrong young leader forged an alliance with Assyria against Israel and Syria. The alliance had disastrous consequences for Judah, costing the nation its independence. Isaiah the prophet counsels the foolish king to return to the ways of God which he has abandoned. The prophet challenges Ahaz to ask God for some sign from the Lord that God will once again return and save Judah. Ahaz responds with sarcasm ("I will not tempt the Lord!"). Isaiah then speaks the most famous prophecy regarding the Messiah (**first reading**). Many interpreted this oracle as referring to Hezekiah, Judah's next king, but Matthew and the New Testament writers see Isaiah's words as fulfilled ultimately in Jesus Christ.

Paul's letter to the Romans was written to introduce himself to the Christian community at Rome in anticipation of his journey there – a journey that Paul eventually made, but as a prisoner. Writing from Greece (most probably Corinth), Paul introduces himself to the Roman community as an apostle of "Jesus Christ, descended from David . . . but made Son of God in power according to the spirit of holiness" (**second reading**). Jesus as the perfect fulfillment of the Mosaic covenant will be a major theme throughout Paul's letter to the Romans.

Themes:

God's promise fulfilled.

The Spirit of God is the principal albeit unseen player in the events of Christmas. Matthew's account is not historical but theological: Jesus' birth is the work of the Holy Spirit – God has directly intervened in human history. God's Spirit, who inspired the prophets to preach, who enabled the nation of Israel to enter into the covenant with Yahweh, continues at work in the world in new and creative ways. Jesus Christ is the ultimate and perfect fulfillment of that covenant.

Emmanuel: 'God is with us.'

The "mystery" of the Incarnation is not that God could become one of us – the inexplicable part is *how* and *why* God could love humankind enough to humble himself to take on the human condition. Christ is born – and human history is changed forever, In profound simplicity and stillness, the light of Christ has dawned and the darkness of hatred, intolerance and ignorance is shattered. We have reason to rejoice and to hope, for in our midst dawns *Emmanuel* – "God is with us."

Joseph, the 'just' and 'upright' man.

Joseph is the hero of Matthew's account; the carpenter is a model of forgiveness and compassion. On learning of Mary's unexpected pregnancy, he does not condemn her but plans to divorce her quietly in order to spare her a formal inquiry into her behavior and certain condemnation. He is also a model of faith: His trust in God's providence transcends the letter of the Law, enabling him to welcome Jesus into his life under very difficult circumstances. God entrusts his Messiah to the care of a man who models the compassion and mercy that Emmanuel will proclaim to all of humanity.

For reflection:

- Share stories of *Emmanuel* – stories of "God with us" in the ordinary and the everyday, stories of God's Spirit present and working in our world as it was in the events of the Incarnation.
- How do our Christmas customs and traditions express the mystery of the Incarnation?
- Have you met men and women like Joseph, whose faith and compassion led them to heroic acts of love and kindness?

Readings:

Mass of the Vigil
Matthew 1: 1-25
Isaiah 62: 1-5
Acts 13: 16-17, 22-25

The readings for the Vigil Mass of Christmas celebrate Jesus' birth as the fulfillment of the First Covenant.

For Matthew, the story of Jesus begins with the promise to Abraham – that Jesus is the ultimate and perfect fulfillment of the Law and Prophets; so Matthew begins his **Gospel** with "a family record" of Jesus, tracing the infant's birth from Abraham (highlighting his Jewish identity) and David (his Messiahship).

Matthew's version of Jesus' birth at Bethlehem follows his detailed genealogy. This is not Luke's familiar story of a child born in a Bethlehem stable, but that of a young unmarried woman suddenly finding herself pregnant and her very hurt and confused husband wondering what to do. In Gospel times, marriage was agreed upon by the groom and the bride's parents, but the girl continued to live with her parents after the wedding until the husband was able to support her in his home or that of his parents. During that interim period, marital intercourse was not permissible.

Yet Mary is found to be with child. Joseph, an observant but compassionate Jew, does not wish to subject Mary to the full fury of Jewish law, so he plans to divorce her "quietly." But in images reminiscent of the First Testament "annunciations" of Isaac and Samuel, an angel appears to Joseph in a dream and reveals that this child is the fulfillment of Isaiah's prophecy. Because of his complete faith and trust in God's promise, Joseph acknowledges the child and names him *Jesus* ("Savior") and becomes, in the eyes of the Law, the legal father of Jesus. Thus, Jesus, through Joseph, is born a descendent of David.

Matthew's point in his infancy narrative is that Jesus is the Emmanuel promised of old – Isaiah's prophecy has finally been fulfilled in Jesus: the "virgin" has given birth to a son, one who is a descendent of David's house (through Joseph). Jesus is truly *Emmanuel* – God is with us.

The promise fulfilled is also the theme of Isaiah's insistence that God will fulfill his promises to the exiled Israelites returning home (**first reading**). Like the great love of a generous spouse, God not only forgives his people but entrusts to them the promise of the Messiah.

Paul's sermon to the Jews at Antioch Pisidia in the Acts of the Apostles (**second reading**) is a concise chronicle of the promise of Emmanuel fulfilled.

Mass at Midnight
Luke 2: 1-14
Isaiah 9: 1-6
Titus 2: 11-14

Centuries of hope in God's promise have come to fulfillment: the Messiah is born!

Luke's account of Jesus' birth (**Gospel**) begins by placing the event during the reign of Caesar Augustus. Augustus, who ruled from 27 B.C. – 14 A.D.), was honored as "savior" and "god" in ancient Greek inscriptions. His long reign was hailed as the *pax Augusta* – a period of peace throughout the vast Roman world. Luke very deliberately points out that it is during the rule of Augustus, the savior, god and peace-maker, that Jesus the Christ, the long-awaited Savior and Messiah, the Son of God and Prince of Peace, enters human history.

Throughout his Gospel, Luke shows how it is the poor, the lowly, the outcast and the sinner who immediately hear and embrace the preaching of Jesus. The announcement of the Messiah's birth to shepherds – who were among the most isolated and despised in the Jewish community – is in keeping with Luke's theme that the poor are especially blessed of God.

In his "Book of Emmanuel" (chapters 6-12), the prophet Isaiah describes Emmanuel as the new David, the ideal king who will free his enslaved people (**first reading**). The "day of Midian" refers to Gideon's decisive defeat of the Midianites, a nomadic nation of outlaws who ransacked the Israelites' farms and villages (Judges 6-8).

Paul's letter to his co-worker Titus articulates the heart of the mystery of the Incarnation: the grace of God himself has come to us in the person of Jesus Christ (**second reading**).

Mass at Dawn
Luke 2: 15-20
Isaiah 62: 11-12
Titus 3: 4-7

Typical of Luke's Gospel, it is the shepherds of Bethlehem – among the poorest and most disregarded of Jewish society – who become the first messengers of the **Gospel.**

As Israel rebuilds its city and nation, the prophet Isaiah calls his people to lift their hearts and spirits to behold the saving power of God (**first reading**).

In a letter to his co-worker Titus, Paul writes that our salvation comes as a result of the initiative of our merciful God (**second reading**).

Mass During the Day
John 1: 1-18
Isaiah 52: 7-10
Hebrews 1: 1-6

The **Gospel** for Christmas day is the beautiful Prologue hymn to John's Gospel. With echoes of Genesis 1 ("In the beginning . . . ," "the light shines on in darkness . . ."), the Prologue exalts Christ as the creative Word

of God who comes as the new light to illuminate God's re-creation.

In the original Greek text, the phrase "made his dwelling place among us" is more accurately translated as "pitched his tent or tabernacle." The image evokes the Exodus memory of the tent pitched by Israelites for the ark of the covenant. God sets up the tabernacle of the new covenant in the body of the Child of Bethlehem.

Israel has been brought to ruin by its incompetent, unfaithful rulers. But God himself leads his people back to Zion (site of the Jerusalem temple) from their long exile in Babylon. Again and again, the Lord restores and redeems Israel (**first reading**).

No prophet could imagine the length God would go to save and re-create humankind. But Christ, "the exact reflection of the Father's glory" and "heir of all things through whom he created the universe," comes as the complete and total manifestation of God's love, fulfilling the promises articulated so imperfectly and incompletely by the prophets (**second reading**).

Themes:

Christmas: a celebration for all of humanity.

From the Christmas story in Luke's Gospel, we have a romantic image of shepherds as gentle, peaceful figures. But that manger scene image is a far cry from the reality: The shepherds of Biblical times were tough, earthy characters who fearlessly used their clubs to defend their flocks from wolves and other wild animals. They had even less patience for the pompous scribes and Pharisees who treated them as second and third-class citizens, barring these ill-bred rustics from the synagogue and courts.

And yet it was to shepherds that God first revealed the birth of the Messiah. The shepherds' vision on the Bethlehem hillside proclaims to all people of every place and generation that Christ comes for the sake of all humankind.

Christmas: the beginning of the Christ event.

A favorite story of Martin Buber, the great Jewish philosopher, concerned a rabbi in Jerusalem to whom it was excitedly announced that the Messiah had come. The rabbi calmly looked out of the window, surveyed the scene carefully, and announced that, to him, nothing seemed to have changed, and then calmly returned to his study.

The Messiah *has* come – but what difference does that make in our lives? If the rabbi were to look out his window tonight, he would certainly see many different things: He would see the lights and decorations and illuminated trees and wreaths, he would hear the carolers sing their songs about "joy to the world" and "peace on earth," he would behold the smiles and joy of people extending greetings to one another.

But what would the rabbi see out of his window tomorrow? or next week? or a day in February? or April? or July?

The Messiah *has* come! What happened one Palestinian night when a son was born to a carpenter and his young bride was the beginning of a profound transformation of humanity. But has it made a difference? Has our world become a better place since the Son of God became incarnate here? Has anything changed? The theologian Martin Buber described the difference this way: "Men [and women] become what they are, sons [and daughters] of God, by *becoming* what they are, brothers of their brothers [and sisters of their sisters]."

'The Word made flesh'/'a life for the light of all.'

The miracle of Christmas is God's continuing to reach out to humankind, his continuing to call us to relationship with him despite out obstinacy, selfishness and rejection of him. In Jesus, the extraordinary love of God has taken our "flesh" and "made his dwelling among us." In his "Word made flesh," God touches us at the very core of our beings, perfectly expressing his constant and unchanging love. Christ is born – and human history is changed forever. In profound simplicity and stillness, the light of Christ has dawned and the darkness of hatred, intolerance and ignorance is shattered.

The 'Bethlehems' of our hearts.

In his acclaimed autobiography, *The Seven Story Mountain,* Thomas Merton wrote about his first Christmas as a monk at Gethsemani Abbey in Kentucky:

> "Christ always seeks the straw of the most desolate cribs to make his Bethlehem. In all other Christmases of my life, I had got a lot of presents and a big dinner. This Christmas I was to get no presents, and not much of a dinner: but I would have indeed, Christ, God, the Savior of the world.

> "You who live in the world: let me tell you that there is no comparing these two kinds of Christmas. . . . The emptiness that had opened up within me, that had been prepared during Advent and laid open by my own silence and darkness, now became filled. And suddenly I was in a new world."

The true miracle of Christmas continues to take place in the Bethlehems of our hearts. The trappings of Christmas, for the most part, do not begin to capture the full magnitude of the Christmas event. In the emptiness of our souls, God forgives us, reassures us, exalts us, elates us, loves us. In the coming of Jesus, God's love becomes real, touchable and approachable to us. The true meaning of Christmas is that simple – and that profound.

'O Holy Night.'

Christmas is a feast that appeals to our senses: the sights of glittering lights, the taste of the many delicacies of Yuletide feasting, the smell of freshly cut evergreen branches, the feel of the crisp winter air and newly-fallen snow, the sound of the magnificent music of Christmas.

But the first Christmas had none of those things. Consider the actual sights and sounds and feels and tastes – and smells! – of that night: the damp, aching cold of a

cave on the Bethlehem hillside; the burning in the eyes and throat from days of traveling along hard, dusty roads; the sudden panic of discovering there is no place to stay in a strange city, the paralyzing fear that robbers and wild animals could strike out of nowhere; the silence of the night, broken only by the cry of wolves and the bleating of sheep; the screaming of a young girl delivering her first child alone, with her carpenter husband offering what help he could; and the overwhelming stench of a cave used as a barn: the smell of animals, of manure, of perspiration.

That first Christmas night was human life at its dreariest, dirtiest and messiest, the human experience at its most painful, most exhausting, most terrifying. The first Christmas was dirty and grimy and, frankly, stunk to high heaven – but it was as holy as the highest heights of heaven. In our imperfections, in our sin, in our obtuse selfishness, God enters our human life and sanctifies it. The glorious sights and sounds, tastes and aromas of this holy night invite us to embrace the great love of God, the love that can transform our humanity from the hopelessness of a lonely birth in a cave to the hope and joy of redeeming grace.

For reflection:

- It has been a busy time, getting to this day. Was it all worth it?
- "We need a little Christmas . . ." so the song goes from the musical *Mame*. Why do we need Christmas *this* year?
- How is the first Christmas as described by Luke at odds with our Christmas celebration? How can we reconcile the difference in the simplicity of the first Christmas and the extravagance of our celebration?
- How can we make "shepherds" (outcasts, the poor and rejected) part of our Christmas?
- What one Christmas tradition, practice or story speaks to you most especially of the holiness of this night/day?
- Share your most memorable Christmas – a memory that even today affects your understanding of the mystery of the Incarnation.

Feast of the Holy Family

Readings:
Matthew 2: 13-15, 19-23
Sirach 3: 2-6, 12-14
Colossians 3: 12-21

Matthew's **Gospel** continues his account of Jesus' early years, focusing on the evangelist's principal theme: that Jesus is the Messiah promised by God long ago. Matthew portrays the Holy Family as outcasts, refugees in their own country. Bound together by love and trust in God and in one another, they embark on the dangerous journey to Egypt to flee the insane rage of Herod. Jesus relives the Exodus experience of Israel: he will come out of Egypt, the land of slavery, to establish a new covenant of liberation for the new Israel.

The Book of Sirach is a collection of carefully-crafted maxims and commentaries based on the Law. The author ("Jesus, son of Eleazar, son of Sirach" – 50: 27), a wise and experienced observer of life, writes on a variety of topics in order to help his contemporaries understand the role of faith in everyday life.

Today's **first reading** is a beautiful reflection on the fourth commandment. To honor one's parents, Ben Sira writes, is to honor the Lord God himself.

Paul wrote his letter to the Colossians (one of Paul's "captivity epistles") at the urging of Epaphras, the leader of the church there. The young church was being torn apart by adherents of Gnosticism ("knowledge"), a philosophy that stressed the superiority of knowledge over faith. Paul writes that such Gnostic teachings are but "shadows"; Christ is "reality," the "image of the invisible God, the first-born of all creation" in whom we are redeemed. In today's **second reading** from Colossians, Paul presents a picture of real community, formed in the perfect, unconditional love of Christ.

Themes:

The family: 'the little church.'

Today's feast is a celebration of family – that unique nucleus of society that gives us life, nurture and support throughout our journey on earth. Families are the first and best places for the love of God to come alive. Within our families we experience the heights of joy and the depths of pain. The Fathers of Vatican II called the family "the first and vital cell of humanity . . . the domestic sanctuary of the Church." Families reflect the love of Christ:

love that is totally selfless, limitless and unconditional, both in good times and (especially) in bad times. Today's Feast of the Holy Family calls us to re-discover and celebrate our own families as harbors of forgiveness and understanding and safe places of unconditional love, welcome and acceptance.

The cross and the crib.

It is easy to welcome Jesus the innocent child of Christmas; much more difficult is to welcome Jesus, the humble Crucified of Holy Week and Easter. Matthew's Gospel of the Holy Family reminds us that the crib is overshadowed by the cross, that this holy birth is the beginning of humankind's re-birth in the Resurrection. With Jesus, we must be about "the Father' house," bringing the justice, reconciliation and compassion won by the cross into our families and communities.

A model of holiness for all families.

In Matthew's and Luke's stories of Jesus' birth and childhood (which were later additions to those Gospels, drawn from the many stories about Jesus' life that were part of the early Christian oral tradition that had developed), life for the family of Joseph, Mary and Jesus is difficult and cruel: they are forced from their home; they are innocent victims of the political and social tensions of their time; they endure the suspicions of their own people when Mary's pregnancy is discovered; their child is born under the most difficult and terrifying of circumstances; Joseph and Mary endure the agony of losing their beloved child. And yet, through it all, their love and faithfulness to one another do not waver. The Holy Family is a model for our families as we confront the many tensions and crises that threaten the stability, peace and unity that are the joys of being a family.

For reflection:

- What rituals and customs in your own family reflect the spiritual dimension of Christmas?
- What experiences has your family shared that have brought you closer together? Consider both the wonderful and the catastrophic; times of trial, tension and tragedy; times that demanded extraordinary efforts to forgive and reconcile.
- Can you, as a parent, identify with Joseph and Mary in today's Gospel?

Solemnity of Mary, Mother of God

Readings:

Luke 2: 16-21
Numbers 6: 22-27
Galatians 4: 4-7

Today's solemnity is the oldest feast of Mary in the Church, honoring her by her first and primary title, "Mother of God."

Jesus is given the name *Yeshua* – "The Lord saves." The rite of circumcision unites Mary's child with the chosen people and makes him an heir to the promises God made to Abraham – promises to be fulfilled in the Child himself (**Gospel**).

From the Book of Numbers (one of the five books of the Law) the Lord gives to Moses and Aaron the words of priestly blessing (**first reading**).

The Church of Galatia is facing defections because of Judaic preachers who insist that pagan converts submit to the Jewish rite of circumcision and the observance of the Law. Paul's letter maintains that salvation is through Christ alone, that Christ's followers are no longer under the yoke of the First Law. Paul puts the Christmas event in perspective: through Christ, born of Mary, we become sons and daughters of "Abba," meaning Father (**second reading**).

Themes:

'Theotokos' – 'God-bearer.'

Today we honor Mary under her most ancient title – "*Theotokos,* Bearer of God." Mary, the mother of the Child of Bethlehem, is the perfect symbol of our own salvation. In accepting her role as mother of the Messiah, she becomes the first disciple of her Son, the first to embrace his Gospel of hope, compassion and reconciliation. She is the promise of what the Church is called to be and will be and seeks to become; she is the hope and comfort of a pilgrim people walking the road of faith. Mary, the "bearer of God," is a genuine and fitting example for us of what it means to be a faithful disciple of the Servant Redeemer – "bearers of God" in our own time and place.

Mary: our mother and sister.

Her statues have always radiated sweetness. She is always young and pink-cheeked and slender, with hair cascading down to her waist.

But the Mary of the Gospels is neither a fairy tale princess nor the romanticized "lovely lady dressed in blue." The flesh-and-blood Mary was an altogether human woman:

- the pregnant adolescent who was painfully misunderstood by the man she loved;
- the young mother, virtually alone, is forced to give birth to her firstborn in a damp cave one night on the outskirts of a place unknown to her;
- the frantic parent searching for her lost child in Jerusalem;
- the caring woman who was not afraid to speak her mind or voice her questions;
- the anguished mother who stood by courageously while, in a travesty of justice, her son was executed.

The figure we venerate in mysterious icons was a woman with her feet firmly planted on earth. Mary of Nazareth knew the pain that only a mother could feel; she knew the joy that only a totally selfless and giving woman of faith could experience.

Luke's Gospel reveals an uneducated adolescent who, in a dusty village in a small backwater of a conquered country, said, *Be it done to me according to your word,* stuck by that decision and changed the course of history. If Mary, the young unmarried pregnant girl, can believe in the incredible thing that she is to be a part of, if she can trust herself and believe in her role in the great story, than the most ordinary of us can believe in our parts in the drama, too.

[Adapted from *The Fire in the Thornbush* by Bishop Matthew H. Clark.]

In the new year 'of our Lord.'

G.K. Chesterton made this observation about New Year's: "The object of a new year is not that we should have a new year. It is that we should have a new soul and a new nose, new feet, a new backbone, new ears and new eyes."

Today a new year lies before us like a blank page or canvas. So many possibilities – much more than just the simple resolutions we are lucky to keep beyond the kick-off of today's first football game. But a whole new year, a new entity of time, begins today. We Christians believe that God has sanctified all time in his work of creation and his loving re-creation of the world in the Risen One. The God who makes all things new in Christ enables us to make this truly a *new* year for each one of us – a time for renewal and re-creation in the love of God, a time for making this year a year of peace in our lives and homes, a time for making this new year truly a "year of our Lord."

For reflection:

- In what ways is the Mary of the Gospels a real companion to us on our journey through the New Year?
- What was your "favorite year"? What made it a special time for you? How can you resolve to bring those elements into the New Year before you?
- Share the hopes, the challenges, the promises that the new year presents. How can we make this new year *anno Domini* – a "year of our Lord"?

Second Sunday after Christmas

Readings:
John 1: 1-18
Sirach 24: 1-4, 8-12
Ephesians 1: 3-6, 15-18

Today's readings call us to pause before the Bethlehem scene and contemplate the great destiny of the Child of Bethlehem.

The **Gospel**, the beautiful Prologue hymn to John's Gospel, with its echoes of Genesis 1 ("In the beginning . . .," "the light shines on in darkness . . ."), exalts Christ as the creative Word of God that comes as the new light to illuminate God's re-creation. In the original Greek text, the phrase "made his dwelling place among is" is more accurately translated as "pitched his tent or tabernacle." The image is also evoked by the teacher Ben Sira in today's **first reading**. In Sirach's hymn to the wisdom of God, holy wisdom is described as present before the Lord at the very beginning of creation and now present within the holy city. The writer's vision foreshadows Christ, God's Wisdom incarnate who, raised by God from the dead, continues, as John describes in his Gospel, to "make his dwelling place (literally, "pitched his tent") among us."

In his introduction to his letter to the Ephesians (today's **second reading**), Paul prays that the Christian community at Ephesus may receive the "spirit of wisdom" in order to realize the "great hope" to which God has called them in Christ Jesus.

Themes:

The 'wisdom' of God incarnate.

In the Child born of Mary at Bethlehem, the wisdom of God becomes real to us. His very birth manifests the constant and inexplicable love of God for his people, present for all time; his ministry as Messiah will teach us how we can transform humanity's dark night of sin and emptiness into the eternal day of God's peace and wholeness; his embracing of the cross will be the ultimate victory of holy wisdom over the Godless wisdom of the world.

The God who 'pitches his tent' among us.

Our God is a God constantly present to us in so many ways. He is present in the gifts of holy creation; he is present to all humanity in the birth of Christ; he is present in the Spirit of wisdom and goodness inspiring us to do the work of the Gospel; he is present to us in prayer and sacrament. The Messiah Jesus is the light who illuminates for us the life and presence of God, who reveals to us the great and unconditional love of God, the Creator who loves us like a parent loves his/her very own sons and daughters.

For reflection:

- How has God's "holy wisdom" influenced or changed or life?
- In what ways have you discovered the preeminence of "holy wisdom" over conventional wisdom?
- Where, when and how is God's "tent" pitched in your midst?

Epiphany

Cycles A, B and C

Readings: *Matthew 2: 1-12*
Isaiah 60: 1-6
Ephesians 3: 2-3, 5-6

Today's **Gospel**, the story of the astrologers and the star of Bethlehem, is unique to Matthew's Gospel. Note that Matthew does not call them kings or "magi" but "astrologers," nor does he give their names or report where they came from – in fact, Matthew never even specifies the number of astrologers (because three gifts are reported, it has been a tradition since the fifth century to picture "three wise men"). In stripping away the romantic layers that have been added to the story, Matthew's point can be better understood.

A great many First Testament ideas and images are presented in this story. The star, for example, is reminiscent of Balaam's prophecy that "a star shall advance from Jacob" (Numbers 24: 17). Many of the details in Matthew's story about the child Jesus parallel the story of the child Moses and the Exodus.

Matthew's story also provides a preview of what is to come. First, the reactions of the various parties to the birth of Jesus augur the effects Jesus' teaching will have on those who hear it. Herod reacts with anger and hostility to the Jesus of the poor who comes to overturn the powerful and rich. The chief priests and scribes greet the news with haughty indifference toward the Jesus who comes to give new life and meaning to the rituals and laws of the scribes. But the astrologers – non-believers in the eyes of Israel – possess the humility of faith and the openness of mind and heart to seek and welcome the Jesus who will institute the Second Covenant between God and the New Israel.

Secondly, the gifts of the astrologers indicate the principal dimensions of Jesus' mission:

• *gold* is a gift fitting for a king, a ruler, one with power and authority;
• *frankincense* is a gift fitting for a priest, one who offers sacrifice (frankincense was an aromatic perfume sprinkled on the animals sacrificed in the Temple);
• *myrrh* is a fitting "gift" for some one who is to die (myrrh was used in ancient times for embalming the bodies of the dead before burial).

Today's **first reading**, from Trito-Isaiah (chapters 56-66), is a song of encouragement to the exiled Jews who are returning to Jerusalem from Babylon to rebuild their nation and their way of life. But Isaiah envisions more for the city than just its rebuilding: Jerusalem will be a light for all nations, a gathering place not only for the scattered Jews but for the entire world, where God will once again dwell in the midst of his faithful people Israel.

The letter to the Ephesians is Paul's "synthesis" on the nature of the Church. In today's **second reading**, Paul writes that the Church transcends national and cultural identities: in Christ, Jew and Gentile form one body and share equally in the promise of the Resurrection.

Themes:

A Messiah for all nations.

In Matthew's Gospel, it is the "Gentile" astrologers who discover the newborn "King of the Jews," while the people of the covenant (Herod, the chief priests and scribes) remain oblivious to his presence in their midst. The prophet Isaiah describes the Messiah as a "light for all nations" (first reading). In Christ, God is present in all of human history – God is not the exclusive property of one nation or people; no religious group holds title to the wonderful things God has done. Epiphany calls us to a new vision of the world that sees beyond walls and borders we have created and to walk by the light which has dawned for all of humankind, a light by which we are able to recognize *all* men and women as our brothers and sisters under the loving providence of God, the Father of all.

The search for God in our lives.

Cardinal Newman said that "to be earnest in seeking the truth is an essential requisite in finding it." The astrologers' following of the star is a journey of faith, a journey that each one of us experiences in the course of our own life. Christ's presence is not confined to Scripture and churches; he is present in everyone and everything that is good. We find the true purpose of this life in our search for God, the great Shepherd of our souls.

The 'stars' we follow.

What we read and watch and listen to in search of wealth, fame and power are the "stars" we follow. The journey of the astrologers in Matthew's Gospel puts our own "stargazing" in perspective. The astrologers set their sights on a star that leads them to God. Where will the our "stars" lead us?

For reflection:

• *Epiphany* comes from the Greek word meaning appearance or manifestation. Think about the "epiphanies" around us – the many ways the Lord "appears" or "manifests" his presence among us.
• How is your particular parish called to be "universal"? In what ways does the Gospel challenge your community to abandon the "safety" of itself to reach out to those considered "outside" of it (new immigrants, the poor, etc.)?
• A popular bumper sticker seen during this time of year reads: "Wise men still seek him." Who are the "wise" men and women in our world who have dedicated themselves to seeking Christ? What are their stories?

13

Readings:

Matthew 3: 13-17
Isaiah 42: 1-4, 6-7
Acts 10: 34-38

Today's **Gospel** is the final revelation of the Epiphany event: Jesus' baptism at the Jordan River by John. The Baptizer's refusal at first to baptize Jesus and Jesus' response to his refusal (a dialogue that appears only in Matthew's Gospel) speak to Matthew's continuing theme of Jesus as the fulfillment of the First Testament prophecies. Jesus clearly did not need to be baptized. But his baptism by John is an affirmation that God was with this Jesus in a very special way (Isaiah's prophecy is fulfilled: "my favor rests on him. Jesus has come to identify with.") sinners, to bring them forgiveness; hence the propriety of Jesus' acceptance of baptism by John.

Baptism was a ritual performed by the Jews, usually for those who entered Judaism from another religion. It was natural that the sin-stained, polluted pagan should be "washed" in baptism, but no Jew could conceive of needing baptism, being born a son of Abraham, one of God's chosen people and therefore assured of God's salvation. But John's baptism – a baptism affirmed by Jesus was not one of initiation, but one of *reformation* – a rejection of sin in one's own life and acknowledgment of one's own need for conversion. In Christ, baptism becomes a sacrament of rebirth, a reception of new life.

Today's **first reading** is the first of the "servant songs" in Deutero-Isaiah in which the prophet tells of the "servant" of God who will come to redeem Israel. In this first song, Isaiah speaks of the servant as God's "chosen one with whom I am pleased" – words that will be heard at the River Jordan.

Cornelius was a Roman centurion, a good and kind man who deeply respected and observed the high moral code and noble style of Judaic worship. In a dream, Cornelius is told to send for Peter and listen to what he has to say. Cornelius invites Peter to address his household. Peter's sermon (today's **second reading**) typifies early Christian preaching to the Gentiles: while God revealed his plan to his chosen nation of Israel, the Lord invites all people and nations to enter into the new covenant of the Risen Christ.

Themes:

Baptism: to become 'servants.'

We tend to view Baptism as an isolated milestone in our lives; but baptism is more than just a "naming" ceremony – it is an ongoing process that continues in every moment of our lives. In baptism, we are "grasped by the hand" of God (first reading) and "called" to become the servants of God; we are formed into God's holy people, a people who rise from the waters of baptism and, with the Spirit upon us, travel his road of justice and mercy to the fulfillment of the Resurrection. In baptism, we claim the name of "Christian" and embrace all that that holy name means: to live for others rather than for ourselves, in imitation of Christ. Our baptism makes each one of us the "servant" described in today's readings: to bring forth in our world the justice, reconciliation and enlightenment of Christ, the "beloved Son" and "favor" of God.

The Spirit of God 'hovering' over us.

In all four Gospel accounts of Jesus' baptism, the evangelists use a similar description of the scene at the Jordan when Jesus is baptized by John: The Spirit of God descended and rested upon him, "hovering" over him like a dove – in other words, the Spirit of God resided within Jesus; that peace, compassion and love of God was a constant presence within the Carpenter from Nazareth. In baptism, we embrace that same Spirit – that same Spirit "hovers" over us giving directive and meaning to every moment of our lives.

The 'work' of Christmas begins.

The Christmas season officially comes to an end today at the banks of the Jordan River with Jesus' baptism by John. The glad tidings and good cheer of the holiday season are long over, Christmas has been packed away for the next 11 months and we can (finally) move on with our lives for another year. But the Messiah remains. Jesus is no longer the child in a Bethlehem manger but the adult Redeemer making his way to Jerusalem. The good news spoken by the angels continues to unfold; the most wondrous part of the Christ story is yet to be revealed. Today, the same Spirit that "anoints" the Messiah for his mission calls us to be about the *work* of Christmas in this new year: to seek out and find the lost, to heal the hurting, to feed the hungry, to free the imprisoned, to rebuild families and nations, to bring the peace of God to all peoples everywhere.

For reflection:

- In practical terms, what does it mean to be the "servant" of God?
- Share stories about people you know in whom the Spirit of God "hovers like a dove."
- What "work" of Christmas remains to be done in your parish community? How have things changed – for the better and for the worse – since we celebrated Christmas?

Readings:

Matthew 6: 1-6, 16-18
Joel 2: 12-18
2 Corinthians 5: 20 – 6: 2

The readings for this first day of the Lenten journey to Easter call us to *turn*.

In Hebrew, the word for repentance is to *turn*, like the turning of the earth to the sun at this time of year, like the turning of soil before spring planting. The Lenten journey that begins on this Ash Wednesday calls us to repentance – to turn away from those things that separate us from God and re-turn to the Lord.

In today's **Gospel**, Jesus, in his Sermon on the Mount, instructs his listeners on the Christian attitude and disposition toward prayer, fasting and almsgiving. Such acts are meaningful only if they are outward manifestations of the essential *turning* that has taken place within our hearts.

Around 400 B.C., a terrible invasion of locusts ravaged Judah. The prophet Joel visualized this catastrophe as a symbol of the coming "Day of the Lord." The prophet summoned the people to repent, to *turn* to the Lord with fasting, prayer and works of charity (**first reading**).

In his second letter to the Corinthians, Paul alternates between anger and compassion, between frustration and affection in defending his authority and mandate as an apostle in the face of attack by some members of the Corinthian community. In today's **second reading**, the apostle appeals for reconciliation among the members of the community, a *return* to the one faith shared by the entire Church.

Themes:

Lenten 'turning': springtime rebirth.

During the next few weeks, the world around us will change dramatically: the days will grow longer and warmer; the ice and snow will melt away and the first buds of spring will appear; the raw winter iciness will be replaced by the warmth of summer; the drab grayness of winter will be transformed into the color and promise of spring. Likewise, the symbols of ashes and somberness that mark today's liturgy will be eclipsed in six weeks by the light and flowers and *Alleluias* of the Easter celebration. In fact, the very word "Lent" has come down to us from the ancient Anglo-Saxon word, *lencten,* meaning *springtime.*

The change we see around us should also be experienced *within* us during these weeks of Lent. We tend to approach Lent as something to be endured rather than to be observed, a time for *not* doing, for avoiding instead of as a time for *doing,* for *becoming;* but, like springtime, Lent should be a time for transformation, for change, for becoming the people that God has called to be. It is a time, as the prophet Joel proclaims in the first reading, for "rending our hearts, not our garments."

The ashes we receive today should be quiet symbols of something much deeper, much more powerful, much more lasting going on within us. In accepting these ashes we acknowledge the fact that we are sinners, that we are less than faithful to our baptismal name of Christian. But in accepting these ashes we also accept the challenge to become, as Paul writes to the Corinthians, "the very holiness of God."

Lenten 'turning': our 'desert' retreat.

The season of Lent that we begin today is a time to stop in the "busy-ness" of our everyday lives, to consider the truly important things in our lives, to realize the many blessings we possess in this world and the promised blessings of the next. Unfortunately, we have been conditioned to see Lent as a time for giving up and not doing, instead of as a time for doing and becoming. As Jesus began his ministry with a 40-day "retreat" in the desert wilderness, Lent should be our own "desert experience," a time to peacefully and quietly renew and re-create our relationship with God, that he might become the center of our lives in every season.

For reflection:

- Can the case be made that we *need* Lent?
- How can we Lent be made a time for doing, for becoming?
- What is your parish doing to make this a meaningful Lent for the community?
- What does the natural cycle of springtime teach us about the seasons of Lent and Easter?

Readings:

Matthew 4: 1-11
Genesis 2: 7-9; 3: 1-7
Romans 5: 12-19

Discerning the will of God is the focus of the three readings for this first Sunday in Lent.

In Matthew's account of Jesus' 40-day desert experience (**Gospel**), Jesus is confronted with several choices. All of the tempter's offers would have Jesus sin against the great commandment of Deuteronomy: "You shall love the Lord your God with all your heart, and with all your soul, and with all your strength" (Deuteronomy 6: 5). The tempter offers comfort, wealth and power, but Jesus chooses, instead, the course of humble and prayerful servanthood that the Father has chosen for him. All of Jesus' responses to the devil's challenges are found in Deuteronomy (8: 3, 6: 16, 6: 13).

The Sunday Lenten journey this year begins quite literally at the beginning – the creation of humankind and the Genesis account of humankind's "fall" from grace (**first reading**). There are two powerful images in this reading: God creates human life by "breathing life" into his new creation. On Easter night, the Risen Christ will "breathe" the new life of the Holy Spirit into the his new creation, the Church.

In the center of the garden, God plants two trees: the tree of life and the tree of the knowledge of good and evil. The serpent's prophecy comes to pass: "God knows well that the moment you eat of it you will be like gods who know what is good and what is bad." With such knowledge comes the awesome responsibility for the choices we make.

Paul's commentary in Romans on Christ as the new Adam (**second reading**) puts the Genesis story in the new perspective of the Resurrection: "God's gift of Jesus reverses the trend of sin and selfishness that humankind has known since the "first Adam," the beginning of time.

Themes:

Lent: making choices.

This First Sunday of Lent confronts us with choices: Eve's choice to eat of the fruit and thus become "like God," Jesus' choices proposed by the "tempter" – personal profit, comfort and glory or the life of God. Every moment of our lives demands that we make hard choices, choices that challenge us to either live the values we believe in the depths of our hearts or forsake those values for things of less worth or permanence. The season of Lent calls us to embrace God's Spirit of truth that we may make the choices demanded by our complicated and complex world with courage, insight and faith.

Lent: a 'desert experience,' the beginning of new things.

Most of us were taught that one "kept a good Lent" by penance and acts of self-denial, but more in keeping with the total spirit of Lent is the idea of freeing ourselves from "business as usual" in order to focus more fully on God's presence in our lives. The season of Lent should be a "desert experience" for us as it was for Jesus – a time to renew our relationship with God, to reset our priorities and values to the things of God.

For reflection:

- How can we make this Lent our own "desert" experience?
- What was the most difficult choice you ever had to make? What values were behind the choice you made?
- How can the same talent or gift be used both for good and for evil, for obtaining both positive and negative results, for the benefit of another and for one's own narrow interests?
- How, in your life or in the life of the community, has a painful, destructive situation become "new" through someone's compassionate determination to "breathe life" into it and thereby transform it?

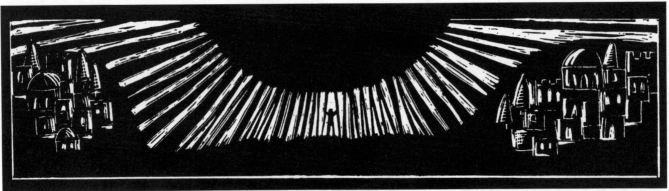

Readings:

Matthew 17: 1-9
Genesis 12: 1-4
2 Timothy 1: 8-10

In today's **Gospel**, Peter, James and John witness the extraordinary transformation of Jesus that we know as the "transfiguration." Matthew's account (which takes place six days after his first prediction of the passion and his first instructions on the call to discipleship) is filled with images from the First Testament: the voice which repeats Isaiah's "Servant" proclamation, the appearance of Moses and Elijah, the dazzling white garments of Jesus. Matthew's primary interest is the disciples' reaction to the event: their awe at this spectacular vision will soon wither into fear at the deeper meaning of the transfiguration – a meaning that they do not yet grasp. As the disciples will later understand, the transfiguration is a powerful sign that the events ahead of them in Jerusalem are indeed the Father's will.

At God's call, Abram (later Abraham) leaves his home for the land God will show him (**first reading**). He forsakes family and friends in Haran, one of the very cultured cities of the time, to create God's new nation. The elderly patriarch places his complete trust in the blessings promised by God.

Paul writes to Timothy, his former traveling companion and now administrator of the church at Ephesus, encouraging his friend to keep faith in the face of inevitable troubles and conflicts, for the Risen Christ is present in his teaching (**second reading**).

Themes:

Our invitation to Lenten 'transformation.'

The use of the Greek word "transfiguration" indicates that what the disciples saw in Jesus on Mount Tabor was a divinity that shone from *within* him. This Lenten season is a time for each of us to experience such a "transfiguration" within ourselves. In the first reading, God reveals to Abram his plan to transform Abram's clan into the Lord's very own special nation; our community is called to be God's own as well, to be his special possession, a sign to the world of God's constant presence. Today's Gospel prefigures Jesus' transformation from the slain Jesus of the cross to the victorious Jesus of the Resurrection; the Lenten journey calls us to transform our lives from the grasp of suffocating self-centeredness and injustice to the complete joy of selfless compassion and reconciliation.

The God of joy and suffering.

Peter's reaction to the Christ of the transfiguration contrasts sharply with his reaction to the Christ of Good Friday. When confronted with the Christ of the cross, Peter is afraid to even acknowledge knowing him. It's easy to accept the God of joy, the God of blessing; but when that God becomes the God of suffering, the God who calls us to give readily and humbly to the poor and unconditional forgiveness to those who hurt us, we begin to back off from the relationship God invites us embrace. Accepting God's many gifts is not a problem, but responding to the call of God to rebuild the world into his kingdom (as Abraham is called to do in the first reading) is much more difficult. Lent calls us to descend Mount Tabor with Jesus and journey with him to Jerusalem and take up our cross with him, so that the divinity we see in the transfigured Jesus may become in us the Easter life of the Risen Christ.

For reflection:

- Do you know of individuals who have *transformed* their part of the world, who have brought joy and hope into desperate situations by their compassion and sense of human dignity?
- Have you experienced times of great suffering or turmoil that have enriched your life, enabling you to do better things?
- Share examples of how both the Christ of the transfiguration and the Christ of the cross are both present in your community.

Readings:

John 4: 5-42
Exodus 17: 3-7
Romans 5: 1-2, 5-8

Jesus' meeting the Samaritan woman at Jacob's well (**Gospel**) illustrates the principal role of Jesus as the Messiah: to reconcile all men and women to the Father. As a Samaritan, the woman is considered an outcast by the Jews; as a known adulteress, she is scorned by her own village. With kindness and dignity, Jesus reconciles her to God.

This Gospel has long had a special place in baptismal catechesis: in revealing himself as the Messiah to the Samaritan woman, Jesus speaks to her of the fountain of water he will give – the life-giving waters of baptism. From Jacob's well springs forth the living waters of the Messiah Christ.

The Samaritan woman is, for the evangelist John, a model of a disciple's experience of faith: In a personal encounter with Jesus, she confronts her own sinfulness and need for forgiveness; she then comes to realize the depth of God's love for her; reconciled with God, her life is transformed; she is then sent forth to share with others her "faith story" of what she has seen and heard of this Jesus.

In today's **first reading**, from the story of Israel's Exodus, the great escape from Egypt doesn't seem so great to the Israelites any more. Lost in the desert and desperate for water, the Israelites are ready to stone Moses for leading them on this foolish adventure. But the Lord instructs Moses to strike the rock in Horeb to bring forth badly-needed water.

In the **second reading**, the apostle Paul rejoices – "boasts" – in the forgiveness obtained for all humanity through Christ, the Perfect Reconciler. This great expression of God's love for us is "poured out in our hearts through the Holy Spirit."

Themes:

The waters of baptism: new life in God.

Water is the predominant symbol in today's readings: God saves the desert-bound Israelites by bringing forth water from the rock at Horeb (first reading); Paul speaks of love "poured out in our hearts through the Holy Spirit" (second reading); and, at Jacob's well, Jesus promises the Samaritan woman a water that will be a "fountain...of eternal life" (Gospel). Water sustains life. It also cleans away the grime and filth that can diminish and destroy life. In the waters of baptism, the sins that alienate us from God are washed away and we are reborn in the Spirit of compassion and community.

Our call to the work of reconciliation.

Jesus tears down walls and breaks down barriers that divide people from one another and from God. He promises water that removes the sin that separates the Samaritan woman from her neighbors; he comes to lead all people to "worship in Spirit and truth," thus removing the barrier that separates the woman and her people from the community of Israel. The Samaritan woman cannot contain her desire to share with her neighbors the Messiah she has met. By telling her neighbors – neighbors who scorned her – she becomes an agent of reconciliation within her own community of Shechem. Like her, we are called not to be a people of judgment or condemnation, but to be a people of reconciliation, reaching out to one another and calling forth from one another the good each one of us possesses. In so many ordinary ways we can bring forth the new life and hope of Christ if we are willing to tear down the walls that divide us, to rebuild homes and hearts, to build bridges over chasms of mistrust and prejudice. But we cannot communicate Christ to others until we have discovered him in ourselves.

Confronting the reality of sin in our lives.

The Paschal mystery begins with a recognition of sin. We confront our sinfulness and, in doing so, we realize our need for God. Remember the Samaritan woman's excited proclamation to her neighbors: "Come and see someone who told me everything I ever did! Could this not be the Messiah?" Jesus prods the woman to confront her sin, without embarrassment or anger; she responds with wonder and joy that God accepts her and forgives her. Sin is a reality in the lives of each one of us; but through Christ, forgiveness, reconciliation and rebirth are just as real and possible.

For reflection:

- How have you experienced or witnessed rebirth and re-creation through forgiveness and reconciliation?
- How can our Church be an agent of reconciliation?
- Do you know individuals who have imitated the "Messiah" by reaching out and giving hope to today's "Samaritan women"?
- Who are the "Samaritans" of our time: those considered different, out of step with the world, outcasts, who can show the rest of us the loving presence and mercy of God?
- Jesus breaks a number of "taboos" in speaking with the Samaritan woman. Are there similar "taboos" today that can and should be broken through the simple act of forgiveness, of taking the first step in reconciliation?

Fourth Sunday of Lent

Readings: *John 9: 1-41, Samuel 16: 1, 6-7, 10-13*
Ephesians 5: 8-14

In his accounts of Jesus' "signs," John displays great skills as a dramatist. His story of the healing of the man born blind is really a play with six scenes: the blind beggar's healing with the mud Jesus mixes on the Sabbath; the townsfolk's reaction to his cure; the beggar's testimony before the Pharisees; the testimony of the blind man's parents; the beggar's second appearance before the Pharisees (resulting in his expulsion); the beggar's return to Jesus.

While his synoptic counterparts recount Jesus' miracles as manifestations of his great love and compassion, John "stages" Jesus' miracle to reveal the deeper meanings of Jesus' mission of redemption as the Messiah.

The healing of the blind beggar (**Gospel**) heightens the tension between Jesus and the Pharisees. Jesus' teaching threatens the structured and exalted life of the scribes and Pharisees. They seek to discredit Jesus – and this "miracle" gives them the opportunity. In using spittle, kneading clay and rubbing it on the man's eyes, Jesus had broken the strict rules prohibiting any kind of manual labor on the Sabbath. The miracle itself is secondary; the issue becomes Jesus' breaking of the Sabbath. The Pharisees are so embittered against Jesus that they are prepared to do anything – even manipulate ecclesiastical procedures – to destroy Jesus.

The inquisition of the blind man and his parents and his expulsion from the temple are significant for the evangelist and his readers. John and his community of Jewish-Christians are experiencing the same rejection – many of them have been expelled from their synagogues and the temple for their belief in Jesus as the Messiah.

Today's **first reading** recounts God's election of David as Saul's successor as king of Israel. The Lord instructs the venerable prophet Samuel to go to the family of Jesse. Samuel assumes that the older and stronger Eliab is to be the king, but God sees in the young shepherd David what people cannot see, for "the Lord looks into the heart."

In today's **second reading**, from his letter to the Ephesians, Paul uses the image of light to describe the Christian's new life in the Risen Christ. The "darkness" of the old life is contrasted with the "illumination" of baptism.

Themes:

'Seeing with eyes of faith': opening our hearts to newness of life.

Plato said: "We can easily forgive a child who is afraid of the dark; the real tragedy of life is when adults are afraid of the light." Sometimes we have so ordered and arranged our lives that we consider anything that disrupts or challenges that order as evil: we cower from change, we create walls around ourselves to keep out people and ideas we don't know or understand, we steel ourselves from demands on our time and compassion. Jesus' restoring the sight of the blind man challenges the Pharisees to open their own eyes to the reality of God's goodness in their midst; but Jesus has so challenged "the system" – a system that was working very well for them – that they are too afraid to be open to the joy and spirit that Jesus proclaimed. The Lenten journey calls us to detach ourselves from anything that causes us to close our minds and hearts to the light and spirit of the Gospel.

'Seeing with eyes of faith': a vision of humility and selflessness.

Our faith, our embracing of the Spirit of God, demands that we see things not with the eyes of practicality, self-interest and profitability alone, but with the eyes of selfless and humble faith, as well. With the eyes of faith, we are able to see beyond appearances and superficialities and look deeper to discover the timeless and profound truths of the human heart. Such a vision empowers us to re-create our world, to shatter the darkness of injustice and hate with the light of justice and compassion.

'Seeing with eyes of faith': faithless myopia.

We can become so absorbed with our own narrow interests that we miss the obvious good that is present before us. Today's Gospel illustrates the destructiveness of such myopia. But Jesus' teachings and healings so threaten the ordered lives of the Jewish leaders that they seek some way to discredit what he has done. Ironically, the more tragic blindness is suffered not by the blind man but by the Pharisees who refuse to see the presence of God among them. This season of Lent calls us to open our eyes to the grace and love of God present to us in everything that is good.

For reflection:

- Challenging institutions and traditions can be frightening and costly, but also liberating. Share stories of people, who in challenging such verities, have enabled institutions to do better things.
- Looking beyond the exterior to the inner motivation of someone is a special grace. Consider times when you misunderstood the motives behind someone's action or behavior, or you were unjustly accused of "ulterior motives."
- Reflecting on the images of light and darkness, sight and blindness, consider situations when it's safer and more comfortable to remain in the dark.

Fifth Sunday of Lent

Cycle A

Readings: *John 11: 1-45*
                 Ezekiel 37: 12-14
                 Romans 8: 8-11

As was the case in John's account of the healing of the man born blind (last Sunday's Gospel), the raising of Lazarus (today's **Gospel**) is more than just a sign of Jesus' love and compassion. Each of the seven miracles that John includes in his Gospel ("the Book of Signs," as this section of John's Gospel is titled) is dramatized by the evangelist to underscore some dimension of the redemptive nature of Jesus' work. The raising of Lazarus, the climactic sign in John's Gospel, is presented in five scenes: Jesus receiving the news of Lazarus' death, the disciples protesting Jesus' return to Judea, Martha's pleading with Jesus, Jesus' emotional arrival at the tomb and the miraculous raising of Lazarus.

The "sign" is clearly intended by John to demonstrate Jesus' power over life and death. The raising of Lazarus plays like a rehearsal for the events next week's liturgies will celebrate.

Ezekiel preached in Babylon to the Jews who had been banished from their homeland six centuries before Christ. Today's **first reading** is the conclusion of Ezekiel's vision of the dry bones which, at God's prophesy, come to life as an immense army. Just as God "breathed" life into the molded clay he formed to create Adam as a living being, so God will breathe his spirit again into the "dry bones" of Israel to restore his people to life.

Resurrection is also the theme of today's **second reading**, from Paul's letter to the Romans. People who live according to the ways of the world are spiritually dead, but those who belong to Christ are alive in the Spirit.

Themes:

Resurrection:
the Easter promise of hope.

The readings for this last Sunday before Holy Week are an affirmation of the promise that "the Spirit of him who raised Jesus from the dead dwells in [us]" (second reading) and through that Spirit we can rise from death to life. Lazarus' experience prefigures the life that Jesus, the "resurrection and the life," (who will, ironically, be put to death because, in part, of his gift of life to Lazarus), will give to all who believe in him once he has been raised from the dead.

Resurrection:
freedom to live in Easter joy and hope.

Many of us are trapped and held hostage by the obsessive pursuit of wealth, status or power; we become "dead" to the life that exists around us. Jesus calls not only to Lazarus but to all of us: *Come out! Go free!* As Jesus called out to Lazarus to be untied from the wrappings of the dead and to be free to live once again, so we are called to be free from those things that keep us from loving and being loved. This season of Lent calls us to such freedom: by embracing the Spirit of resurrection, we can bring new life and joy into our homes and communities.

Resurrection:
bringing forth new life in the present.

While very few of us can heal the sick or bring the dead back to life as Jesus did, there are many situations in our lives into which we can bring forth healing and resurrection. We can bring forth resurrection by spending some time with a child or an elderly relative or neighbor, by sharing what we have with someone in need, by taking the first step toward reconciliation with someone who has hurt us or by asking forgiveness of someone we have hurt. There are so many people who are awaiting resurrection – to rise from despair, cynicism and alienation to joy, hope and a sense of belonging. Such is the resurrection and healing that we can bring to our world as we await the promise of Christ's resurrection.

For reflection:

- Share stories of *resurrection* – experiences of people who have been "dead" (as Paul describes death in the second reading) but have been freed from the "bindings" of death.
- How can we bring "resurrection" to our everyday lives?
- John writes that although the raising of Lazarus caused many of the Jews "to put their faith in Jesus," the raising of Lazarus was cause for alarm among the leaders of the Jewish people. Consider the diverse and contradictory reactions people might have about the raising of Lazarus and what those reactions say about the human condition.

Passion (Palm) Sunday

Readings: *Blessing and Procession of Palms:*
Matthew 28: 1-11
Liturgy of the Word: Matthew 26: 14 – 27: 66
Isaiah 50: 4-7
Philippians 2: 6-11

Matthew's **Gospel** of Jesus' entry into the city of Jerusalem is framed by the prophecy of Zechariah (9: 9). The Messiah will come, not as a conquering warrior astride a noble steed, but in lowliness and peace, riding on an ass. Jesus' entry into Jerusalem in such a public and deeply symbolic way sets up the final confrontation between Jesus and the chief priests and scribes.

While the Blessing and Procession of Palms commemorates Jesus' triumphant entry into Jerusalem, the Liturgy of the Word focuses on the passion and death of the Messiah. In his **Passion** narrative, Matthew frames his account in the context of the First Testament prophecies concerning the Messiah. Matthew's Jesus is totally alone, abandoned by everyone, but is finally vindicated by God (the portrait of the Messiah depicted in Isaiah and Psalm 22).

Scripture scholars believe Matthew (and Luke) adapted their material from the evangelist Mark. Most of Matthew's Passion account is identical in vocabulary and content to Mark's. Matthew, however, adds several details not found in Mark's Gospel, including the death of Judas, Pilate's washing his hands of responsibility for Jesus' death, Pilate's wife's dream and the guards assigned to watch the tomb after Jesus' burial.

Matthew is writing his Gospel for Jewish Christians who themselves have suffered greatly at the hands of the Jewish establishment. Many have been expelled from their synagogues and the temple for their insistent belief in Jesus as the Messiah. Jesus' trial before the Sanhedren is pivotal in Matthew. Matthew alone names Caiaphas as high priest during the proceedings and details the chief priests' manipulation of Pilate and crowds. Matthew presents Jesus to his Jewish Christian community as a model of suffering at the hands of the Jews (it is Matthew's Passion account includes the troubling line spoken by the crowds, "Let his blood be upon us and our children"). The tearing of the sanctuary veil symbolizes, for Matthew's community, a break with their Jewish past.

As is the case throughout Matthew's Gospel, Gentiles and not the people of Israel recognize the truth about Jesus: only Pilate and his wife recognize the innocence of the condemned Jesus.

The **first reading** is taken from the "Servant songs," Isaiah's foretelling of the "servant of God" who will redeem Israel. In this third song, Isaiah portrays the servant as a devoted teacher of God's Word who is ridiculed and abused by those who are threatened by his teaching.

In his letter, Paul quotes what many scholars believe is an early Christian hymn (**second reading**). As Christ totally and unselfishly "emptied himself" to accept crucifixion for our sakes, so we must "empty" ourselves for others.

Themes:

The faith we profess and the faith we live.

There is a certain incongruity about today's liturgy. We begin with a celebration – we carry palm branches and echo the *Hosannas* shouted by the people of Jerusalem. But Matthew's Passion confronts us with our complicity in the injustice that leads ultimately to the cross. We welcome the Christ of victory, the Christ of Palm Sunday; but we turn our backs on the Christ of suffering and of the poor, the Christ of Good Friday. These branches of palm are symbols of the incongruity between the faith we profess on our lips and the faith we profess in our lives.

The 'attitude' of Christ: 'the Suffering Servant'.

The Gospel calls us to take on the "attitude of Christ Jesus": to "empty" ourselves of our own interests, fears and needs for the sake of others; to realize how our actions affect *them* and how our moral and ethical decisions impact the common good; to reach out to heal the hurt and comfort the despairing, despite betrayal; to carry on, with joy and in hope, despite rejection, humiliation and suffering. The celebration of Holy Week calls us to become servants of God by being servants to one another.

For reflection:

- Consider examples of individuals who possessed the courage to maintain their convictions and beliefs while left abandoned and alone in the face of opposition, ridicule and popular belief.
- In what ways are we confronted today with the reality of the cross?
- How is Christ's "attitude," as articulated in Paul's hymn in Philippians, the antithesis to the "attitude" of today's world?
- Which character in the Passion narrative do you identify with especially? What is it about their heroism – or failure – that strikes you?

Readings:
John 13: 1-15
Exodus 12: 1-8, 11-14, 1 Corinthians 11: 23-26

The centerpiece of John's **Gospel** account of the Last Supper is the *mandatum* – from the Latin word for "commandment," from which comes our term for this evening, *Maundy* Thursday. At the Passover seder, the night before he died, Jesus established a new Passover to celebrate God's covenant with the new Israel. The special character of this second covenant is the *mandatum* of the washing of the feet – to love one another as we have been loved by Christ.

(John makes no mention of the establishment of the Eucharist in his account of the Last Supper. The Johannine theology of the Eucharist is detailed in the "bread of life" discourse following the multiplication of the loaves and fish at Passover, in chapter 6 of his Gospel.)

Tonight's **first reading** recounts the origin and ritual of the feast of Passover, the Jewish celebration of God breaking the chains of the Israelites' slavery in Egypt and leading them to their own land, establishing a covenant with them and making of them a people of his own.

The deep divisions in the Corinthian community have led to abuses and misunderstandings concerning the "breaking of the bread." In addressing these problems and articulating the proper spirit in which to approach the Lord's Supper, Paul provides us with the earliest written account of the institution of the Eucharist, the Passover of the new covenant (this evening's **second reading**). If we fail to embrace the spirit of love and servanthood in which the gift of the Eucharist is given to us, then "Eucharist" becomes a judgment against us.

Themes:

Becoming 'Eucharist' for one another.

Tonight's liturgy is like a song that is out of tune or a photograph out of focus. Things are "out of sync" tonight. Jesus' last Passover seder sinks into betrayal, denial and abandonment. The holy kiss of peace is desecrated. While his twelve closest friends carry on a petty squabble over who is the greatest among them, Jesus gives them the gift of perfect unity, the Eucharist. With his ultimate triumph at hand, Jesus stuns his disciples by washing their feet – a humiliating task usually relegated to the lowliest of slaves – as a model of the selfless love that should characterize the new community of the Resurrection.

True, this is the night on which the Lord Jesus gave us himself in the Eucharist and instituted the ministerial priesthood. But there are shadows: the joy of the Eucharist is shadowed by Christ's challenge to become Eucharist for one another; the authority and dignity of priesthood is shadowed by the stark command to "wash one another's feet" not as overseers but as servants.

As we gather to remember the night of the Last Supper, we confront how "out of sync," how shadowed our lives are in relation to the life to which God calls us. We partake of the Eucharist tonight vowing to become the body of Christ to our hurting world and renewing our baptismal promise to become the priestly people of the new Israel – to do for others as our Teacher and Lord has done for us.

The parable of the 'Mandatum.'

Tonight, the Rabbi who taught in parables teaches what is perhaps his most touching and dramatic parable.

In the middle of the meal, Jesus – the revered Teacher, the Worker of miracles and wonders, the Rabbi the crowds wanted to make a king just a few days before – suddenly rises from his place as presider, removes his robe, wraps a towel around his waist and – like the lowliest of slaves – begins to wash the feet of the Twelve. We can sense the shock that must have shot through that room. But, quietly, Jesus goes about the task. Jesus on his knees, washing the dirt and dust off the feet of the fisherman, then the tax collector, and so on. Despite Peter's embarrassment and inability to comprehend what is happening, Jesus continues the humiliating and degrading task.

The Teacher, who revealed the wonders of God in stories about mustard seeds, fishing nets and ungrateful children, on this last night of his life – as we know life – leaves his small band of disciples his most beautiful parable: As I, your Teacher and Lord, have done for you, so you must do for one another. As I have washed your feet like a slave, so you must wash the feet of each other and serve one another. As I have loved you without limit or condition, so you must love one another without limit or condition. As I am about to suffer and die for you, so you must suffer and, if necessary, die for one another.

Tonight's parable is so simple, but its lesson is so central to what being a real disciple of Christ is all about. When inspired by the love of Christ, the smallest act of service done for another takes on extraordinary dimensions.

For reflection:

- How can we be "Eucharist" to one another?
- In what ways can we "wash the feet" of others?
- Consider the ways our faith is "out of sync" with our human experience.
- Explore the range of emotions that are present both in the scene depicted in tonight's Gospel and in the elements of tonight's liturgy.

Readings:

John 18:1 – 19:42
Isaiah 52:13 – 53:12
Hebrews 4:14-16; 5:7-9

John's deeply theological **Passion** account portrays a Jesus who is very much aware of what is happening to him. His eloquent self-assurance unnerves the high priest and intimidates Pilate ("You have no power over me"), who shuttles back and forth among the various parties involved, desperately trying to avoid condemning this innocent holy man to death. Hanging on the cross, Jesus entrusts his mother to his beloved disciple, thus leaving behind the core of a believing community. He does not cry out the psalm of the abandoned (Psalm 22); rather, his final words are words of decision and completion: "It is finished." The crucifixion of Jesus, as narrated by John, is not a tragic end but the beginning of victory, the lifting up of the Perfect Lamb to God for the salvation of humankind.

Isaiah's fourth and final oracle of the "servant of God" (today's **first reading**) is a hauntingly accurate description of the sufferings that the innocent one will endure to atone for the sins of his people. Only in Jesus Christ is Isaiah's prophecy perfectly fulfilled.

The priesthood and sacrifice of Jesus are the themes of the letter to the Hebrews (scholars are unanimous in their belief that this letter, while reflecting Pauline Christology, was not written by Paul himself). The verses taken for today's **second reading** acclaim Jesus, Son of God and Son of Man, as the perfect mediator between God and humankind.

Themes:

The broken body of Christ.

The broken body of Jesus – humiliated, betrayed, scourged, abused, slain – is the central image of today's liturgy. Today, Jesus teaches us through his own broken body.

As a Church, as a community of faith, we are the body of Christ. But we are a broken body. We minister as broken people to broken people. The suffering, the alienated, the unaccepted, the rejected, the troubled, the confused are all part of this broken body of Christ.

This is the day to reflect on the reality of pain and suffering. This is the day to realize that the source of such brokenness – sin – is also a reality. But the "goodness" of "Good" Friday teaches us that there are other realities. For us who believe, the broken body of Christ is forever transformed into the full and perfect life of the Risen Christ. In conquering life's injustices and difficulties, we are healed and made whole in the reality of the Resurrection.

The cross: the tree of life.

Actually, it is a plank hoisted up on a pole anchored in the ground, but the wood of the cross is nevertheless a life-giving tree.

The tree of Good Friday repulses us, horrifies us and, possibly, shames us. The tree that is the center of today's liturgy confronts us with death and humiliation, with the injustice and betrayal of which we are all capable.

But through the tree of the cross we are reborn. The tree of defeat becomes the tree of victory. Where life was lost, there life will be restored. The tree of Good Friday will blossom anew, bringing life, not death; bringing light that shatters centuries of darkness; bringing Paradise, not destruction.

Crucifying the 'problem' Jesus.

This Jesus had become a problem. His ramblings about love and forgiveness and neighbor were fine, up to a point; but things were getting out of hand. To the highly sensitive leaders of Judaism his parable about "Good" Samaritans (!), his associating with prostitutes and tax collectors, his scorning of the intricate traditions of the cherished Law threatened the very foundation of their Jewish identity and society. So, very methodically and quite legally, a strategy developed. Even a fall-back plan – co-opting the Roman government – was set into motion. The result: The problem is "solved" on a cross on the outskirts of the town.

Two millennia later, Good Friday confronts us with the reality that the crucifixion of the "problem" Jesus takes place again and again in our own time and place:

- when people's lives and futures are cast aside for the sake of profit or political expediency, the problem Jesus is crucified again;
- when self-righteous anger stifles compassionate charity and strangles efforts at healing reconciliation, the problem Jesus is crucified again;
- when unjust laws and dehumanizing social systems are allowed to continue because "I've got mine," the problem Jesus is crucified again.

Good Friday calls us to follow the "problem" Jesus, "to die with him so that we may also rise with him."

For reflection:

- Have you experienced, in your own life, suffering that has been, somehow, life-giving?
- How is each one of us a member of the broken body of Christ?
- Where is the crucifixion of Jesus taking place now, in our own time and place?

Readings:

Gospel: Matthew 28:1-10
First Testament Readings:
  Genesis 1:1 – 2:2
  Genesis 22:1-18
  Exodus 14:15 – 15:1
  Isaiah 54:5-14
  Isaiah 55:1-11
  Baruch 3:9-15, 32 – 4:4
  Ezekiel 36:16-28
Epistle: Romans 6:3-11

In his **Gospel**, Matthew presents Jesus' resurrection as a great intervention by God, inaugurating a new order throughout creation and history. The empty tomb is surrounded by miraculous phenomena: the earthquake, the angel whose appearance resembles a "flash of lightning" with garments as "dazzling as snow," the rolled back stone and the collapse of the guards.

In Matthew's account, Mary Magdalene and the "other" Mary come to the tomb for no other reason than to mourn (the guards no doubt would have prevented any attempt to go near the body for additional anointing). The disciples have not gone near the tomb. The women's courageous and compassionate presence is rewarded by their being the first to hear the astonishing news of the Resurrection. The angel explains that Jesus has been "raised up" exactly as he foretold on three occasions in Matthew's Gospel (16:21, 17:23 and 20:19). The two women then become "apostles to the apostles," sent to tell the others what they have seen.

On their way, the Risen One appears to them. In bidding the two Marys peace and in calling the cowering disciples his "brothers," Jesus offers the forgiveness and reconciliation that are hallmarks of the Easter promise.

The **First Testament readings** all recount God's first creation and covenant with the people of Israel. In the passion, death and resurrection of his Son, the faithful God re-creates creation and vows a new covenant to his people.

Paul's **Epistle** to the Romans includes this brief catechesis on the Easter sacrament: in baptism, we die with Christ to our sinfulness and we rise with him to the life of God.

Themes:

The resurrection: a new creation.

Did the universe begin with a bang or a whimper?

Is God the master firemaker who ignited a big bang that set creation on its journey through the cosmos? Or is God the meticulous craftsman who carefully formed one single cell – a thousandfold smaller than a single particle of dust – that contained within its microscopic walls the power to give birth to planets and stars and plants and animals – and us?

The scientists among us journey to the last frontiers of thought to discover how creation began. But the point is: it began. God set it all in motion. **The first Genesis.**

Nobody saw Jesus leave the tomb. Nobody saw life return to the crucified body. Nobody saw the massive stone roll away. Theories abound, scenarios have been devised to explain it away. Some say that the apostles stole the body – but could that band of hapless fishermen and peasants devise such a hoax? Maybe Jesus didn't die – maybe he revived three days later. But re-read the events of Good Friday. He didn't have a chance. Ponder the whys and hows, but you cannot escape the reality: the empty tomb, the eyewitness accounts of his appearances to Mary, Peter, the disciples traveling to Emmaus, the Eleven. Jesus is risen. **The second Genesis.**

On this night in early spring, we celebrate God's new creation. Death is no longer the ultimate finality but the ultimate beginning. The Christ who taught forgiveness, who pleaded for reconciliation, who handed himself over to his executioners for the sake of justice and mercy, has been raised up by God. We leave behind in the grave our sinfulness, our dark side, our selfishness, our pettiness – the evil that mars God's first creation.

Tonight, we join our renewed hearts and re-created voices in the "Alleluia!" of the new creation.

The empty tomb: ultimate hope.

In the light of Easter morning, we realize unmistakably the depth of God's love for us and understand the profound truth of Jesus' Gospel of compassion, love, forgiveness, reconciliation and selflessness for the sake of others. God's "raising up" of his Son affirms our redemption through the power of the Gospel spirit of love; the empty tomb of Easter is the ultimate victory of the Gospel over humanity's dark tendency toward despair, isolation, prejudice and selfishness. With Easter faith, we can transform the darkness of Good Friday's hatred into the light of Easter's *Alleluia*; we can awaken the promise of the empty tomb in every place and moment and heart we encounter on our journey to Easter's fulfillment in our own lives.

For reflection:

- Tonight we celebrate with symbols: fire (light), story (Scripture), water (baptism) and bread (Eucharist). What do these symbols teach us about the Paschal mystery?
- "The Lord has been raised from the dead and now goes ahead of you to Galilee, where you will see him," the angel reports. How do we "see" the Risen Lord today in our own "Galilee?"
- How would our lives be different if tonight had never happened?

Readings:
John 20: 1-9
Acts 10: 34, 37-43
Colossians 3: 1-4
or 1 Corinthians 5: 6-8

[NOTE: The Gospel for the Easter Vigil may be read in place of John 20: 1-9.]

John's Easter **Gospel** says nothing of earthquakes or angels. His account begins before daybreak. It was believed that the spirit of the deceased hovered around the tomb for three days after burial; Mary Magdalene was therefore following the Jewish custom of visiting the tomb during this three-day period. Discovering that the stone has been moved away, Mary Magdalene runs to tell Peter and the others. Peter and the "other disciple" race to get there and look inside.

Note the different reactions of the three: Mary Magdalene fears that someone has "taken" Jesus' body; Peter does not know what to make of the news; but the "other" disciple – the model of faithful discernment in John's Gospel – immediately understands what has taken place. So great are the disciple's love and depth of faith that all of the strange remarks and dark references of Jesus now become clear to him.

In this sermon recorded in Luke's Acts (**first reading**), Peter preaches the good news of the "Christ event" to the Gentile household of Cornelius. The resurrection of Jesus is the ultimate sign of God's love for all of humanity. The apostles' mandate to preach the Gospel is about to cross into the Gentile world beyond Jerusalem.

The imprisoned Paul writes (**second reading: Colossians**) that because we are baptized into Christ's death and resurrection, our lives should be re-centered in new values, in the things of heaven.

Paul's first letter to the Corinthians includes one of the earliest Easter homilies in Christian literature (**second reading: 1 Corinthians**). The custom in many Jewish households at Passover was to discard old yeast (leaven) and bake new unleavened bread for the feast. For Paul, this is a fitting symbol for the Christian community at Corinth: They must rid themselves of the self-centeredness and corruption which destroys their community and, together, share "the unleavened bread of sincerity and truth."

Themes:

The empty tomb: reason to hope.

While the Easter mystery does not deny the reality of suffering and pain, it does proclaim reason for hope in the human condition. The empty tomb of Christ trumpets the ultimate *Alleluia* – that love, compassion, generosity, humility and selflessness will ultimately triumph over hatred, bigotry, prejudice, despair, greed and death. The Easter miracle enables us, even in the most difficult and desperate of times, to live our lives in hopeful certainty of the fulfillment of the Resurrection at the end of our life's journey.

The empty tomb: the ultimate victory.

Today we stand, with Peter and John and Mary, at the entrance of the empty tomb; with them, we wonder what it means. The Christ who challenged us to love one another is risen and walks among us! All that he taught – compassion, love, forgiveness, reconciliation, sincerity, selflessness for the sake of others – is vindicated and affirmed in the Father raising him from the dead. The empty tomb should not only console us and elate us, it should challenge us to embrace the life of the Gospel. With Easter faith, we can awaken the promise of the empty tomb in every place and moment we encounter on our journey through this life.

The Church: the Resurrection community.

The Risen Christ is present to us in the faithful witness of every good person who shares the good news of the empty tomb by their living of the Gospel of selflessness and compassion. The empty tomb should inspire us to bring resurrection into this life of ours: to rise above life's sufferings and pain to give love and life to others, to renew and re-create our relationships with others, to proclaim the Gospel of *Christ who died, Christ who has risen, Christ who will come again!*

For reflection:

- Have any stories in the news this week struck you as examples of resurrection in our own time – of bringing hope, new life, new possibilities to once dark, hopeless places?
- Where is the Risen Lord present among us? How is the good news of the Risen Jesus proclaimed in the faithfulness and compassionate charity of people around you?
- How should our belief in the empty tomb affect our everyday outlook and attitudes?

Second Sunday of Easter

Cycle A

Readings:
John 20:19-31
Acts 2:42-47
1 Peter 1:3-9

The **Gospel** for the Second Sunday of Easter (for all three years of the Lectionary cycle) is Act 2 of John's Easter drama.

Scene 1 takes place on Easter night. The terrified disciples are huddled together, realizing that they are marked men because of their association with the criminal Jesus. The Risen Jesus appears in their midst with his greeting of "peace." John clearly has the Genesis story in mind when the evangelist describes Jesus as "breathing" the Holy Spirit on his disciples: Just as God created man and woman by breathing life into them (Genesis 2: 7), the Risen Christ re-creates humankind by breathing the new life of the Holy Spirit upon the eleven.

In scene 2, the disciples excitedly tell the just-returned Thomas of what they had seen. Thomas responds to the news with understandable skepticism. Thomas had expected the cross (see John 11: 16 and 14: 5) – and no more.

The climactic third scene takes place one week later, with Jesus' second appearance to the assembled community – this time with Thomas present. He invites Thomas to examine his wounds and to "believe." Christ's blessing in response to Thomas' profession of faith exalts the faith of every Christian of every age who "believes without seeing"; all Christians who embrace the Spirit of the Risen One possess a faith that is in no way different or inferior from that of the first disciples. The power of the Resurrection transcends time and place.

The first readings for the Sundays of the Easter seasons are taken from Luke's Acts of the Apostles. Acts has been called the "Gospel of the Holy Spirit" because it recounts how the Spirit of God was at work forming this small group on the fringes of Judaism into the new Israel, the Church of the Risen Christ. Today's **first reading** is one of several brief "snapshots" Luke includes of the Jerusalem Church, a community united in heart and mind, in charity to all and in their witness to the Resurrection. Instruction, sharing, Eucharist and prayer were the hallmarks of this first church, this first "parish."

On the Sundays of Easter during this (Cycle A) Easter season the second reading will be taken from the first letter attributed to Peter (although the letters were probably written by Silvanus, a companion of Paul's). The letter, addressed to converts from paganism and the predominantly Gentile Christian communities of Asia Minor, is a collection of exhortations, especially on faithfulness in the midst of persecution and suffering. It presents a beautiful catechesis on the Paschal dimensions of baptism.

Today's **second reading** is a prayer of thanksgiving that outlines the major themes of the Peter's message: God has given us a new birth in the resurrection of Jesus, which leads to a "heavenly inheritance" incapable of fading, despite the trials and persecutions of the world.

Themes:

Called to be Easter communion and community.

The Risen Christ calls us to communion with God through him and to community with one another. We trace our roots as parish and faith communities to Easter night when Jesus "breathed" his spirit of peace and reconciliation upon his frightened disciples, transforming them into the new Church; today's first reading from Acts is a snapshot of the ideal of the Church they became. Jesus' gift of peace and his entrusting to the disciples the work of forgiveness are what it means to be a church, a parish, a community of faith: to accept one another, to affirm one another, to support one another as God has done for us in the Risen Christ. What brought the apostles and first Christians together as a community – unity of heart, missionary witness, prayer, reconciliation and healing – no less powerfully binds us to one another as the Church of today.

Transforming skepticism into trust.

All of us, at one time or another, experience the doubt and skepticism of Thomas. While we have heard the good news of Jesus' empty tomb, all of our fears, problems and sorrows overwhelm us and prevent us from realizing it in our own lives. In raising his beloved Son from the dead, God also raises our spirits to the realization of the totality and limitlessness of his love for us. As Thomas experiences, Easter transforms our crippling sense of skepticism and cynicism into a sense of trust and hope in the providence of God.

For reflection:

- Have you ever known someone (or yourself) whose life was almost swallowed up in destructive skepticism, cynicism or despair? How was that skepticism transformed into hope and trust?
- In what ways can your parish community become like the first Christian communities portrayed in today's readings?
- How can we "breathe" new life into situations and relationships?

Third Sunday of Easter

Readings:

Luke 24: 13-35
Acts 2: 14, 22-28
1 Peter 1: 17-21

Today's **Gospel** begins on the afternoon of that miraculous Easter Sunday. Having just completed the observance of the Passover Sabbath, two disciples of Jesus (one identified as Cleopas) are making the seven-mile trip to the village of Emmaus. By identifying them as disciples, Luke is emphasizing that these two were more than just impartial observers of the events of Holy Week.

Luke writes that their exchange was "lively" – we can well imagine! As well as anger at the great travesty of justice that had taken place, they must have felt emotionally shattered at what had befallen their revered Rabbi Jesus. The two are suddenly joined by a stranger who asks the subject of their "lively" conversation. The stranger then explains, to their astonishment, the *why* of each of the events of the past week. When they reach the village, the two disciples ask the stranger to stay with them. And, in the words from Luke's Gospel that we have come to treasure, the two disciples "come to know (the Risen Christ) in the breaking of the bread."

Today's **first reading** from Acts is Peter's Pentecost sermon in which the apostle preaches that the First Testament prophecies of a Messiah who will descend from David are fulfilled in Christ Jesus. Peter cites Psalm 16 (today's responsorial psalm) as David's own prophesy of the Messiah's resurrection.

Delivered by God from the "futile ways" of their ancestors, the Gentile converts of Asia Minor are expected to be out of step with their former pagan culture ("your sojourn in a strange land"). Peter writes in today's **second reading** that they are to live lives "spotless and unblemished" like the Lamb who redeemed them.

Themes:

'Bread blessed and broken' for us.

Luke's Easter night story parallels our own experience of the Eucharist: Sometimes we come to the Lord's table feeling angry, hurt, despairing, alone, but at this table, coming to "know him in the breaking of the bread," we can experience the peace and presence of the Risen Christ.

Bound by the living memory of Jesus.

It has been said that true friendship begins when people share a memory. The joy of friendship comes to life when one can say to another, *Do you remember the time when...?* The first Christian communities were bound together by the apostles' memories of Jesus, like the story we read in today's Gospel and the *kerygma* ("proclamation") of Peter in Acts. We are bound together by memory – the memory of the great Paschal event of Christ. In the word we hear together and the bread we share together, God's love is both remembered and relived; the experience of the altar gives us direction, meaning and hope in the marketplaces of our lives. Like the two disciples who recognize Jesus in the breaking of bread, we, too, are bound as a community by the same memory of the Risen One.

Pilgrim people of the new covenant.

The people of God have always been a pilgrim people, journeying from slavery to freedom, from discernment to commitment, from death to life. Like the disciples journeying to Emmaus, we are disciples journeying. It is never an easy journey – but we never journey alone. The ever-faithful God has revealed his presence to us in fire and cloud, in bread from heaven and water from the rock, in the word of the prophets. The journey reaches its zenith in the great Paschal journey from crucifixion to resurrection. As the disciples traveling to Emmaus discover, the journey is not ended. It continues through the wilderness and deserts, and is often marked by the cross; but God is always very much present to us.

For reflection:

- Put yourself in the place of the two disciples in today's Gospel. What do you think they were saying and feeling? Can you identify with those emotions?
- How is this place (this altar, this church) a place of peace, of hope, of healing?
- What memories bind you as a parish community?
- How is life like the two disciples' Emmaus experience?

Fourth Sunday of Easter

Readings:
John 10: 1-10
Acts 2: 14, 36-41
1 Peter 2: 20-25

Chapter 10 of John's **Gospel** is Jesus' "Good Shepherd" discourse. In today's Gospel reading, two kinds of sheepfolds or corrals are mentioned: In the community or town sheepfold, the real shepherd was recognized by the gatekeeper and his flock knew his voice and followed; out in the fields, the shepherd slept across the corral opening – his body became the corral gate. Both "gates" are beautiful images of the Redeeming Christ, the "Good Shepherd" who lays down his own life to become the very source of life for his people.

There is another important dimension to this discourse. John places these words of Jesus right after the curing of the man born blind (the Gospel read a few weeks ago on the Fourth Sunday of Lent). The evangelist uses these references about shepherds, sheep and sheepgates to underline the miserable job of "shepherding" being done by the Pharisees and the temple authorities as in the case of the blind man. John is writing in the spirit of the prophet Ezekiel (Ezekiel 34): God will raise up a new shepherd to replace the irresponsible and thieving shepherds who feed themselves at the expense of the flock.

The reaction to Peter's Pentecost sermon (**first reading**) parallels the response to John the Baptist's exhortation in Luke's Gospel (Luke 3: 10-11). Whereas John spoke of a baptism of Spirit to come, Peter proclaims that it is now a realty.

Luke, the author of Acts, describes salvation both in terms of community and individual commitment. Each person has to accept his/her call to salvation. But salvation never remains a private matter between the individual and God; rather, one is baptized into God's people ("added") and saved as a member of the Church.

Peter's letters are addressed especially to slaves. Suffering is a bitter fact of the slave's life, but Peter attempts to give them hope by interpreting their experience in light of the suffering Christ (**second reading**). In verses 22-24, Peter repeats Isaiah's Song of the Servant (Isaiah 53: 1-12, first reading for Good Friday): Christ was truly innocent, there was no justification for what he was forced to endure, but he endured it all for the sake of humankind. So Christians – even slaves – are called to imitate Christ. Peter uses the image of the shepherd to describe Christ's work of redemption ("the guardian of your souls").

Themes:

The 'shepherd': the servant-leader.

Today's Gospel is a lesson in servanthood, in realizing our responsibility to hear and follow the "voice" of the Jesus of courage and selflessness. To do otherwise is to become "thieves [who come] only to steal and slaughter and destroy" their own selfish interests and profit. As disciples, we are called first and always to imitate the humble servanthood of Christ by our dedication to the Gospel values of compassion, reconciliation and justice.

The 'gate': the hard demands of the Gospel.

Sometimes we look at the Gospel from our modern, sophisticated perspective and quietly dismiss what Jesus says as too unrealistic or too simplistic to deal with the complex problems we must face. We are too involved in finding high-tech answers to high-tech problems to be concerned with such things like love for one another, forgiveness, compassion and justice. But there is no high-tech, comfortable, convenient road to living the Gospel. "To have life to the full" demands that we journey by way of the "gate" of Gospel wisdom, charity, reconciliation, compassion and justice.

For reflection:

- Share stories about individuals who are true "shepherds" – leaders and teachers in the spirit of the Good Shepherd.
- What trends do you see in society today as running counter to the Gospel demands of selfless and compassionate giving to others?
- How do you reconcile the *personal* and the *communal* dimensions of faith?

Readings:

John 14: 1-12
Acts 6: 1-7
1 Peter 2: 4-9

The scene of today's **Gospel** is the Last Supper. John's account of that night is the longest in the Gospels – five chapters in length (but with no account of the institution of the Eucharist). The evangelist uses a literary device common in Scripture: A leader (Moses, Joshua, David, Tobit) gathers his own (family, friends, disciples) to announce his imminent departure, offer advice and insight into the future and give final instructions.

At the time John is writing his Gospel, Christians are being harassed by both the Jews and the Romans. Proclaiming the crucified Jesus as the Messiah is blasphemy to Judaism, while accusing the Romans of "judicial murder" in the death of Jesus threatened the new faith's chances of survival as a "lawful religion" tolerated by their Roman occupiers.

The dominant themes here are consolation and encouragement: *Be faithful, remember and live what I have taught you, for better days are ahead for you.* Christ – the Way to God, the Truth of God and Life incarnate of God – will return for the faithful "who do the works that I do."

The ordination of the first seven deacons (**first reading**) is a watershed for the young Church – leadership is now being passed on to a new kind and generation of minister. The community realizes that it is growing beyond just the Hebrew-speaking and now includes the Greek-speaking Christians. This is especially significant because Greek was one of the major world languages at the time.

The numbers *twelve* and *seven* are important symbols of the nature of the Church: the apostles, twelve in number like the tribes of Israel, are the leaders of the new Israel; the seven deacons (the same in number as the world's seas) are signs of the Church's outreach to the whole world.

Peter continues his baptismal catechesis (**second reading**), using the First Testament images of the rejected stone and nationhood (community) to explain to new Christians the nature of their membership in the Church. To those who do not believe, Jesus is "a stumbling block" and an "obstacle," while for the faithful, Jesus is the "cornerstone." Baptized into Christ's death and resurrection, we, too, are "living stones" that make up the Church of the Risen One; we, too, are raised up to be "priests," called to proclaim the Gospel throughout the earth.

Themes:

Christ: 'the way, the truth and the life.'

The Jesus of the Gospel does not only show us the way – his life of humble and generous servanthood *is* the way; he does not only philosophize about a concept of truth – he *is* the perfect revelation of the truth about a God of enduring and unlimited love for his people; he is not just a preacher of futuristic promises – he has been raised up by God to a state of existence in God to which he invites all of us. In embracing the Spirit of his Gospel and living the hope of his Word, we encounter, in Christ, God himself.

Discipleship: 'to do the work I do.'

Regardless of the career path we choose – doctor, laborer, bank teller, teacher, parent or priest – if we truly consider ourselves disciples of the Risen Jesus, we are called "to do the work I do." In our homes, workplaces, city halls and playgrounds, we are called to bring the miracle of Easter life: the reconciliation, justice and peace of the Risen One in whom God has revealed himself to all of humanity.

Our return 'home.'

Seldom do we think of death as a return home, but today's Gospel image of the "house with many dwelling places" helps us to realize that we were created for a life beyond this one – we were created by God for life in and with him. The Risen Jesus is the way to our return "home" to the Father.

For reflection:

- How is God, as revealed by Jesus, "real" to us today?
- Consider ways your parish is or should be a "edifice of spirit."
- How does Jesus' image of "many dwelling places" alter or change our childhood image of heaven?
- What does the story of the first seven deacons and the Apostles' decision to "lay hands" upon them teach today's parish communities about ministry?

Sixth Sunday of Easter

Readings:
John 14: 15-21
Acts 8: 5-8, 14-17
1 Peter 3: 15-18

A "paraclete" (from the Greek *parakletos*, meaning "beside" and "to call") is one who intervenes and intercedes in favor of what is right or good. In legal terminology, a paraclete is an advocate who defends the accused on trial. For John, Christ is the first "Paraclete," who comes to liberate humanity from the slavery of sin. The second "Paraclete," promised by Jesus in today's **Gospel**, is the Spirit of truth, the Church's living, creative memory in which the mystery of God's love, revealed by and in Christ, lives for all time.

The universal mission of the Church takes its first steps outside of the Jewish world in today's **first reading** from Acts. Philip the deacon ("ordained" in last week's first reading) goes to Samaria, where his preaching about Jesus the Messiah is enthusiastically received. This was an unlikely and unexpected place for such a beginning – the Samaritans, remember, were the despised outcasts of Judaism. The acceptance of the Samaritans as equals in the Christian community was suspect by many of the Jewish members of the Church.

Peter tells his readers – many of whom are slaves – that the best witness to Christ is an honest and holy life that refutes defamation and libel by its clear and evident goodness (**second reading**).

Themes:

The Paraclete: faith that transforms our world.

Jesus acknowledges in his farewell to his disciples that their witness to him will be costly. He promises to send, from the Father, a *Paraclete* who will stand by them (and us) during the difficult times ahead. The Spirit of truth, "whom the world cannot accept," illuminates our vision and opens our hearts to discern the will and wisdom of God. The Paraclete advocates within us what is good, what is right and what is just, despite the skepticism and rejection of those who are blind to what is good.

The bishops of the United States wrote in their 1986 pastoral, *Economic Justice for All*: "After Jesus had appeared to them and when they received the gift of the Spirit, they became apostles of the good news to the ends of the earth. In the face of poverty and persecution they transformed human lives and formed communities which became signs of the power and presence of God. Sharing this same resurrection faith, contemporary followers of Christ can face the struggles and challenges that await those who bring the Gospel vision to bear on our complex economic world."

The demanding love of the Risen Christ.

In his Gospel, John never allows love, as taught by Jesus, to remain at the level of sentiment or emotion. Its expression is always highly moral and is revealed in obedience to the will of the Father. To love as Jesus loved – in total and selfless obedience, without conditions and without expectation of that love ever being returned – is the difficult love that Jesus expects of those who claim to be his disciples. The world might say that only fools love like that, but such "hard" love is the recognition of the true nature of love. In dying to our own interests we can become fully alive, fully human in the image of the Risen Christ.

The Spirit of truth: the Church's living memory.

The Spirit of truth, the Paraclete, is the creative, living memory of the Church. Through that "living memory," the Church enters into the mystery of Christ himself. The Spirit/Paraclete unites us and energizes us as we come together to share, re-live and learn from our memory of Christ, the Risen Son of the Father. Jesus – the wise Rabbi, the compassionate Healer, the Friend of rich and poor and saint and sinner, the obedient and humble Servant of God – is a living presence among us to give us hope, strength and light as we struggle to balance and direct our lives until he calls us to the new life of his Resurrection.

For reflection:

- Have you every felt the brunt of the world's inability to "accept" the Spirit of truth?
- How is the memory of Jesus more than a recollection of a story but a living presence touching us all?
- In today's reading from Acts, Peter and John "impose hands on (the Samaritans) and they received the Holy Spirit." Recall your own confirmation, however many years ago. What images of that ceremony come to mind as you consider today's readings?
- Share an experience of "hard love," when loving someone was painful or difficult, or when following the instincts of the "Spirit" was met with opposition.

Readings: *Matthew 28: 16-20,*
Acts 1: 1-11, Ephesians 1: 17-23

Today's readings include two accounts of Jesus' return to the Father:

The **first reading** is the beginning of the Acts of the Apostles, Luke's "Gospel of the Holy Spirit." Jesus' Ascension begins volume two of Luke's masterwork. The words and images here recall the First Covenant accounts of the ascension of Elijah (2 Kings 2) and the forty years of the Exodus. Luke considers the time that the Risen Lord spent with his disciples a sacred time, a "desert experience" for the apostles to prepare them for their new ministry of preaching the Gospel of the resurrection. (Acts alone places the Ascension forty days after Easter; the synoptic Gospels – including, strangely, Luke's – specifically place the ascension on the day of Easter; John writes of the "ascension" not as an event but as a new existence with the Father.)

Responding to their question about the restoration of Israel, Jesus discourages his disciples from guessing what cannot be known. Greater things await them as his "witnesses." In the missionary work before them, Christ will be with them in the presence of the promised Spirit.

Matthew's **Gospel** begins with the promise of Emmanuel – "God is with us." It concludes on the Mount of the Ascension with Emmanuel's promise, "I am with you always."

Paul's letter to the Ephesians celebrates the union of all men and women in and with Christ, as members of his mystical body. In the opening chapter of his letter to the Ephesians (**second reading**), the apostle prays that the Christian community at Ephesus may be united by the great "hope" they share in the Risen Christ, whom the Father has made sovereign over all creatures and head of the Church.

Themes:

The Ascension: an ending and a beginning.

Jesus' Ascension is both an ending and a beginning. The physical appearances of Jesus are at an end; his revelation of the "good news" is complete; the promise of the Messiah is fulfilled. Now begins the work of the disciples to teach what they have learned and to share what they have witnessed. It is not a very promising start. Like any beginning or transition in life, it is a moment of great uncertainty, confusion and apprehension. Christ places his Church in the care of a rag-tag collection of fishermen, tax collectors and peasants. And yet, what began with those eleven has grown and flourished through the centuries to the very walls of our own parish family. The Church Je-

sus leaves to them is rooted not in buildings or wealth or formulas of prayer or systems of theology but in faith nurtured in the human heart, a faith centered in joy and understanding that is empowering and liberating, a faith that gives us the strength and freedom to be authentic and effective witnesses of the Risen One, who is present among us always.

The commission to 'teach,' to 'witness,' to 'heal.'

Christ entrusts to his disciples of every time and place the sacred responsibility of teaching others everything he has taught and revealed about the Father: God's limitless love, his unconditional forgiveness and acceptance of every person as his own beloved child and our identity as God's sons and daughters and brothers and sisters to one another. Christ also calls us to be witnesses of God's presence in our lives. He sends us to bring into the lives of others his healing forgiveness and reconciliation with God and one another. The words Jesus addresses to his disciples on the mountain of the Ascension are addressed to all of us two millennia later. We are called to teach, to witness and to heal in our own small corners of the world, to hand on to others the story that has been handed on to us about Jesus and his Gospel of love and compassion.

Celebrating Christ's continuing presence.

The Ascension of the Lord is not the observance of a departure but the celebration of a presence. Matthew's Gospel begins with the promise of *Emmanuel* – "God is with us"; it concludes with the promise of the Risen Christ, "I am with you always, even to the end of time." While Jesus returns to the Father from whom he comes, he remains present to us in the Spirit of his love, his hope, his compassion "With a spirit of wisdom and insight to know him clearly...[and an] innermost vision [to] know the great hope to which he has called you" (first reading), we can discover Christ's presence at every turn of our lives' journeys to his final return at the end of time.

For reflection:

- What emotions and feelings do you think the eleven experienced as they walked down the mountain and returned to Jerusalem? Can you relate to such feelings?
- Who are the "apostles" to the small, hidden places of earth?
- What are the different ways we "teach" the good news? Two thousand years after it happened, can we be effective "witnesses" of the resurrection? How do we bring "healing" as Christ did into the lives of others?

Seventh Sunday of Easter

Readings:

John 17: 1-11
Acts 1: 12-14
1 Peter 4: 13-16

Today's reading from John's **Gospel**, the climax of the Last Supper discourse, is the "high priestly prayer" of Jesus. As his "hour" of glory approaches, Jesus prays to the Father for the unity of present and future disciples, a union rooted in the love of the Father and the Son.

In today's brief passage from Acts (**first reading**), the stage is set for the Pentecost event to be celebrated next week. After Jesus' Ascension, the small company returns to the upstairs room in Jerusalem "devoting themselves to constant prayer." This reading also contains the last New Testament reference to Mary, the mother of God. Her role in Jesus' birth parallels her presence at the birth of the Church, the body of Christ.

In today's final Easter reading from Peter's first letter (**second reading**), the writer concludes the letter with this exhortation for those who suffer and are persecuted. Their joy and hope in the promise of the Resurrection will not be in vain.

Themes:

The Church: 'one, holy, Catholic, apostolic.'

When Jesus left this world, he had little reason to hope. He seemed to have achieved so little and to have won so few. And the Twelve – soon to be the Eleven – to whom he has entrusted his new Church are certainly not among the most capable of leaders nor the most dynamic of preachers. Yet with so small a beginning, Jesus changed the world. As Jesus returns to the Father, he leaves a portion of the Father's glory behind: the community of faith. Jesus' priestly prayer, which we hear on this Sunday before Pentecost, is a prayer not only for his followers at table with him then but also for us at this table: that we may be united and consecrated in the truth Jesus has revealed and that we may reveal to the world the love and care of the Father for all of the human family.

Prayer: the awareness of God's presence.

The Church as a community of prayer is at the heart of today's readings – prayer that is, first and foremost, an attitude of trust and acceptance of God's presence in the community, an attitude that is not occasional but constant and continuing, an attitude not limited to asking for something but of thanksgiving for what is and for what has been. The prayer of Jesus at the Last Supper and the prayer of the company of disciples seek not God's acquiescence to their will but that God's will might be done effectively through them.

The Gospel entrusted to us and every generation.

In today's Gospel, Jesus prays that his disciples will be worthy and effective witnesses of the Gospel he has entrusted to them. That same Gospel has been passed on to every generation of the Church ever since. In baptism, that Gospel was passed on to us – we became witnesses of the great Easter event and accepted responsibility for telling our children and people of our time and place the good news of the empty tomb. Not in words alone but in our attitude of joy, our work for reconciliation among all, our commitment to what is right and just and our simplest acts of generosity and compassion, do we witness the Father's name and presence to the generations who follow us.

For reflection:

- How is Jesus' priestly prayer "answered" in our parish?
- In what places has the Church survived and flourished where there was little or no expectation that it would?
- What do today's readings teach us about prayer?

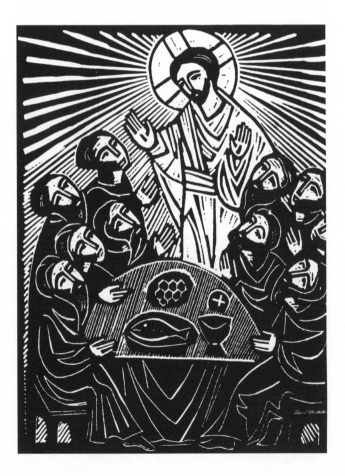

Readings:

John 20: 19-23
Acts 2: 1-11
1 Corinthians 12: 3-7, 12-13

Pentecost was the Jewish festival of the harvest (also called the Feast of Weeks), celebrated 50 days after Passover, when the first fruits of the corn harvest were offered to the Lord. A feast of pilgrimage (hence the presence in Jerusalem of so many "devout Jews of every nation"), Pentecost also commemorated Moses' receiving of the Law on Mount Sinai. For the new Israel, Pentecost becomes the celebration of the Spirit of God's compassion, peace and forgiveness – the Spirit that transcends the Law and becomes the point of departure for the young Church's universal mission (the planting of a new harvest?).

Today's **Gospel**, the first appearance of the Risen Jesus before his ten disciples (remember Thomas is not present), on Easter night is John's version of the Pentecost event. In "breathing" the Holy Spirit upon them, Jesus imitates God's act of creation in Genesis. In the Resurrection, the Spirit re-creates the band of disciples into the new Israel; the "peace" of understanding, enthusiasm and joy and shatters all barriers among them to make of them a community of hope and forgiveness. By Christ's sending them forth, the disciples become *apostles* – "those sent."

In his Acts of the Apostles (**first reading**), Luke invokes the First Testament images of wind and fire in his account of the new Church's Pentecost: God frequently revealed his presence in fire (the pillar of fire in the Sinai) and in wind (the wind that sweeps over the earth to make the waters of the Great Flood subside). The Hebrew word for spirit, *ruah*, and the Greek word *pneuma* also refer to the movement of air, not only as wind, but also of life-giving breath (as in God's creation of man in Genesis 2 and the revivification of the dry bones in Ezekiel 37). Through this life-giving "breath," the Lord begins the era of the new Israel on Pentecost.

Appealing for unity in the badly-splintered Corinthian community, Paul reminds the Corinthians of the presence of the Holy Spirit in their midst, which brings together the different charisms each possesses for the good of the whole community and the glory of God (**second reading**).

Themes:

The Spirit: the *ruah* of God.

The feast of Pentecost celebrates the unseen, immeasurable presence of God in our lives and in our church – the *ruah* that animates us to do the work of the Gospel of the Risen One, the *ruah* that makes God's will our will, the *ruah* of God living in us and transforming us so that we might bring his life and love to our broken world. God "breathes" his Spirit into our souls that we may live in his life and love; he ignites the "fire" of his Spirit within our hearts and minds that we may seek God in all things in order to realize the coming of his reign.

The Spirit: the powerful and enabling love of God.

Today we celebrate the Spirit – the great love that binds the Father to the Son and now binds us to God and to one another. It is a love that transcends words but embraces the heart and soul of each one of us; it gives voice to the things we believe but are too afraid to speak; it gives us the courage and grace to work for the dreams we are sometimes too cynical or fearful to hope for. The Spirit of God enables us to re-create our world in the love of the God who loved us enough to become one of us, to die for us and to rise for us. The theologian and scientist Teilhard de Chardin noted that "love is the only force that can make things one without destroying them. . . . Some day, after mastering the winds, the waves, the tides and gravity, we shall harness for God the energies of love, and then, for the second time in the history of the world, man will have discovered fire."

The Spirit: the 'birth' of the Church.

Pentecost is a moment of profound realization and transformation for the community of disciples. The faith they had received, the wonders they had witnessed and the Word they had heard came together in a new understanding, clarity, unity and courage to begin the work Jesus had entrusted to them. In Jesus' "breathing" upon them the new life of the Spirit, the community of the Resurrection – the Church – takes flight. That same Spirit continues to "blow" through today's Church to give life and direction to our mission and ministry to preach the Gospel to every nation, to proclaim the forgiveness and reconciliation in God's name, to baptize all humanity into the life of Jesus' Resurrection.

For reflection:

- The Spirit of God reveals itself in today's readings in the forms of fire, wind and breath. What other images can help us understand the Spirit of God working within us?

- How does the presence of the Holy Spirit make your parish "different" from other groups and organizations of people?

- Share stories of God's Spirit alive around you. How would those stories be different if God's Spirit was not present there?

Readings:

John 3: 16-18
Exodus 34: 4-6, 8-9
2 Corinthians 13: 11-13

As Ordinary Time resumes, two "solemnities of the Lord" are celebrated on the next two Sundays.

Today's celebration of the Trinity originated in France in the eighth century and was adopted by the universal Church in 1334. The solemnity focuses on the essence of our faith: the revelation of God as Creator, the climax of his creation in Jesus the Redeemer, the fullness of the love of God poured out on us in the Sustainer Spirit.

Nicodemus, a Pharisee and member of the Sanhedrin, comes under the cover of darkness to meet the remarkable Rabbi he has heard so much about. In their discussion (today's **Gospel**) Jesus speaks of the need to be reborn "from above" and of the great love of God who gives the world his own Son, not to condemn humankind but to save it.

In today's **first reading**, an angry and frustrated Moses returns to the summit of Mount Sinai. Having received the Law from God, Moses descended to the Israelite camp to find the people worshiping a golden calf. In his anger, Moses slammed the tablets to the ground, shattering them. God has instructed Moses to make a new set of tablets and return to the mountain, where the Lord will once again inscribe the Law on the new tablets. In his great mercy, God will forgive Israel and renew his covenant with them.

Paul's second letter to the Corinthians is his most personal and stormiest epistle. As in 1 Corinthians, Paul confronts the troubled community at Corinth with the issues dividing it and its strained relationship with Paul. The verses that make up today's **second reading** are the conclusion of Paul's letter, a final greeting of peace and prayer for unity in the Father, Son and Spirit.

Themes:

Trinity: the love of God revealed.

Many metaphors have been used to explain and depict the Trinity. St. John of Damascus, the great Eastern theologian of the eighth century, suggested that we think "of the Father as a root, of the Son as a branch, and of the Spirit as a fruit, for the substance of these three is

one." Today we celebrate the essence of our faith manifested in our lives: the loving providence of the Creator who continually invites us back to him; the selfless servanthood of the Redeemer who "emptied" himself to become like us in order that we might become like him; the joyful love of the Spirit that is the unique unity of the Father an Son.

The God of 'new beginnings.'

The three readings today all speak of a God who is motivated by a love we mortals cannot fathom. As revealed to us by Jesus, our God is a God not of endings but beginnings; a God who does not demand the payment of debts but who constantly offers unconditional and unlimited chances to begin again; a God who does not take satisfaction in our failures but rejoices in lifting us up from our brokenness, despair and estrangement from him and from one another. Despite our ignorance, displacement and sometimes outright rejection of him, God continues to call us back to him, always making the first move to welcome us back: God readily forgives Israel and renews his covenant with them (Exodus); God is the ultimate source of loving community, even for the deeply divided Corinthian church (2 Corinthians); God re-creates humankind in touching human history in the Christ event (John). Today's celebration is an invitation to share in God's work of reconciliation, of creating communion and community among all his people.

For reflection:

- Share stories of people who have been able to re-create their lives because they have experienced the mercy of God who always calls us back to him.
- The shamrock, the triangle and the fruit tree (St. John of Damascus, cited above) have been all been used to depict the mystery of the Trinity. Are there any contemporary images that help you understand and appreciate the Triune God?
- How has God – Father, Son and Spirit – made his presence known to you? How would you explain this presence to a non-believer?
- John's Gospel (John 3) tells the story of Jesus' meeting with Nicodemus, the Pharisee who comes at night to meet Jesus. In what ways do we approach God and the whole question of faith like Nicodemus approaches Jesus?

The Body and Blood of the Lord

Readings:
John 6: 51-58
Deuteronomy 8: 2-3, 14-16
1 Corinthians 10: 16-17

Today's celebration of the Body and Blood of the Lord originated in the Diocese of Liege in 1246 as the feast of Corpus Christi. In the reforms of Vatican II, the feast was joined with the feast of the Precious Blood (July 1) to become the Solemnity of the Body and Blood of the Lord. We celebrate today the Christ's gift of the Eucharist, the source and summit of our life together as the Church.

In the "bread of life" discourse in John's **Gospel**, Jesus' revelations concerning his Messianic ministry take on a Eucharistic theme. The image of Jesus as "bread from heaven" echoes two dimensions of the same First Testament image: the wisdom of God's Law nourishing all who accept it and God's blessing of manna to feed the journeying Israelites.

Today's **first reading** is taken from Moses' second address in Deuteronomy, as the Israelites emerge from their 40-year journey through the desert to the Promised Land. Moses and his people are standing on the high plateaus of Moab; stretching below them is the land God gives them. At this long awaited moment of fulfillment, Moses exhorts Israel to remember forever the goodness and mercy of God during their sojourn and cites many examples of God's providence, including the gift of manna in the desert.

In appealing to the Corinthians to heal their divisions, Paul cites the gift of the Eucharist as the ultimate expression of the unity of the Christian community (today's **second reading**).

Themes:

Eucharist: becoming the body of Christ.

"If you have received worthily," St. Augustine preached, "you are what you have received." The gift of the Eucharist comes with an important "string" is attached: it must be shared. In *sharing* the body of Christ, we *become* the body of Christ. If we partake of the "one loaf" (Reading 2), then we must be willing to become Eucharist for others – to make the love of Christ real for all.

Eucharist: the table of the Lord.

Christ calls us to his table, offering his peace, affirmation, support and love. We come to the Eucharist to celebrate our identity as his disciples and to seek the sustaining grace to live the hard demands of such discipleship; we come to the Eucharist seeking the peace and hope of the Risen One in the compassion and support we offer and receive from one another. At Christ's table, we are always welcome. In celebrating the Eucharist, we make our parish family's table the Lord's own table, a place of reconciliation and compassion.

Eucharist: united in 'memory.'

Before entering the Promised Land, Moses admonished the Israelites to become a people bound together by the memory of the great things God has done for them; at the Last Supper, Jesus instituted the new Passover of the Eucharist "in memory of me." Our coming to the table of the Eucharist is even more than just reliving the memory of Christ's great sacrifice for our redemption – in sharing the Eucharist we re-enter the inexplicable love of God who gives us eternal life in his Son, the Risen Christ.

Eucharist: the new manna, food for the journey.

The God who breathed his life into each one of us also gives us a world filled with all that is necessary to maintain that life. The people of Israel remember especially how God sustained them during their sojourn through the Sinai with the gift of manna. In raising Christ from the dead, God has effectively re-created humankind: We live in the hope that we will share in the life of the Risen One. The Eucharist is the new manna which sustains us on our journey to the eternal life of the Resurrection.

For reflection:

- How can we be "Eucharist" to one another? How can we bring the Eucharist from our altar into our world?
- Of all the foods of the earth, why is bread the perfect food to become the body of Christ?
- The word *Eucharist* means "thanksgiving." How can our sharing of the Body and Blood of the Lord be an act of thanksgiving, even when we gather under the most painful of circumstances?

The Sundays of the Year – Cycle A

Second Sunday of the Year

Readings:
John 1: 29-34
Isaiah 49: 3, 5-6
1 Corinthians 1: 1-3

The Fourth **Gospel** emphasizes John the Baptizer's role as the bridge between the First Testament and its fulfillment in Christ. In his vision of the Spirit of God "resting" upon and within Jesus, the Baptizer realizes that this is the chosen Servant of God who has come to inaugurate the Messianic era of forgiveness and reconciliation (today's **first reading**, the second of Isaiah's "servant" songs, describes the mission of the servant: to bring Israel back to the Lord and, through her, extend the Lord's salvation to every nation and people on earth).

On the first seven Sundays of Cycle A the second reading is taken from Paul's first letter to the Church at Corinth. Corinth was one of the great cities of the ancient world, a commercial crossroads between east and west, a melting pot of Jewish, Roman and Greek cultures, religions and influences. Corinth had all of the best and the worst of a bustling pagan capital: the high ideals of Greek spirituality existed side by side with a decadence and moral depravity that were reactions to the ancient Greek ascetic scorn of the physical.

Paul stayed in Corinth for almost two years during his second missionary journey. He wrote this letter, probably from Ephesus, in response to a communication he received outlining the problems and rivalries dividing the Corinthian community. In today's **second reading**, the introduction to 1 Corinthians, Paul describes the great dignity of those called to be part of the "consecrated . . . holy people" in Christ. Using First Testament images, Paul targets the two major themes of his letter to the Corinthians: the common call to holiness and the community's unity in the same Lord.

Themes:

The call to be witnesses and prophets of the 'Lamb of God.'

For most of us, John the Baptizer is an Advent character. He appears in the Advent readings admonishing us to prepare the way of the Lord who comes at Christmas. Although Christmas has been over for some weeks now, John is back in today's Gospel. Christ comes now to do the *work* of Christmas – to bring forgiveness and reconciliation to our hurting world. We have been called, as the Baptizer was called, to declare to our contemporaries that the "Lamb of God" has come. John declared his witness in preaching and baptizing; our witness can be declared in less vocal but no less effective vehicles: in our unfailing compassion for others, in our uncompromising moral and ethical convictions, in our everyday sense of joy and purpose.

Gospel hope in new possibilities and new beginnings.

Christ the Light dawns upon us, opening our eyes to see beyond ourselves and realize our kinship with one another as children of the same God and Father. Christ's presence among us is a time for new beginnings: an invitation to walk from the shadows of hatred and mistrust to the light of understanding and peace, a chance for healing our brokenness and mending our relationships with one another, a call to be seekers of hope and enablers of reconciliation in our own time and place.

Our call to be a 'consecrated' people.

The human life we are given is a gift from God "who formed [us] as his servant[s] from the womb" (first reading). Jesus, who began his public ministry by submitting to the baptism of John, came to sanctify and "consecrate" all humanity. We, too, are consecrated in our own baptisms: we have been set apart as a sacred and holy people by our God. This sacred dimension of all human life should profoundly affect every human contact and relationship we have.

For reflection:

- Have there been times in your life when you have experienced the presence of the "Lamb of God" in another's kindness, in their heroic charity, in their selfless attitude?
- Who are the witnesses of Christ among us now, whose perseverance and suffering say to the world: "Look there! The Lamb of God!"?
- The word *consecrate* comes from the Latin words meaning to set apart for the use of the sacred or holy. If we are a "consecrated" people, what difference should that "setting apart" make in our lives?

Third Sunday of the Year

Readings:
Matthew 4: 12-23
Isaiah 8: 23 – 9: 3
1 Corinthians 1: 10-13, 17

Galilee is the centerpiece of today's **Gospel** and First Testament readings.

In Jesus' time, Galilee was the most populated and productive region of Palestine. The great roads of the world passed through Galilee, making it a strategic target for invasion. White-sailed ships crept up the Mediterranean coast from Alexandria and caravans traveled through the region from Mesopotamia and Egypt.

Galilee, unlike the rest of Palestine, had an international perspective, in touch with many non-Jewish ideas and influences. Josephus, the Roman historian, wrote of the people of Galilee: "They were fond of innovation and, by nature, disposed to change and delighted in sedition...The Galileans were never destitute of courage...They were ever more anxious for honor than for gain."

In a few lines, Matthew sketches a new beginning in human history: the arrest of John and the end of the First Testament; the beginning of a "new" testament in the teaching and healing ministry of Jesus in Galilee and the call of the first disciples from their fishing nets along the Sea of Galilee. Jesus' beginning his public ministry in Galilee is, for Matthew, yet another fulfillment of an ancient oracle concerning the Messiah: that, through the darkness of Galilee's Assyrian captivity, the "great light" of their deliverance will appear (**first reading**).

The Christian community at Corinth was terribly divided. The factions were set up along lines of allegiance to the individual ministers who introduced them to Christianity – and each side was proud of their loyalty. "Disciples" of Cephas (Peter) would tend to be Jews, while the Gentiles would look to Paul for leadership; Greek converts, raised in the ascetic philosophy of the ancients, were devoted to Apollos, a fellow Greek. Paul minces no words in reminding them that the Church is one community by the cross of Christ: It was Christ – not Paul or Apollos or Cephas or anyone else – who redeemed them and reconciled them with God (**second reading**).

Themes:

A new era begins.

Today's Gospel marks a turning point in human history: the age of the prophets is fulfilled and the work of the Messiah begins; the "Old" Testament in John the Baptizer meets the "New" Testament in Jesus. The "great light of the Christ has finally dawned! The Messiah Jesus comes with a Gospel of healing that binds up ancient wounds, hatreds and despair. The challenge to those of every time and place who hear the Gospel is the same as when it was heard for the first time by the people of Galilee: to walk out of the darkness of self-centeredness, hopelessness and alienation and into the light of reconciliation, justice and hope, to be open to the Spirit of newness and the possibilities for forgiveness, reconciliation and rebirth.

Our invitation to discipleship: 'Follow me.'

Like Peter, James and John, we are asked by Jesus to take on the work of discipleship; we are asked to leave our "fishing nets" – our own needs and wants – to follow the example of love and servanthood given to us by Jesus; we are asked to rebuild our lives, homes and cities in the justice and peace that Jesus proclaims. Discipleship is risky, difficult and costly. But in inviting us to "follow" him, Jesus appeals to the goodness within each one of us and to our own hopes and dreams of living lives of fulfillment and grace. The Gospel is addressed to each one of us; we must look to our own hearts and spirits to respond to Jesus' invitation to "follow" him as his disciples.

Building dynamic Christian community.

Today's readings tell us about two very different groups of people: the Galileans, a people open to new ideas and change, and the Corinthians, a people torn apart by factionalism. Galilee and Corinth should challenge our parish families to be genuine Christian communities: welcoming the Gospel with inquisitive openness to change and renewal in our lives; recognizing in one another the faith we share and the humanity we have in common, given to us by the same God, the Father of us all.

For reflection:

- How is discipleship "risky"? What are the costs of abandoning our "fishing nets" to proclaim the Gospel?
- In what ways is the Gospel message "new" today, two thousand years after Jesus proclaimed it?
- How does your parish community resemble the Galileans? How does your parish community resemble the Corinthians?

Fourth Sunday of the Year

Readings:
Matthew 5: 1-12
Zephaniah 2: 3; 3: 12-13
1 Corinthians 1: 26-31

The Gospel readings for the next few Sundays will be taken from the Sermon on the Mount, Matthew's compilation of the discourses of Jesus.

Today's **Gospel** is the beautiful "Beatitudes" reading. The word "blessed," as used by Jesus in the eight maxims, was written in Greek as *makarios*, a word which indicates a joy that is God-like in its serenity and totality.

Specific Greek words used throughout the text indicate several important meanings:

* *the poor in spirit:* those who are detached from material things, who put their trust in God.
* *the sorrowing:* this Beatitude speaks of the value of caring and compassion – the hallmarks of Jesus' teaching.
* *the lowly:* the Greek word used here is *praotes* – true humility which banishes all pride; the "blessed" who accept the necessity to learn and grow and realize their need to be forgiven.
* *they who show mercy:* the Greek word *chesedh* used here indicates the ability to get "inside a person's a skin" until we can see things from his/her perspective, consider things from his/her experience mind and feel his/her joys and sorrows.
* *the peacemakers:* peace is not merely the absence of trouble or discord; peace is a positive condition – it is everything which provides and makes for humanity's highest good. Note, too, that the "blessed" are described as peace-*makers* and not simply peace-*lovers.*

Today's **first reading** is not typical of the firebrand Zephaniah who preached passionately to a Jerusalem corrupted by a return to old pagan practices (such as worshiping the sun and moon and stars) and political intrigue with their Assyrian occupiers. The Book of Zephaniah is a terrifying warning of the coming Day of the Lord (Zephaniah's descriptions of the final judgment inspired the Christian hymn *Dies Irae*). But in today's reading, the doomsayer Zephaniah speaks of hope: the Lord will protect "the remnant of Israel," the "people humble and lowly" who remain faithful to their covenant with him.

For the most part, the Christians in Corinth were non-entities, the most non-influential people in a very power conscious city. But in today's **second reading**, Paul assures them that worldly influence and wisdom do not matter. God did not choose the intellectual, the powerful and the noble for his own. To "boast in the Lord" (a favorite expression of Paul's) means to acknowledge that we live because of God's goodness and we live only for him.

Themes:

The Beatitudes: the Gospel system of values.

The Beatitudes call us to a very different set of values than those of our dog-eat-dog/success-is-everything/get-them-before-they-get-you/bottom-line-based world. We are called, as Zephaniah preaches, "to seek the Lord in all things." Rabbi Harold Kushner writes in his book, *When All You've Ever Wanted Isn't Enough:* "Our souls are not hungry for fame, comfort, wealth or power. Those rewards create almost as many problems as they solve. Our souls are hungry for meaning, for the sense that we have figured out how to love so that our lives matter."

The exaltation of the 'humble and lowly.'

Today's readings describe the people of God in less-than-exhilarating terms: "a remnant, humble and lowly" (first reading); absurd, weak, lowborn and despised (second reading); and poor, lowly, sorrowing and persecuted (Gospel). As a people of faith we are called to focus our lives on the "blessedness" of the Sermon on the Mount: to seek our joy and fulfillment in God above all things. Our "blessedness" cannot be measured by our portfolios, celebrity or intellect, but in our ability to grasp that we exist not in and of ourselves but by and in the love of God.

For reflection:

* The literary form used by Jesus in the Beatitudes, "Blessed are . . . for they . . ." is used frequently in the First Testament, especially in the Wisdom literature and the Psalms. How would Jesus "compose" the Beatitudes if he were speaking to your parish community?
* How can we realistically and pragmatically be the people of the Beatitudes, "a remnant, humble and lowly" in the marketplaces of our world?
* Which of the eight Beatitudes is especially meaningful to you?
* Who are among the "remnant" of our world, the "Blessed" of the Beatitudes, who remain faithful while living in a faithless world?

Fifth Sunday of the Year

Readings:

Matthew 5: 13-16
Isaiah 58: 7-10
1 Corinthians 2: 1-5

Unsalted popcorn and an electrical power outage are all that we need to appreciate Jesus' message in today's **Gospel** reading (the continuation of the Sermon on the Mount). Through the images of salt and light, Jesus impresses upon his listeners the vocation of Christians: *as I am salt and light to the world, so you, as my disciples, must reflect me to the world.*

Isaiah exhorts his listeners that they will realize their call to become a light for the nations only when they become a community of justice and charity (**first reading**). The prophet continues to speak of the Messiah's coming, not as a time of political or military victory for Israel, but as a time of justice, mercy and reconciliation.

Continuing his letter to the strife-torn Christian community at Corinth, Paul remembers his first disastrous preaching there (**second reading**). As recounted in the Acts of the Apostles, Paul's "weakness and fear" was in sharp contrast to the "eloquence" of Apollos. While the Corinthians responded favorably to Apollos' preaching, they were put off by Paul. The community began to splinter into factions. But regardless of whose preaching they heard and accepted, whatever effect the Gospel has had on them, Paul writes, is not due to the preacher's own "wisdom" or "eloquence" but to the Spirit of God giving life to those words.

Themes:

The Christian vocation: 'salt.'

As well as being the best thing that ever happened to French fries, the chemical compound salt has thousands of other uses. Not only does salt flavor food, salt also preserves such foods as meat and fish by drawing up the moisture from microorganisms that cause decay (without moisture, the bacteria die, thus keeping food from spoiling). Salt, a vital element in our blood, sweat and tears, bathes the billions of cells in our bodies. Salt has even more industrial uses: it is found in shoe leather and clothing dye; it softens water; it is used in making glass, building roads, manufacturing shampoo, bleaching paper and cooling nuclear reactors; it is used both in freezing and in de-icing. There are over 14,000 uses of salt – but by itself, salt is useless. Only when it mixes with something else is the value of salt realized. When Jesus tells us that we are to be "salt for the earth," he calls us to bring his compassion, justice and forgiveness into our homes, workplaces, schools and communities. Like salt, faith should be an active ingredient in every dimension of our lives. It means little if it is kept in its Sunday "shaker"; faith un-

locks the meaning and purpose of this life God has given us.

The Christian vocation: 'light.'

Since antiquity, light has been a powerful symbol of goodness shattering the "darkness" of evil, injustice and ignorance. Isaiah frequently uses light as a sign both of good conquering evil and of the Messiah's coming to restore Israel to its sacred character. Jesus invokes the image of light in the same way, but makes the additional point that we should not be afraid to be "light to the world" ("one does not light a lamp and then put it under a bushel basket"). Our simplest acts of charity can be a "light" for our world and unmistakable evidence of the presence of God among us.

For reflection:

- When and how are we salt-*less* Christians?
- Do you know people who have been "light" to others?

Sixth Sunday of the Year

Readings:
Matthew 5: 17-37
Sirach 15: 15-20
1 Corinthians 2: 6-10

Today's **Gospel** is the first indication of trouble between Jesus and the leaders of the Jews. The role of the scribes evolved from that of recorders and codifiers of the Torah into that of interpreters of the specific rules and regulations of the Torah. The Pharisees, the "separated brethren," removed themselves from everyday activity in order to keep the Law assiduously, thereby serving as a model to the Jewish people who held them in great esteem.

While the scribes and Pharisees were extreme legalists in their interpretation of the Law, Jesus is the ultimate *supra*-legalist. He takes their legalities a step further: The Spirit of God, which gives life and meaning to the Law, transcends the letter of the Law. Jesus preaches that we cannot be satisfied with merely avoiding the act of murder but must also curb the insults and anger that lead to murder; we cannot be satisfied with justifying separation and estrangement but must actively seek reconciliation and forgiveness; we cannot be satisfied with just fulfilling contracts in order to avoid being sued but must seek to become honest and trustworthy persons in all our dealings. Jesus comes to teach an approach to life that is motivated neither by edict nor fear but by the recognition and celebration of the humanity we share with all men and women.

For Jesus, the human heart is decisive. It is the "new" Law's emphasis on the attitude of the heart that perfects and fulfills the principles and rituals of the "old."

Life is a series of choices: between light and darkness, between good and evil, between life and death. True wisdom (Ben Sira's theme throughout this First Testament book) is seeking and choosing the things of God (**first reading**).

The Corinthian Church is a broken community, divided by different loyalties and philosophies. These verses would appear to be addressed to the Greeks who were schooled in the philosophical approaches of Aristotle, Sophocles and Plato. Echoing Ben Sira's theme, Paul writes that the source of true and eternal wisdom is God, who has revealed, in Christ Jesus, truth far beyond any "wisdom" the world teaches (**second reading**).

Themes:

Embracing the God's attitude of humble love.

While the scribes and Pharisees were obsessed with the meticulous keeping of the letter of the Law, Jesus taught the importance of the more difficult task of embracing the Spirit of God, the attitude of love and humility that endows all just laws with life and meaning. We often see laws and rules as the minimum required of us – beyond what is specifically defined and clearly spelled out, anything goes. But for Jesus, the human heart is decisive in determining what is right and wrong. Our faithfulness to prayer and worship means nothing if hatred and selfishness separate us from family and friends; anger is more than an emotion but the beginning of a potentially destructive chain of events in human relationships; sins of a sexual nature are not dismissed as mere "failings" but as an unacceptable degrading of men and women. Christ speaks not of rules and regulations but of the most profound values of the human heart. "What else are the laws of God," St. Augustine said, "but the very presence of the Holy Spirit."

Confronting the reality of 'truth.'

The truth is not contained in laws, oaths, statistics or rituals; it is found in the Spirit that prompts us in the decisions we make, the wisdom that leads us to the enactment of just laws and the celebrations of rituals that meaningfully remember and celebrate God's great love for us. All of us, at some point in our lives, are confronted by the truth: when the "safe" path we have chosen leads us to a sense of emptiness, when the values we pursue no longer square with the values of God. Authentic faith gives us a new vision to see the truth clearly and a spirit to embrace that truth with integrity and courage.

Taking responsibility for the choices we make.

On his deathbed, the noted cynic and agnostic W.C. Fields was discovered reading a Bible. When asked why his sudden interest in the Good Book, Fields explained, "I'm looking for a loophole." Ben Sira's words (first reading) strike at the "loophole detector" in all of us. We must take responsibility for the choices we make in this life. Similarly, Jesus' sermon in today's Gospel makes clear that more is expected of us than the scrupulous following of the letter of the Law. God holds us accountable not only for what we do but for the sincerity of the love that motivates us. God looks beyond excuses and rationalizations to the selflessness (or the self-centeredness) within our hearts.

For reflection:

- Have you experienced or witnessed love and commitment that transcended legal or moral expectations?
- How do we rationalize our way around or explain away ethical and moral dilemmas?
- How can getting "hung up" with technicalities and organizational structure limit our ability to accomplish something good?
- When have you had to accept responsibility reluctantly for some behavior or action? What did you learn from the experience?

Readings:
Matthew 5: 38-48
Leviticus 19: 1-2, 17-18
1 Corinthians 3: 16-23

In today's **Gospel**, Jesus continues to take the Law beyond the boundaries, narrow definitions and measurements of the official interpreters.

Of course, nowhere in the New Testament does the phrase "hate your enemy" appear – the concept of "enemy" was an assumption on the part of the scribes and Pharisees, who defined an enemy as anyone not a Jew. But Jesus challenges that assumption: God's love unites all men and women, on whom the Father's "sun rises and sets as well." However justified retaliation might appear to be, Jesus calls us to seek reconciliation instead of vengeance.

The Book of Leviticus is the Torah's "Sacramentary." A good portion of this third book of the Bible consists of laws governing rituals and sacrifices offered by for the priests of the tribe of Levi. The few verses that make up today's **first reading** reflect on charity towards one's "neighbor." Jews considered their "neighbors" to be exclusively Jewish; but Jesus made the concept of "neighbor" universal.

Paul's words in today's **second reading** are targeted at the different factions who are crippling the Church in Corinth. Paul minces no words: regardless of who baptized you or whose "brand" of Christianity you find attractive, in the faith all Christians share we form **one** "temple of God" – and woe to anyone who tries to destroy that temple, Paul warns.

The apostle's cryptic remarks about becoming a "fool" are addressed to a people who are considered outsiders in their own city. Corinth is an influential, cosmopolitan capital – the Corinthians pride themselves on their sophistication and wisdom in the affairs of the world. But Paul reminds the Christians of Corinth that true wisdom is of God and not of this world: We should purposely seek to be "fools" in the eyes of the world in order to be "wise" for the sake of the reign of God.

Themes:

The ministry of reconciliation.

Christ calls us to be more than just "law abiding" citizens – he calls us to be a people of reconciliation: to love the unlovable, to reach out to the alienated, to dismantle whatever walls divide and isolate people and build bridges that bring people together. The challenge of the Gospel is to be ready and willing to take the first step towards reconciliation – even towards people we would prefer having little or nothing to do with. Such a commitment to reconciliation and forgiveness is the cutting edge of the Gospel.

Forgiving our 'enemies.'

The Jesus of the Gospel instills within us a vision that sees beyond stereotypes, politics and appearances and recognizes and honors the goodness possessed by every human being. In the Greek text of Matthew's Gospel, the word used in today's text is *agape* (love). The word indicates not a romantic or emotional kind of love we have for the special ones in our lives but, rather, a state of benevolence and good will. The love that Jesus asks us to have for our "enemies" means that no matter how they hurt us, we will never let bitterness close our hearts to them nor will we seek anything but good for those "enemies." *Agape* begins with recognizing the humanity we share with all people who call God "Father." God's reign of justice and peace can only be realized when individuals freely surrender their own interests, needs and "just" due for the good of others.

For reflection:

- How does Jesus' teaching on loving one's enemies square with today's headlines?
- How can we realistically "love" our enemies?
- Is retaliation or vengeance ever justified?
- How do factions destroy unity of purpose in any organization or community?

Eighth Sunday of the Year

Readings:
Matthew 6: 24-34
Isaiah 49: 14-15
1 Corinthians 4: 1-5

Jesus' **Gospel** homily on serving "two masters" and the parables of the birds and wild flowers challenge our scale of values: Do we exist to acquire the holiness of God or the riches of life? Jesus does not deny the reality of basic human needs for food and clothing, but to displace the holiness of God with the perishables of wealth and power is the ultimate human tragedy.

Second Isaiah's prophetic mission was to give consolation to the Israelites who had been deported to Babylon by Nebuchadnezzar after the fall of Jerusalem in 597 B.C. Today's **first reading**, from Isaiah's poems of return, assures Israel that Yahweh has not forgotten them and that he is about to liberate his people again. The passage beautifully uses the image of a mother's love for her child to celebrate humanity's relationship with God.

In today's **second reading** – the last in this series of weekly readings from Paul's first letter to the Corinthians – the apostle continues his appeal to the many factions within the Church at Corinth to put aside their differences and remember their common call to be servants to another in Christ. Questioning another's commitment to the Gospel and sincerity of faith is a meaningless and fruitless exercise; such judgments are the domain of Christ alone.

Themes:

Gospel values: becoming slaves to things.

So much of our time and energy is spent worrying about and securing *things*. We can become so absorbed with the pursuit of money, prestige and power that we miss the sense of purpose God's presence gives our lives and fail to realize the richness of the love of those who are most important to us. Jesus does not condemn work, but he places it all in perspective. Material wealth is, rightly, a tool we use to cooperate with God in the work of completing creation; but money and power which become barriers between our lives and the life of God are idols to be condemned.

Trusting in the providence of God.

All three readings today speak of the providence of God: the God who does not forget us but constantly loves us as a mother who loves her child (Isaiah); the Lord who knows the "intentions of hearts" (1 Corinthians); and the Father who will provide for us (Matthew). In realizing God's care for all his people, we should, in turn, realize our own worth and the worth of every man, woman and child, who are also loved and cared for by God. This understanding of God's providence should have a profound impact on the values we embrace, helping us to see the world as one human family and leading us to seek what is good and just for all of God's people.

For reflection:

- Do you know of individuals whose climb up the ladder of success left them feeling empty, jaded and unfulfilled?
- We all know incessant worriers – people who deprive themselves of so much joy because of their often needless anxieties and groundless fears. What does today's Gospel say to them?
- How can we make life "simpler" in this complicated, fast-paced world of ours?
- What are the "warning signs" that one's pursuit of fame and fortune is out of control, that one is losing perspective as to what is genuinely important and of value in this life God has given us?

Readings:
Matthew 7: 21-27
Deuteronomy 11: 18, 26-28
Romans 3: 21-25, 28

In today's **Gospel**, Jesus concludes the Sermon on the Mount by exhorting his listeners to put the words of the Gospel into action. The depth of one's conviction of faith is the foundation of religion: The faith we actually live is the faith we really believe. One's sincerity is reflected in one's deeds; words can never substitute for actions.

The Book of Deuteronomy is a collection of Moses' exhortations to the Israelites on the plains of Moab as they prepared to enter the Promised Land. Today's **first reading** concludes Moses' explanation of the Covenant and its implications for the new nation of Israel. In their desert experience, Israel learned the great fidelity and power of God – despite their own infidelity and weakness. Now, as they are about to become a nation, Moses reminds his people that their very existence and identity as a people are dependent upon their response to the great love of God for them.

For 16 consecutive Sundays in this Cycle A of the lectionary, the second reading is taken from Paul's letter to the Christian community at Rome. The apostle wrote this, the longest of his letters, at the end of his third missionary journey. Writing from Corinth in 58 A.D., Paul is looking westward – all the way to what is now Spain – to new missionary challenges. This epistle was written to prepare the way for a journey to the imperial city, to introduce himself and his teaching to a Christian community he did not know.

Paul's letter to the Romans is a systematic treatise explaining how God's plan of salvation, ever since First Testament times, is fulfilled in Jesus Christ. This Sunday's **second reading** effectively summarizes a key theme of Romans: One's "justification" before God is not determined by the observance of all the detailed requirements of the Jewish Torah but by the depth of one's faith.

Themes:

The 'rock' of personal conviction.

Many older Catholics still remember a Church where every detail of faith was codified, measured and outlined for us – from the amount of money one could steal before the theft became a mortal sin (we were taught that $5 was the cut-off point, based on 1960 prices) to how much time we could save ourselves in Purgatory with the right combination and timing of prayers. The Jews of Jesus' time had the same experience: The rabbis had counted 613 separate laws and precepts specified in the Pentateuch, the Decalogue and Moses' explanation of them. To be a good and faithful Jew, then, was determined in one's observance of these 613 *mitzvoth*.

But Jesus says that authentic faith begins in one's heart, with an understanding of God's love for us and the irrepressible longing to respond to that love. The Fathers at Vatican II saw this in terms of the dignity of one's conscience: "Man has in his heart a law inscribed by God. His dignity lies in observing this law, and by it he will be judged. His conscience is man's most secret core, his sanctuary. There he is alone with God, whose voice echoes in his depths. In a wonderful way, conscience reveals that law which is fulfilled by love of God and neighbor." (*The Church in the Modern World*, 16)

Living the Gospel of the cross.

Jesus challenges us to bridge the chasm that often exists between what we say we belief and the values we actually live and practice. All of us, at one time or another, are guilty of rationalizing and hypocrisy; we find comfort in rhetoric and abstractions that shield us from the hard demands made by the Jesus of the cross. Throughout the Gospel, Jesus upholds the attitude of one's heart as the measure by which God will judge us. The faithful disciple understands that the love of God is the center of all things and seeks to bring that love into his/her life and the lives of others with conviction, integrity and perseverance.

For reflection:

- Some people's faith helps them withstand the storms of life, while others' faith fails them. Have you experienced or witnessed both kinds of faith? Why did faith remain? Why did it collapse?
- Recall times when your parish, as a whole, acted with the faith of "a house solidly set on rock."
- When have you been confronted with the reality of your own failure to live the values your profess?

Tenth Sunday of the Year

Cycle A

Readings:
Matthew 9: 9-13
Hosea 6: 3-6
Romans 4: 18-25

Tax collectors like Matthew were despised by the Jews of Palestine. Realizing it could never efficiently collect taxes from every subject in its far-flung empire, the Roman government auctioned off the right to collect taxes in a given area. Whoever bought that right was responsible to the Roman government for the agreed upon amount; whatever the purchaser could collect over and above that sum was his commission. How he "collected" those taxes was of little concern to the Romans. It was a system that effectively legalized corruption, extortion and bribery. The Jews considered tax collectors (also known as publicans) collaborators with their nation's occupiers who became wealthy men by taking advantage of their people's misfortune.

That Jesus should invite a tax collector to join his closest circle (today's **Gospel**), as well as welcoming known sinners into his company, scandalized the Pharisees. Citing the words of the prophet Hosea (today's first reading), Jesus states unequivocally that his Messianic mission is universal in nature and spirit and not limited to the coldly orthodox and piously self-righteous of Israel. Christ comes to call all men and women – Jew and Gentile, rich and poor, saint and sinner – back to the Father.

One of the twelve "minor prophets" of the First Testament, Hosea was the first to describe the relationship between Yahweh and Israel in terms of marriage. Hosea preached in the eighth century before Christ in the northern kingdom of Israel, which he refers to as Ephraim (Judah is the southern kingdom). In today's **first reading** the prophet warns the Israelites that their community's offering of sacrifices and holocausts to God should reflect the community's interior spirit of obedience and praise. Without love and knowledge of God, such worship is a sham.

Both Abraham and Christians know a God who brings forth life out of death. For Abraham, God brought life out of Sarah's dead womb; in raising Jesus from the dead, God restored us to life. For the apostle Paul, Abraham is a model of faith for us who have witnessed God's covenant promises to the First Testament patriarchs and prophets fulfilled in the Risen Christ (today's **second reading**).

Themes:

Worship: expressing the faith of our hearts.

Each week we gather around our altars to celebrate, in word and sacrament, our relationship with God. God does not demand but invites us to celebrate with him. Our worship means very little if we are conscious of our faith only for this one hour each week. (Sometimes our sense of Christian love and community doesn't even make it out of the church parking lot!). Our worship should reflect and celebrate the joy and love we live every day of every week; otherwise, as Hosea says, our worship is "like the dew that early passes away."

To rejoice in what is good and right.

Jesus came to show fishermen and farmers, peasants and prostitutes, tax collectors and shepherds, widows and children that they are all special in God's eyes. What is especially sad about the incident recorded in today's Gospel is the Pharisees' inability to rejoice with and for those who have been restored to hope by the forgiveness of God. These "professional religious" could not accept the fact that God loves these people as much as he does those who considered themselves the "separated brethren" because of their fastidious keeping of the Law. Because of their concern with criticism instead of encouragement and condemnation instead of forgiveness, the Pharisees failed to understand, not through legal entities and impersonal theological treatises, but through compassion and reconciliation to all human hearts.

For reflection:

- When do we become a society of "Pharisees," critical and intolerant of other individuals and groups we consider "different" and "unworthy" to be part of our community?
- How should our celebration of the Eucharist each week affect the everyday dimensions of our lives?
- Have you ever found yourself suspicious over someone's "conversion" or wary of someone's sudden kindness? What made you suspicious? Did it turn to anger? Why?

11th Sunday of the Year

Readings:
Matthew 9: 36 – 10: 8
Exodus 19: 2-6
Romans 5: 6-11

Today's **Gospel** serves as a narrative transition from Matthew's recounting of Jesus' miraculous deeds (chapters 8 and 9) to Jesus' missionary discourse (chapters 10 and 11). The missionary dimension of discipleship is underscored by two images: the people who are "like sheep without a shepherd" and the need for laborers to gather the harvest. Having established his great powers as a healer, Jesus now passes on to the Twelve the "gift" of their own call and mission to the people of Israel.

The covenant God makes with Israel during the Exodus transformed the Israelites from a band of ex-slaves into a nation. It gave them an identity and a destiny. The God who brought them out of the land of Egypt to a promised land now invites them to enter into a special relationship with him – a covenant of intimacy, holiness and freedom (**first reading**).

In the giving of his Son to renew and re-create that covenant by his passion, death and resurrection, God continues to call humanity back to him (**second reading**).

Themes:

The disciple's vocation to share the 'gift' of faith.

The Twelve whom Jesus "summons" in today's Gospel are very ordinary men. They possess neither wealth, scholarship nor social standing; yet they are given the "gift" of leadership to share with all people the Gospel they have received. Whether ordained or not, all who are baptized share in this "priestly" work (first reading) of sharing the gift of faith with others. In even the smallest and simplest act of love and compassion we announce that "the reign of God is upon us."

The ministry of 'healing' reconciliation.

In today's Gospel, Jesus commissions the apostles to a ministry of healing. But to see this commission as involving physical healing alone is to miss an important dimension of Jesus' ministry. Jesus commissions the apostles and his Church to heal hearts and souls in a ministry of reconciliation:

* *cure the sick:* bring back to God those who are alienated, those are weak in faith (the word used in the Greek text *asthenes* means "weak");
* *raise the dead:* bring back those hopelessly and helplessly dead because of sin and blind and deaf to the goodness and love of God.
* *heal the leprous:* bring back those who have been rejected or are separated from God's people;
* *expel demons:* liberate those enslaved by sin and evil.

A Shepherd for 'sheep without a shepherd.'

People are thirsting, yearning for a God in whom they can center their lives, a Shepherd to lead them to community, compassion and purpose. Jesus' compassion for the "shepherdless" confronts us with our own commitment to bring to others the Gospel spirit of justice, compassion and reconciliation. Today's Gospel also reaffirms our responsibility to welcome rather than judge others who have not heard the voice of the Shepherd, to seek reconciliation with those from whom we are estranged or separated for whatever reason. Faithfulness to the call of discipleship compels us to lead others to the joy, healing and hope of Christ, our Shepherd, by the joy, healing and hope we live.

For reflection:

* Would you consider your own call to ministry a gift?
* How is your parish community – both those ordained and those not ordained – a "kingdom of priests, a holy nation"?
* Is there one of the Twelve Apostles, listed by Matthew in today's Gospel, with whom you especially identify?
* Do any of today's headlines indicate to you that we are still "sheep without a shepherd"?

Readings:

Matthew 10: 26-33
Jeremiah 20: 10-13
Romans 5: 12-15

In Matthew's missionary discourse (**Gospel**), Jesus instills in his disciples the need for openness and courage in their preaching of the Gospel. The disciple who faithfully proclaims the Gospel will likely be denounced, ridiculed and abused; but Jesus assures his followers that they have nothing to fear from those who can deprive "the body of life," for their perseverance and courage in proclaiming the Gospel of Jesus will be rewarded in the reign of God.

Jeremiah recognized that the Babylonian empire rising in the north posed a serious threat to Judah. Jeremiah prophesied that Judah's pride and infidelity would lead to the fall of Jerusalem and the destruction of the temple. The king, enraged that Jeremiah could suggest such an unthinkable thing, had the prophet whipped and placed in the stocks. Though denounced and persecuted by the people he loved, the deeply sensitive Jeremiah remains faithful to his prophetic call, confident that God is with him and that his persecutors will not triumph (**first reading**).

In his letter to the Romans (**second reading**), Paul contrasts the figures of Adam and Christ. Adam is the first human who unleashed the power of sin into the world and, consequently, humankind's alienation from God; for Paul, Jesus is the first human of God's new creation. By the gracious gift of Jesus Christ, sin and death are destroyed and grace and life are restored.

Themes:

'Do not be afraid . . .'

Today's first reading and Gospel are powerful assurances that we have nothing to fear before God. Three times in today's Gospel Jesus tells his disciples not to be afraid. Imagine living your life fearing no person, group or institution anywhere, "fearing" only God – God who has already proven his love and acceptance of us unreservedly, the Father who watches over the smallest of creatures. Such a realization is the ultimate liberation and empowerment. Fear is most destructive when it chokes us off from creating or accomplishing what is right, just and good. In overcoming such fears do we begin to become faithful disciples of Christ Jesus.

As the late Dr. Martin Luther King Jr. preached: "Courage is an inner resolution to go forward despite obstacles; cowardice is submissive surrender to circumstances. Courage breeds creative self-affirmation; cowardice produces destructive self-abnegation. Courage faces fear and masters it; cowardice represses fear and is mastered by it."

The courage to proclaim the truth.

Diogenes, the Greek philosopher, observed that, for many, "truth is like light to sore eyes." Jesus does not sugar-coat his warning: The Gospel demands the courage to stand up for its principles in the face of society's skepticism and disapproval. Like the Jews' rejection of Jeremiah's unpopular message, many segments of society cannot abide the idea of unconditional love nor the constant call to forgive demanded by Jesus in the Gospel. If we take our role as disciples seriously, then, we are probably going to do time in the "stocks" of public disapproval and derision for the Gospel we live.

Important to understand, too, is the call of Jesus to "acknowledge me before others." We can "disown" Jesus actively by our words and actions, but we can also "disown" him passively by our silence.

For reflection:

- Who are the martyrs of our own time, whose sacrifice and death proclaim their faith in the mercy and love of God?
- How do we "disown" Jesus by silence?
- In what ways are today's readings "liberating"?
- What community and national concerns today need the perseverance and faith of a prophet like Jeremiah or a faithful disciple of Jesus?

Readings:

Matthew 10: 37-42
2 Kings 4: 8-11, 14-16
Romans 6: 3-4, 8-11

Today's **Gospel** is the conclusion of Matthew's collection of Jesus' missionary discourses, in which Jesus speaks of the sacrifice demanded of his disciples and the suffering they will endure for their faith. In today's reading, Jesus clearly is not attacking family life; he is warning his disciples of the conflict and misunderstanding they will experience for their proclaiming the word. To be an authentic disciple of Jesus means embracing the suffering, humility, pain and selflessness of the cross; to be an authentic disciple of Jesus means taking on the often unpopular role of prophet for the sake of the kingdom; to be an authentic disciple of Jesus means welcoming and supporting other disciples who do the work of the Gospel.

Elisha was ordained by God to be the successor the great prophet Elijah (1 Kings 19: 15-21). Today's **first reading** is one of several delightful First Testament stories about Elisha the "miracle worker" and his assistant Gehazi. The woman of Shunem recognizes the sacred nature of Elisha's calling and assists him as she is able, offering him the hospitality of her home. Elisha, in turn, rewards her for her kindness with the promise of a child.

In today's **second reading**, from the letter to the Romans, Paul writes that, although sin is still very much a reality in our lives, it is no longer a permanent, hopeless condition. We Christians live always in the hope and power of Christ's resurrection.

Themes:

The disciple's call to seek reconciliation.

The true disciple of Christ takes a very different approach to resolving conflict — an approach totally at odds with the win-at-all-costs philosophy of the world: We are called to work for reconciliation regardless of the cost. Christ's challenge to us is to look beyond stereotypes and labels to see, instead, brothers and sisters. Christ calls us to rise from the grave of self-centeredness, putting the needs of others first and our own interests last.

'Welcoming' the prophet/disciple's call.

God calls every one of us to the work of the prophet – to proclaim his presence among his people. Jesus demands that anyone who would be his disciple put themselves "to ruin" and "nought" for the sake of something far greater – God's reign of compassion and justice for all. Some are called to be witnesses of God's justice in the midst of profound evil and hatred; others are called to be witnesses of his hope and grace to those in pain and anguish; and many share in the work of the prophet/witness by enabling others to be effective witnesses and ministers of God's love. The gift of faith opens our spirits to realize and accept our call to be witnesses of God's love borne on the cross and prophets of the hope of his Son's resurrection.

Taking up the cross of Jesus.

We all try to live our faith as best we can, but most of us will readily concede that we have our limits. The most difficult part of imitating Jesus is the cross and what it stands for: unconditional forgiveness, the totally emptying of ourselves of our wants and needs for the sake of another, the spurning of safety and popular convention to do what is right and just. To imitate Jesus with faithfulness and integrity means to take up his cross and live, regardless of the cost and pain, the values of that cross and the Gospel of the Crucified.

For reflection:

- When was the last time you experienced a genuine crisis of conscience – a situation when you felt social convention pressuring you to act in a way contrary to your sense of the Gospel?
- In what ways can we welcome the "prophets" present among us today?
- How do we discover ourselves in "bringing ourselves to nought" for the sake of the Gospel?

Readings:
Matthew 11: 25-30
Zechariah 9: 9-10
Romans 8: 9, 11-13

Rarely outside of John's Gospel is Jesus' intimacy with the Father so clearly portrayed as in today's **Gospel** from Matthew. Jesus offers a hymn of praise to his Father, the holy Creator of all who deeply loves his creation as a father loves his children. The great love of God for all of humanity is revealed in the love of his Son, the Messiah.

Religion as a "yoke" was exactly how Jesus' Jewish listeners saw the Law. They saw their faith as a burden, a submission to a set of endless rules and regulations dictating every dimension of their lives. But Jesus describes his "yoke" as "easy." The Greek word used here that we translate as "easy" more accurately means "fitting well." In Palestine, ox yokes were custom-made of wood, cut and measured to fit a particular animal. Jesus is proposing here a radical change in attitude regarding religion: Our relationship with God is not based on how meticulously we keep a certain set of rules and regulations (a direct challenge to the long-held views of the scribes and Pharisees) but in the depth of our love for God, reflected in our love for others. Our relationship with God is not based on subjugation and weariness but on hope and joy.

There is also an important political dimension to these verses. Matthew's Gospel was written a short time after the destruction of Jerusalem in the year 70 A.D. by the soldier-emperor Vespasian. For both the Jewish and the new Christian communities, it was a time of painful introspection: Would Israel's hope for the political restoration of the Jewish state never be realized? While orthodox Jews maintained unwavering fidelity to their people, language and sense of nationalism, the Christian "cult" saw their ultimate destiny not in the political restoration of Israel but in the coming of the reign of God – a reign that embraces not just Jews but all men and women, even Israel's most despised enemies. Jewish suspicion of the Christian community was growing as the new group would have no part of the Jewish political agenda. Jesus' words on gentleness and humility set off sparks between loyal Jews and Christians who were abandoning the cause.

The prophecy by Zechariah in today's **first reading** was cited by the evangelists as fulfilled in Jesus' entry into Jerusalem. The prophecy is not only fulfilled literally but, more importantly, in spirit: the Messiah comes, not in fire and fury, but in quiet humility; he comes, not armed with military might, but with peace and justice, banishing the implements of war forever.

The image of a king riding on an ass strikes today's listener as a contradiction, but, in Zechariah's time, a ruler riding on an ass was a symbol of great dignity and author-ity (hence, Jesus is hailed as a king in the Palm Sunday Gospel). There is also an irony in this image that is not lost on Zechariah's hearers: The Jews were despised by their Persian and Egyptian enemies who ridiculed the Jews as "donkey drivers." Among this nation of "donkey drivers" God's own light will dawn for the world.

Paul assures the Christians of Rome in today's **second reading** that we are people of the Spirit of God – we live constantly in the hope of the Resurrection, not in the hopelessness of this world of ours.

Themes:

The 'burden' and 'yoke' of discipleship: service.

At the entrance to Father Flanagan's Boys' Town, there is a sculpture of an older boy carrying a younger child on his shoulders. The inscription at the base of the statue reads, "He ain't heavy, Father, he's my brother" (the inscription was also the title of a popular song recorded by Neil Diamond and by the Hollies in the early 1970s). The statue (and song) are the perfect responses to the "burden" Christ proposes for us. To love one another as God has loved us, to serve one another as Christ the Savior serves God's people, is a yoke that is "easy" in its sense of fulfillment and "light" in its sense of joy.

The 'child-like' dimension of faith: humility.

There is most definitely a child-like dimension to faith: We are called to see the wonders of God's love in everyone and everything. But we consider ourselves too sophisticated, too wise, too busy to see and hear and feel the presence of God in our world: in the love and laughter of children, in the simple kindness of friends, in the heroic but little recognized charity of the real disciples and prophets among us. In calling us to be "gentle" and "humble of heart," Jesus does not call us to be simpletons and anti-intellectuals but to embrace his attitude and spirit of hearts open to the Word of God and hands open to sharing and giving to all people – sons and daughters of our Father in Heaven, our brothers and sisters in Christ.

For reflection:

- How do we needlessly approach our faith as a "burden"? How do we take the joy out of religion?
- How is the disciple of Christ to be a strong and tireless witness to the Gospel and, at the same time, "gentle and humble of heart"?
- What does the image of the "king riding on an ass" teach us about the crises and challenges facing our world today?

15th Sunday of the Year

Readings:
Matthew 13: 1-23
Isaiah 55: 10-11
Romans 8: 18-23

Chapter 13 of Matthew's **Gospel** is the evangelist's collection of Jesus' parables. The word parable comes from the Greek word *parabole* which means putting two things side by side in order to confront or compare them. And that is exactly how Jesus uses parables: He places a simile from life or nature against the abstract idea of the reign of God. The comparison challenges the hearer to consider ideas and possibilities greater and larger than those to which they might be accustomed.

Jesus' hearers expected God's kingdom to be the restoration of Israel to great political and economic power; the Messiah would be a great warrior-king who would lead Israel to such triumph. Jesus' parables subtly and delicately led people, without crushing or disillusioning them, to rethink their concept of God's kingdom.

In Palestine, sowing was done before the plowing. Seed was not carefully or precisely placed in the ground. The farmer scattered the seed in all directions, knowing that, even though much will be wasted, enough will be sown in good earth to ensure a harvest nonetheless. The parable of the sower (which appears in all three synoptic gospels) teaches that the seed's fruitfulness (God's word) depends on the soil's openness (the willingness of the human heart to embrace it).

Deutero-Isaiah, the prophet of the exile, concludes his section of the Book of Isaiah with the description of God's word enriching our lives like the rains of heaven enrich the earth for the harvest (**first reading**).

Paul assures the church at Rome (**second reading**) that the glory that awaits Christ's faithful far exceeds the sufferings of the present. All of creation, which "groans (in) agony," joins humanity in anticipating the completion of our redemption.

Themes:

The harvest: opening our hearts to God.

In order to grow, a seed must be placed *inside* the earth so that its roots may take hold as its stem reaches for the sun above the surface. The parable of the sower challenges us to see how deeply the word of God has taken root in our lives, how central God is to the very fabric of our day-to-day existence: Are we too obtuse to understand the meaning of God's word in our lives (like the seed on the footpath)? Maybe our faith is a "Sunday mornings only" experience and has no practical application in the real world of Monday through Saturday (the seed on the rocky soil); or perhaps we're too intent on "making it" in the world that we refuse to allow the presence of God to alter our agenda for wealth and power (the seed among the briars). As the dry earth yearns for the water to bring forth the harvest (first reading), so must our hearts be open to receive the word of God.

Hope: the unexpected harvest.

The farmer of the parable confidently seeds his fields knowing that, although some seed will be lost to the footpaths, rocks and thorns, a harvest will come. God's word of love and healing will go forth and be fruitful (first reading) – sometimes in soil in which such growth is unexpected. We must not be discouraged or intimidated from what is right or good because it might be misinterpreted, misunderstood or rejected. Sometimes we may never realize what good will be realized from the smallest "seed" of kindness we plant. Christ invites us, his followers, to embrace the faith of the sower: to trust and believe that our simplest acts of kindness and forgiveness, our humblest offer of help and affirmation to the needy, our giving of only a few minutes to listen to the plight of another soul may be the seeds that fall "on good soil" and yield an abundant harvest.

For reflection:

- Consider how different people react to the messages of the Gospel. Why the different reactions? What dimensions of people's backgrounds and experiences affect how – and how much – of the Gospel takes root?
- Share stories of how a simple act of kindness – a good word, a smile, a moment to listen – yielded an unexpected harvest of growth and goodness.
- Reflect on the ways in which the "harvest" we desire differs from the "seeds" we sow.

16th Sunday of the Year

Readings:
Matthew 13: 24-43
Wisdom 12: 13, 16-19
Romans 8: 26-27

Matthew's Gospel has been called the "Gospel of the Kingdom," containing some 51 references to the kingdom or reign of God. Three of Jesus' "kingdom" parables make up today's **Gospel**: *The parable of the wheat and the weeds:* God's kingdom will be "harvested" from among the good which exists side-by-side with the bad. Palestinian farmers were plagued by *tares* – weeds that were very difficult to distinguish from good grain. The two would often grow together and become so intertwined that it was impossible to separate them without ripping both weed and plant from the ground. Jesus teaches his impatient followers that the Lord of the harvest is more concerned with the growth of the wheat than with the elimination of the weeds. The time for separation and burning will come in God's own time; our concern should be that of our own faithfulness.

The parable of the mustard seed: The smallest and humblest are enabled by the Holy Spirit to do great things in the kingdom of God. From small and humble beginnings, God's kingdom will grow.

The parable of the yeast: A small amount of yeast mixed with three measures of flour can make enough bread to feed over one hundred. In the same way, God's reign is a powerful although unseen force.

Matthew's Gospel was written some 50 years after Jesus' death and 15 years after the destruction of Jerusalem. By this time it is clear to the community of Christians that Jesus is not going to be accepted by all of Israel as the Messiah. In citing these parables, the evangelist encouraged the largely Jewish Christian community to see itself as the legitimate heir to God's promises to Israel. They were the "good wheat" existing side by side with the "weeds" that would destroy it, the small mustard seed that would give rise to the great and mighty tree of the Church, the small amount of yeast that would become bread for the world.

The Book of Wisdom, written less than 100 years before Christ, is addressed to the Jewish community that settled in Alexandria during the exile. The author makes Solomon, the wise king of Hebrew tradition, his mouthpiece in order to give more credence to his teachings. The Book of Wisdom exhorts Greek-speaking Jews who have abandoned their faith to enter the mainstream of Greek philosophy and thought to seek again the true wisdom of God.

Today's **first reading** speaks of the mercy and justice of God as signs of his great power. The author reminds his readers that as the chosen of God they are to be compassionate and merciful as God has been compassionate and merciful toward Israel throughout its history. The truly powerful do not intimidate others with displays of might but use their power to inspire others to do what is good and right.

In today's **second reading**, from his letter to the Romans, Paul reflects on the role of the Spirit as an inspiration to prayer. The awareness of God's Spirit within us gives both meaning and focus to our prayers.

Themes:

'The wheat and weeds': embracing the joy of faith.

We often approach religion as a deadly serious business; we lose the spirit of joy and the sense of hope that are part of the promise of the Risen Christ. We become so concerned about pulling out the weeds that we forget to harvest the grain; we become so focused on the evil and abuses that surround us and "threaten" us that we fail to realize and celebrate the healing and life-giving presence of God in our very midst; we become so intent in upbraiding and punishing sinners that our own lives become mired in gloom and despair. The Lord of the harvest is more concerned about the growth of the good wheat than the elimination of the weeds. The task of judging sinners belongs to God; to us belongs the work of compassion and reconciliation.

'Mustard seeds': trusting in small beginnings.

All of us, at some time, are called to be "mustard seeds": to do the small, thankless things that are necessary to bring a sense of wholeness and fulfillment to our homes and communities. History records many examples of seemingly small acts of courage that ignited revolutions on behalf of what is right and just. From such "mustard seeds" are yielded great harvests of peace and reconciliation.

The Christian vocation of being 'yeast' to our world.

The parable of the yeast speaks to us of our vocation as Christians in the world. In baptism, we accept God's call to be "yeast," giving life to a world which is often lifeless in its despair and aimlessness. The call to holiness becomes more and more difficult as society becomes less and less tolerant of the spiritual. What the world values is often at odds with Christ's call to selflessness and simplicity. Our faith in the God of forgiveness and redemption gives us the courage to carry on until the harvest.

For reflection:

- In light of today's first reading from the Book of Wisdom, if we are the "wheat of the field," how should we deal with the "weeds"?
- Share stories you have found especially inspiring of small "seeds" giving rise to great things, of individuals who have realized the full potential of the Gospel mustard seed.
- Looking through today's newspaper, do you see, in the midst of war, terrorism, poverty, etc., traces of the "yeast" of the kingdom of God?

Readings:

Matthew 13: 44-52
1 Kings 3: 5, 7-12
Romans 8: 28-30

The first two parables in today's **Gospel** – the parables of the buried treasure and the pearl – are lessons in the total *attach*ment to Christ and *detach*ment from the things of the world demanded of the disciple to make the reign of God a reality. The parable of the dragnet is similar in theme to last week's parable of the wheat and weeds. Again, Matthew makes the point that the kingdom of God is neither an instant happening nor a static event, but a dynamic movement toward completion and fulfillment which Jesus set into motion.

Solomon succeeded his father David in 961 B.C. to become the third and last king of the twelve tribes. Today's **first reading** underscores the promise of the young king, who requests from the Lord the wisdom and understanding to fulfill his role as a kind and just ruler of God's people.

The **second reading**, from Paul's letter to the Romans, outlines the Christian vocation as it was designed by God: to be conformed to the image of his Son. The references to "predestination" do not refer to an arbitrary decision by God of who will and who will not be saved but to the fact that God's offer of salvation to all of humanity transcends the confines of time.

Themes:

Risking all things for the values of God.

Today's readings speak of the discovery of the "meaning of life," the search for lasting values. As Solomon understood in asking the Lord for wisdom and "an understanding heart" (first reading), the "treasures" and "pearls" of lasting value are the things of God: the love of family and friends, the support of community, the sense of fulfillment from serving and giving for the sake of others. In order to attain such treasure, we must take the risk of the speculator and "sell off" our own interests, ambitions and agendas in order to free ourselves to embrace the lasting values of the compassion, love and reconciliation of God.

Wisdom: the search for God in all things.

The institutions and beliefs in which we place our faith can let us down; the present confounds us and the future bewilders us. As today's readings make clear, true wisdom begins with seeking God's ways of justice and mercy first in all things.

For reflection:

- Do you know of individuals who have discovered a "treasure" of insight that remained hidden to others around them?
- How have your values changed over the years?
- When God offers Solomon anything he wants, Solomon asks God for wisdom; in the parable of the buried treasure, the finder sells every possession he has to buy the field. Consider the high cost of embracing the wisdom and values of God.
- Have you ever doubted the "wisdom of God" because it seemed so contrary to prevailing popular opinion or conventional wisdom – only to realize later that the truth did, in fact, lie with God?

18th Sunday of the Year

Readings:
Matthew 14: 13-21
Isaiah 55: 1-3
Romans 8: 35, 37-39

The multiplication of the loaves and fish (**Gospel**) is the only one of Jesus' miracles recorded in all four Gospels. The early Christian community especially cherished this story because they saw this event as anticipating the Eucharist and the final banquet in the kingdom of God. This miracle also has strong roots in the First Testament: Just as the merciful God feeds the wandering Israelites with manna in the desert, Jesus, "his heart moved with pity," feeds the crowds who have come to hear him.

In Matthew's account, Jesus acts out of his great compassion on the crowds. First, he challenges the disciples to give what they have – five loaves and two fish. Then he performs the four-fold action that prefigures the Eucharist: Jesus takes, blesses, breaks and gives the bread and fish to the assembled multitude, making of them a community of the Lord's banquet.

King Cyrus of Persia defeated the Babylonians in 539 B.C. Unlike conquerors before him, Cyrus did not deport defeated peoples for slave labor nor did he suppress their religious traditions; instead, he allowed them to remain in their homeland and he himself honored what his people held as sacred. And so Cyrus permitted the Jews who were exiled by the Babylonians to return to Jerusalem and rebuild the temple the Babylonians sacked and destroyed five decades before. Deutero-Isaiah, the prophet of the exile, rejoices in the repatriation of his people. Using the image of a great feast (**first reading**), the prophet preaches that the land God gave Israel will once again be fruitful if God's justice and mercy are allowed to prevail.

In the continuation of his letter to the Romans (**second reading**), Paul offers a hymn of praise to Christ, the supreme hope of the Christian community. Nothing in this world nor outside of it has the power or authority to "separate" us from the love of Christ.

Themes:

The banquet of heaven.

For the peoples of both the First and New Testament, the image of a great banquet was an important visualization of the reign of God: the gifts of the land were unmistakable signs of their God's great Providence; the Messiah's coming was often portrayed as a great banquet with choice food and wines; the miracle of the loaves and fishes is a clear affirmation in God's providence. The bread of the Eucharist, which we share together in charity and faith, is a prelude to the great banquet of the next world to which our loving Father invites us.

Building a community of faith though sharing.

In today's Gospel, Jesus feeds the crowds with the little that the apostles could scrape together – five pieces of bread and two fish. Because someone was willing to share what he or she had, Jesus was able to make a miracle happen. But the real wonder of the event transcended the physical act of feeding so many people – the real miracle was the creation of a community. We, in turn, must be motivated by that same spirit of compassion to bring to the table whatever bread and fish we possess that they may be transformed and shared for the good of all. Faithful to the call of discipleship, we must give totally and completely, without judgment or conditions, with the same loving compassion of Jesus.

For reflection:

- Is our contemporary concept of mealtime still a fitting image for the providence of God and the reign of God to come?
- Consider the ways we misuse food and drink – from self-destruction to exploitation.
- How is the crowd in today's Gospel like your own parish community?
- Have you ever experienced the act of sharing as a transforming event within a group or community?

19th Sunday of the Year

Readings: Matthew 14: 22-33
1 Kings 19: 9, 11-13
Romans 9: 1-5

In Matthew's **Gospel**, the storm at Gennesaret and Peter's walking on the water immediately followed the multiplication of the loaves and fishes. The depth of Peter's love for Jesus is not matched by a depth of faith; but Jesus nonetheless raises the sinking disciple up from the waters of fear and death.

The prophet Elijah, in today's **first reading**, is on the run. His preaching against the idolatrous practices of King Ahab and Queen Jezebel made him a marked man. Forced into hiding, Elijah is a broken man. He begs God to take his life; but instead, God saw that he had whatever food he needed and sent him on a 40-day journey to Horeb, the same mountain upon which Moses encountered God. Elijah does not hear God in the tornado, earthquake and fire, but in a "tiny whispering sound" that speaks not to the senses but to the heart.

The five verses from his letter to the Romans that make up today's **second reading** reveal Paul's deep sensitivity to his Jewish roots and his anguish over his people's inability to see Jesus as the Messiah and the fulfillment of the God's promise of old. Paul says he would gladly undergo some curse himself for the sake of his people's coming to the knowledge of Christ.

Themes:

Christ calming the storms of our lives.

We have all experienced "storms" in our lives when things seemed especially hopeless, when the pressure is on to compromise our values and integrity, when we are sinking in anger and confusion. But Jesus is present to us in the offerings of compassionate and loving support from family and friends. Just as he was there to catch the sinking Peter during the storm, Jesus is there to "catch" us if we have the trust and faith to seek his hand and reach for it.

The 'quiet' voice of the God of peace.

Like his disciples and the Jews of Jesus' time, we expect a God of power, a God who will save us from every cataclysm. But as Elijah discovers in the first reading, the Lord's voice is often heard most distinctly in the quiet. God speaks and works his wonders through individuals who recognize him as a light in the midst of darkness, who hear him as the "whisper" in the midst of a storm. The quiet power of the Lord inspires us to do powerful things in bringing his love and compassion to our world.

For reflection:

- Share stories of men and women whose faith and values have calmed humanity's storms.
- How are we like Peter in today's Gospel – strong in love but weak in our ability to trust?
- When have you heard the voice of God "in a tiny whispering sound"?

20th Sunday of the Year

Readings:
Matthew 15: 21-28
Isaiah 56: 1, 6-7
Romans 11: 13-15, 29-32

The story of the Canaanite woman (**Gospel**) was very important to the Christians of the predominately Gentile Christian communities. Jesus' healing of the daughter of the persistent Canaanite mother became a prophetic model for the relationship between Jewish and Gentile Christians. The woman is not only a Gentile, but a descendent of the Canaanites, one of Israel's ancient and most despised enemies. Despite Jesus' rebuff of her (equating Gentiles with "dogs," as Jews referred to anyone who was not a Jew), the woman has the presence of mind to point out that "even dogs are given crumbs and scraps from their masters' tables." She is a model of both great faith in Jesus (addressing him by the Messianic title of "Son of David") and great love for her daughter (subjecting herself to possible ridicule and recrimination for approaching Jesus).

As the Israelites return to Jerusalem from exile, the prophet Isaiah announces a new, "international" vision of salvation that includes, not only Jews, but "foreigners" and non-Jews who believe in the Lord's goodness and keep his commandments (**first reading**).

Paul acknowledges his joy over the acceptance of the Gospel by the Gentiles, but he expresses his hope that his own people, the Jews, will realize that Christ is not the rejection of Israel's covenant with God but the fulfillment of that covenant (**second reading**).

Themes:

Seeing one another as God sees us.

Because she is a Canaanite, the woman in today's Gospel is despised by the Jewish community. But Jesus does not see in her an old enemy; he sees, in her great compassion and love for her sick daughter, a loving mother; he sees, in her courage to come forward in the face of imminent rejection and denunciation, a woman of great faith. The Lord calls every person who possesses such compassion and love, regardless of nationality or heritage or stereotype or label, to his holy mountain.

'Subtle' bigotry: to be 'human together.'

Archbishop Desmond Tutu explained the turmoil that plagued his South African homeland for many years this way: "Many years ago...we [blacks] were thought to be human, but not quite as human as white people, for we lacked what seemed indispensable to that humanity – a particular skincolor. We have a wonderful country with truly magnificent people, if only we could be allowed to be human together."

Most of us would consider ourselves fair-minded and unbiased, neither bigots nor racists; but, if we're honest, we would probably recognize times we have treated people as if they were "a little less human" because they did not possess some quality or ingredient we consider iperative. We underestimate people because they are somehow different; we treat them as inferiors because they don't quite measure up to what we think they should or should not be. The Lord does not measure his people by our standards but welcomes to his holy mountain all who do what is "right" and "just." The Canaanite woman possesses the depth of faith and compassion by which we can be "human together."

For reflection:

- The Canaanite woman in today's Gospel is a figure of great courage, love and perseverance. Do you know of individuals who have possessed the same depth of courage, love and perseverance?
- We all think of ourselves as open-minded, fair and tolerant, without bias or prejudice. But can we be prejudiced, biased and intolerant of others without even realizing it?
- How can a parish make itself a "house of prayer for all peoples"?

21st Sunday of the Year

Readings: *Matthew 16: 13-20*
Isaiah 22: 15, 19-23
Romans 11: 33-36

In Matthew's Gospel, Peter's confession of faith is a turning point in the ministry of Jesus. Jesus will now concentrate on preparing his disciples to take on the teaching ministry and leadership of the Church he will establish.

The scene of today's **Gospel**, Caesarea Philippi, was the site of temples dedicated to no less than 14 different pagan gods, ranging from the Syrian god Baal to Pan, the Greek god of nature. In the middle of the city was a great white temple built by Herod and dedicated to the "divinity" of Caesar (hence the name of the city). In the midst of this marketplace of gods and temples, Jesus first indicates his plans and hopes for his church.

Jesus "sets up" Peter's declaration of faith by asking his disciples what people are saying about him. Many believed that Jesus is the reincarnation of John the Baptizer or the long-awaited return of the prophet Elijah or Jeremiah (Malachi 4: 5-6), whose return would signal the restoration of Israel. Simon Peter, however, has been given the gift of faith ("no mere man has revealed this to you") and unequivocally states that Jesus is the Messiah.

Jesus blesses Simon with the new name of "rock" (*Kepha* in Aramaic, *Petros* in Greek), the foundation for Jesus' new Church. Peter is entrusted with the keys of the kingdom of heaven (an image drawn from Isaiah 22: 15-25, today's first reading) and the mission to bring sins to consciousness and to proclaim to sinners the love and forgiveness of God.

Shebna is scribe to King Hezekiah and superintendent of the palace. With the Assyrians threatening Jerusalem's borders, Shebna has advised the king to enter into a conspiracy of agreements with the Egyptians, despite God's promise to protect his people. Isaiah is incensed at Shebna's refusal to trust God, as well as the scribe's ostentation (the opulent tomb Shebna has built for himself) and his obsession with chariots and armaments. Isaiah prophesies (today's **first reading**) how Shebna will be replaced by the faithful Eliakim, Hezekiah's royal chamberlain. This passage parallels the description of the office Jesus intends for Peter.

The meditation that is today's **second reading** concludes Paul's treatise on Christ as Redeemer of Jew and Gentile alike. Quoting Isaiah 40: 13, Paul praises God's goodness and grace as defying human comprehension; all we can do is praise God and accept his wondrous invitation to faith.

Themes:

'Who do you say I am?'

The question Jesus asks Peter and his disciples is asked of us every minute of every day. Every decision we make is ultimately a response to the question, *Who do you say I am?* Our love for family and friends, our dedication to the cause of justice, our commitment to the highest moral and ethical principles, our taking the first step toward reconciliation and forgiveness, our simplest acts of kindness and charity declare most accurately and effectively our belief in the Gospel Jesus as the Messiah and Redeemer.

'You are rock . . .'

Peter is the first of the disciples to grasp the divinity of Christ. On the faith of Peter "the rock" Christ establishes his Church. Peter becomes, then, the first stone in the foundation of the Church. We who are baptized into the faith handed down to us by Peter and the apostles become stones in this "edifice of Spirit"; the faith we live and the hope we cherish in the empty tomb of Easter are the foundation of the Church of the Risen One.

'The keys of the kingdom of heaven.'

The "keys of the kingdom of heaven" entrusted by Christ to us, his Church, are hope, trust and understanding; they are the authority to proclaim, in our personal works of charity and various ministries, the presence of God in our midst. These "keys" are entrusted to us to enable others to discover the presence of God in their own lives; they can open up to us the mysteries of God's great love for all of humanity as revealed to us in the Risen Christ. Heaven's "keys" focus our vision as a Church not on the present but on the age to come; we live in constant hope of the kingdom of heaven and the reign of God. In every moment of our lives, we proclaim to the world the promise of the resurrection and the life of the world to come.

For reflection:

- In what ways do our actions give different and conflicting answers to Jesus' question to his disciples, *Who do you say I am?*

- Since Scriptural times, to entrust someone with keys is the ultimate sign of trust. To accept such a trust demands authority, responsibility, courage and strength – perhaps more so in ancient times, when keys were so large and heavy one had to carry them on one's shoulder (first reading). What past or present leaders of the Church have been especially heroic and effective custodians of the "keys of the kingdom of heaven"?

- Jesus tells Simon Peter that his realization of Jesus' divinity is a gift from God – "no mere man has revealed this to you." How can such faith be considered a "gift?"

- How does the Church today "declare bound on earth [what] shall be bound in heaven" and "loosed on earth [what] shall be loosed in heaven"?

22nd Sunday of the Year

Readings:
Matthew 16: 21-27
Jeremiah 20: 7-9
Romans 12: 1-2

Peter's confession of faith (last Sunday's Gospel) begins a new phase of Matthew's Gospel. Jesus' teachings will now be addressed primarily to his disciples, as Jesus makes his way to Jerusalem. The hostility between Jesus and the leaders of Judaism is about to reach the crisis stage.

In today's **Gospel**, Jesus proclaims unambiguously that his mission as the Messiah includes suffering and death. Peter is sharply rebuked by Jesus for his seemingly innocent remark that Jesus should be spared such a fate, but Jesus sees Peter's refusal to accept such a possibility as a "satanic" attempt to deflect the Messiah from his mission of redemption. To avoid suffering and hardship in order to opt for the easy and safe course is purely human thinking, an obstacle to experiencing the life of the Spirit. Authentic discipleship involves taking on the cross and "denying oneself" – disowning ourselves as the center of our existence and realizing that God is the object and purpose of our lives.

Jeremiah has had enough of the prophetic office. His warnings of Jerusalem's fall and the destruction of the temple at the hands of the Babylonians on their northern border are met first with ridicule, derision and then anger – Jeremiah is imprisoned and beaten for his unpopular oracles. In today's **first reading**, taken from Jeremiah's "Confessions," the prophet opens his soul to God with a bluntness and boldness seldom read in Scripture. He considers abandoning his office of prophet, but admits that God's word is too powerful to be ignored.

In chapter 12 of his letter to the Romans (this Sunday's **second reading**), Paul discusses the practical implications of the Gospel in everyday life. Paul begins the chapter by pointing out that, while the Mosaic code included elaborate directions on sacrifices and other rituals, the Gospel invites believers to present their very selves as a "living sacrifice of praise" to God.

Themes:

Discipleship: taking up the cross.

One is not a Christian only because he/she claims to be one. There is no mistaking Jesus's point in today's Gospel: *If you wish to be considered my follower, you must make yourself second for the sake of others, take up your cross and follow in my footsteps.* The cross we are asked to take up is not easy: it represents a value system that runs counter to our own; it compels us to make choices we would rather not make or opt for. The life of the true disciple of Christ is one of generous, selfless and sacrificial service to others in order to bring the joy and hope of the resurrection into our lives and theirs.

Self-denial: to discover God.

Christ calls each one of us to let go of our own needs and wants in order to bring God's grace into our lives and the lives of others. This attitude of discipleship compels us to make choices we would rather make, to embrace values that run counter to the world's, to take the difficult, painful first step toward reconciliation and peace, to put aside our own sense of victimization in order to seek peace and justice and healing for others. In "denying" ourselves we discover the life and love of God.

For reflection:

- What experiences in your life reflect the wisdom of the Chinese proverb: "The diamond cannot be polished without friction, nor the individual perfected without trials"?
- What "crosses" are we called to take up today?
- Do you know of people who have accomplished or taught great things because of the suffering they endured?
- How can "self denial" be a positive growth experience?

Readings:
Matthew 18: 15-20
Ezekiel 33: 7-9
Romans 13: 8-10

Chapter 18 of Matthew's Gospel is a collection of Jesus' sayings on the practical challenges facing the Christian community, such as status-seeking, scandal, division and, the topic of today's reading, conflict.

Today's **Gospel** reading sounds more like regulations devised by an ecclesiastical committee than a teaching of Jesus (this chapter has been called the "church order discourse" of Jesus). But the point of Jesus' exhortation is that we must never tolerate any breech of personal relationship between us and another member of the Christian community. At each stage of the process – personal discussion, discussion before witnesses, discussion before the whole community – the aim is to win the erring Christian back to the community (the three-step process of reconciliation outlined by Jesus here corresponds to the procedure of the Qumran community).

Jesus' exhortation closes with a promise of God's presence in the midst of every community, regardless of size, bound together by faith.

In today's **first reading**, Ezekiel, who preached to the Jews exiled from their homeland by the Babylonians (after the fall of Jerusalem in 587 B.C.), is called by God to be Israel's "watchman" – not to warn of a coming military invasion but to proclaim the forgiveness of God to an Israel defeated by its loss of faith and sinfulness.

Paul repeats, in the **second reading** today, the teaching of Jesus that so infuriated the Jewish leaders of his time: that all 613 commandments derived from the Torah are fulfilled if one's spiritual and moral outlook are directed by the virtue of love. The one thing we owe to one another as Christians is to love one another as Christ has loved us.

Themes:

Building Christ-centered community.

We have become very good at drawing lines and boundaries around our lives, at keeping ourselves insulated from others, at remaining comfortable and safe in our own world surrounded by our own interests and concerns. But Jesus envisions his Church becoming a community of reconciliation, mercy and forgiveness. Jesus calls us to the hard struggle of building communities that are *inclusive*, not *exclusive*; of bringing back the lost, not out of pride or zealousness but out of "the debt that binds us to love one another"; of welcoming the neediest, the helpless and the alienated into our midst as we would welcome Christ himself. Within such faithful communities of prayer and servanthood the Risen One promises to dwell.

The work of reconciliation.

Today's Gospel outlines a process of reconciliation in order to heal divisions within the community and to bring back the lost, the alienated, the disaffected. The excommunication of anyone is always the last resort – excommunication indicates failure on the part of both the individual and the community. Jesus calls his hearers to seek honesty and sincerity in all relationships, to put aside self-interest, anger and wounded pride in order to take those first, difficult steps in healing the rifts that destroy that Spirit of love that is God's gift of unity and peace.

For reflection:

- Consider the situations and crises in the world that cry out for reconciliation.
- How is today's Gospel a lesson in "conflict management"?
- Have you ever experienced Christ's presence in some unexpected or surprising way in another person?
- Is there anyone you know who could be considered a "hero" of reconciliation?

Readings:

Matthew 18: 21-35
Sirach 27: 30 – 28: 7
Romans 14: 7-9

It is ironic that Peter should ask the question about forgiveness that introduces the parable of the merciless steward (**Gospel**), since Peter himself will be so generously forgiven by Jesus for his denial of Jesus on Good Friday. It was common rabbinical teaching that one must forgive another three times; the fourth time, the offender was not to be forgiven. Perhaps Peter was anticipating Jesus' response to his question by suggesting seven rather than the conventional three times; but Jesus responds that there should be no limit to the number of times we must be ready to forgive those who wrong us ("seventy times seven times"), just as there is no limit to the Father's forgiveness of us. As the king in the parable withdraws his forgiveness of his official because of the official's failure to forgive another, so will God withdraw his forgiveness of the unforgiving and merciless among us. God's forgiveness is not entirely unconditional: if we do not share it, we will lose it.

In the **first reading**, meditating on anger and vengeance, the holy teacher Ben Sirach, writing 200 years before Christ, challenges the ancient proscription of "an eye for an eye." We can only obtain mercy and forgiveness from God if we forgive our neighbors.

This weekly series of **second readings** from Paul's letter to the Romans concludes with a meditation on the Lordship of Jesus. If God has accepted each one of us, how can we not accept one another as brothers and sisters?

Themes:

Forgiveness: the gift of love.

The cutting edge of Jesus' teaching on love is that nothing is unforgivable nor should there be limits to forgiveness. Forgiveness can only be given out of love and, therefore, demands sacrifice on the part of the forgiver. To forgive as God forgives means to intentionally act to purge the evil that exists between us and those who harm us, to take the first, second and last steps toward bridging divisions, to work ceaselessly to mend broken relationships and to welcome and accept the forgiven back into our lives unconditionally, totally and joyfully. Such forgiveness is often difficult and sometimes painful; but Christ calls us to look beyond our own hurt to the other person's healing, to look beyond our own loss to the loss of relationship and the weakening of community, to look beyond our own pride to the dignity and goodness of those who wrong us.

To forgive as God forgives us.

Before our merciful Father in heaven, every one of us is an insolvent debtor. But the great mystery of our faith is that God continues to love us, continues to call us back to him, continues to seek not retribution but reconciliation with us. All God asks of us is that we forgive one another as he forgives us, to help one another back up when we stumble as he lifts us back up. To forgive as God forgives means to move beyond the harm and pain done to us and to seek reconciliation regardless of the cost, without setting limits or conditions. Such God-like forgiveness can be painful and humiliating, but it is truly life-giving and liberating.

For reflection:

- Share stories of heroic, extraordinary forgiveness.
- How is anger, of itself, a destructive, dehumanizing emotion?
- What are the practical implications of today's readings? Can forgiveness ever be withheld? When is restitution justified?
- When is forgiveness NOT forgiveness? When is forgiveness whole and complete?

Lord, How many times shall I forgive my brother?

Readings:

Matthew 20: 1-16
Israel 55: 6-9
Philippians 1: 20-24, 27

The parable of the generous vineyard owner (which appears only in Matthew's **Gospel**) is the first of several parables and exhortations challenging the Pharisees and scribes and those who criticized Jesus for preaching to tax collectors and sinners.

Jesus makes two points in this parable: The parable speaks of the primacy of compassion and mercy in the kingdom of God. The employer (God) responds to those who have worked all day that he has been just in paying them the agreed-upon wage; they have no grievance if he chooses to be generous to others. God's goodness and mercy transcends the narrow and limited laws and logic of human justice; it is not the amount of service given but the attitude of love and generosity behind that service.

The parable also illustrates the universality of the new Church. The contracted workers, Israel, will be joined by the new "migrant workers," the Gentiles, who will share equally in the joy of the kingdom of God.

Today's **first reading** is from the collection of oracles and hymns composed by the writer known only as Deutero-Isaiah ("Second Isaiah"), who prophesied hope and salvation to Israel toward the end of the Babylonian exile. God's goodness, love and mercy defy human expectations and reasoning – we cannot understand why God continues to call us back to him, why he constantly forgives us, why he continues to love us.

Paul's letter to the Philippians has been called the "epistle of joy." The apostle speaks with the pride of a founding father to his beloved community at Philippi (located in what is now Northern Greece), which Paul established in 50 A.D. The epistle to the Philippians is really three short letters which have been edited together somewhat haphazardly. Philippians (the **second reading** for the next four Sundays) reveals a sensitive, tender, caring side to Paul that is seldom seen in his other letters.

Paul is writing to the community at Philippi from prison (probably in Ephesus). Conscious of the imminence of his own death, Paul finds consolation and joy in his faith that "life means Christ."

Themes:

The mercy of God transcending human justice.

Faith is a gift that should give joy and direction to our lives, but it fails as a standard for measuring, judging and condemning others. We have our scales, time clocks and computer print-outs to measure what is just and what is not; but God is generous, loving and forgiving with an extravagance that offends our sense of justice. Genuine forgiveness and reconciliation are the ways of God, no matter what our own sense of justice and fair play may tell us. Christ calls us to rejoice in those who have been healed, to welcome as co-workers all who have come to work in the vineyard. The attitude of the faithful disciple celebrates the goodness and mercy of God rather than feel slighted or cheated because others we consider "less worthy" find peace in him.

Welcoming all workers into the 'vineyard.'

Today's readings admonish those who consider themselves "pillars" of the Church that there is no elite or aristocracy in the kingdom of God. The faith we have received is a gift that should deflate pretensions, intolerance and self-righteousness and, instead, instill a sense of joy, peace and direction to our lives. Christ calls us to embrace the Gospel, not as ideologues or zealots, but as disciples who love him through our love for others. We are called to share Christ, not to manipulate or control others through him.

For reflection:

- Oscar Wilde said that "a cynic is someone who knows the price of everything and the value of nothing." Would Isaiah and Matthew agree?
- Who are the "new" workers who come into the vineyard to work side-by-side with us? How do we "contract workers" patronize and diminish them?
- How can people be manipulated, used and controlled through Scripture? How can such misuse of Scripture be prevented?

Readings:

Matthew 21: 28-32
Ezekiel 18: 25-28
Philippians 2: 1-11

Today's parable of the two sons (**Gospel**) is a devastating condemnation of the Jewish religious leaders whose faith is confined to words and rituals. Jesus states unequivocally that those the self-righteous consider to be the very antithesis of religious will be welcomed by God into his presence before the "professional" religious.

Prostitutes and tax collectors were the most despised outcasts in Judaism. In light of the First Testament tradition of God's relationship with Israel as a "marriage" and Israel's disloyalty as "harlotry," prostitution was considered an especially heinous sin. Tax collectors were, in the eyes of Palestinian Jews, the very personification of corruption and theft. According to the Roman system of tax collection, publicans (tax collectors) would pay the state a fixed sum based on the theoretical amount of taxes due from a given region. The publican, in return, had the right to collect the taxes in that region – and they were not above using terrorism and extortion to collect. Tax collectors, as agents of the state, were also shunned as collaborators with Israel's Roman captors.

Jesus' declaration that those guilty of the most abhorrent of sins would enter God's kingdom before them deepened the Jewish establishment's animosity toward Jesus.

Ezekiel writes during the wrenching years of the Israelites' exile from Jerusalem (sixth century B.C.). But the prophet admonishes his people to recognize that their exile from God – an exile they have imposed on themselves by their "wickedness" – is far more devastating than their political exile from their homeland. The exiled Jews of Ezekiel's time blamed everyone from their ancestors to Yahweh for their plight. Ezekiel reminds them that each individual is responsible for his or her life, that each generation receives life or death according to its own actions; but God offers forgiveness and reconciliation to all people of all times (**first reading**).

Imprisoned in Ephesus and distressed by the divisions plaguing the Church at Corinth, Paul begs his beloved Philippians to be united in humility and selflessness, and quotes what many scholars believe is the text of an ancient hymn praising Christ as the supreme example of the selfless Servant of God (**second reading**).

Themes:

The authority of deeds over words.

Promises can never take the place of performance, words are never a substitute for deeds. Christ demands that we who would be his followers give voice to our faith not just in the prayers and rituals we utter but in the positions and candidates we support, the deals we make and the relationships we form with one another. The challenge of discipleship is to translate the many "good intentions" we have into the actual work of being Christ's followers.

Conversion of spirit: the personal commitment of faith.

Albert Schweitzer wrote that we "must cease attributing [our] problems to the environment, and learn again to exercise [our] will – [our] personal responsibility in the realm of faith and morals." In today's Gospel, Jesus teaches that genuine faith begins with a conversion of spirit, a personal conviction and commitment to do the will of God in all things. We cannot take refuge in the mores of the tribe or bow to peer pressure; we cannot say we acted under orders; we cannot claim that our theft becomes a crime only when a judge or jury says so. True faith – the Spirit of God that renews and transforms – transcends the letter of law, the safety of social convention and the capriciousness of popular opinion.

The measure of the human heart.

We are often too quick to gauge people according to our own very dubious and often inaccurate standards. The externals of dress, speech and pedigree fail to take into account the true measure of a person's worth: the love that is contained in the heart. Christ calls us to look beyond labels and stereotypes like "tax collectors" and "prostitutes" and recognize, instead, the holiness that resides within every person, who is, like us, a child of God.

For reflection:

- Who among us today are the most unlikely but most certain to enter the kingdom of God?
- How do we "exile" ourselves from God?
- In what ways do people tend to blame the Church, their parish, the pastor for their lack of faith?
- How do our "measures" of individuals and groups differ from that of God's measures?

Readings:

Matthew 21: 33-43
Isaiah 5: 1-7
Philippians 4: 6-9

Today's **Gospel** parable "updates" Isaiah's allegory of the friend's vineyard (**first reading**). God is the owner of the vineyard who has "leased" the property to the religious and political leaders of Israel. Many servants (prophets) were sent to the tenants, but all met the same fate. The owner finally sends his own Son, who is brutally murdered "outside" the vineyard (a prediction of his crucifixion outside the city of Jerusalem?). With this parable, Jesus places himself in the line of the rejected prophets. The owner finally comes himself and destroys the tenants and leaves the vineyard to others (the Church) who yield an abundant harvest. This parable is intended to give hope and encouragement to Matthew's Christian community, which is scorned and persecuted by its staunchly Jewish neighbors.

Today's reading from Paul's letter to the Philippians (**second reading**) continues his words of encouragement to his beloved converts at Philippi. In order that God's peace may reign in their lives they must put into practice all that they have learned, received, heard and seen.

Themes:

Harvesting our corner of the 'vineyard.'

Each one of us has been given a portion of God's vineyard to cultivate. Fear, selfishness and bigotry can kill whatever chances we have of turning our part of the vineyard into something productive; but, through justice, generosity and compassion, we can reap a rich and fulfilling harvest, regardless of how small or poor or insignificant our piece of the vineyard is.

The cost of faithful discipleship.

Faith can be costly. Throughout our lives we are challenged to sacrifice the treasures of God in order to embrace the values deemed important by society. The witness we are called to give can subject us to misunderstanding, suspicion, abuse, intimidation and ridicule from others. Living the values of the Gospel can be discouraging, humiliating and isolating. Yet everyone of us who claims to be a disciple of Jesus and a witness of his Resurrection is called to pay whatever price is demanded for the sake of the reign of God, for we believe that love rather than greed, peace rather than hostility, forgiveness rather than vengeance will yield the harvest of God's reign.

For reflection:

- In what ways are we responsible and irresponsible "tenants" of the vineyard?
- Share stories of individuals who have made even the most "arid" sections of the "vineyard" bloom.
- How can your parish community become a more "productive" section of the vineyard?

Readings:

Matthew 22: 1-14
Isaiah 25: 6-10
Philippians 4: 12-14, 19-20

Jesus' parable of the wedding feast (today's **Gospel**) is another portrayal of Israel's rejection of God's promise. The invitation is therefore extended to everyone – Gentiles, foreigners and those who do not know God – to come to the Lord's table. (Matthew's readers would see the "destruction of those murderers" and the "burning of their city" as references to the destruction of Jerusalem by the Romans in 70 A.D.)

Jesus tells a second parable within the parable of the wedding feast. The wedding garment is the conversion of heart and mind required for entry into the kingdom. The Christian who does not wear this mantle of repentance and good deeds will suffer the same fate as those who reject outright the invitation to the wedding. As the apostle Paul writes (Romans 13: 14), we must "put on" the garment of Christ.

The image of the universal banquet has a long history in the mythological and folkloric traditions of the world. Eight centuries before Christ, Isaiah pictures for his Jewish hearers (today's **first reading**) the richness of the Messianic banquet on the heavenly mountain of God, when Yahweh will remove the sorrow and humiliation of Israel.

Imprisoned in Ephesus, Paul offers words of thanks to the Philippians for their gift of money sent through Epaphroditus. In today's **second reading**, Paul assures his good friends and benefactors that he is able to cope with whatever hardship because of the strength he receives from God.

Themes:

Accepting God's invitation to his Son's wedding banquet.

We can be so busy making a living that we fail to make a life; we can become so obsessed with organizing life that we overlook the essence of life itself. God has invited each of us to his Son's wedding feast – the fullness of God's life in the Resurrection. The only obstacle is our inability to hear his invitation amid the noisy activity that consumes our time and attention.

The one wedding feast.

All of us deeply admire Mother Teresas, the Father Damians, the Albert Schweitzers and the St. Francises of the world. Yet the same God who called each of them to their work calls us to do the same. The parables of the king's wedding feast and wedding garment confront us with the reality that we cannot be Christian without conversion; we cannot come to the feast of heaven while remaining indifferent to the empty plates before so many of the world's children; we cannot love the God we cannot see if we cannot love those we can see. The question posed by today's readings is how we respond to the invitation: with excuses? with rationalizations? with refusals? Every one of us – saint and sinner, faithful communicant and lost soul – are invited by God to be his guests at the banquet of heaven.

Putting on the wedding garment.

In accepting an invitation to a wedding, we must dress accordingly. The wedding garment of today's Gospel is the garment of good works we make for ourselves for the Lord's banquet: the garment sewn of repentance, joyful expectation and humble service to others.

For reflection:

- In what ways do today's Christians miss or refuse their invitations to the Lord's wedding feast?
- How should the images in today's readings of the banquet and wedding feast affect our understanding of *church?*
- What elements of the wedding feast might be brought to your parish life and liturgy?
- How would the "perfect" wedding garment be pictured or designed for the Lord's wedding banquet?

Readings:
Matthew 22: 15-21
Isaiah 45: 1, 4-6
1 Thessalonians 1: 1-5

Two opponents of Jesus, the Pharisees and Herodians (supporters of Herod's dynasty), join forces to trap Jesus (**Gospel**). If Jesus affirms that taxes should be paid, he alienates the religious nationalists; if he denies that taxes should be paid, then he is subject to arrest by the Romans as a political revolutionary. But the very fact that his inquisitors could produce the emperor's coin from out of their purses was to admit a Roman obligation: If one used the sovereign's coin then one automatically took an obligation to the sovereign; in other words, the Pharisees and Herodians, in trying to trap Jesus, answered their own question. But Jesus takes the debate to an even higher level by challenging them to be just as obedient in paying their debt to God.

The 50-year exile of the Jews under the Babylonians is about to end. King Cyrus of Persia has defeated the Babylonians and has announced the liberation of the Jews (538 B.C.). Isaiah sees Cyrus as the instrument by which Yahweh reasserts his presence in Israel's history (**first reading**). Just as a foreign nation served as the rod of his anger (Isaiah 10: 5), so, through the foreigner King Cyrus, Yahweh liberates his people.

Scholars believe that Paul's first letter to the Christian community at Thessalonica in Northern Greece is the first of the 27 books of the New Testament book to be written. On behalf of his co-workers Silvanus and Timothy, Paul greets the Thessalonians and offers a prayer of thanks for the Holy Spirit, which made the apostle's teaching effective and the community's acceptance possible (**second reading**).

Themes:

'To give to God . . .': values of the heart.

The confrontation over Caesar's coin is not a solution to any church-versus-state controversy; Jesus' response to the Pharisees confronts them – and us – with the demand to act out of our convictions and to take responsibility for our actions. While we yearn for easy answers to complicated questions and "soundbite" solutions to complex problems, the real purpose and meaning of life are found in the intricacies of our consciences and the things we believe in the depths of our hearts. Jesus appeals to us to look beyond the simplistic politics and black-and-white legalisms represented by the coin and realize that we are called to embrace the values centered in a faith that sees the hand of God in all things and every human being as part of a single family under the providence of God. As Thomas Merton wrote: "We are warmed by fire not by the smoke of the fire. We are carried over the Sea by a ship, not by the wake of a ship. So, too, what we are is to be sought in the invisible depths of our own being, not in our outward reflection in our own acts. We must find our real selves not in the froth stirred up by the impact of our beings upon the beings around us, but in our own soul which is the principle in our acts."

'To give to Caesar . . .': the covenant of citizenship.

The Pharisees who confront Jesus with Caesar's coin are trying to trap him into making a choice between one's country and God. But Jesus' response indicates that one's citizenship does not have to be at odds with one's faith; in fact, when government seeks to provide for the just welfare of its citizens, it is doing the "things" of God.

The Preamble to our nation's Constitution reads more like a covenant we Americans have made with one another than a legal outline of how our government will operate. Although God is not mentioned at all, we can sense his Spirit in the Preamble:

We the people of the United States, in order to form a more perfect union, establish justice, insure domestic tranquility, provide for the common defense, promote the general welfare, and secure the blessings of liberty for ourselves and our posterity...

To strike that balance between the things of Caesar's and the things of God demands that we participate in the affairs of government responsibly and intelligently, in order that our public policies reflect the wisdom and justice of our God.

For reflection:

- We hear a great deal from fundamentalist organizations about "Christian" candidates, "Christian" issues, the "Christian" way to vote. What does the Gospel demand of the authentic Christian in terms of his/her citizenship?
- Can patriotism ever be contrary to the Gospel?
- Are there times when you find yourself using social convention or common practice as an excuse for acting in a way you know is contrary to the Gospel?
- How can the "labels" we ascribe to people be unjust?

30th Sunday of the Year

Readings:

Matthew 22: 34-40
Exodus 22: 20-26
1 Thessalonians 1: 5-10

In this week's **Gospel**, as in last week's, the Jewish leaders seek to trip up Jesus. The question the lawyer poses was much discussed in rabbinical circles: *Which is the greatest commandment?* The Pharisees' intention in posing the question was to force Jesus into a single rabbinical school, thereby opening him up to criticism from all other sides. Jesus' answer, however, proves his fidelity to both the Jewish tradition and to a spirituality that transcends the legal interpretations of the commandments: the "second" commandment is the manifestation of the first. If we love the Lord God with our whole being, that love will manifest itself in our feeding of the hungry, our sheltering of the homeless and our liberating of the oppressed.

Today's **first reading** is from the section of the Book of Exodus known as the "Code of the Covenant," a detailed explanation of the moral, civil and ritual legislation by which the Israelites were to become a holy people. Today's reading outlines the laws of charity toward the poor and "aliens" and the promise of Yahweh's protection of the helpless and defenseless.

In today's **second reading**, Paul encourages the young Church at Thessalonica to be a model of faithful community for the new churches in the region.

Themes:

The 'great' commandment: to love as God loves.

As our society becomes more and more diverse, as science continues to make once unimaginable advances in all forms of technology, the ethical and moral questions we face become more complicated, difficult and challenging. The Great Commandment gives us the starting point for dealing with such issues: we are called to love as God loves us – without limit, without condition, without counting the cost, completely and selflessly. The implication of such love is staggering: personal agendas collapse, bottom-line consideration pale in importance. If we really understand the depth of God's great love for us, we cannot help but embrace, his Spirit of love – love that is unconditional and selfless, love that gives joyfully and thankfully.

To love the 'foreigner' and the 'alien.'

In today's first reading, Yahweh reminds Israel that they should not "oppress and abuse an alien, for you were once aliens yourself in the land of Egypt." In today's Gospel, Jesus' command to love our neighbor means seeing one another as we see ourselves: realizing that our hopes and dreams for ourselves and our families are the same dreams others have for themselves and their families. The fact is that all of us, at one time or another, are aliens, outsiders, foreigners and strangers. The commandment to "love your neighbor as yourself" calls us to look beyond the suspicions, doubts and stereotypes we use to makr people and recognize every person as a child of God, worthy of respect, love and compassion.

For reflection:

- When is loving someone as we love ourselves most difficult?
- Have you ever been the "alien," "the foreigner," the outsider?
- Has your perspective of another person ever changed dramatically as a result of considering how you would cope in that person's situation?

Readings:

Matthew 23: 1-12
Malachi 1: 14 – 2: 2, 8-10
1 Thessalonians 2: 7-9, 13

Today's **Gospel** is another powerful indictment of the scribes and Pharisees. The scribes were the religious intellectuals of the time, skilled in interpreting the Law and applying it to everyday life; the Pharisees belonged to a religious fraternity ("the separated brethren") who prided themselves on the exact, meticulous observance of the Law. Jesus condemns them for their failure to live up to their teachings: In their eagerness to be revered, they seek to dominate rather than to serve. Religious ostentation and pretension are rejected in favor of the Christian ideal of leadership contained in loving service to the community.

In warning his disciples not to use of the titles "Rabbi," "teacher" and "Father," Jesus condemns the spirit of pride and superiority such titles connote. Those who minister as teachers and leaders should be humbled by the fact that they are not teachers or leaders in their own right but by the inspiration and grace of God. In the reign of God, those who exercise authority have a particular responsibility to lead by serving.

The Jews have returned to Jerusalem after the exile. The temple has been rebuilt. But things are not like they were before. Shaken by the experience, Israel has re-made God in *their* image and likeness. Yahweh, the living God of the covenant, has become, instead, a symbol of Jewish nationalism. In today's **first reading**, the prophet Malachi ("messenger of God"), the last of the minor prophets, sharply rebukes the priests of Israel for their poor and irresponsible leadership, their indifference and their failure to correct the abuses in worship and the spiritual, moral and social problems Israel faces.

Paul fondly remembers the time he spent among the Thessalonians in Northern Greece, during his second missionary journey around 50 B.C. Though Paul and his companions are warmly received by many Gentile converts, the Jews of Thessalonica harassed Paul and accused the new Christians of treason before the Roman authorities. Paul is forced to leave the city. Timothy later returned to Thessalonica to keep the community together. Timothy's positive report to Paul is reflected in the apostle's loving and encouraging words. In today's **second reading**, Paul says he loves his Thessalonian brothers and sisters as a mother who cares for her children and a father who exhorts them to live lives worthy of the teaching they have received.

Themes:

The authority of service.

Today's readings exalt the leader who leads by example:

The prophet Malachi criticizes those priests and leaders of Israel whose empty words ("you do not lay it to heart") have caused many to abandon their faith; Paul recalls his days preaching among the Thessalonians when "we wanted to share with you not only God's tidings but our very lives, you had become so dear to us; and Jesus minces no words when he says "the greatest among you will be the one who serves the rest." In the Gospel perspective, the greatest leaders and teachers are those who share their vision of faith not in words alone but by the power and authority of their example.

Gospel 'greatness': the joy of Christ-like service.

Jesus' whole life is a parable of humble and selfless service to others. For the person of faith, joy is found not in the recognition or honor that one receives in doing good but in the act of doing good itself, in realizing that we imitate Christ in such service, in the assurance that we are bringing the love of God into the lives of others. Christ-like service sees with the eyes of another, walks the path of another. Jesus, who welcomed to his side the rejected and scorned of society, who washed the feet of his disciples and taught them to do the same, leaves the legacy of such "greatness" to us, his Church.

For reflection:

- Share stories of people you have known who have effectively led others by the power and inspiration of their example and humility.
- In light of today's readings, how would you define the term "religious authority"?
- Our Church's tradition includes the use of many beautiful ornate symbols in worship: incense, music, bells, vestments, etc. How do we keep these things in perspective if we are to be faithful to Jesus' words in today's Gospel?

32nd Sunday of the Year

Readings:

Matthew 25: 1-13
Wisdom 6: 12-16
1 Thessalonians 4: 13-18

These last Sundays of the year focus on the *Parousia*, the Lord's return at the end of time. The parable of the bridesmaids, found only in Matthew's **Gospel**, is taken from Jesus' fifth and final discourse in Matthew, the great eschatological discourse.

According to the Palestinian custom, the bridegroom would go to the bride's house on their wedding day to finalize the marital agreement with his father-in-law. When the bridegroom would return to his own home with his bride, the bridesmaids would meet them as they approached, signaling the beginning of the wedding feast.

The image of the approaching wedding feast is used by Jesus to symbolize his coming at the end of time. Jesus' return will take many by complete surprise. The love we have for others as evidenced in works of kindness and compassion is the "oil" we store in our lamps awaiting for Christ's return.

Today's **first reading** is a poetic vision of true wisdom as a paradox: to seek wisdom – God's word – is to discover her.

The Thessalonians believed that the Second Coming was imminent. But what would happen to those Christians of the community who have already died? In today's **second reading**, Paul assures them that they, too, will share in the resurrection and be united with the Lord.

Themes:

Christ's return: the 'oil' of loving service.

In considering the "end" of time and the inevitability of our own deaths, our first thoughts may be of work never to be completed and dreams never to be realized. Instead of terrifying us or intimidating us or driving us to despair, the inevitability of the return of Christ "the bridegroom" should make us realize the preciousness of the time we have been given and inspire us to make the most of this time, filling our "lamps" with the "oil" of compassion, justice and forgiveness as we await his coming. Today's readings remind us that the end of this life is the beginning of a new one – the eternal life of the "Bridegroom," the Risen Christ. He must be the axis around which our whole being and life turn.

Christ's return: the limited gift of time.

The playwright Ben Hecht wrote that "time is a circus that keeps packing up and moving away." Time is a gift that God gives us through which we might come to discover him and the things that are of God. The "busyness" of our days can derail us from embracing the important things of life itself – like the love of family and friends. The wisdom of God (first reading) compels us to seek Christ the Bridegroom in every moment we have been given in this life until the wedding feast of the life to come.

For reflection:

- In November (the month of All Saints and All Souls), when the dark final days of autumn give way to the cold of winter, our thoughts naturally turn to the reality of death. Share stories of people you have known who have taught you important lessons about death and dying through their encounters with death.
- Is there anything reassuring in these last Scriptural readings of November?
- Ours is a society and culture that tends to deny the reality of death. Why?

Readings:
Matthew 25: 14-30
Proverbs 31: 10-13, 19-20, 30-31
1 Thessalonians 5: 1-6

The "measure" of Christ's judgment in the world to come is made clear in the parable of the talents (**Gospel**): The Lord will judge us according to how well we have used the "talents" and gifts every one of us has been given. The greater the "capital" we have been given, the greater God's expectations.

The First Testament Book of Proverbs is a collection of wise sayings, collected over a period of 500 years from sources throughout the world. Today's **first reading**, from the final chapter of Proverbs, is part of a poem envisioning the ideal wife as wisdom in action: a woman of prayer, of loving service to her family and of charity to all. Read in the light of today's Gospel, it is a portrait of the faithful servant of God.

More important to Paul is not the exact time of the Lord's return in the future but the attitude of expectation we must adopt in the present. Paul exhorts the Christian community at Thessolonica, (today's **second reading**) to remember that they have been called, in baptism, to live in the daylight of knowledge and hope in the Risen Christ. We do not live in fear but in joyful expectation of his return at the end of time.

Themes:

The 'stewardship' of talent and ability.

Every one of us possesses some degree of talent, ability and skill. The "talents" we possess have been "entrusted" to us by the "Master." Jesus teaches in today's Gospel that our place in the reign of God will depend on our stewardship of those gifts from God. The "good wife" in today's reading from Proverbs and the two industrious servants of the Gospel are successes in God's eyes because their lives are of benefit to others. Their greatness will be exalted by God. But those servants who cannot see beyond themselves, who squander their talents, who use their talents irresponsibly for personal profit or self-gratification, are useless and will have no share in the joy of God's reign.

The opportunities we have to 'reap and gather.'

Each one of us is given many opportunities to "reap and gather." Some of us have the opportunity to influence public policy and provide for the common good; some have the skills to bring healing, hope and wisdom to others; some possess the ability to help others understand, affirm and celebrate the humanity we share. Most of the opportunities we have, however, are quiet, ordinary and unseen, perhaps having no discernible effect beyond our immediate families; but we can still bring a measure of hope to others in the sincerity, kindness and joy we bring to the everyday dimensions of life. The challenge of the Gospel is to be ready and willing to respond to the opportunities we have to give joyfully and generously of ourselves for the sakes of others.

For reflection:

- Share stories of individuals whose "investments" of their talents – abilities and skills the world considered relatively small and insignificant – yielded extraordinary returns.
- What "talents" do we possess that our world is crying out for? What talents do people possess that they tend to underestimate or ignore as valueless?
- What talents do you see in your parish community that are being buried in the ground? Why does that happen? What can be done to bring them out?

Solemnity of Christ the King

Readings:
Matthew 25: 31-46
Ezekiel 34: 11-12, 15-17
1 Corinthians 15: 20-26, 28

Matthew's is the only description of the Last Judgment in any of the Gospels. It is Jesus' last discourse recorded by Matthew before the events of the Passion begin to unfold. In the vision he presents in this **Gospel**, Christ is the king who sits in judgment "as a shepherd separates sheep from goats." Mercy and charity will be the standards for determining one's entry into the future kingdom of God.

The people of Israel, exiled from their homeland and living in servitude under the Babylonians, cry out for a king to lead them. In today's **first reading**, Ezekiel offers an oracle of consolation and hope: God will no longer entrust his people to evil and incompetent leaders, but will himself look after and "tend" his chosen and faithful people. The theme of personal responsibility of one's life (a major teaching of Ezekiel) and the judgment between one "sheep" and another reflect today's Gospel description of the Last Judgment.

Some of the Corinthians are denying the resurrection of the dead, apparently because of their inability to imagine how any kind of bodily existence could be possible after death. Paul addresses this issue in chapter 15 of his first letter to the Corinthians. In the verses that make up today's **second reading**, Paul praises Christ as the "first fruits" of the Resurrection – the triumphant, living Christ represents the promise that is the future of all the faithful. The Risen Christ who has vanquished death now reigns over all forever.

Themes:

The Risen Christ in the 'disguise' of nameless poor.

Christ the Shepherd-King clearly and unequivocally identifies himself with the poor. Our "greatness" lies in our ability to reach beyond ourselves to bring justice, peace and reconciliation into the lives of everyone. Mother Teresa of Calcutta put today's Gospel theme so succinctly when she said: "At the end of life we will not be judged by how many diplomas we have received, how much money we have made, how many great things we have done. We will be judged by 'I was hungry and you gave me to eat . . . I was naked and you clothed me . . . I was homeless and you took me in.' Hungry not only for bread – but hungry for love; naked not only of clothing – but naked of human dignity and respect; homeless not only for want of a room of bricks, but homeless because of rejection. This is Christ in distressing disguise."

The 'kingship' of Christ.

We Americans don't take kindly to kings – just ask George III. So what are we to make of today's feast of Christ the *King?* The very title of today's celebration smacks of a certain "triumphalism" that many of us want nothing to do with.

In nations ruled by a royal family, the concept of monarchy is based on two premises: that the king rules by "divine right," that is, by the authority of God; and that the character of the entire nation is vested in their king, sometimes expressed in the idea of the sovereign being the "father" of his children, the governed.

In this light, Christ is indeed King. Jesus is the anointed one of God, the *Christus*, the Messiah raised up by the Father. And he is the very essence of his people, the Church. His Gospel is the bond that unites us as Church; the Eucharist, his body, gives life to that Church. To claim that Christ is our "King," to proclaim ourselves to be "Christians," demands a clear and conscious decision by each of us, not passive compliance to a "herd" spirituality. To truly celebrate this feast means to welcome Christ not just into the compartments and slots of our lifestyles marked "religion" but into every thread and fiber of the fabric of our lives.

For reflection:

- Who are the people in whom we are *least* likely to recognize Christ?
- How can we make God's kingdom a reality in our own communities?
- What impact should our claim that Christ is our King have on our lives, we who inhabit the earth 2,000 years after our "King"?

Lectionary Cycle B
The Year of Mark

The Proper of the Seasons – Cycle B

First Sunday of Advent

Readings:
Mark 13: 33-37
Isaiah 63: 16-17, 19; 64: 2-7
1 Corinthians 1: 3-9

The beginning of the Christian year begins at the end – the promised return of Christ at the end of time. In this brief **Gospel** parable of the master of the house, Jesus articulates the Advent themes of waiting, watchfulness and readiness. Jesus calls us to realize our responsibilities in the present as we dare to look forward to the promise of the future.

Today's **first reading** from Trito-Isaiah is a prayer of hope at a very desperate and overwhelming time for the prophet's listeners. The long night of the Babylonian exile is over; now begins the hard and difficult work of restoration. Isaiah and the Jewish community who have returned to what is left of Jerusalem acknowledge their sinfulness and faithlessness, but plead not for justice but for mercy from the God who reveals himself as Father to his people. In the beautiful image of God as "potter," Israel asks God to re-create and re-form them into a people and nation worth of the covenant.

In his opening words of thanksgiving (to what will be a very stern letter of reprimand and reproof for the divisions plaguing the Christian community in Corinth), Paul reminds his readers, in the **second reading**, that the Lord's promised return is not a reason for fear and despair but a cause for hope, for the promise of the covenant renewed in Christ Jesus will be fulfilled. It is not the date of the *Parousia* that should concern us but our readiness to stand before the coming "Son of Man."

Themes:

'Be on watch! Stay awake!'

Life is a constant Advent experience: the world is not as just, not as loving, not as whole as we know it can and should be; we are constantly waiting to become, to discover, to understand, to change, to complete, to fulfill. Hope, struggle, fear, expectation and fulfillment are all part of life's Advent. But the coming of Christ and his presence among us – as *one* of us – give us reason to live in hope: that light will shatter the darkness, that we can be liberated from our fears and prejudices, that we are never alone or abandoned by our merciful Father in heaven. We are not a Christmas people but an *Advent* people living our lives in patient faith and joyful hope for the Lord's coming in our lifetimes.

'An Advent people.'

The season of Advent confronts us with both the preciousness and precariousness of life, the inevitable – yet still always difficult – changes that we must contend with in the course of the time we are given. We begin the liturgical season of Advent at the end: The first Sunday of Advent (and of a new liturgical year) focuses on the last day, when Christ returns to lead us into a new time – the eternity of God's reign. The theologian Karl Rahner said that we are an "Advent Church," a Church that lives always in hopeful anticipation of the Christ who comes in its faithfulness to the Gospel of justice and reconciliation.

For reflection:

- How can we make this Advent a time of transformation, of re-creation?
- Do you have any intense experience of *waiting*, of *watching*?
- What did it teach you about the preciousness of life?
- Have you ever "slept" through an experience in which your inattention proved costly?
- How is Christmas an "adult" feast?

Second Sunday of Advent

Readings:
Mark 1: 1-8
Isaiah 40: 1-5, 9-11
2 Peter 3: 8-14

John's brief appearance in Mark's **Gospel** begins a new era in the history of salvation. Mark's details about John's appearance recall the austere dress of the great prophet Elijah (2 Kings 1: 8). The Jews believed that Elijah would return from heaven to announce the long-awaited restoration of Israel as God's kingdom. For Mark and the synoptics, this expectation is fulfilled in John the Baptizer. In the Baptizer's proclamation of Jesus as the Messiah, the age of the prophets is fulfilled and the age of the Messiah begins. His baptism with water is an act of hope and expectation in the very Spirit and life of God.

Today's **first reading** begins the second section of the Book of Isaiah, (Deutero-Isaiah), often called the Book of Consolation. The prophet preaches that the long night of exile at the hands of the Babylonians is at an end and the Israelites will soon be able to return to their homeland. It is a time for joy and expectation, of course, but also a time for realizing the difficult work that lies ahead in rebuilding their nation.

In today's **second reading**, Peter confronts the notion that somehow Christ's return has been "delayed." The point is not the exact timetable of the Parousia (for our concept of measured time means nothing to God), but that God's "delay" is a gift of grace to allow time for repentance and reconciliation with God. This time of grace marks our identity as an "Advent people."

Themes:

Our call to be 'prophets' of the Lord.

Each one of us is called to be a prophet of Christ. The word *prophet* comes from the Greek word meaning "one who proclaims." Not all prophets wear camel skins and eat locusts – there are prophets among us right now who proclaim in their ministries, in their compassion and their kindness, in their courageous commitment to what is right that Jesus the Messiah has come.

A season of both comfort and warning.

As an "Advent people," we are caught (like the Israelites returning to Jerusalem) between a world that is dying and, at the same time, waiting to be reborn. The work of Advent is to bring about that rebirth: to prepare a world that is ready for the Lord's coming. Christ's coming is both a comfort and a threat: the Messiah comes with a Gospel that proclaims the love of God and the hope of his Son's Resurrection – but it is a Gospel that imposes the cross of humble, loving servanthood. There is a highway to be built for our God through the wilderness of individual hearts and societies; there are valleys of want to be filled in and mountains of injustice to be brought low. Christ comes as the light that shatters the darkness of old animosities and hatreds and creates a new heaven and a new earth in the justice and peace of God.

'Making straight the wastelands . . .'

There are so many wastelands and barren places into which we can bring life, so many roads and avenues we can transform into highways through our charity and forgiveness. In giving the needs of others priority over our own interests, in taking the first humbling steps toward reconciliation with another, in seeing in other people the face of Christ, we make a "highway" in our world for the Lord who comes.

For reflection:

- Who are the "prophets" among us now who proclaim the Messiah in our community and our world today?
- How is the Gospel both a message of hope and a warning?
- What are the "wastelands" of our community and society into which we can create a "highway" for the God of mercy, peace and justice?

Readings:
John 1: 6-8, 19-28
Isaiah 61: 1-2, 10-11
1 Thessalonians 5: 16-24

God has revealed himself to his people through the incarnation of his Word, Jesus Christ. In today's **Gospel**, John the Baptizer points to this revelation as one standing "among you whom you do not recognize."

Forms of "baptism" were common in the Judaism of Gospel times – in some Jewish communities, it was through baptism rather than circumcision that a Gentile became a Jew. But John's baptism was distinctive. His baptism at the Jordan was a rite of repentance and *metanoia* – a conversion of heart and spirit. The Baptizer's ministry fulfilled the promise of Ezekiel (Ezekiel 36: 25-26): that, at the dawn of a new age, the God of Israel would purify his people from their sins with clear water and instill in them a new heart and spirit.

Today's **first reading** is the prophet Trito-Isaiah's hopeful proclamation of his mission to the exiles returning to Jerusalem. In Luke's Gospel, Jesus himself reads these words at the beginning of his preaching and healing ministry (Luke 4: 16-20).

The **second reading** is the conclusion of what Scripture scholars recognize as the earliest writing in the New Testament and therefore, the oldest surviving document of Christianity (written around 51 A.D.). The apostle Paul has spoken sternly to the Church at Thessalonica that they cannot wait for the Lord's return passively. He ends his letter with a series of exhortations urging the Thessalonians to embrace the ideals of Christian community: joy, thanksgiving, wise sincere discernment, seeking the common good.

Themes:

Our call to be 'Christ bearers.'

Through baptism, we take on the role of "Christ bearers." Like John's proclamation at the River Jordan, we are called to be witnesses of God's love by the love we extend to others; precursors of his justice by our unfailing commitment to what is right and good; lamps reflecting the light of God's Christ in our forgiveness, mercy and compassion.

The Advent call to joy.

The Christ event calls us to joy – to realize and celebrate the joy of God's presence that we are often too busy or too jaded or too overwhelmed to see. God desires much more than a cold, submissive "Creator/created" relationship with us; he seeks the kind of loving and trusting relationship that exists between devoted parents and their children. While realizing our failings, God does not abandon us to sink in hopelessness and despair. We have so much to celebrate, so much to be thankful for, so much to be hopeful about. "God saw the world falling in ruin because of fear and immediately acted to call it back with love. God invited it by grace, preserved it by love and embraced it with compassion." (Peter Chrysologus)

The Christmas 'Spirit.'

All three readings speak of the transforming Spirit of God: the Spirit of justice and peace re-creating post-exile Jerusalem (first reading); the Spirit of unity and joy transforming the Thessalonian gathering into a community of faith (second reading); the Spirit of humble servanthood, forgiveness and compassion to be proclaimed by the "one who is to come." (Gospel) The true Spirit of Christmas dwells among us, calling to bring hope, healing and joy to the poor, the brokenhearted and the enslaved, to witness in our own love for others God's love and mercy.

For reflection:

- Where and when have you witnessed the true Spirit of Christmas?
- Who are the Isaiahs and "Christ-bearers" of our age – those who bring "glad tidings," healing, liberty and hope to our world, whose lives proclaim the justice and mercy of God?
- How can we capture and uphold the real joy of this holy season?

Readings:

Luke 1: 26-38
2 Samuel 7: 1-5, 8-11, 16
Romans 16: 25-27

Today's **Gospel** on this Sunday before Christmas is Luke's account of the Gabriel's appearance to Mary. The Annunciation story is filled with First Testament imagery. (For example, the announcement by the angel parallels the announcements of the births of many key figures in salvation history, such as Isaac and Samuel; the "overshadowing" of Mary recalls the cloud of glory covering the tent of the ark and temple in Jerusalem.) Mary's *yes* to Gabriel's words sets the stage for the greatest event in human history: God's becoming human.

At last installed in his own palace, King David begins the planning for an equally magnificent edifice for the Ark of the Covenant. But, in today's **first reading**, the prophet Nathan refocuses the king's plans: God will establish his own house, not of stone, but of faithful men and women – David's descendants.

Today's **second reading**, from the conclusion of Paul's theologically detailed epistle to the Romans, expresses the apostle's praise of God for the final and complete revelation of his Word in the Jesus of the Gospel.

Themes:

Mary's *'yes'* to God's will.

The final chapter of the Christmas event begins with Mary's simple *yes* to God. Despite feelings of confusion and fear, it is a "yes" offered in complete faith and trust. The eminent Scripture scholar Raymond Brown has written that Mary's faithful assent to Gabriel's words makes her the "first disciple" of her Son. Mary of Nazareth is, for all of us, a model of discipleship: saying *yes* to the voice of God calling all of us to make his presence real in our own time and place.

God's 'favor' among his most humble servants.

In today's Gospel, God begins the "Christ event" with Mary, a simple Jewish girl who is at the very bottom of her people's social ladder; the God who created all things makes the fulfillment of his promise dependent upon one of the most dispossessed and powerless of his creatures. Yet God exalts her humility, her simplicity, her trust in his love and mercy. God is most present among the poor, the rejected, the abandoned and the forgotten among us today. They have a great deal to teach us about the "favor" of God.

For reflection:

- In what small and hidden places is God especially present?
- What have you learned from the poor and humble about the mystery of God's love?
- In what ways is Mary a model of faithful discipleship to the contemporary Church?

Readings:

Mass of the Vigil   *Matthew 1: 1-25*
Isaiah 62: 1-5
Acts 13: 16-17, 22-25

The readings for the Vigil Mass of Christmas celebrate Jesus' birth as the fulfillment of the First Covenant.

For Matthew, the story of Jesus begins with the promise to Abraham – that Jesus is the ultimate and perfect fulfillment of the Law and Prophets; so Matthew begins his **Gospel** with "a family record" of Jesus, tracing the infant's birth from Abraham (highlighting his Jewish identity) and David (his Messiahship).

Matthew's version of Jesus' birth at Bethlehem follows his detailed genealogy. This is not Luke's familiar story of a child born in a Bethlehem stable, but that of a young unmarried woman suddenly finding herself pregnant and her very hurt and confused husband wondering what to do. In Gospel times, marriage was agreed upon by the groom and the bride's parents, but the girl continued to live with her parents after the wedding until the husband was able to support her in his home or that of his parents. During that interim period, marital intercourse was not permissible.

Yet Mary is found to be with child. Joseph, an observant but compassionate Jew, does not wish to subject Mary to the full fury of Jewish law, so he plans to divorce her "quietly." But in images reminiscent of the First Testament "annunciations" of Isaac and Samuel, an angel appears to Joseph in a dream and reveals that this child is the fulfillment of Isaiah's prophecy. Because of his complete faith and trust in God's promise, Joseph acknowledges the child and names him *Jesus* ("Savior") and becomes, in the eyes of the Law, the legal father of Jesus. Thus, Jesus, through Joseph, is born a descendent of David.

Matthew's point in his infancy narrative is that Jesus is the Emmanuel promised of old – Isaiah's prophecy has finally been fulfilled in Jesus: the "virgin" has given birth to a son, one who is a descendent of David's house (through Joseph). Jesus is truly *Emmanuel* – God is with us.

The promise fulfilled is also the theme of Isaiah's insistence that God will fulfill his promises to the exiled Israelites returning home (**first reading**). Like the great love of a generous spouse, God not only forgives his people but entrusts to them the promise of the Messiah.

Paul's sermon to the Jews at Antioch Pisidia in the Acts of the Apostles (**second reading**) is a concise chronicle of the promise of Emmanuel fulfilled.

Mass at Midnight   *Luke 2: 1-14*
Isaiah 9: 1-6
Titus 2: 11-14

Centuries of hope in God's promise have come to fulfillment: the Messiah is born!

Luke's account of Jesus' birth (**Gospel**) begins by placing the event during the reign of Caesar Augustus. Augustus, who ruled from 27 B.C. - 14 A.D.), was honored as "savior" and "god" in ancient Greek inscriptions. His long reign was hailed as the *pax Augusta* – a period of peace throughout the vast Roman world. Luke very deliberately points out that it is during the rule of Augustus, the savior, god and peace-maker, that Jesus the Christ, the long-awaited Savior and Messiah, the Son of God and Prince of Peace, enters human history.

Throughout his Gospel, Luke shows how it is the poor, the lowly, the outcast and the sinner who immediately hear and embrace the preaching of Jesus. The announcement of the Messiah's birth to shepherds – who were among the most isolated and despised in the Jewish community – is in keeping with Luke's theme that the poor are especially blessed of God.

In his "Book of Emmanuel" (chapters 6-12), the prophet Isaiah describes Emmanuel as the new David, the ideal king who will free his enslaved people (**first reading**). The "day of Midian" refers to Gideon's decisive defeat of the Midianites, a nomadic nation of outlaws who ransacked the Israelites' farms and villages (Judges 6-8).

Paul's letter to his co-worker Titus articulates the heart of the mystery of the Incarnation: the grace of God himself has come to us in the person of Jesus Christ (**second reading**).

Mass at Dawn   *Luke 2: 15-20*
Isaiah 62: 11-12
Titus 3: 4-7

Typical of Luke's Gospel, it is the shepherds of Bethlehem – among the poorest and most disregarded of Jewish society – who become the first messengers of the **Gospel.**

As Israel rebuilds its city and nation, the prophet Isaiah calls his people to lift their hearts and spirits to behold the saving power of God (**first reading**).

In a letter to his co-worker Titus, Paul writes that our salvation comes as a result of the initiative of our merciful God (**second reading**).

Mass During the Day   *John 1: 1-18*
Isaiah 52: 7-10
Hebrews 1: 1-6

The **Gospel** for Christmas day is the beautiful Prologue hymn to John's Gospel. With echoes of Genesis 1 ("In the beginning . . . ," "the light shines on in darkness . . ."), the Prologue exalts Christ as the creative Word

of God who comes as the new light to illuminate God's re-creation.

In the original Greek text, the phrase "made his dwelling place among us" is more accurately translated as "pitched his tent or tabernacle." The image evokes the Exodus memory of the tent pitched by Israelites for the ark of the covenant. God sets up the tabernacle of the new covenant in the body of the Child of Bethlehem.

Israel has been brought to ruin by its incompetent, unfaithful rulers. But God himself leads his people back to Zion (site of the Jerusalem temple) from their long exile in Babylon. Again and again, the Lord restores and redeems Israel (**first reading**).

No prophet could imagine the length God would go to save and re-create humankind. But Christ, "the exact reflection of the Father's glory" and "heir of all things through whom he created the universe," comes as the complete and total manifestation of God's love, fulfilling the promises articulated so imperfectly and incompletely by the prophets (**second reading**).

Themes:

Christmas: a celebration for all of humanity.

From the Christmas story in Luke's Gospel, we have a romantic image of shepherds as gentle, peaceful figures. But that manger scene image is a far cry from the reality: The shepherds of Biblical times were tough, earthy characters who fearlessly used their clubs to defend their flocks from wolves and other wild animals. They had even less patience for the pompous scribes and Pharisees who treated them as second and third-class citizens, barring these ill-bred rustics from the synagogue and courts.

And yet it was to shepherds that God first revealed the birth of the Messiah. The shepherds' vision on the Bethlehem hillside proclaims to all people of every place and generation that Christ comes for the sake of all humankind.

Christmas: the beginning of the Christ event.

A favorite story of Martin Buber, the great Jewish philosopher, concerned a rabbi in Jerusalem to whom it was excitedly announced that the Messiah had come. The rabbi calmly looked out of the window, surveyed the scene carefully, and announced that, to him, nothing seemed to have changed, and then calmly returned to his study.

The Messiah *has* come – but what difference does that make in our lives? If the rabbi were to look out his window tonight, he would certainly see many different things: He would see the lights and decorations and illuminated trees and wreaths, he would hear the carolers sing their songs about "joy to the world" and "peace on earth," he would behold the smiles and joy of people extending greetings to one another.

But what would the rabbi see out of his window tomorrow? or next week? or a day in February? or April? or July?

The Messiah *has* come! What happened one Palestinian night when a son was born to a carpenter and his young bride was the beginning of a profound transformation of humanity. But has it made a difference? Has our world become a better place since the Son of God became incarnate here? Has anything changed? The theologian Martin Buber described the difference this way: "Men [and women] become what they are, sons [and daughters] of God, by *becoming* what they are, brothers of their brothers [and sisters of their sisters]."

'The Word made flesh'/'a life for the light of all.'

The miracle of Christmas is God's continuing to reach out to humankind, his continuing to call us to relationship with him despite out obstinacy, selfishness and rejection of him. In Jesus, the extraordinary love of God has taken our "flesh" and "made his dwelling among us." In his "Word made flesh," God touches us at the very core of our beings, perfectly expressing his constant and unchanging love. Christ is born – and human history is changed forever. In profound simplicity and stillness, the light of Christ has dawned and the darkness of hatred, intolerance and ignorance is shattered.

The 'Bethlehems' of our hearts.

In his acclaimed autobiography, *The Seven Story Mountain,* Thomas Merton wrote about his first Christmas as a monk at Gethsemani Abbey in Kentucky:

> "Christ always seeks the straw of the most desolate cribs to make his Bethlehem. In all other Christmases of my life, I had got a lot of presents and a big dinner. This Christmas I was to get no presents, and not much of a dinner: but I would have indeed, Christ, God, the Savior of the world.
>
> "You who live in the world: let me tell you that there is no comparing these two kinds of Christmas. . . . The emptiness that had opened up within me, that had been prepared during Advent and laid open by my own silence and darkness, now became filled. And suddenly I was in a new world."

The true miracle of Christmas continues / take place in the Bethlehems of our hearts. The trap gs of Christmas, for the most part, do not begin to c e the full magnitude of the Christmas event. In the er ness of our souls, God forgives us, reassures us, exal , elates us, loves us. In the coming of Jesus, God's l becomes real, touchable and approachable to us. The meaning of Christmas is that simple – and that profou

'O Holy Night.'

Christmas is a feast that appeals to r senses: the sights of glittering lights, the taste of th any delicacies of Yuletide feasting, the smell of fre cut evergreen branches, the feel of the crisp winter nd newly-fallen snow, the sound of the magnificent music of Christmas.

But the first Christmas had none of those things. Consider the actual sights and sounds and feels and tastes – and smells! – of that night: the damp, aching cold of a

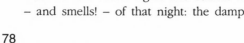

cave on the Bethlehem hillside; the burning in the eyes and throat from days of traveling along hard, dusty roads; the sudden panic of discovering there is no place to stay in a strange city, the paralyzing fear that robbers and wild animals could strike out of nowhere; the silence of the night, broken only by the cry of wolves and the bleating of sheep; the screaming of a young girl delivering her first child alone, with her carpenter husband offering what help he could; and the overwhelming stench of a cave used as a barn: the smell of animals, of manure, of perspiration.

That first Christmas night was human life at its dreariest, dirtiest and messiest, the human experience at its most painful, most exhausting, most terrifying. The first Christmas was dirty and grimy and, frankly, stunk to high heaven – but it was as holy as the highest heights of heaven. In our imperfections, in our sin, in our obtuse selfishness, God enters our human life and sanctifies it. The glorious sights and sounds, tastes and aromas of this holy night invite us to embrace the great love of God, the love that can transform our humanity from the hopeless-ness of a lonely birth in a cave to the hope and joy of redeeming grace.

For reflection:

- It has been a busy time, getting to this day. Was it all worth it?
- "We need a little Christmas . . ." so the song goes from the musical *Mame*. Why do we need Christmas *this* year?
- How is the first Christmas as described by Luke at odds with our Christmas celebration? How can we reconcile the difference in the simplicity of the first Christmas and the extravagance of our celebration?
- How can we make "shepherds" (outcasts, the poor and rejected) part of our Christmas?
- What one Christmas tradition, practice or story speaks to you most especially of the holiness of this night/day?
- Share your most memorable Christmas – a memory that even today affects your understanding of the mystery of the Incarnation.

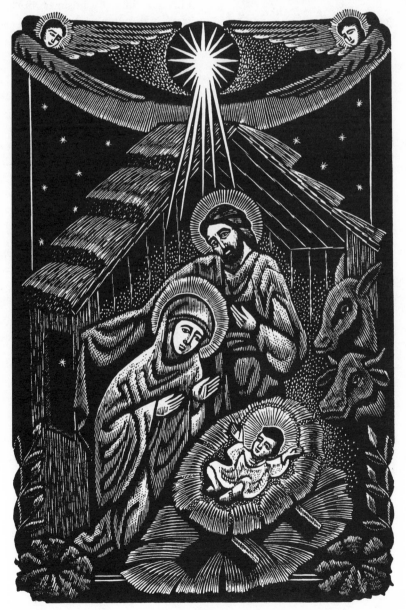

Readings:

Luke 2: 22-40
Sirach 3: 2-6, 12-14
Colossians 3: 12-21

today's **Gospel**, the faithful Joseph and Mary bring their son to the temple for his presentation to the Lord ritual required by the Law. The Book of Exodus taught that a family's first-born son "belonged" to the Lord who saved them when the first-born sons of the Egyptians were destroyed at the first Passover (Exodus 13: 15).

The holy man Simeon and the prophetess Anna are idealized portraits of the faithful "remnant" of Israel awaiting the Messiah's coming. Simeon's canticle praises God for the universal salvation that will be realized in Jesus; in his prophecy, the shadow of the cross falls upon the Holy Family.

Anna, as an elderly widow, is considered among the most vulnerable and poor of society. Her encounter with the child typifies the theme woven throughout Luke's Gospel — the exaltation of society's poorest and most humble by God.

The Book of Sirach is a collection of carefully-crafted maxims and commentaries based on the Law. The author — "Jesus, son of Eleazar, son of Sirach" – 50: 27), a wise and experienced observer of life, writes on a variety of topics in order to help his contemporaries understand the role of faith in everyday life.

Today's **first reading** is a beautiful reflection on the fourth commandment. To honor one's parents, Ben Sira writes, is to honor the Lord God himself.

Paul wrote his letter to the Colossians (one of Paul's "captivity epistles") at the urging of Epaphras, the leader of the church there. The young church was being torn apart by adherents of Gnosticism ("knowledge"), a philosophy that stressed the superiority of knowledge over faith. Paul writes that such Gnostic teachings are but "shadows"; Christ is "reality," the "image of the invisible God, the first-born of all creation" in whom we are redeemed. In today's **second reading** from Colossians, Paul presents a picture of real community, formed in the perfect, unconditional love of Christ.

Themes:

The family: 'the little church.'

Today's feast is a celebration of family – that unique nucleus of society that gives us life, nurture and support throughout our journey on earth. Families are the first and best places for the love of God to come alive. Within our families we experience the heights of joy and the depths of pain. The Fathers of Vatican II called the family "the first and vital cell of humanity...the domestic sanctu-

ary of the Church." Families reflect the love of Christ: love that is totally selfless, limitless and unconditional, both in good times and (especially) in bad times. Today's Feast of the Holy Family calls us to re-discover and celebrate our own families as harbors of forgiveness and understanding and safe places of unconditional love, welcome and acceptance.

The cross and the crib.

We all have great hopes and dreams for our children; but we also seek to protect them from the realities that can destroy such dreams. Joseph and Mary confront those same hopes and fears in today's Gospel. Their spirits must have soared when Simeon proclaimed that their child would be a "light" for Israel; but that joy shattered into anxiety and horror when Simeon prophesied the suffering ahead for them. It is easy to welcome Jesus the innocent Child of Christmas; but God calls us to welcome Jesus, the humble Crucified of Holy Week and Easter. Luke's Gospel of the Child Jesus reminds us that the crib is overshadowed by the cross, that this holy birth is the beginning of humankind's re-birth in the Resurrection.

A model of holiness for all families.

In Matthew and Luke's stories of Jesus' birth and childhood (which were later additions to those Gospels, drawn from the many stories about Jesus' life that were part of the early Christian oral tradition that had developed), life for the family of Joseph, Mary and Jesus is difficult and cruel: they are forced from their home; they are innocent victims of the political and social tensions of their time; they endure the suspicions of their own people when Mary's pregnancy is discovered; their child is born under the most difficult and terrifying of circumstances; Joseph and Mary endure the agony of losing their beloved child. And yet, through it all, their love and faithfulness to one another do not waver. The Holy Family is a model for our families as we confront the many tensions and crises that threaten the stability, peace and unity that are the joys of being a family.

For reflection:

- What rituals and customs in your own family reflect the spiritual dimension of Christmas?
- What experiences have your family shared that have brought you closer together? Consider both the wonderful and the catastrophic; times of trial, tension and tragedy; times that demanded extraordinary efforts to forgive and reconcile.
- Can you, as a parent, identify with Joseph and Mary in today's Gospel?

Solemnity of Mary, Mother of God

Readings:

Luke 2: 16-21
Numbers 6: 22-27
Galatians 4: 4-7

Today's solemnity is the oldest feast of Mary in the Church, honoring her by her first and primary title, "Mother of God."

Jesus is given the name *Yeshua* – "The Lord saves." The rite of circumcision unites Mary's child with the chosen people and makes him an heir to the promises God made to Abraham – promises to be fulfilled in the Child himself (**Gospel**).

From the Book of Numbers (one of the five books of the Law) the Lord gives to Moses and Aaron the words of priestly blessing (**first reading**).

The Church of Galatia is facing defections because of Judaic preachers who insist that pagan converts submit to the Jewish rite of circumcision and the observance of the Law. Paul's letter maintains that salvation is through Christ alone, that Christ's followers are no longer under the yoke of the First Law. Paul puts the Christmas event in perspective: through Christ, born of Mary, we become sons and daughters of "Abba," meaning Father (**second reading**).

Themes:

'Theotokos' – 'God-bearer.'

Today we honor Mary under her most ancient title – "*Theotokos*, Bearer of God." Mary, the mother of the Child of Bethlehem, is the perfect symbol of our own salvation. In accepting her role as mother of the Messiah, she becomes the first disciple of her Son, the first to embrace his Gospel of hope, compassion and reconciliation. She is the promise of what the Church is called to be and will be and seeks to become; she is the hope and comfort of a pilgrim people walking the road of faith. Mary, the "bearer of God," is a genuine and fitting example for us of what it means to be a faithful disciple of the Servant Redeemer – "bearers of God" in our own time and place.

Mary: our mother and sister.

Her statues have always radiated sweetness. She is always young and pink-cheeked and slender, with hair cascading down to her waist.

But the Mary of the Gospels is neither a fairy tale princess nor the romanticized "lovely lady dressed in blue." The flesh-and-blood Mary was an altogether human woman:

- the pregnant adolescent who was painfully misunderstood by the man she loved;
- the young mother, virtually alone, is forced to give birth to her firstborn in a damp cave one night on the outskirts of a place unknown to her;
- the frantic parent searching for her lost child in Jerusalem;
- the caring woman who was not afraid to speak her mind or voice her questions;
- the anguished mother who stood by courageously while, in a travesty of justice, her son was executed.

The figure we venerate in mysterious icons was a woman with her feet firmly planted on earth. Mary of Nazareth knew the pain that only a mother could feel; she knew the joy that only a totally selfless and giving woman of faith could experience.

Luke's Gospel reveals an uneducated adolescent who, in a dusty village in a small backwater of a conquered country, said, *Be it done to me according to your word,* stuck by that decision and changed the course of history. If Mary, the young unmarried pregnant girl, can believe in the incredible thing that she is to be a part of, if she can trust herself and believe in her role in the great story, than the most ordinary of us can believe in our parts in the drama, too.

[Adapted from *The Fire in the Thornbush* by Bishop Matthew H. Clark.]

In the new year 'of our Lord.'

G.K. Chesterton made this observation about New Year's: "The object of a new year is not that we should have a new year. It is that we should have a new soul and a new nose, new feet, a new backbone, new ears and new eyes."

Today a new year lies before us like a blank page or canvas. So many possibilities – much more than just the simple resolutions we are lucky to keep beyond the kick-off of today's first football game. But a whole new year, a new entity of time, begins today. We Christians believe that God has sanctified all time in his work of creation and his loving re-creation of the world in the Risen One. The God who makes all things new in Christ enables us to make this truly a *new* year for each one of us – a time for renewal and re-creation in the love of God, a time for making this year a year of peace in our lives and homes, a time for making this new year truly a "year of our Lord."

For reflection:

- In what ways is the Mary of the Gospels a real companion to us on our journey through the New Year?
- What was your "favorite year"? What made it a special time for you? How can you resolve to bring those elements into the New Year before you?
- Share the hopes, the challenges, the promises that the new year presents. How can we make this new year *anno Domini* – a "year of our Lord"?

Readings:
John 1: 1-18
Sirach 24: 1-4, 8-12
Ephesians 1: 3-6, 15-18

Today's readings call us to pause before the Bethlehem scene and contemplate the great destiny of the Child of Bethlehem.

The **Gospel**, the beautiful Prologue hymn to John's Gospel, with its echoes of Genesis 1 ("In the beginning . . .," "the light shines on in darkness . . ."), exalts Christ as the creative Word of God that comes as the new light to illuminate God's re-creation. In the original Greek text, the phrase "made his dwelling place among is" is more accurately translated as "pitched his tent or tabernacle." The image is also evoked by the teacher Ben Sira in today's **first reading**. In Sirach's hymn to the wisdom of God, holy wisdom is described as present before the Lord at the very beginning of creation and now present within the holy city. The writer's vision foreshadows Christ, God's Wisdom incarnate who, raised by God from the dead, continues, as John describes in his Gospel, to "make his dwelling place (literally, "pitched his tent") among us."

In his introduction to his letter to the Ephesians (today's **second reading**), Paul prays that the Christian community at Ephesus may receive the "spirit of wisdom" in order to realize the "great hope" to which God has called them in Christ Jesus.

Themes:

The 'wisdom' of God incarnate.

In the Child born of Mary at Bethlehem, the wisdom of God becomes real to us. His very birth manifests the constant and inexplicable love of God for his people, present for all time; his ministry as Messiah will teach us how we can transform humanity's dark night of sin and emptiness into the eternal day of God's peace and wholeness; his embracing of the cross will be the ultimate victory of holy wisdom over the Godless wisdom of the world.

The God who 'pitches his tent' among us.

Our God is a God constantly present to us in so many ways. He is present in the gifts of holy creation; he is present to all humanity in the birth of Christ; he is present in the Spirit of wisdom and goodness inspiring us

to do the work of the Gospel; he is present to us in prayer and sacrament. The Messiah Jesus is the light who illuminates for us the life and presence of God, who reveals to us the great and unconditional love of God, the Creator who loves us like a parent loves his/her very own sons and daughters.

For reflection:

- How has God's "holy wisdom" influenced or changed or life?
- In what ways have you discovered the preeminence of "holy wisdom" over conventional wisdom?
- Where, when and how is God's "tent" pitched in your midst?

FOR HE CHOSE US IN HIM BEFORE THE CREATION OF THE WORLD TO BE HOLY AND BLAMELESS IN HIS SIGHT.

EPHESIANS 1:4 NIV

Readings:
Matthew 2: 1-12
Isaiah 60: 1-6
Ephesians 3: 2-3, 5-6

Today's **Gospel**, the story of the astrologers and the star of Bethlehem, is unique to Matthew's Gospel. Note that Matthew does not call them kings or "magi" but "astrologers," nor does he give their names or report where they came from – in fact, Matthew never even specifies the number of astrologers (because three gifts are reported, it has been a tradition since the fifth century to picture "three wise men"). In stripping away the romantic layers that have been added to the story, Matthew's point can be better understood.

A great many First Testament ideas and images are presented in this story. The star, for example, is reminiscent of Balaam's prophecy that "a star shall advance from Jacob" (Numbers 24: 17). Many of the details in Matthew's story about the child Jesus parallel the story of the child Moses and the Exodus.

Matthew's story also provides a preview of what is to come. First, the reactions of the various parties to the birth of Jesus augur the effects Jesus' teaching will have on those who hear it. Herod reacts with anger and hostility to the Jesus of the poor who comes to overturn the powerful and rich. The chief priests and scribes greet the news with haughty indifference toward the Jesus who comes to give new life and meaning to the rituals and laws of the scribes. But the astrologers – non-believers in the eyes of Israel – possess the humility of faith and the openness of mind and heart to seek and welcome the Jesus who will institute the Second Covenant between God and the New Israel.

Secondly, the gifts of the astrologers indicate the principal dimensions of Jesus' mission:

* *gold* is a gift fitting for a king, a ruler, one with power and authority;
* *frankincense* is a gift fitting for a priest, one who offers sacrifice (frankincense was an aromatic perfume sprinkled on the animals sacrificed in the Temple);
* *myrrh* is a fitting "gift" for some one who is to die (myrrh was used in ancient times for embalming the bodies of the dead before burial).

Today's **first reading**, from Trito-Isaiah (chapters 56-66), is a song of encouragement to the exiled Jews who are returning to Jerusalem from Babylon to rebuild their nation and their way of life. But Isaiah envisions more for the city than just its rebuilding: Jerusalem will be a light for all nations, a gathering place not only for the scattered Jews but for the entire world, where God will once again dwell in the midst of his faithful people Israel.

The letter to the Ephesians is Paul's "synthesis" on the nature of the Church. In today's **second reading**, Paul writes that the Church transcends national and cultural identities: in Christ, Jew and Gentile form one body and share equally in the promise of the Resurrection.

Themes:

A Messiah for all nations.

In Matthew's Gospel, it is the "Gentile" astrologers who discover the newborn "King of the Jews," while the people of the covenant (Herod, the chief priests and scribes) remain oblivious to his presence in their midst. The prophet Isaiah describes the Messiah as a "light for all nations" (first reading). In Christ, God is present in all of human history – God is not the exclusive property of one nation or people; no religious group holds title to the wonderful things God has done. Epiphany calls us to a new vision of the world that sees beyond walls and borders we have created and to walk by the light which has dawned for all of humankind, a light by which we are able to recognize *all* men and women as our brothers and sisters under the loving providence of God, the Father of all.

The search for God in our lives.

Cardinal Newman said that "to be earnest in seeking the truth is an essential requisite in finding it." The astrologers' following of the star is a journey of faith, a journey that each one of us experiences in the course of our own life. Christ's presence is not confined to Scripture and churches; he is present in everyone and everything that is good. We find the true purpose of this life in our search for God, the great Shepherd of our souls.

The 'stars' we follow.

What we read and watch and listen to in search of wealth, fame and power are the "stars" we follow. The journey of the astrologers in Matthew's Gospel puts our own "stargazing" in perspective. The astrologers set their sights on a star that leads them to God. Where will the our "stars" lead us?

For reflection:

* *Epiphany* comes from the Greek word meaning appearance or manifestation. Think about the "epiphanies" around us – the many ways the Lord "appears" or "manifests" his presence among us.
* How is your particular parish called to be "universal"? In what ways does the Gospel challenge your community to abandon the "safety" of itself to reach out to those considered "outside" of it (new immigrants, the poor, etc.)?
* A popular bumper sticker seen during this time of year reads: "Wise men still seek him." Who are the "wise" men and women in our world who have dedicated themselves to seeking Christ? What are their stories?

Baptism of the Lord

Readings:

Mark 1: 7-11
Isaiah 42: 1-4, 6-7
Acts 10: 34-38

Today's **Gospel** is the final revelation of the Epiphany event: Jesus' baptism at the Jordan River by John. The fact that Mark begins his Gospel with the baptism of Jesus indicates its importance. In the "renting of the sky," the Spirit "descending on him like a dove" and the voice heard from the heavens, God "anoints" his Messiah (the word *Messiah* means "anointed") for the work he is about to do.

Today's **first reading** is the first of the "servant songs" in Deutero-Isaiah in which the prophet tells of the "servant" of God who will come to redeem Israel. In this first song, Isaiah speaks of the servant as God's "chosen one with whom I am pleased" – words that will be heard at the River Jordan.

Cornelius was a Roman centurion, a good and kind man who deeply respected and observed the high moral code and noble style of Judaic worship. In a dream, Cornelius is told to send for Peter and listen to what he has to say. Cornelius invites Peter to address his household. Peter's sermon (today's **second reading**) typifies early Christian preaching to the Gentiles: while God revealed his plan to his chosen nation of Israel, the Lord invites all people and nations to enter into the new covenant of the Risen Christ.

Themes:

Baptism: to become 'servants.'

We tend to view Baptism as an isolated milestone in our lives; but baptism is more than just a "naming" ceremony – it is an ongoing process that continues in every moment of our lives. In baptism, we are "grasped by the hand" of God (Reading 1) and "called" to become the servants of God; we are formed into God's holy people, a people who rise from the waters of baptism and, with the Spirit upon us, travel his road of justice and mercy to the fulfillment of the Resurrection. In baptism, we claim the name of "Christian" and embrace all that that holy name means: to live for others rather than for ourselves, in imi-

tation of Christ. Our baptism makes each one of us the "servant" described in today's readings: to bring forth in our world the justice, reconciliation and enlightenment of Christ, the "beloved Son" and "favor" of God.

The Spirit of God 'like a dove' upon us.

In all four Gospel accounts of Jesus' baptism, the evangelists use a similar description of the scene at the Jordan when Jesus is baptized by John: The Spirit of God descended and rested upon him "like a dove" – in other words, the Spirit of God resided within Jesus; that peace, compassion and love of God was a constant presence within the Carpenter from Nazareth. In baptism, we embrace that same Spirit – that same Spirit descends upon us giving direction and meaning to every moment of our lives.

The 'work' of Christmas begins.

The Christmas season officially comes to an end today at the banks of the Jordan River with Jesus' baptism by John. The glad tidings and good cheer of the holiday season are long over, Christmas has been packed away for the next 11 months and we can (finally) move on with our lives for another year. But the Messiah remains. Jesus is no longer the child in a Bethlehem manger but the adult Redeemer making his way to Jerusalem. The good news spoken by the angels continues to unfold; the most wondrous part of the Christ story is yet to be revealed. Today, the same Spirit that "anoints" the Messiah for his mission calls us to be about the *work* of Christmas in this new year: to seek out and find the lost, to heal the hurting, to feed the hungry, to free the imprisoned, to rebuild nations, to bring peace to all peoples everywhere.

For reflection:

- In practical terms, what does it mean to be the "servant" of God?
- Share stories about people you know upon whom "rests" the the Spirit of God.
- What "work" of Christmas remains to be done in your parish community? How have things changed – for the better and for the worse – since we celebrated Christmas?

Readings:
Matthew 6: 1-6, 16-18
Joel 2: 12-18
2 Corinthians 5: 20 – 6: 2

The readings for this first day of the Lenten journey to Easter call us to *turn*.

In Hebrew, the word for repentance is to *turn,* like the turning of the earth to the sun at this time of year, like the turning of soil before spring planting. The Lenten journey that begins on this Ash Wednesday calls us to repentance – to turn away from those things that separate us from God and re-turn to the Lord.

In today's **Gospel**, Jesus, in his Sermon on the Mount, instructs his listeners on the Christian attitude and disposition toward prayer, fasting and almsgiving. Such acts are meaningful only if they are outward manifestations of the essential *turning* that has taken place within our hearts.

Around 400 B.C., a terrible invasion of locusts ravaged Judah. The prophet Joel visualized this catastrophe as a symbol of the coming "Day of the Lord." The prophet summoned the people to repent, to *turn* to the Lord with fasting, prayer and works of charity (**first reading**).

In his second letter to the Corinthians, Paul alternates between anger and compassion, between frustration and affection in defending his authority and mandate as an apostle in the face of attack by some members of the Corinthian community. In today's **second reading**, the apostle appeals for reconciliation among the members of the community, a *return* to the one faith shared by the entire Church.

Themes:

Lenten 'turning': springtime rebirth.

During the next few weeks, the world around us will change dramatically: the days will grow longer and warmer; the ice and snow will melt away and the first buds of spring will appear; the raw winter iciness will be replaced by the warmth of summer; the drab grayness of winter will be transformed into the color and promise of spring. Likewise, the symbols of ashes and somberness that mark today's liturgy will be eclipsed in six weeks by the light and flowers and *Alleluias* of the Easter celebration. In fact, the very word "Lent" has come down to us from the ancient Anglo-Saxon word, *lencten,* meaning *springtime.*

The change we see around us should also be experienced *within* us during these weeks of Lent. We tend to approach Lent as something to be endured rather than to be observed, a time for *not* doing, for avoiding instead of as a time for *doing,* for *becoming;* but, like springtime, Lent should be a time for transformation, for change, for becoming the people that God has called to be. It is a time, as the prophet Joel proclaims in the first reading, for "rending our hearts, not our garments."

The ashes we receive today should be quiet symbols of something much deeper, much more powerful, much more lasting going on within us. In accepting these ashes we acknowledge the fact that we are sinners, that we are less than faithful to our baptismal name of Christian. But in accepting these ashes we also accept the challenge to become, as Paul writes to the Corinthians, "the very holiness of God."

Lenten 'turning': our 'desert' retreat.

The season of Lent that we begin today is a time to stop in the "busy-ness" of our everyday lives, to consider the truly important things in our lives, to realize the many blessings we possess in this world and the promised blessings of the next. Unfortunately, we have been conditioned to see Lent as a time for giving up and not doing, instead of as a time for doing and becoming. As Jesus began his ministry with a 40-day "retreat" in the desert wilderness, Lent should be our own "desert experience," a time to peacefully and quietly renew and re-create our relationship with God, that he might become the center of our lives in every season.

For reflection:

- Can the case be made that we *need* Lent?
- How can we Lent be made a time for doing, for becoming?
- What is your parish doing to make this a meaningful Lent for the community?
- What does the natural cycle of springtime teach us about the seasons of Lent and Easter?

Readings:

Mark 1: 12-15
Genesis 9: 8-15
1 Peter 3: 18-22

The Lenten season begins in the wilderness. Mark's brief account of Jesus' 40 days in the wilderness (today's **Gospel**), takes place immediately after Jesus' baptism at the Jordan by John. "Led by the Spirit," Jesus' going to the desert is an act of obedience to the Father. This is a time for contemplation and discernment regarding the tremendous task before him.

The word *Satan* comes from the Hebrew word for *adversary*. Satan serves as the adversary of God, advocating those values that contradict and oppose the love and mercy of God. Mark's portrait of Jesus in the desert is one of a Messiah coming to terms with the paradox of the human condition.

Jesus begins his ministry in Galilee by proclaiming "fulfillment" – God's long-awaited promised Messiah has come.

Throughout salvation history, God will not be defeated by humanity's failure. The First Testament readings on these Sundays of Lent during the "B" cycle of the lectionary recall Yahweh's constant offerings of covenant to his people Israel.

The **first reading** today recounts God's covenant with Noah. After their 40 days and nights adrift in the ark during the great flood, Noah and his family begin the task of re-establishing God's creation. As Peter preaches in his first letter (**second reading**), Christians read Noah's story as an Easter/baptismal story: under the sign of the rainbow, God promises never to destroy the world again by water; in fact, God restores life through the waters of baptism.

Themes:

Lent: our 'desert experience' with the Lord.

These 40 days of Lent are the Spirit's call to us for a "desert experience," to be alone with God, to dare to wonder if our lives are all they could and should be. Lent calls us away from business as usual (the real motivation behind giving up one's favorite confection or pastime) in order to seek out our own "desert place" to renew our relationship with God, to focus on his presence in our lives, to consider the values of the heart, to determine if our lives are all they can and should be.

Lent: a time for making choices.

As Jesus was "put to the test," so, too, are we confronted with the many different choices and goals life presents us. Every moment of our lives demands that we make hard choices – choices between the values of God and the values of the "adversary," choices between the values we believe in the depths of our hearts or the "marketplace" values of prestige, wealth and security. Lent challenges us to ask ourselves what we *really* believe in, what we *really* want our lives to be, what are we willing to sacrifice for, fight for, die for. In confronting these questions honestly, openly and faithfully, we come to a new realization of God as the center of our lives and hopes and to a new yearning for the fulfillment of the Easter promise at the end of our lives' journey.

For reflection:

- How can we make this Lent our own "desert experience"?
- What role does fasting, acts of penance and sacrifice for the poor play in Lent's call to the desert?
- What are some of the issues and decisions that life confronts us with that ultimately come down to a choice between the ways of God and the ways of the "adversary"?
- What values advocated by the "adversary" do you find yourself struggling with in your own life?

Readings:
Mark 9: 2-10
Genesis 22: 1-2, 9, 10-13, 15-18
Romans 8: 31-34

Today's **Gospel** is Mark's account of the transfiguration of Jesus. In the event witnessed by Peter, James and John on the mountain, the promise of the first covenant (Moses the great lawgiver and Elijah the great prophet) converges with the fulfillment of the new covenant (Jesus the Messiah).

Throughout Israel's history, God revealed his presence to Israel in the form of a cloud (for example, the column of cloud that led the Israelites in the desert during the Exodus – Exodus 15). On the mountain of the transfiguration, God again speaks in the form of a cloud, claiming the transfigured Jesus as his own Son.

Returning down the mountain, Jesus urges the three not to tell of what they had seen, realizing that their vision would confirm the popular misconception of an all powerful, avenging Messiah. The mission of Jesus the Messiah means the cross and resurrection, concepts Peter and the others still do not grasp.

With its many parallels to the sacrifice of Christ, the Son of God, the Genesis story of Abraham's sacrifice of his son Isaac (**first reading**) is also read each year at the Easter Vigil. The God of limitless love and forgiveness demands of himself what he does not demand of the ever trusting and faithful Abraham: the death of his own son.

The **second reading** is a hymn celebrating the great love of the God who "did not spare his own Son but handed him over for the sake of us all." With such a God on our side, Paul preaches, what have we to fear?

Themes:

The 'transfiguring' love of God within us.

What the disciples saw in Jesus on the mountain was the divinity – the very life and love of God – that dwelled within him. That love of God lives within each one of us, as well, calling us beyond our own needs, wants and interests. Love that calls us beyond ourselves is transforming. The challenge of the call to discipleship is to allow that love to "transfigure" our lives and our world. In the transforming love of Christ the Messiah-Servant, we can "transfigure" despair into hope, sadness into joy, anguish into healing, estrangement into community.

Accepting both the Risen Christ and the Crucified Christ.

The Jesus of the Gospel comes with a heavy price: the glorious Christ of the Transfiguration will soon become the Crucified Christ of Good Friday. Accepting the God of blessing is easy, but when that God becomes the God of suffering who asks us to give readily and humbly to others and to forgive one another without limit or condition, then we begin to insulate ourselves from the relationship God invites us to embrace. This Lenten season calls us to descend the mountain with the "transfigured" Jesus and to take up our cross with him in Jerusalem. In risking the pain and demands of loving one another as Christ has loved us, the divinity we recognize in the Jesus of the transfiguration becomes for us the eternal life of the Jesus of Easter.

For reflection:

- How can selfless love be "transfiguring"?
- When, in your life, have you been confronted with both the transfigured Jesus and the crucified Jesus?
- What have you learned from your own experiences of suffering, anguish and pain that made a profound difference in your life?

Readings:

John 2: 13-25
Exodus 20: 1-17
1 Corinthians 1: 22-25

The temple is the focus of today's **Gospel**. Whereas the Synoptic Gospels place Jesus' cleansing of the temple immediately after his Palm Sunday entrance into Jerusalem, John places the event early in his Gospel, following Jesus' first sign at Cana. While the synoptics recount only one climactic journey to Jerusalem, the Jesus of John's Gospel makes several trips to the holy city.

Pilgrims to the temple were expected to make a donation. Because Roman currency was considered "unclean," Jewish visitors had to change their money into Jewish currency in order to make their temple gift. Money changers, whose tables lined the outer courts of the temple, charged exorbitant fees for their service.

Visiting worshipers who wished to have a sacrifice offered on the temple altar would sometimes have to pay 15 to 20 times the market rate for animals purchased inside the temple. Vendors could count on the cooperation of the official temple "inspectors" who, as a matter of course, would reject as "unclean" or "imperfect" animals from outside the temple.

Jesus' angry toppling of the vendors' booths and tables is a condemnation of the injustice and exploitation of the faithful in the name of God. So empty and meaningless has their worship become that God will establish a new "temple" in the resurrected body of the Christ.

Of course, the leaders and people do not understand the deeper meaning of Jesus' words, nor did the people who witnessed his miracles understand the true nature of his Messianic mission. John's closing observations in this reading point to the fact that the full meaning of many of Jesus' words and acts were understood only later, in the light of his resurrection.

The Israelites' encounter with God on Mount Sinai transformed their identity from a nomadic tribe into a nation. The wisdom of the commandments given by God to the Israelites (**first reading**) became the spirit of their covenant with Yahweh.

For the Jews, who expect signs and miracles, and for the Greeks, who expect great wisdom, a crucified Jesus makes no sense. Paul writes to the Corinthians (**second reading**) that, in the light of the Gospel of the Risen Christ, God's apparent weakness becomes power and conventional wisdom becomes foolishness.

Themes:

Driving out the 'money changers' from our lives.

In the temple precincts of our lives are "money changers" and connivers – fear, ambition, addictions, selfishness, prejudice – that distort the meaning of our lives and debase our relationships with God and with one another. Lent is a time to invite the "angry" Jesus of today's Gospel into our lives to drive out those things that make our lives less than what God created them to be.

A spiritual 'spring cleaning.'

At this point in the year, spring can't come soon enough. Our late winter yearning for newness, freshness, warmth and light puts Jesus' angry expulsion of the merchants from the temple into perspective. Christ comes to bring newness to humankind, to bring a springtime of hope to a people who have lived too long in a winter of alienation and despair. The business of the merchants distorted the sacred role of the temple as a meeting place for God and his people. Lent (which comes from the old English word for *springtime*) is the time for a "spring cleaning" of our spirits and souls – driving out the useless, the meaningless, the destructive from our lives, as we prepare for the great festival of Easter life and hope.

For reflection:

- How can anger be channeled into a positive emotion?
- Have you ever struggled to "drive out" of your life some attitude, situation or set of circumstances that deadened you to the real joy and purpose of life?
- How do the "winter blues" we all experience at this time of year reflect the "blues" we sense in our souls and spirits?
- How is "spring cleaning" a good metaphor for Lent?

Readings:

John 3: 14-21
2 Chronicles 36: 14-17, 19-23
Ephesians 2: 4-10

Nicodemus is a Pharisee, a member of the ruling Sanhedren. Like so many others who heard Jesus, he is fascinated by this worker of wonders. He arranges to meet Jesus at night, so as not to attract undue attention.

In their meeting, Jesus tries to make Nicodemus understand the mission of the Messiah in a new light:

- It is not Israel's strict adherence to the ancient Law but the love of God that is the vehicle of salvation. God is motivated by a love so great that he gives the world his only Son, not to destroy but to transform the world. Redemption begins with God; reconciliation and healing are God's work, filled with possibilities that are as limitless as they are undeserved.

- Yahweh is not the God of condemnation and destruction but the God of forgiveness, mercy and reconciliation. The Messiah comes as a "light" to enable humankind to realize the great love and mercy of God.

- Contrary to the image Nicodemus and Judaism have of a powerful, triumphant Messiah who will restore Israel's political fortunes, the real Messiah will suffer and die in order to conquer death and restore life. Jesus invokes the image of Numbers 21: 4-9: as Yahweh directs, Moses lifts up the image of a serpent on a pole to heal those who suffer from a deadly plague caused by the bite of serpents. The crucified Messiah, too, will be "lifted up" to bring healing and wholeness to this hurting world.

In the conclusion of the Chronicles of the First Testament (**first reading**), God uses Judah's conqueror, King Cyrus, to restore the Jews to nationhood and to covenant with Yahweh. Despite Judah's unfaithfulness and rejection of God, God's love is so great that he uses surprising means to save his people.

In his eloquent letter to the Ephesians (**second reading**), Paul echoes Jesus' words to Nicodemus: that we owe our salvation, not to anything we have done to deserve it, but only to the great love and mercy of God.

Themes:

Trusting God, not fearing him.

Too often, we approach faith as a series of "thou shalt nots" – religion is equated with guilt, spirituality with that nagging little conscience in the depths of our souls that serves as a safety valve to stop us from becoming the wicked people we know we're capable of becoming. Jesus challenges such a limited concept of faith that imagines God scowling at us and just waiting to push the button to send us straight to the depths of hell. God is not a cosmic tyrant that revels in seeing us suffer; God has revealed himself as the loving Father of a perfect creation that has made itself imperfect in so many ways through sin. Christ does not come to put the "fear of God" into us but to place his spirit of life and love within us.

Christ, the Word of God to us.

Humanity was and still is in kind of a mess: We are not the loving, caring people we should be to one another; we vacillate in making the moral, ethical decision; we rationalize our failure to live the values we profess to believe in. Despite our rejection of the ways of God, our demeaning of the values of God, God continues to call us and seek us out. God loves his creation too much to write it off or condemn it; instead, God raises up his Son as a new light to illuminate our hearts, to make us see things as God sees them, to share God's hope for humanity's redemption.

For reflection:

- Contrast the attitudes and beliefs of those who live a faith based on fear and those who live a faith based on joy and gratitude.

- In what ways do we approach Jesus like Nicodemus in today's Gospel?

- Have you ever been made aware of the life and love of God in a surprising, unexpected way?

Fifth Sunday of Lent

Readings:
John 12: 20-33
Jeremiah 31: 31-34
Hebrews 5: 7-9

Today's **Gospel** is a pivotal moment in John's narrative. Jesus' words about the "coming" of his "hour" marks the end of John's "Book of Signs" and prefaces of "The Book of Glory" – the passion, death and resurrection of Jesus.

The Passover is about to begin; many Jews (including some Greek Jews) have arrived in Jerusalem for the festival. Meanwhile, Jesus' conflict with the Jewish establishment has reached the crisis stage. The events of Holy Week are now in motion. Jesus obediently accepts his fate and is prepared for the outcome.

Jesus compares his "glorification" to a grain of wheat that is buried and dies to itself in order to produce new life. The sacrifice and harvest of the grain of wheat are the fate and glory of anyone who would be Jesus' disciple. The "voice" heard from the sky expresses the unity of Jesus' purpose and God's will.

In today's **first reading**, the prophet Jeremiah prophesies a "new covenant" (this is the only time in the First Testament that such a phrase appears). This new covenant will be written not on stone but on human hearts. Jeremiah's vision will be realized in the resurrection of Christ Jesus.

Today's **second reading** from the letter to the Hebrews praises Christ for his obedience to the will of God his Father. In his sufferings, Christ is the perfect high priest who restores humanity to relationship with God.

Themes:

The grain of wheat: the risk of love.

The risk of being hurt is the price of love. Suffering, of itself, is of little value; but suffering and pain endured out of love is life-giving. That is the challenge of the grain of wheat: only by loving is love returned, only by reaching out and trying do we learn and grow, only by giving to others do we receive, only by dying do we rise to new life.

The grain of wheat: transforming our lives.

To transform our lives in order to become the people we are meant to be begins by dying to those prejudices, fears and ambitions we cling to. Christ gave his life on the tree of the cross in order that new life might come forth. His death gave rise to a new heart and spirit for humanity. The Gospel of the grain of wheat is Christ's assurance to us of the great things we can do and the powerful miracles we can work by letting go of our prejudices, fears and ambitions in order to imitate the compassion and love of the crucified Jesus, the Servant Redeemer.

For reflection:

- The grain of wheat is a beautiful illustration of the price and glory of Easter faith. What do other popular Easter symbols (the egg and the butterfly, for example) teach us about faith in the Risen Christ?
- What has suffering and "dying" in your own life taught you about the ways of God?
- Have you ever had difficulty accepting a situation, a challenge, another person? How did things change after you accepted – however reluctantly – what you would have preferred to walk away from?
- How is loving another person risky? How is that risk rewarded?

Passion (Palm) Sunday

Readings: *Blessing and Procession of Palms:*
Mark 11: 1-10 or John 12: 12-16
Liturgy of the Word: Mark 14: 1 – 15:47
Isaiah 50: 4-7
Philippians 2: 6-11

Mark's **Gospel** of Jesus' entry into Jerusalem is the most subdued version of the event in Scripture. Mark downplays the crowd's enthusiasm surrounding Jesus' arrival; he is acclaimed neither as the Messiah nor the king, but as a great prophet.

In John's version, however, Jesus is enthusiastically welcomed as the Messiah-king by the crowds, many of whom had seen or heard about Jesus' raising of Lazarus. John also makes a specific reference to Zephaniah's prophecy that the Messiah-king will enter the city seated on "a donkey's colt."

Jesus' entry into the holy city and his "cleansing" of the temple with the demand that it be a "house of prayer for all people" will bring his clash with the ruling class to a head. In his account of the **Passion**, Mark portrays the anguish of Jesus who has been totally abandoned. Mark's Jesus is resigned to his fate. He makes no response to Judas when he betrays him nor to Pilate during his interrogation (and Pilate makes no effort to save him, as the procurator does in the other three Gospels). As he does throughout his Gospel, Mark pointedly portrays the utter failure of the disciples to provide any assistance or support to Jesus or to even understand what is happening. The "last" disciple who flees naked into the night when Jesus is arrested is a powerful symbol of the disciples who left family and friends behind to follow Jesus but now leave everything behind to get away from him.

The **first reading** is taken from Deutero-Isaiah's "Servant songs," the prophet's foretelling of the "servant of God" who will come to redeem Israel. In this third song, Isaiah portrays the servant as a devoted teacher of God's Word who is ridiculed and abused by those who are threatened by his teaching.

In his letter to the Christian community at Philippi (in northeastern Greece), Paul quotes what many scholars believe is an early Christian hymn (**second reading**). As Christ totally and unselfishly "emptied himself" to accept crucifixion for our sakes, so we must "empty" ourselves for others.

Themes:

The faith we profess and the faith we live.

There is a certain incongruity about today's Palm Sunday Liturgy. We begin with a sense of celebration – we carry palm branches and echo the *Hosannas* (from the Hebrew for *God save [us]*) shouted by the people of Jerusalem as Jesus enters the city. But Mark's account of the Passion confronts us with our complicity in the injustice, fear and hatred that leads ultimately to the cross. We welcome the Christ of victory, the Christ of Palm Sunday; but we turn our backs on the Christ of suffering and of the poor, the Christ of Good Friday. These branches of palm are symbols of that incongruity that often exists between the faith we profess on our lips and the faith we profess in our lives.

The 'attitude' of Christ, the 'Suffering Servant.'

The Gospel calls us to take on the "attitude of Christ Jesus" in his passion and death: to "empty" ourselves of our own interests, fears and needs for the sake of others; to realize how our actions affect *them* and how our moral and ethical decisions impact the common good; to reach out to heal the hurt and comfort the despairing around us despite our own betrayal; to carry on, with joy and in hope, despite rejection, humiliation and suffering. The celebration of Holy Week calls us to embrace the attitude of Christ's compassion and total selflessness, becoming servants of God by being servants to one another.

The abandoned Jesus: the lonely way of the cross.

In his account of the Passion, Mark portrays a Jesus who has been totally abandoned by his disciples and friends. There is no one to defend him, to support him, to speak for him. He endures such a cruel and unjust death alone. Yet, amid the darkness, a light glimmers: The prophecy of a new temple "not made by human hands" is fulfilled in the shreds of the temple curtain; a pagan centurion confesses his new-found realization that this crucified Jesus is indeed the "son of God"; and a member of the Sanhedren, Joseph of Arimathea, is embolden to break with his fellow councilors and request of Pilate the body of Jesus. The Passion of Jesus should be a reason for hope and a moment of grace for all us as we seek the reign of God in our own lives – however lonely and painful our search may be.

For reflection:

- Consider stories and examples of individuals who possessed the courage to maintain their convictions and beliefs while left abandoned and alone in the face of opposition, ridicule and popular belief.
- In what ways are we confronted today with the reality of the cross?
- How is Christ's "attitude," as articulated in Paul's hymn in Philippians, the antithesis to the "attitude" of today's world?
- Which character in Mark's Passion narrative do you identify with especially? What is it about his or her heroism – or failure – before the cross that strikes you?

Readings: *John 13: 1-15*
Exodus 12: 1-8, 11-14, 1 Corinthians 11: 23-26

The centerpiece of John's **Gospel** account of the Last Supper is the *mandatum* – from the Latin word for "commandment," from which comes our term for this evening, *Maundy* Thursday. At the Passover seder, the night before he died, Jesus established a new Passover to celebrate God's covenant with the new Israel. The special character of this second covenant is the *mandatum* of the washing of the feet – to love one another as we have been loved by Christ.

(John makes no mention of the establishment of the Eucharist in his account of the Last Supper. The Johannine theology of the Eucharist is detailed in the "bread of life" discourse following the multiplication of the loaves and fish at Passover, in chapter 6 of his Gospel.)

Tonight's **first reading** recounts the origin and ritual of the feast of Passover, the Jewish celebration of God breaking the chains of the Israelites' slavery in Egypt and leading them to their own land, establishing a covenant with them and making of them a people of his own.

The deep divisions in the Corinthian community have led to abuses and misunderstandings concerning the "breaking of the bread." In addressing these problems and articulating the proper spirit in which to approach the Lord's Supper, Paul provides us with the earliest written account of the institution of the Eucharist, the Passover of the new covenant (this evening's **second reading**). If we fail to embrace the spirit of love and servanthood in which the gift of the Eucharist is given to us, then "Eucharist" becomes a judgment against us.

Themes:

Becoming 'Eucharist' for one another.

Tonight's liturgy is like a song that is out of tune or a photograph out of focus. Things are "out of sync" tonight. Jesus' last Passover seder sinks into betrayal, denial and abandonment. The holy kiss of peace is desecrated. While his twelve closest friends carry on a petty squabble over who is the greatest among them, Jesus gives them the gift of perfect unity, the Eucharist. With his ultimate triumph at hand, Jesus stuns his disciples by washing their feet – a humiliating task usually relegated to the lowliest of slaves – as a model of the selfless love that should characterize the new community of the Resurrection.

True, this is the night on which the Lord Jesus gave us himself in the Eucharist and instituted the ministerial priesthood. But there are shadows: the joy of the Eucharist is shadowed by Christ's challenge to become Eucharist for one another; the authority and dignity of priesthood is shadowed by the stark command to "wash one another's feet" not as overseers but as servants.

As we gather to remember the night of the Last Supper, we confront how "out of sync," how shadowed our lives are in relation to the life to which God calls us. We partake of the Eucharist tonight vowing to become the body of Christ to our hurting world and renewing our baptismal promise to become the priestly people of the new Israel – to do for others as our Teacher and Lord has done for us.

The parable of the 'Mandatum.'

Tonight, the Rabbi who taught in parables teaches what is perhaps his most touching and dramatic parable.

In the middle of the meal, Jesus – the revered Teacher, the Worker of miracles and wonders, the Rabbi the crowds wanted to make a king just a few days before – suddenly rises from his place as presider, removes his robe, wraps a towel around his waist and – like the lowliest of slaves – begins to wash the feet of the Twelve. We can sense the shock that must have shot through that room. But, quietly, Jesus goes about the task. Jesus on his knees, washing the dirt and dust off the feet of the fisherman, then the tax collector, and so on. Despite Peter's embarrassment and inability to comprehend what is happening, Jesus continues the humiliating and degrading task.

The Teacher, who revealed the wonders of God in stories about mustard seeds, fishing nets and ungrateful children, on this last night of his life – as we know life – leaves his small band of disciples his most beautiful parable: As I, your Teacher and Lord, have done for you, so you must do for one another. As I have washed your feet like a slave, so you must wash the feet of each other and serve one another. As I have loved you without limit or condition, so you must love one another without limit or condition. As I am about to suffer and die for you, so you must suffer and, if necessary, die for one another.

Tonight's parable is so simple, but its lesson is so central to what being a real disciple of Christ is all about. When inspired by the love of Christ, the smallest act of service done for another takes on extraordinary dimensions.

For reflection:

- How can we be "Eucharist" to one another?
- In what ways can we "wash the feet" of others?
- Consider the ways our faith is "out of sync" with our human experience.
- Explore the range of emotions that are present both in the scene depicted in tonight's Gospel and in the elements of tonight's liturgy.

Readings:
John 18:1 – 19:42
Isaiah 52:13 – 53:12
Hebrews 4:14-16; 5:7-9

John's deeply theological **Passion** account portrays a Jesus who is very much aware of what is happening to him. His eloquent self-assurance unnerves the high priest and intimidates Pilate ("You have no power over me"), who shuttles back and forth among the various parties involved, desperately trying to avoid condemning this innocent holy man to death. Hanging on the cross, Jesus entrusts his mother to his beloved disciple, thus leaving behind the core of a believing community. He does not cry out the psalm of the abandoned (Psalm 22); rather, his final words are words of decision and completion: "It is finished." The crucifixion of Jesus, as narrated by John, is not a tragic end but the beginning of victory, the lifting up of the Perfect Lamb to God for the salvation of humankind.

Isaiah's fourth and final oracle of the "servant of God" (today's **first reading**) is a hauntingly accurate description of the sufferings that the innocent one will endure to atone for the sins of his people. Only in Jesus Christ is Isaiah's prophecy perfectly fulfilled.

The priesthood and sacrifice of Jesus are the themes of the letter to the Hebrews (scholars are unanimous in their belief that this letter, while reflecting Pauline Christology, was not written by Paul himself). The verses taken for today's **second reading** acclaim Jesus, Son of God and Son of Man, as the perfect mediator between God and humankind.

Themes:

The broken body of Christ.

The broken body of Jesus – humiliated, betrayed, scourged, abused, slain – is the central image of today's liturgy. Today, Jesus teaches us through his own broken body.

As a Church, as a community of faith, we are the body of Christ. But we are a broken body. We minister as broken people to broken people. The suffering, the alienated, the unaccepted, the rejected, the troubled, the confused are all part of this broken body of Christ.

This is the day to reflect on the reality of pain and suffering. This is the day to realize that the source of such brokenness – sin – is also a reality. But the "goodness" of "Good" Friday teaches us that there are other realities. For us who believe, the broken body of Christ is forever transformed into the full and perfect life of the Risen Christ. In conquering life's injustices and difficulties, we are healed and made whole in the reality of the Resurrection.

The cross: the tree of life.

Actually, it is a plank hoisted up on a pole anchored in the ground, but the wood of the cross is nevertheless a life-giving tree.

The tree of Good Friday repulses us, horrifies us and, possibly, shames us. The tree that is the center of today's liturgy confronts us with death and humiliation, with the injustice and betrayal of which we are all capable.

But through the tree of the cross we are reborn. The tree of defeat becomes the tree of victory. Where life was lost, there life will be restored. The tree of Good Friday will blossom anew, bringing life, not death; bringing light that shatters centuries of darkness; bringing Paradise, not destruction.

Crucifying the 'problem' Jesus.

This Jesus had become a problem. His ramblings about love and forgiveness and neighbor were fine, up to a point; but things were getting out of hand. To the highly sensitive leaders of Judaism his parable about "Good" Samaritans (!), his associating with prostitutes and tax collectors, his scorning of the intricate traditions of the cherished Law threatened the very foundation of their Jewish identity and society. So, very methodically and quite legally, a strategy developed. Even a fall-back plan – co-opting the Roman government – was set into motion. The result: The problem is "solved" on a cross on the outskirts of the town.

Two millennia later, Good Friday confronts us with the reality that the crucifixion of the "problem" Jesus takes place again and again in our own time and place:

- when people's lives and futures are cast aside for the sake of profit or political expediency, the problem Jesus is crucified again;
- when self-righteous anger stifles compassionate charity and strangles efforts at healing reconciliation, the problem Jesus is crucified again;
- when unjust laws and dehumanizing social systems are allowed to continue because "I've got mine," the problem Jesus is crucified again.

Good Friday calls us to follow the "problem" Jesus, "to die with him so that we may also rise with him."

For reflection:

- Have you experienced, in your own life, suffering that has been, somehow, life-giving?
- How is each one of us a member of the broken body of Christ?
- Where is the crucifixion of Jesus taking place now, in our own time and place?

Readings:

Gospel: Mark 16:1-8
First Testament Readings:
Genesis 1:1 – 2:2, Genesis 22:1-18,
Exodus 14:15 – 15:1, Isaiah 54:5-14,
Isaiah 55:1-11, Baruch 3:9-15, 32 – 4:4,
Ezekiel 36:16-28
Epistle: Romans 6:3-11

In Mark's account, Jesus was buried quickly because sundown was approaching and the sabbath was about to begin. The three faithful women came to complete the ritual anointings that had to be omitted two nights before. They are not prepared for what they find.

A "young man" proclaims to the terrified women (**Gospel**) that all that God has promised and all that Jesus taught has been fulfilled. Easter morning is the dawning of a new day of hope for a re-created humanity.

The "young man" instructs the three women to go and tell the disciples "and Peter" what has happened. Remember that throughout his Gospel, Mark has made a point of the disciples' constant failure to understand and grasp the meanings of the Servant-Messiah's words and actions. Mark's singling out of Peter indicates the new life of forgiveness and reconciliation Peter will receive from the Risen Christ. That same resurrection experience is offered to every disciple of every place and time.

The **First Testament readings** all recount God's first creation and covenant with the people of Israel. In the passion, death and resurrection of his Son, the faithful God re-creates creation and vows a new covenant to his people.

Paul's **Epistle** to the Romans includes this brief catechesis on the Easter sacrament: in baptism, we die with Christ to our sinfulness and we rise with him to the life of God.

Themes:

The resurrection: a new creation.

Did the universe begin with a bang or a whimper? Is God the master firemaker who ignited a big bang that set creation on its journey through the cosmos? Or is God the meticulous craftsman who carefully formed one single cell that contained within its microscopic walls the power to give birth to planets and stars and plants and animals – and us?

The scientists among us journey to the last frontiers of thought to discover how creation began. But the point is: it began. God set it all in motion. **The first Genesis.**

Nobody saw Jesus leave the tomb. Nobody saw life return to the crucified body. Nobody saw the massive stone roll away. Theories abound, scenarios have been devised to explain it. Some say that the apostles stole the body – but could that band of hapless fishermen and

peasants devise such a hoax? Maybe Jesus didn't die – maybe he revived three days later. But re-read the events of Good Friday. He didn't have a chance. Ponder the whys and hows, but you cannot escape the reality: the empty tomb, the eyewitness accounts of his appearances to Mary, Peter, the disciples traveling to Emmaus, the Eleven. Jesus is risen. **The second Genesis.**

On this night in early spring, we celebrate God's new creation. Death is no longer the ultimate finality but the ultimate beginning. The Christ who taught forgiveness, who pleaded for reconciliation, who handed himself over to his executioners for the sake of justice and mercy, has been raised up by God. We leave behind in the grave our sinfulness, our dark side, our selfishness, our pettiness – the evil that mars God's first creation. Tonight, we join our renewed hearts and re-created voices in the "Alleluia!" of the new creation.

Easter hope: rolling away the 'stone.'

The problem confronting Mary Magdalene, Mary and Salome was not a minor one. Tombs in Gospel times were large caves in which several bodies could be laid. The entrance to the cave would then be closed off with a large, flat, round stone fitted into a track dug into the ground.

But the three faithful women will not be deterred by a stone. They were focused on their task: to properly complete the burial of their slain friend and teacher.

When it comes to living our faith, we often find "stones" in our way. The "stones" may be the fear of ridicule or humiliation, social conventions, or the quest for profit and power. But Christ's Resurrection is the complete victory of reconciliation, love, humility and selflessness over the "tombs" of despair, hatred and greed. In our Easter celebration of the women's discovery of the rolled-backed stone we come to realize that such stones in our own lives are obstacles only if we let them. The Easter miracle opens the love and hope of God we have entombed within us and rolls away the stones that prevent us from experiencing the joy of the Resurrection.

For reflection:

- Tonight we celebrate with symbols: fire (light), story (Scripture), water (baptism) and bread (Eucharist). What do these symbols teach us about the Paschal mystery?
- What "stones" have you encountered in your living out the good news of the empty tomb?
- The Risen Christ "is going ahead of you to Galilee, where you will see him just as he told you," the angel reassures the women. How do we "see" the Risen Lord today in our own "Galilee?"
- How would our lives be different if tonight had never happened?

Easter Sunday

Readings:

John 20: 1-9
Acts 10: 34, 37-43
Colossians 3: 1-4
or 1 Corinthians 5: 6-8

[NOTE: The Gospel for the Easter Vigil may be read in place of John 20: 1-9.]

John's Easter **Gospel** says nothing of earthquakes or angels. His account begins before daybreak. It was believed that the spirit of the deceased hovered around the tomb for three days after burial; Mary Magdalene was therefore following the Jewish custom of visiting the tomb during this three-day period. Discovering that the stone has been moved away, Mary Magdalene runs to tell Peter and the others. Peter and the "other disciple" race to get there and look inside.

Note the different reactions of the three: Mary Magdalene fears that someone has "taken" Jesus' body; Peter does not know what to make of the news; but the "other" disciple – the model of faithful discernment in John's Gospel – immediately understands what has taken place. So great are the disciple's love and depth of faith that all of the strange remarks and dark references of Jesus now become clear to him.

In this sermon recorded in Luke's Acts (**first reading**), Peter preaches the good news of the "Christ event" to the Gentile household of Cornelius. The resurrection of Jesus is the ultimate sign of God's love for all of humanity. The apostles' mandate to preach the Gospel is about to cross into the Gentile world beyond Jerusalem.

The imprisoned Paul writes (**second reading: Colossians**) that because we are baptized into Christ's death and resurrection, our lives should be re-centered in new values, in the things of heaven.

Paul's first letter to the Corinthians includes one of the earliest Easter homilies in Christian literature (**second reading: 1 Corinthians**). The custom in many Jewish households at Passover was to discard old yeast (leaven) and bake new unleavened bread for the feast. For Paul, this is a fitting symbol for the Christian community at Corinth: They must rid themselves of the self-centeredness and corruption which destroys their community and, together, share "the unleavened bread of sincerity and truth."

Themes:

The empty tomb: reason to hope.

While the Easter mystery does not deny the reality of suffering and pain, it does proclaim reason for hope in the human condition. The empty tomb of Christ trumpets the ultimate *Alleluia* – that love, compassion, generosity, humility and selflessness will ultimately triumph over hatred, bigotry, prejudice, despair, greed and death. The Easter miracle enables us, even in the most difficult and desperate of times, to live our lives in hopeful certainty of the fulfillment of the Resurrection at the end of our life's journey.

The empty tomb: the ultimate victory.

Today we stand, with Peter and John and Mary, at the entrance of the empty tomb; with them, we wonder what it means. The Christ who challenged us to love one another is risen and walks among us! All that he taught – compassion, love, forgiveness, reconciliation, sincerity, selflessness for the sake of others – is vindicated and affirmed in the Father raising him from the dead. The empty tomb should not only console us and elate us, it should challenge us to embrace the life of the Gospel. With Easter faith, we can awaken the promise of the empty tomb in every place and moment we encounter on our journey through this life.

The Church: the Resurrection community.

The Risen Christ is present to us in the faithful witness of every good person who shares the good news of the empty tomb by their living of the Gospel of selflessness and compassion. The empty tomb should inspire us to bring resurrection into this life of ours: to rise above life's sufferings and pain to give love and life to others, to renew and re-create our relationships with others, to proclaim the Gospel of *Christ who died, Christ who has risen, Christ who will come again!*

For reflection:

- Have any stories in the news this week struck you as examples of resurrection in our own time – of bringing hope, new life, new possibilities to once dark, hopeless places?
- Where is the Risen Lord present among us? How is the good news of the Risen Jesus proclaimed in the faithfulness and compassionate charity of people around you?
- How should our belief in the empty tomb affect our everyday outlook and attitudes?

Second Sunday of Easter

Readings:

John 20: 19-31
Acts 4: 32-35
1 John 5: 1-6

The **Gospel** for the Second Sunday of Easter (for all three years of the Lectionary cycle) is Act 2 of John's Easter drama.

Scene I takes place on Easter night. The terrified disciples are huddled together, realizing that they are marked men because of their association with the criminal Jesus. The Risen Jesus appears in their midst with his greeting of "peace." John clearly has the Genesis story in mind when the evangelist describes Jesus as "breathing" the Holy Spirit on his disciples: Just as God created man and woman by breathing life into them (Genesis 2: 7), the Risen Christ re-creates humankind by breathing the new life of the Holy Spirit upon the eleven.

In scene II, the disciples excitedly tell the just-returned Thomas of what they had seen. Thomas responds to the news with understandable skepticism. Thomas had expected the cross (see John 11: 16 and 14: 5) – and no more.

The climactic third scene takes place one week later, with Jesus' second appearance to the assembled community – this time with Thomas present. He invites Thomas to examine his wounds and to "believe." Christ's blessing in response to Thomas' profession of faith exalts the faith of every Christian of every age who "believes without seeing"; all Christians who embrace the Spirit of the Risen One possess a faith that is in no way different or inferior from that of the first disciples. The power of the Resurrection transcends time and place.

The first readings for the Sundays of the Easter seasons are taken from Luke's Acts of the Apostles. Acts has been called the "Gospel of the Holy Spirit" because it recounts how the Spirit of God was at work forming this small group on the fringes of Judaism into the new Israel, the Church of the Risen Christ. Today's **first reading** is one of several brief "snapshots" Luke includes of the Jerusalem Church, a community united in heart and mind, in charity to all and in their witness to the resurrection.

On the Sundays of this (cycle B) Easter season, the second readings are taken from the brief first letter attributed to John (although probably not written by the evangelist himself, the letter does echo many of the themes of his Gospel). The letter appeals to Christians in the Johannine Church to remain faithful to the love that unifies them in Christ Jesus – a unity that has been undermined by dissident teachers. In today's **second reading**, the writer reminds his brothers and sisters that they have been reborn in the Risen Christ and are now sons and daughters of God the Father.

Themes:

Called to be Easter communion and community.

The Risen Christ calls us to communion with God through him and to community with one another. We trace our roots as parish and faith communities to Easter night when Jesus "breathed" his spirit of peace and reconciliation upon his frightened disciples, transforming them into the new Church; today's first reading from Acts is a snapshot of the ideal of the Church they became. Jesus' gift of peace and his entrusting to the disciples the work of forgiveness are what it means to be a church, a parish, a community of faith: to accept one another, to affirm one another, to support one another as God has done for us in the Risen Christ. What brought the apostles and first Christians together as a community – unity of heart, missionary witness, prayer, reconciliation and healing – no less powerfully binds us to one another as the Church of today.

Transforming skepticism into trust.

All of us, at one time or another, experience the doubt and skepticism of Thomas. While we have heard the good news of Jesus' empty tomb, all of our fears, problems and sorrows overwhelm us and prevent us from realizing it in our own lives. In raising his beloved Son from the dead, God also raises our spirits to the realization of the totality and limitlessness of his love for us. As Thomas experiences, Easter transforms our crippling sense of skepticism and cynicism into a sense of trust and hope in the providence of God.

For reflection:

- Have you ever known someone (perhaps yourself) whose life was almost swallowed up in destructive skepticism, cynicism or despair? How was that skepticism transformed into hope and trust?
- In what ways is your parish community like – or can become like – the first Christian communities portrayed in today's readings?
- How can we "breathe" new life into situations and relationships?

35-48

15, 17-19

2: 1-5

...ount of Jesus' first post-
...sciples. The two disci-
... Emmaus have returned
...'s story of the Resurrec-
... telling their story, Jesus

... in his Easter accounts to
... was not the fantasy of
...ection story a plot con-
...nehow managed to spirit
...ing to Luke's account, the
...one near the tomb them-
...kind of "resurrection.") In
...ke is countering the argu-
...way the resurrection myth.
...Resurrection of Jesus Christ
... all of the Scriptures – the
...ritings – find their ultimate

...esus' resurrection is realized
...eart and mind to understand
... Word and to fully embrace
... and trust in the Risen Christ,
...he mercy and forgiveness of

...(**first reading**), Peter gives
...rgiveness of God, inviting his
Jewish hearers to ....e life of the Servant Jesus, in
whom the promises of their ancient faith are fulfilled.

The writer of the first letter of John (**second reading**) also proclaims the mercy and forgiveness of God,
reminding his community that in Jesus Christ we have before God a "just intercessor."

Themes:

Easter: the fulfillment of God's love for humanity.

In the passion, death and resurrection of Jesus, God
reveals in a specific moment of history, in a specific loca-
tion on earth, the limitless and eternal love the Father has
for his people. God continues to make the miracle of the
empty tomb present to us in the caring, compassion and
love we receive and give – the love we have witnessed in
the suffering of Christ, a love that is victorious even over
death.

Learning to hope in Easter despite life's many Good Fridays.

"We learn as much from sorrow as from joy," the
novelist Pearl S. Buck wrote, "as much from illness as
from health, as much from handicap as from advantage –
and indeed, perhaps more." Through dealing with life's
difficulties, disappointments and injustices we come to understand and appreciate what this gift of life is all about.
In today's Gospel, the Risen Jesus challenges his disciples
– and us – to recall what he taught and what they had
witnessed. The Easter miracle is God's assurance that love
and forgiveness, even in the most difficult situations, are
never offered in vain; in learning to cope without losing
hope, in learning from the painful realities of life and in
accepting the lessons learned in God's Spirit of humility
and patience, we become capable of growth, re-creation,
transformation – and resurrection.

The transforming vision of Easter.

In today's Gospel, the Risen Jesus challenges his disciples – and us – to recall what he taught and what they
had witnessed in his time among them. Authentic Easter
faith transforms our vision to see God's hand in every
moment, transforms our attitudes to recognize God's compassion and forgiveness in every human encounter from
politics to raising children, transforms our spirits to realize
that there is always a reason to hope even in the face of
life's most painful and traumatic moments. True resurrection faith is complete and total, re-creating even the most
jaded and desperate moments of our lives.

For reflection:

- Have you known someone who has been able to
  transform the suffering and injustice they encountered
  into hope and justice for others?
- Have you ever witnessed love that persevered in the
  most difficult and trying circumstances and was finally
  victorious?
- Where and when in your life have you witnessed or
  experienced *resurrection*?

Readings:

John 10: 11-18
Acts 4: 8-12
1 John 3: 1-2

Jesus' portrait of the Good Shepherd (**Gospel**) is not an idyllic, serene image. Palestinian shepherds were held absolutely liable for every single sheep entrusted to their care; "good" shepherds, motivated by a sense of responsibility rather than money, considered it a matter of honor to lay down their lives for the sheep in their charge, wild beast and bandit in defense of the flock. While the shepherd/sheep metaphor is well-known throughout Scripture, Jesus's vow to lay down his life for his sheep is something new. It completes Jesus' break with the mercenary religious leaders of the Jewish establishment who care little for the flock they have been entrusted to serve.

Invoking the name of Jesus Christ, Peter and John cured a crippled man they met in the temple precincts; they then began to explain to the crowds who had witnessed this miracle just who this Jesus was. The two apostles were quickly hauled before an angry Sanhedren who demanded an explanation as to these rantings about the resurrection of this dead Jesus. Peter responds (today's **first reading**) that in healing the cripple in Jesus' name, God manifests the same power he revealed in raising Jesus from the dead.

A common theme among Hellenistic religions was that to truly know and understand someone or something was to become "like" them. In today's **second reading**, the writer of 1 John teaches that to "know" Christ is to know God; in Christ, we become God's own "children."

Themes:

The 'Good Shepherd': the call to servanthood.

"Good" shepherding is hard work – it means being involved in the pain and grit of life. Christ calls us to the vocation of being "good shepherds" in his image of loving servanthood: seeking out and bringing back the lost, the scattered and forgotten; enabling people to move beyond their fears and doubts to become fully human; willingly paying the price for justice and mercy for all members of the "one fold."

The 'Good Shepherd': the Spirit of humility and compassion.

Jesus' model of the Good Shepherd calls us to look beyond our own expectations, needs and fears in order to become "shepherds" of reconciliation, compassion and charity to others. To be a disciple of Jesus is not to be simply a "hired hand" who acts only to be rewarded; real followers of Jesus realize that every person of the "one fold" possesses the sacred dignity of being children of God and rejoices in knowing that in serving others he/she serves God. In embracing the Gospel attitude of humility and compassion for the sake of others – in "laying down our own lives" for others – our lives will one day be "taken up again" in the Father's Easter promise.

For reflection:

- Who have you known in your life who exemplifies the model of the "Good Shepherd"?
- What does the Gospel of the Good Shepherd say to us about the nature and role of leadership and authority?
- What does it mean to "know" someone? In what ways is knowing Christ being *like* Christ?
- Who or what are the "wolves" who force us to run away from our responsibilities as "shepherds"?

Fifth Sunday of Easter

Readings:

John 15: 1-8
Acts 9: 26-31
1 John 3: 18-24

From the music of the psalms to the engravings on the temple pediments, vines were a symbol of Yahweh's many blessings to Israel. In his Last Supper discourse (**Gospel**), Jesus appropriates the image of the vine to explain his eternal connectedness to his disciples, their connectedness through him to God the Father and their connectedness to one another.

Acts 9 tells the story of the conversion of Saul from being the Church's principal persecutor to becoming Paul, the Church's premiere missionary. Barnabas serves as a mediator between Paul and the distrusting Jerusalem community (**first reading**).

Echoing John's Gospel teachings on love, the writer of the epistles bearing John's name (**second reading**) urges his readers to remain faithful to the sacred commandment to love one another in the spirit of Christ Jesus.

Themes:

Our connectedness to God and one another.

In Christ, we are connected to God and to one another. We cannot live our faith in a vacuum: Unless Jesus becomes the center of our lives, the faith we profess is doomed to wither and die in emptiness; unless we embrace the Gospel and its demanding spirit of selflessness, compassion and forgiveness, our profession of faith is meaningless. The Risen One calls us to community, to be branches on the same vine, to realize our life in Christ is also life in one another.

The harvest of the Word within us.

The Easter season speaks to us of the eternal presence of Christ in our midst, present to us in the Word we have heard and has taken root in our hearts. Our faithfulness to the call to discipleship demands that we work to enable that Word within us to produce a "yield" of compassion, forgiveness, justice and reconciliation. In the "fruit" we bear as "branches" of Christ we glorify God the "vinegrower."

For reflection:

- How can individuals and churches be "barren" branches? How can they be "fruitful" branches?
- How does our "connectedness" to Christ affect the work we do as a Church? How does it make the Church different from other humanitarian organizations?
- In what ways do the life cycles of plants mirror our own experience as a community of faith?

Sixth Sunday of Easter

Readings:
John 15: 9-17
Acts 10: 25-26, 34-35, 44-48
1 John 4: 7-10

Chapters 13 through 17 of John's Gospel, Jesus' Last Supper discourse, might be described as Jesus' last will and testament to his fledgling church.

Continuing last Sunday's theme of the vine and branches, Jesus speaks of the love of God that is to be the bonding agent of the new Israel (**Gospel**). The model of love for the faithful disciple – "to love one another as I have loved you" – is extreme, limitless and unconditional. The love manifested in the Gospel and the Resurrection of Christ creates an entirely new relationship between God and humanity. Again Christ, the obedient Servant – Redeemer, is the great "connector" between God and us.

In Christ, we are not "slaves" of a distant, divine Creator but "friends" of a loving God who hears the prayers and cries made to him in Jesus' name. As "friends of God," we are called to reflect that love to the rest of the world.

Cornelius, a Roman centurion, was a religious man – the kind of Gentile whom the Jews called a "God fearer." One day, Cornelius has a dream in which an angel instructs him to send for Simon Peter. Peter's meeting with Cornelius (**first reading**) is a revelation to the apostle: he begins to understand that God calls all men and women to himself. This is a significant development in the growth of the new Church, which was still wrestling with its deeply ingrained Jewish identity and practices.

The author of the Johannine epistles (**second reading**) writes eloquently of the love of God manifested in the gift of his Son.

Themes:

To love one another as Christ loved us.

Loving one another as Christ loved us begins by putting aside our own hopes and wants and seeking instead the hopes and wants of others; caring for and about others with selflessness and understanding, regardless of the sacrifice; always ready to make the first move to forgive and to heal. That kind of love can be so overwhelmingly demanding that we may shy away from the prospect. But most of us have known some time when we have been able to love like that or when someone has loved us like that. It is an incredible joy. We experience a profound sense of purpose and wholeness in giving and receiving that kind of love – the depth and love Christ has had for us.

To be 'friends' of God.

Christ transforms creation's relationship with its Creator. God is not the distant, aloof, removed architect of the universe; God is not the cruel taskmaster; God is not the unfeeling judge who seeks the destruction of the wicked. God is creative, reconciling, energizing love. And Jesus is the perfect expression of that love. All that God has done in the first creation of Genesis and the re-creation of Easter has been done out of limitless, unfathomable love. Such love invites us not to fear God but to accept his offering of "friendship"; not to self-loathing for our unworthiness but to grateful joy at what God has done for us.

For reflection:

- What does it mean to be a "friend" of God, as opposed to simply believing in the existence of God?
- How does the "love of Christ" differ from the popular notion of "love"?
- How have your ideals and beliefs about love changed as you have gotten older?
- Who have you known in your life who have been able to love others as Christ has loved?

Ascension of the Lord

Readings:

Mark 16: 15-20
Acts 1: 1-11
Ephesians 1: 17-23

Today's readings include two accounts of Jesus' return to the Father.

The **first reading** is the beginning of the Acts of the Apostles, Luke's "Gospel of the Holy Spirit." Jesus' Ascension begins volume two of Luke's masterwork. The words and images here recall the First Covenant accounts of the ascension of Elijah (2 Kings 2) and the forty years of the Exodus: Luke considers the time that the Risen Lord spent with his disciples a sacred time, a "desert experience" to prepare the apostles for their new ministry of preaching the Gospel of the resurrection. (Acts alone places the Ascension forty days after Easter; the synoptic Gospels – including, strangely, Luke's – specifically place the ascension on the day of Easter; John writes of the "ascension" not as an event but as a new existence with the Father.)

Responding to their question about the restoration of Israel, Jesus discourages his disciples from guessing what cannot be known. Greater things await them as his "witnesses." In the missionary work before them, Christ will be with them in the presence of the Spirit to come.

Scholars call today's **Gospel** the "longer ending" of Mark's text. In style and substance, these six verses are very unlike Mark; the best guess is that these verses were added sometime in the first century to "complete" Mark's account to include the tradition of the Ascension of Jesus. Before returning to the Father, Jesus commissions his new church to continue Christ's presence on earth through their proclamation of the "good news."

Paul's letter to the Ephesians celebrates the union of all men and women in and with Christ, as members of his mystical body. In the opening chapter of his letter to the Ephesians (**second reading**), the apostle prays that the Christian community at Ephesus may be united by the great "hope" they share in the Risen Christ, whom the Father has made sovereign over all creatures and head of the Church.

Themes:

The Ascension: an ending and a beginning.

Jesus' Ascension is both an ending and a beginning. The physical appearances of Jesus are at an end; his revelation of the "good news" is complete; the promise of the Messiah is fulfilled. Now begins the work of the disciples to teach what they have learned and to share what they have witnessed. It is not a very promising start. Like any beginning or transition in life, it is a moment of great uncertainty, confusion and apprehension. Christ places his Church in the care of a rag-tag collection of fishermen, tax collector and peasants. And yet, what began with those eleven has grown and flourished through the centuries to the very walls of our own parish family. The Church Jesus leaves to them is rooted not in buildings or wealth or formulas of prayer or systems of theology but in faith nurtured in the human heart, a faith centered in joy and understanding that is empowering and liberating, a faith that gives us the strength and freedom to be authentic and effective witnesses of the Risen One, who is present among us always.

The commission to 'teach,' to 'witness,' to 'heal.'

Christ entrusts to his disciples of every time and place the sacred responsibility of teaching others everything he has taught and revealed about the Father: God's limitless love, his unconditional forgiveness and acceptance of every person as his own beloved child and our identity as God's sons and daughters and brothers and sisters to one another. Christ also calls us to be witnesses of God's presence in our lives. He has also asks us to bring into the lives of others his healing forgiveness and reconciliation with God and one another. The words Jesus addresses to his disciples on the mountain of the Ascension are addressed to all of us two millennia later. We are called to teach, to witness and to heal in our own small corners of the world, to hand on to others the story that has been handed on to us about Jesus and his Gospel of love and compassion.

For reflection:

- What emotions and feelings do you think the eleven experienced as they walked down the mountain and returned to Jerusalem? Can you relate to such feelings?
- Who are the "apostles" to the small, hidden places on earth?
- What are the different ways we "teach" the good news? Two thousand years after it happened, how can we be effective "witnesses" of the resurrection? How do we bring "healing" as Christ did into the lives of others?

Seventh Sunday of Easter

Readings:

John 17: 11-19
Acts 1: 15-17, 20-26
1 John 4: 11-16

In the John account of the Last Supper, after his final teachings to his disciples before his passion, Jesus addresses his Father in heaven. Today's **Gospel** is from Chapter 17 of John's Gospel, the "high priestly prayer" of Jesus in which he prays for his disciples, that they may be united in love, persevere despite the world's "hatred" of them for the Word that they will proclaim and "consecrated" in the "truth."

After Jesus' Ascension, the Eleven return to Jerusalem. Peter calls upon the "brothers" to restore their number to the sacred number of twelve (**first reading**). Nominating two to serve as "witnesses" with them, they prayerfully place the final selection in the hands of God. Drawing lots was a common Biblical process of election between equal or like things (see, for example, the distribution of the land of Canaan among the tribes of Israel in Numbers 26: 55 and Zechariah's designation to offer incense in the temple sanctuary in Luke 1: 9). The use of lots was considered an act of faith in God's judgment instead of subjecting important decisions to the vagaries of human manipulation or prejudice. What is important is not *how* Matthias is chosen by *why:* Matthias to called to witness the Resurrection of Jesus.

The final selection for this Easter season from the first letter of John (**second reading**) celebrates the Spirit of God's love that binds us to God and to one another.

Themes:

The high price of the 'truth.'

Discovering and proclaiming the "truth" often comes at a price. A world that is more than willing to bend, shape, rework, edit, manipulate and rationalize life's challenges, difficulties and inconveniences to fit its own concept of what life and truth should be often does not appreciate the prophet/disciple's unvarnished, austere proclamation of the truth. The Gospel challenges us to recognize the prejudices, biases and ambitions that exist within each one of us and to realize how they affect the decisions we make based on "truth." We are called to uphold, regardless of the cost, the holiness of truth – truth that is rooted in the reality of God's love and in the sacredness of every person as created in the image and life of God.

The profound simplicity of the 'truth.'

"The truth is so simple," Dag Hammarksjold observed, "that it is regarded as pretentious banality." The truth of our faith is too low-tech for our high-tech world; the values of God are too slight to calibrate on our scales and too small to account for in our ledgers; we can even become so absorbed in the process and details of expressing the truth that we overlook the essence of truth. But the empty tomb of Easter speaks to the simple yet profound truth of God's great love for us. Christ calls us, his Church, to speak the joy of that truth to a world hungry to hear it.

For reflection:

- How can we make Jesus' prayer our own prayer for our parish and faith community?
- Who have you known in your life who has paid dearly for proclaiming the truth?
- Why are institutions, businesses, society, etc., suspicious and wary of the 'truth' as proclaimed in the Gospel?

Pentecost

Readings:
John 20: 19-23
Acts 2: 1-11
1 Corinthians 12: 3-7, 12-13

Pentecost was the Jewish festival of the harvest (also called the Feast of Weeks), celebrated 50 days after Passover, when the first fruits of the corn harvest were offered to the Lord. A feast of pilgrimage (hence the presence in Jerusalem of so many "devout Jews of every nation"), Pentecost also commemorated Moses' receiving of the Law on Mount Sinai. For the new Israel, Pentecost becomes the celebration of the Spirit of God's compassion, peace and forgiveness – the Spirit that transcends the Law and becomes the point of departure for the young Church's universal mission (the planting of a new harvest?).

Today's **Gospel**, the first appearance of the Risen Jesus before his ten disciples (remember Thomas is not present), on Easter night is John's version of the Pentecost event. In "breathing" the Holy Spirit upon them, Jesus imitates God's act of creation in Genesis. In the Resurrection, the Spirit re-creates the band of disciples into the new Israel; the "peace" of understanding, enthusiasm and joy and shatters all barriers among them to make of them a community of hope and forgiveness. By Christ's sending them forth, the disciples become *apostles* – "those sent."

In his Acts of the Apostles (**first reading**), Luke invokes the First Testament images of wind and fire in his account of the new Church's Pentecost: God frequently revealed his presence in fire (the pillar of fire in the Sinai) and in wind (the wind that sweeps over the earth to make the waters of the Great Flood subside). The Hebrew word for spirit, *ruah*, and the Greek word *pneuma* also refer to the movement of air, not only as wind, but also of life-giving breath (as in God's creation of man in Genesis 2 and the revivification of the dry bones in Ezekiel 37). Through this life-giving "breath," the Lord begins the era of the new Israel on Pentecost.

Appealing for unity in the badly-splintered Corinthian community, Paul reminds the Corinthians of the presence of the Holy Spirit in their midst, which brings together the different charisms each possesses for the good of the whole community and the glory of God (**second reading**).

Themes:

The Spirit: the *ruah* of God.

The feast of Pentecost celebrates the unseen, immeasurable presence of God in our lives and in our church – the *ruah* that animates us to do the work of the Gospel of the Risen One, the *ruah* that makes God's will

our will, the *ruah* of God living in us and transforming us so that we might bring his life and love to our broken world. God "breathes" his Spirit into our souls that we may live in his life and love; he ignites the "fire" of his Spirit within our hearts and minds that we may seek God in all things in order to realize the coming of his reign.

The Spirit: the powerful and enabling love of God.

Today we celebrate the Spirit – the great love that binds the Father to the Son and now binds us to God and to one another. It is a love that transcends words but embraces the heart and soul of each one of us; it gives voice to the things we believe but are too afraid to speak; it gives us the courage and grace to work for the dreams we are sometimes too cynical or fearful to hope for. The Spirit of God enables us to re-create our world in the love of God who loved us enough to become one of us, to die for us and to rise for us. The theologian and scientist Teilhard de Chardin noted that "love is the only force that can make things one without destroying them. . . . Some day, after mastering the winds, the waves, the tides and gravity, we shall harness for God the energies of love, and then, for the second time in the history of the world, man will have discovered fire."

The Spirit: the 'birth' of the Church.

Pentecost is a moment of profound realization and transformation for the community of disciples. The faith they had received, the wonders they had witnessed and the Word they had heard came together in a new understanding, clarity, unity and courage to begin the work Jesus had entrusted to them. In Jesus' "breathing" upon them the new life of the Spirit, the community of the Resurrection – the Church – takes flight. That same Spirit continues to "blow" through today's Church to give life and direction to our mission and ministry to preach the Gospel to every nation, to proclaim the forgiveness and reconciliation in God's name, to baptize all humanity into the life of Jesus' Resurrection.

For reflection:

- The Spirit of God reveals itself in today's readings in the forms of fire, wind and breath. What other images can help us understand the Spirit of God working within us?
- How does the presence of the Holy Spirit make your parish "different" from other groups and organizations of people?
- Share stories of God's Spirit alive around you. How would those stories be different if God's Spirit was not present there?

Trinity Sunday

Readings:

Matthew 28: 16-20
Deuteronomy 4: 32-34, 39-40
Romans 8: 14-17

As Ordinary Time resumes, two "solemnities of the Lord" are celebrated on the next two Sundays. Today's celebration of the Trinity originated in France in the eighth century and was adopted by the universal Church in 1334. The solemnity focuses on the essence of our faith: the revelation of God as Creator, the climax of his creation in Jesus the Redeemer, the fullness of the love of God poured out on us in the Sustainer Spirit.

Before returning to God, the Risen Jesus commissions his fledgling Church to teach and baptize in the name of the Holy One who reveals himself as Father, Son and Spirit (**Gospel**). In the Trinity we find our identity as the people of God.

Israel encountered God, first, in God's act of creation, and then in his redemption of the Israelites and his raising up of the nation of Israel. Moses exhorts the Israelites to remain faithful to the commandments of this great God they have encountered (**first reading**).

The Spirit is that unique love that exists between God the Father and Son. Christ invites us to embrace that same Spirit, which enables us to cry out to God as "Father" and to one another as brothers and sisters, children of the same God (**second reading**).

Themes:

Trinity: the love of God revealed.

Many metaphors have been used to explain and depict the Trinity. St. John of Damascus, the great Eastern theologian of the eighth century, suggested that we think "of the Father as a root, of the Son as a branch, and of the Spirit as a fruit, for the substance of these three is one." Today we celebrate the essence of our faith manifested in our lives: the loving providence of the Creator who continually invites us back to him; the selfless servanthood of the Redeemer who "emptied" himself to become like us in order that we might become like him; the joyful love of the Spirit that is the unique unity of the Father and Son.

The commission to 'teach' others about God.

Christ has revealed to us the depth of the Creator's love and has called us to share with one another the unique Spirit of love that unites Father and Son. As disciples of the Risen Christ, we have been called now, in our time and place, to teach what we have seen and heard, to pass on to others "everything I have commanded you" through our imitation of the Teacher's compassion, forgiveness and servanthood.

Called to be 'children of God.'

The core of all of Jesus' teaching is the revelation of God as *Father* to humanity. God calls us, not as the all-powerful Creator demanding homage from the lowly slaves he created, but as a loving parent welcoming one's own children. God invites us to a relationship with him not based on fear and judgment but centered in love, mercy and trust. Today's celebration of the Trinity confronts us with our response to God's invitation and our worthiness to be called God's "children."

For reflection:

- The shamrock, the triangle and the fruit tree have been all been used to depict the mystery of the Trinity. Are there any contemporary images that help you understand and appreciate the Triune God?
- How has God – Father, Son and Spirit – made his presence known to you? How would you explain this presence to a non-believer?
- In what ways do we "teach" others about God without the use of a catechism or theological tome?

The Body and Blood of the Lord

Readings:
Mark 14: 12-16, 22-26
Exodus 24: 3-8
Hebrews 9: 11-15

Today's celebration of the Body and Blood of the Lord originated in the Diocese of Liege in 1246 as the feast of Corpus Christi. In the reforms of Vatican II, the feast was joined with the feast of the Precious Blood (July 1) to become the Solemnity of the Body and Blood of the Lord. Today, we celebrate the Christ's gift of the Eucharist, the source and summit of our life together as the Church.

Today's **Gospel** is Mark's account of the Last Supper. At the Passover meal marking the First Covenant, Jesus, the Lamb of the New Covenant, institutes the New Passover of the Eucharist.

The ancients believed the source of life was contained in blood – blood, therefore, belonged to God alone (that is why even today a devout Jew will never eat any meat which is not completely drained of blood). In marking Israel's covenant with the Lord who brought them out of slavery and into freedom, Moses splashes half of the offerings' blood on the altar, the symbol of God, and sprinkles the other half on the people, joining the covenanted people to their God (**first reading**).

This understanding of the sacredness of blood is central to the theme of the letter to the Hebrews (**second reading**). Jesus is both priest and victim on the cross, whose own blood seals a new covenant and creates a new Israel.

Themes:

Eucharist: becoming the body of Christ.

"If you have received worthily," St. Augustine preached, "you are what you have received." The gift of the Eucharist comes with an important "string" is attached: it must be shared. In *sharing* the body of Christ, we *become* the body of Christ. If we partake of the one bread and cup, then we must be willing to become Eucharist for others – to make the love of Christ real for all.

Eucharist: the table of the Lord.

Christ calls us to his table, offering his peace, affirmation, support and love. We come to the Eucharist to celebrate our identity as his disciples and to seek the sustaining grace to live the hard demands of such discipleship; we come to the Eucharist seeking the peace and hope of the Risen One in the compassion and support we offer and receive from one another. At Christ's table, we are always welcome. In celebrating the Eucharist, we make our parish family's table the Lord's own table, a place of reconciliation and compassion.

Eucharist: entering the life and love of God.

Our coming to the table of the Eucharist is more than just reliving the memory of Christ's great sacrifice for our redemption – in sharing his "body" in the bread of the Eucharist we re-enter the inexplicable love of God who gives us eternal life in his Son, the Risen Christ; in drinking his "blood" in the wine of the Eucharist we take his life into the very core of our beings. We are called not to accept faith like some article of clothing we can take on or off at will but to let the life of God become part of our very beings, like the flesh on our bones and the blood flowing through our veins. To receive the bread and wine of the Eucharist is to receive the very life of God in Christ.

Eucharist: the new manna, food for the journey.

The God who breathed his life into each one of us also gives us a world filled with all that is necessary to maintain that life. The people of Israel remember especially how God sustained them during their sojourn through the Sinai with the gift of manna. In raising Christ from the dead, God has effectively re-created humankind: We live in the hope that we will share in the life of the Risen One. The Eucharist is the new manna which sustains us on our journey to the eternal life of the Resurrection.

For reflection:

- How can we be "Eucharist" to one another? How can we bring the Eucharist from our church to our world?
- What do our own family rituals at dinner time and around the family table teach us about the Eucharist?
- The word *Eucharist* means "thanksgiving." How can our sharing of the Body and Blood of the Lord be an act of thanksgiving, even when we gather under the most painful of circumstances?

The Sundays of the Year – Cycle B

Readings:

John 1: 35-42
1 Samuel 3: 3-10, 19
1 Corinthians 6: 13-15, 17-20

A new beginning and a sacred invitation mark today's **Gospel**. In John's proclamation of Jesus as the "Lamb of God," the age of the prophets ends and the era of the Messiah begins.

Jesus' invitation to Andrew to "Come and see" so moves Andrew that he invites his brother Simon Peter to "come and see" for himself. This is the first of three episodes in John's Gospel in which Andrew introduces someone to Christ: Andrew brings to Jesus the lad with the five barley loaves and a couple of dried fish (John 6: 8-9) and it is Andrew who asks Jesus to meet the Greeks who have requested, "Sir, we would like to meet Jesus. (John 12: 22).

The **first reading** also marks a call/invitation: the beginning of the work of one of Israel's great prophets, Samuel. The Lord directly calls the young Samuel to the vocation of prophet – the Holy One ignores the priest Eli, who "sleeps" like the faithless Israel to whom Samuel has been called to "awaken" in its covenant with God.

The second reading for Sundays 2 through 14 in Cycle B of the lectionary is taken from Paul's two letters to the Christian community of Corinth. Corinth was considered the gateway between the east and west of antiquity, a city of unusual ethnic and cultural diversity. The city had a well-earned reputation for great licentiousness and moral depravity – in large part a reaction to the classic Greek exaltation of the ascetic and scorn of the physical. In his two years there, Paul came to know the city and its reputation well.

Paul's first letter to the Corinthians is a series of admonitions on morality. In the **second reading**, he exhorts his Christian family at Corinth to remember the dignity of the human body as "a temple of the Holy Spirit."

Themes:

God's persistent invitation to us to 'Come and see.'

The mystery of God's love is its limitlessness; throughout human history, despite our rejection of God and obtuseness to his ways, God never ceases to call us back to him, to "come and see." Our God is a God of newness and beginnings, who constantly extends his grace to "start over" and begin again.

"Come and see" is both an invitation and a challenge. Jesus dares us, really, to *come* – to leave behind the things that deter us from God – and *see* – to focus not on what the world exalts as important but on the values of God.

To be disciples in our own time and place.

Henry Ward Beecher observed that "if a person cannot be a Christian in the place where they are, they cannot be a Christian anywhere." The challenge of the call to discipleship/prophecy (as Samuel hears in today's first reading and the disciples hear in the Gospel) is to discern and respond to that call within our own lives, in the context of our own experiences. Regardless of social standing or lifestyle, regardless of where we live, God calls every one of us to life in him. Whether we are creatures of Wall Street or denizens of Sing-Sing, we can make God's reign a reality in our own time and place through our faithfulness to the Gospel values of servanthood, reconciliation, justice and compassion.

Reflecting the 'light' of Christ.

To be an authentic disciple of Jesus means to look at the world with a vision of hope, to recognize the dignity of every human being as a son and daughter of God, to joyfully take on the challenge of bringing justice and peace into our homes, schools and workplaces. We can illuminate the Jerusalems and Nazareths of our own time and place with the goodness, healing, reconciliation and justice of Christ, the Light and Word of God living among us.

For reflection:

- When have you heard the voice of God inviting you to make a new beginning?
- Think about ways in which God provides opportunities for new beginnings that overcome the trauma of change and the pain of broken relationships.
- How can we, like Andrew, invite others to "come and see" the Lord? How does the "voice of God" call today's man and woman of faith to be prophets?

Third Sunday of the Year

Readings:
Mark 1: 14-20
Jonah 3: 1-5, 10
1 Corinthians 7: 29-31

The day of the Messiah has dawned; but newness demands change: a "turning away" (the original meaning of the word *repentance*) from business as usual and a complete trust in the life and love of God. Simon and Andrew's "abandoning" their nets and James' and John's "abandoning" their father in today's **Gospel** illustrate the total trust and commitment Jesus demands of those who would be his disciples.

Jonah (of the three-days-in-the-belly-of-the-whale fame) is a reluctant prophet. Nineveh was the capital of the despised Assyrians, Israel's one-time occupier and bitter enemy. When first sent by God to Nineveh, Jonah refused, believing that Nineveh deserved to be destroyed. But Jonah is made to realize that every nation and every people who *turn* to the Lord (as even wicked Nineveh does in today's **first reading**) are precious to the loving Creator and Father of all. To be God's holy people, Israel must abandon its sense of intolerance and vindictiveness.

For Paul and many of the early Christians, Jesus Christ's return was imminent – they fully expected Christ to appear in their lifetimes. Despite the near alarmist urgency of today's brief **second reading**, Paul makes an important point about the impermanence of our relationships and material goods in this world, a world that "as we know it is passing away."

Themes:

Our value and worth before God.

Jesus began his ministry by calling simple fishermen to be his most trusted friends. Although the Twelve were hardly scholars or men wise in the ways of the world, Jesus saw beyond their gruff simplicity to call forth from them faith, sincerity and integrity. As Mark's Gospel unfolds each Sunday this year, the first disciples will misunderstand Jesus (if not miss his point entirely), desert him and even deny and betray him. But Jesus entrusts to them, for all of humankind, the proclamation of his Gospel. We, too, possess such value and trust in the eyes of our God.

Jesus' call to 'abandonment' for the sake of the Gospel.

Their families must have thought that the first disciples were crazy for just dropping everything to follow the itinerant rabbi from Nazareth. (We can only imagine Zebedee's reaction when his sons James and John suddenly walk out on the family's fishing business!) To be a disciple of Jesus means abandoning the world's values to embrace the demanding values of the Gospel. Thomas Merton wrote: "How many fear to follow their consciences because they would rather conform to the opinion of others than to the truth they know in their souls? How can I be sincere if I am constantly changing my mind to conform with the shadow of what I think others expect of me? Others have no right to demand that I be anything other than what I ought to be in the sight of God."

The possibilities of change through the Gospel.

The Gospel is about possibilities. Christ came to show us how it is possible to love life to the fullest, if we dare to make forgiveness, reconciliation and selfless charity the center of our lives. It is difficult to move beyond our biases and prejudices and to rise above the pressures and deadlines imposed on us to hear that small voice of the Spirit within us. That is the challenge of discipleship: to seek forgiveness when the rest of the world demands vengeance; to see Christ in the faces of those who have been "written off" by society; to work for justice when there is nothing in it for us; to embrace the role of servant when the conventional wisdom dictates "me first." Jesus' Gospel is challenging, demanding and unreasonable – but, oh, the possibilities. . . !

For reflection:

- What "fishing nets" are we called to abandon today by Jesus in order to follow him?
- Who are Jesus' most unlikely "disciples" among us today?
- How have the Gospel teachings on forgiveness, love and healing been the beginning of new possibilities in your life?

Readings:

Mark 1: 21-28
Deuteronomy 18: 15-20
1 Corinthians 7: 32-35

For the poor Jews of Jesus' time, the scribes were the voices of authority, the final arbiters of the Law in which God had revealed himself. Their interpretation of the Law was considered absolute.

"Demons" are encountered many times in Mark's Gospel. Anything that the people of Jesus' time could not understand or explain, such as disease, mental illness or bizarre or criminal behavior, were considered the physical manifestations of the evil one – "demons" or "unclean spirits."

Both demons and scribes are silenced in today's **Gospel**. Jesus' casting out the unclean spirit from the man possessed silences the voices of the demons that plague humanity. In his compassionate outreach to the poor and sick, Jesus "silences" the scribes by redefining the community's understanding of authority: whereas the "authority" of the scribes' words is based solely on their perceived status and learnedness, the authority of Jesus is born of compassion, peace and justice. The casting out of the demons and his curing of the sick who come to him are but manifestations of the power and grace of his words.

Note that the people of the Bible viewed miracles differently than we do. While we, in our high technology, scientific approach to the world, dismiss miracles as some kind of disruption or "overriding" of the laws of nature, the contemporaries of Jesus saw miracles as signs of God's immediate activity in his creation. While we ask, *How could this happen?*, they asked, *Who is responsible?* Their answer was always the same: the God of all creation. Those who witnessed Jesus' healings, then, saw them as God directly touching their lives.

The **first reading**, from the Book of Deuteronomy, recounts God's promise to raise up a successor to Moses – a promise ultimately fulfilled in Jesus. But Moses cautions his people to listen with careful and wise discernment to those who claim to speak with the authority of the prophetic office.

Keeping in mind the social mores regarding marriage and family life in Paul's time as well as the expectation of the first Christians that Jesus would return in their time, today's excerpt from 1 Corinthians (**second reading**) makes the point that relationships and bonds are secondary to our constant search for God.

Themes:

The 'authority' of selflessness and justice.

Mark writes in today's Gospel that the people marveled at Jesus' "teaching in a spirit of authority." Authority comes not from power to enforce but from the ability to inspire. In the reign of God, the poor saint who gives his or her last penny to feed society's forgotten speaks with an authority far more compelling than the powerful industrialist who writes a check for an amount he or she will hardly miss. "The words of Jesus would remain an impossible, abstract ideal were it not for two things: the actions of Jesus and his gift of the Spirit. In his actions, Jesus showed the way of living in God's reign; he manifested the forgiveness which he called for when he accepted all who came to him, forgave their sins, healed them, released them from the demons who possessed them. In doing these things, he made the tender mercy of God present in a world which knew violence, oppression and injustice." [*The Challenge of Peace: God's Promise and Our Response*, #48, National Conference of Catholic Bishops, 1983.]

The voice of 'unclean spirits' within us.

The "unclean spirit" that Jesus casts out of the poor man in today's Gospel serves as a symbol of the voice of evil that sometimes speaks within us – the voice of revenge, self-centeredness, self-righteousness, greed, anger. We can be "possessed" by "demons" who discourage us and plague us with fear when we consider the unpopular position that we know is right and just; or the "demon" of rationalization that falsely justifies actions – or inactions – we know in the core of our being are contrary to the spirit of the Gospel. The compassionate Jesus of the today's Gospel speaks to those "unclean spirits" as well, offering us the grace and courage to cast them out of our minds and hearts forever.

For reflection:

- Recall individuals you have known who possessed an authority based, not on fame, power or wealth, but on their heroic and committed sense of justice, compassion and charity.
- What "demons" do we hear "speaking" out today that can most effectively be silenced, not by anger and retribution, but by the example of Jesus' compassionate outreach?
- Who are the "prophets" among us today – those men and women of faith into whose mouth God "places his word"?

Fifth Sunday of the Year

Readings:
Mark 1: 29-39
Job 7: 1-4, 6-7
1 Corinthians 9: 16-19, 22-23

Throughout his **Gospel**, Mark portrays Jesus as somewhat uncomfortable with his growing renown as a miracle worker. He clearly values time away from the crowd to be alone to pray – even though that time is cut short by the needs of those around him.

Jesus works miracles not out of any need of his own for the adulation of the masses but out of an extraordinary sense of compassion, a deep love for his brothers and sisters, especially those in crisis or pain. The miracles he works are not to solicit acclaim for himself but to awaken faith and trust in the word of God, to restore in humankind God's vision of a world united as brothers and sisters under his providence ("that is what I have come to do"). Jesus' compassion for those who come to him breaks down stereotypes and defenses that divide, segregate and marginalize people; his ministry is not to restore bodies to health but to restore spirits to wholeness.

Jesus comes to restore hope and meaning to those overcome by despair and who are estranged from God and alienated from community – like the pitiful Job (today's **first reading**).

Today's **second reading**, again this Sunday from 1 Corinthians, includes Paul's insightful description of the selflessness demanded of the faithful disciple of Jesus: to become "weak" for the sake of the weak, to make oneself a "slave" to others for the sake of the Gospel.

Themes:

The Gospel as 'good news' to a broken world.

The word *Gospel* means "good news." It is a story that ends not in death but in life; it is centered not in humiliating sorrow but in liberating joy; it does not demand blind adherence to laws and rituals but invites us to welcome the Spirit of compassion and love into our lives. The Gospel of Jesus is about the re-creation and transformation that are possible through reconciliation, justice, mercy and community.

Called to be both a people of prayer and of compassion.

Jesus' life was one of both contemplative prayer and total giving to those in need. It can be a very difficult balance to strike. St. Augustine put it this way: "No one should be so contemplative as to be unmindful of the needs of his neighbor, nor should a person be so active as not to seek the contemplation of God." We are called not just to hear the Gospel but to live it in both the quiet of our hearts and the clamor of our everyday lives.

Christ the Healer: making us whole again.

Jesus does not perform miracles to dazzle the crowds and glory in their acclaim but to awaken his hearers' faith and trust in the word of God, to restore all of humanity to God's vision of one world in which all men and women love and respect one another as brothers and sisters under the Father's loving providence. Living, active faith opens our eyes to see the world as God sees it, opens our minds to understand the world by God's touchstone of love and forgiveness and opens our hearts to seek the will of God in all things.

Prayer: God speaking to *us*.

Prayer, Teresa of Avila taught her sisters, is the "conformity of our will to the will of God." In other words, prayer is not so much *our* talking to God but *God* talking to us. A true spirit of prayer is not a collection of rituals and words we recite for God's benefit; prayer is the opening up of our hearts and minds to try and understand God's will for us, to realize God's presence in our lives and the sacredness of every moment God has given us. Thomas More's prayer is the heart of all prayer: "Give us, O Lord, the grace to work for the things we pray for."

For reflection:

- Have you known people who, despite the pain and trauma they have endured, can still be called people of joy?
- How should the Gospel realistically be expected to affect our lives in such arenas as politics, business, education, sports, family life?
- How can a parish community successfully balance the need we feel for personal prayer and relationship with God and the call of the Gospel to work for justice and peace? How does one demand serve the other?
- Have you ever experienced God's talking to you in prayer?

Sixth Sunday of the Year

Readings:

Mark 1:40-45
Leviticus 13:1-2, 44-46
1 Corinthians 10:31 – 11:1

The cleansing of the leper is a climactic moment in Mark's **Gospel**. By just touching the leper Jesus challenges one of the strictest proscriptions in Jewish society (today's **first reading** provides the context for understanding the social and religious revulsion of lepers).

The leper is a one of the heroic characters of Mark's Gospel (along with such figures as the poor widow who gives her only penny to the temple and the blind Bartimaeus). The leper places his entire trust in Jesus. For him, there is no doubt: this Jesus is the Messiah of hope, the Lord of life. His request for healing is more than a cry for help – it is a profession of faith: "You *can* cure me."

Consider what Jesus does after curing the leper. He sends the newly-cleansed leper to show himself to the priest "and offer for your cure what Moses prescribed." This leper's healing is a message for the Jewish establishment, represented by the priest: that the Messiah has come and is present among you.

A great debate raged in the Church of Corinth. After animal sacrifices were offered before Greek idols, the burned meat often found its way into the marketplace. The more scrupulous among the Christians saw eating such pagan offerings as an affront to the one true God; others thought that it was meaningless. In today's **second reading**, Paul counsels that the matter is too trivial to risk dividing the people of God. In all things, the apostle writes, respect one another's viewpoints and perspectives while focusing together on the faith they share in God as revealed in Christ Jesus.

Themes:

The 'lepers' among us.

Jesus' curing of the leper shocked those who witnessed it. Jesus did not drive the leper away as would be the norm (the leper, according to the Mosaic Law, had no right to even address Jesus); instead, Jesus stretched out his hand and touched him. Jesus did not see an unclean leper but a human soul in desperate need. Mother Teresa of Calcutta has said that "the biggest disease of today is not leprosy or tuberculosis, but rather the feeling of being unwanted, uncared for and deserted by everybody. The greatest evil is the lack of love and charity, the terrible indifference toward one's neighbor who lives at the roadside assaulted by exploitation, corruption, poverty and disease."

The 'uncleanliness' of our own faithlessness.

Our prejudices, selfishness, dishonesty and obtuseness to the needs of the poor is a "leprosy" that eats away at our humanity and makes us less than the people God calls us to be. In his Gospel of charity and compassion, Jesus makes our spirits whole again, restores our hearts to hope and mends our broken attitudes and value systems.

For reflection:

- Who are the "lepers" in our own society, who "frighten" us and cause us to run, lest we somehow become "contaminated"?
- Have you ever felt like a "leper" – cut off, segregated, estranged, isolated?
- Have you ever found yourself in a situation in which God's presence was somehow unmistakably clear to you and you were reluctant or even afraid to acknowledge it?

Seventh Sunday of the Year

Readings:
Mark 2: 1-12
Isaiah 43: 18-19, 21-22, 24-25
2 Corinthians 1: 18-22

Today's **Gospel** reading is the first of six episodes in Mark's Gospel in which Jesus and his teachings become the center of controversy. The popular Wonder-worker becomes a threat to the leadership and stature of the Pharisees and scribes.

The paralyzed man becomes – both literally and figuratively – the center of the first controversy. Jesus again makes the point that he comes not to heal bodies but to heal spirits, to restore the relationship between God and humankind, to mend the brokenness and estrangement afflicting the people of God.

The physical miracles worked by Jesus validate his Gospel of compassion and love and prefigures the great Easter miracle of God's reign to come. The paralyzed man, therefore, is first offered forgiveness by Jesus. The legalistic, tradition-bound scribes and Pharisees protest that only God can forgive sins. Exactly, Jesus says. And to emphasize the sacred mandate he has received, Jesus orders the paralytic to "pick up your mat and walk."

The four friends who help the paralyzed man meet Jesus are among the unknown saints of the Gospel. Consider how much they loved and cared for their friend: fighting through the crowds, maneuvering him up the outside stairs of the house and, removing the thatch and mud covering the roof, lowering him on his mat into the midst of Jesus and the gathering. Their task demanded considerable planning, skill and coordination. Jesus himself praises their effort on their friend's behalf as a profound profession of faith in him as the Messiah.

Today's **first reading** from the prophet Isaiah calls Israel to embrace a new vision of a second Exodus experience. The Lord who led their ancestors from Egyptian captivity now comes to free their hearts and spirits from the captivity of their selfishness and faithlessness.

Twice Paul had planned to return to visit the community at Corinth, but twice postponed his plans. Instead, he sent the stern letter the New Testament canon titled 1 and 2 Corinthians. The community became very critical of Paul, considering the difficult apostle somewhat unstable; the relationship between Paul and the Corinthian church was becoming increasingly strained. In today's **second reading**, Paul responds to charges of fickleness by restating that the permanence and divine origin of the Word of God he originally preached to them binds them together.

Themes:

The enslavement of sin / the liberation of forgiveness.

We can become so caught up with our own ambitions and interests that our lives become paralyzed: we become closed to the joy of giving, we find ourselves removed from the love of family and friends, we are "entombed" by the pressures of deadlines and bottom lines. Christ the Reconciler reveals to us a compassionate God who enables us to break the strangulation of sin and to wake from the paralysis that deadens us to the love and joy of God's presence.

Forgiveness: 'I am doing something new.'

Isaiah's prophecy of "something new" is fulfilled in Christ who proclaims God's ready forgiveness. Through our own readiness to forgive one another we can remove the pall of estrangement that many families suffer, we can tear down walls of separation, we can heal brokenness and hurt, we can replace dysfunction with dialogue and healing.

Proclaiming our faith in acts of giving.

Like the efforts of the paralyzed man's friends, our acts of selfless kindness and committed justice are acts of faith in the Risen Christ. In carrying the mats of the helpless, in reaching out to the outcast and the forgotten, in seeking to tear down the walls (rooftops?) that separate families and friends, we bring them to the Jesus of compassion.

For reflection:

- Have you ever experienced the sense of "newness" as a result of forgiveness given or received?
- Why is forgiveness such a difficult thing to ask for – and accept?
- Have you had friends in your life like the four friends of the paralyzed man in today's Gospel?

Eighth Sunday of the Year

Readings:

Mark 2: 18-22
Hosea 2: 16-17, 21-22
2 Corinthians 3: 1-6

Throughout Scripture, the covenant to which God calls Israel is compared to the love of husband and wife, that special intimacy experienced by the "espoused" (today's **first reading** from Hosea is an example). The images of the bridegroom and wedding feast that Jesus uses in today's **Gospel** resonated with his hearers. But the implication that he is the bridegroom widened the growing gulf between Jesus and the Jewish establishment.

In Jesus' time, faithful Jews fasted twice a week; the Law stipulated, however, that wedding receptions were exceptions to the fast. Jesus justifies his words regarding fasting under this exception: with the Messiah's presence among them, God's promised "wedding banquet" has begun.

Jesus indicts the Pharisees' practice of fasting because it was often an act devoid of praise; it was merely an ostentatious display of religiosity, a "badge of honor" identifying them as the "separated" (the meaning of the word *Pharisee*). Jesus' point, missed by the Pharisees, is that any ritual or pietistic practice must come from the heart; it must be grounded in that special love God calls us to embrace, a love that transcends that of stipulated law and contracts and consumes one totally (like that special love between spouses who are completely and wholly in love).

The images of the patched cloak and the new wine in old wineskins speak to that point: in Christ, God calls us to a new attitude and a renewed spirit of intimate relationship with him that cannot be confined or diminished by the legalistic religiosity adhered to by the Pharisees.

The superficiality of empty ritual is also the focus of Paul's admonition in today's **second reading**. The new covenant of Christ "is not of a written law but of spirit."

In our faithfulness to the call to discipleship, we become "a letter of Christ...a letter written not with ink but by the Spirit of the living God."

Themes:

Faith: the meaning of our rituals.

Christ comes to re-infuse the dusty legalisms and empty rituals of the Mosaic Law with the Spirit of love and thanksgiving for all that God has done for us. The values in which we center our lives are the substance of our faith. Prayer formulas, rituals, liturgies and traditions that are truly holy express and celebrate the substance of that faith we profess.

Christ the 'Bridegroom.'

The depth and constancy of God's love for us is probably best understood in the person of Jesus, the "Bridegroom." He is the always relevant and active reason for living lives of joyful thanksgiving and hopeful celebration of the limitless and unconditional love of God for us his people, his "beloved."

For reflection:

- How does your parish community manifest the presence of Christ, the Bridegroom? What elements of a "wedding feast" are always part of the mission and ministry of your community?
- What have happily married couples taught you about love and human relationship?
- Consider the reasons why some people find the practice of "organized religion" an empty, meaningless experience. How can we renew religious rituals and practices from which we have become detached because of constant repetition and superficial instruction?

Readings: *Mark 2: 23 - 3: 6*
Deuteronomy 5: 12-15
2 Corinthians 4: 6-11

The observance of the Sabbath is the third controversy between Jesus and the Pharisees recorded in Mark's **Gospel**. The Pharisees are appalled that the disciples are pulling grain off wheat stalks as they walk along on the Sabbath. According to the Pharisees' strict observance, this seemingly innocent and mindless activity is considered work and, therefore, profanes the Sabbath. Jesus' response radically redefines the nature of the Sabbath: that even the Sabbath's proscriptions against work and play are second to acts of charity and mercy.

And to make the point, Jesus again performs a miracle. Immediately after his confrontation with the Pharisees, Jesus goes to the synagogue where he meets a man with a "shriveled hand." Strict rabbinical interpretation stipulated that "healings" could take place on the Sabbath if it is a matter of life and death. The poor man here, while in great suffering, is hardly at death's door. But Jesus again emphasizes the sacredness of mercy and compassion by healing the man's hand on the Sabbath.

In this encounter, it is Jesus who responds angrily. The Pharisees cannot grasp the profound meaning of what Jesus has done. They are too centered in themselves to rejoice in the love and mercy of God manifested before them. The tensions between Jesus and the Pharisees set the stage for his destruction.

Today's **first reading** from the Book of Deuteronomy outlines the covenant's laws regarding the Sabbath's observance. While work of any kind is forbidden, the Lord also sets aside the day as one for "remembering" and giving joyful thanks for all that God has done. The holiness of the Sabbath day is extended not only to Jews but to slaves, non-Jews and "aliens." The keeping of the Sabbath demands not only a change in lifestyle but a change in attitude and perspective.

The Corinthians, like most people, are attracted to easy answers and painless solutions to life's problems. Paul is no such preacher, but there are smooth-talking, polished preachers offering their Corinthian converts just such a message. Paul, however, steadfastly maintains (in today's **second reading**) that the Risen Jesus is the ultimate source of our hope and joy.

Themes:

Keeping the Sabbath 'holy.'

The Sabbath is a concept that demands more than a notation on our calendars or an hour or so set aside for "church." The holiness of the Sabbath is kept in attitude and spirit: a realization that we have much for which to be grateful to God and that both sacred time and space should be set aside to allow ourselves to contemplate our gratitude.

The sacredness of compassion and mercy.

Jesus exalts compassion and mercy as fitting praise to the Father whose compassion and mercy to us knows no end. In healing the man with the shriveled hand on the Sabbath, Christ calls us to "remember" the goodness of God in our dedication to justice, reconciliation and peace.

For reflection:

- Consider ways we "remember" the love of God in acts of mercy and compassion.
- Have you experienced any unique but meaningful ways to make Sunday "different" from the other six days of the week?
- With the secularization of our society in recent years, what have we lost in our understanding of and respect for sacred time and space?

Tenth Sunday of the Year

Readings:
Mark 3: 20-35
Genesis 3: 9-15
2 Corinthians 4: 13 – 5: 1

A central theme of Mark's Gospel is how Jesus' hearers (especially the Twelve) fail to comprehend the deeper meaning of his words and actions. The wild charges made by the scribes and the sad apologies offered by his family in today's **Gospel** indicate just how misunderstood Jesus was by those closest to him.

First, the Jesus who calls his disciples to be a united "house" and community, is dismissed by his own "house" as "out of his mind." They apologize for him and his exorbitant claims about himself and his challenging of their most cherished institutions and traditions and try to bring him home.

Second, the Jesus who has cast out demons and cured the sick is charged with being possessed himself. The scribes cannot grasp the single-minded dedication of Jesus to the will of God without the "filters" of their interpretations and traditions; hence, he must be an agent of Satan, the prince of demons. (Remember that whatever the people of Gospel Palestine could not understand or explain was considered the work of "demons.")

Jesus comes to be a vehicle of unity among God's people and calls on his hearers to be united in faith and spirit in him in seeking God's will in all things.

The **first reading** is the Genesis story of God's censure of the serpent for destroying the harmony between the Creator and creation by "tricking" Adam and Eve into selfishness and disobedience. Jesus the Redeemer will restore that harmony through his complete selflessness and obedience to God's will.

In the **second reading**, Paul exhorts the Corinthian community to remain focused on the things of God and not of the earth, to remember that faith ultimately triumphs over misery and death.

Themes:

The Church: family/community of faith.

Christ comes to restore humanity to a sense of community, to a deeper understanding of our sacred dignity as being made in God's image, to a renewed commitment to relationships and belonging with one another. Christ destroys the barriers created by race, tribe, wealth and social status. He speaks of a new, united human family: the family of God. We are called, as the Church of the new covenant, to seek in every person the humanity we all share that comes from God, the Father of all and the Giver of everything that is good.

The 'lunatic' Christ.

Jesus the "lunatic" comes with the crazy idea that love will triumph over hatred, that light will shatter the darkness, that life will conquer death. This "crazy" Jesus seeks to heal us of what is, in fact, our "lunacy" – the lunacy of allowing pettiness, pride, anger, prejudice and self-centeredness to alienate us from one another, the lunacy of exalting "me first" at the expense of others' basic necessities, the lunacy of constantly grabbing as much as we can as fast as we can while most people on this planet have nothing. Jesus calls us to become "alive" in his lunatic sense of reconciliation, community and joy.

'Possessed' by the Spirit of truth.

Jesus is surrounded by people who are afraid and threatened by his message. The scribes' assertion that he is "possessed" by demons masks their fear that Jesus may well be right about their self-serving beliefs and empty values. Jesus' call to discipleship demands the courage to overcome our fears of the truth, and to risk the censure and judgments of others in order to proclaim what is right, just and good.

For reflection:

- What commonly-held practices and beliefs, social conventions and public policies fly in the face of truth?
- If Jesus were to speak at your parish, would he be considered "out of his mind" for what he would say? Why?
- Have you ever found it in your best interests to overlook the truth?

11th Sunday of the Year

Readings:

Mark 4: 26-34
Ezekiel 17: 22-24
2 Corinthians 5: 6-10

The mustard seed – that tiny speck containing the chemical energy to create the great tree – is a natural parable for the greatness that God raises up from small beginnings.

Farming is a matter of hard work and patient faith: All the farmer can do is plant the seed and nurture it with water and care; God's unseen hand in creation transforms the tiny seed into a great harvest. This **Gospel** parable, then, is a call to patience, hope and readiness.

Jesus may have intended this parable especially for the Zealots, a Jewish sect that sought the political restoration of Israel. Many Zealots were terrorists, employing murder and insurrection to destabilize the Roman government. The Zealots dreamed of a Messiah who would restore the Jewish nation. Jesus, however, calls them to see their identity as God's people not in terms of political might but of interior faith and spiritual openness to the love of God.

Ezekiel's allegory of the cedar crest in today's **first reading** speaks to this "replanting" of the kingdom of Israel in the wake of the Babylonian occupation and destruction – from this small "branch" of Gospel humility and servanthood will grow a nation of "majestic" faith.

The apostle Paul's focus in the **second reading** is the present reality of the reign of God: We anticipate Christ's return by bringing his light and life into our own time and place.

Themes:

Harvesting the small seeds we plant.

The faith Jesus calls us to live, more often than not, is a matter of planting mustard seeds of kindness, compassion and understanding. We may never realize what the harvest will yield; but it is from such seeds that the reign of God will flourish.

Harvesting the good found even in the smallest and lowliest.

We are also called to harvest the seeds planted by others, to recognize the potential good in all persons. Dom Helder Camara, the compassionate fighter for the rights of Brazil's poor, has urged Christians: "Become an expert in the art of discovering good in every person. No one is entirely bad. Become an expert in the art of finding the truthful core in views of every kind."

Called to be teachers and students of the Gospel.

Like sowing seed, teaching and learning are matters of patient faith, persevering hope and committed hard work. In baptism, we become both students and teachers: We become students of the Rabbi Jesus, who reveals to us the wonders of the God of love; we also become teachers, called to help others realize the presence of God in their lives through our compassion, support and understanding. We are invited to seek the wisdom of God with the patience and dedication of the sower; we are called to make the reign of God a reality in our own lives with the hope and faith of the mustard seed.

For reflection:

- Do you recall any "small seeds" you or someone you know unconsciously "planted" that resulted in an unexpected harvest?
- Recall stories of individuals society would consider "small" who, in their simple, undistinguished ways revealed the presence of God to those around them.
- What does gardening and the planting and nurturing of seeds teach us about the reign of God?

12th Sunday of the Year

Readings:

Mark 4: 35-41
Job 38: 1, 8-11
2 Corinthians 5: 14-17

The Sea of Galilee is actually a land-locked lake 600 feet below sea level. Ravines in the hills and mountains surrounding the Galilee act as natural wind tunnels. In the evening, as the warm air of the day rises above the water, cool air rushes in through the ravines. The effect is amazing: the tranquil lake is whipped into a fury of white-capped, six-foot waves. In the midst of this terrorizing experience, Jesus calms both the sea and his disciples' fear.

The evangelist is recounting this story to a terrified and persecuted community. Today's **Gospel** is intended to reassure them of the Risen Christ's constant presence in the storms they struggle through for the sake of their faith in his reign to come.

Addressing the long-suffering Job "out of the storm," the Lord proclaims the mastery of his word over wind, rain and sea **(first reading)**.

Paul repeats this exhortation to have faith in Christ and not lose heart to pressures from social standards and conventions; "to live no longer for themselves." **(second reading)**.

Themes:

The 'awakened' Jesus 'stilling the storms' of our own lives.

Throughout the journeys of our lives, we encounter many "storms" – the adversities and tragedies that can either help us grow in understanding life or consume us in despair and hopelessness. Within each of us is the voice of Jesus: *Be still.* Within each of us is the grace of the "awakened" Jesus: the wisdom, patience and grace to discern the presence of God amid the winds of anxiety, tension and fear. The grace of the Risen Christ enables us to discern the presence of God amid the roar of anger and mistrust and to recognize the light of God in the darkness of selflessness and prejudice.

Making time for 'stillness.'

The words Jesus addresses to the storm could just as well be addressed to us: *Peace! Be still!* In our stormy whirlwind lives, we need to make time for peace, for stillness, for quiet, in order to hear the voice of the Spirit, to reset our compass as we navigate our small boats through life's stormy Galilee sea, to check our bearings to make sure that we are living our lives in the hope and joy in which God created us to live them.

For reflection:

* How do we create "storms" in our lives and the lives of others through our anxietiy, fear and self-absorption?
* What can we learn from the storms that blow through our lives?
* In what ways can we bring "stillness" into our lives?

Readings:
Mark 5: 21-43
Wisdom 1: 13-15; 2: 23-24
2 Corinthians 8: 7, 9, 13-15

Both Jairus and the unnamed woman in today's **Gospel** are held up by Mark as models of faith. The message of the two healings is clear: "Do not be afraid; have faith."

The poor, sick woman is so convinced that Jesus not only can help her but *will* help her that she fights her way through the pushing and shoving crowds just to touch the cloak of Jesus. She realizes not only the power of Jesus to heal her but the depth of his love and compassion to *want* to heal her. Her faith is rewarded.

Jairus was a man of considerable authority and stature in the Jewish community. Yet for the sake of his daughter, he puts aside his pride and his instinctive distrust of an "anti-establishment" rabbi like Jesus and becomes a "beggar" on her behalf before Jesus. Despite the ridicule of the mourners and the depth of his despair, Jarius places his hope in Jesus – and hope is not disappointed.

Today's **first reading**, from the Book of Wisdom, reminds its hearers that our God is a God not of death but of life, a God who does not rejoice in our destruction but created us in his image that he might share his life with us.

Paul, in today's **second reading**, urges his Corinthian brothers and sisters to learn charity and generosity from the example of Christ Jesus, the compassionate and humble healer.

Themes:

The 'uselessness' of fear.

In today's Gospel, Jesus tells the distraught Jairus: "Fear is useless. What is needed is trust." Fear, worry, clinging to our own needs are paralyzing – nurturing and healing are impeded, attempts to transform bad into good is futile, resurrection is impossible. Like the wailing mourners at the little girl's bedside, we sometimes resign ourselves to defeat as the regular order of things, to death as the only and final conclusion. In the healings of Jairus' daughter and the hemorrhaging woman, Jesus shows us the life and hope we can bring into our world through the providence of God and the goodness possessed by everyone as a son and daughter of God.

A parent's love.

Every parent can identify with Jairus. Jairus is described by Mark as "an official of the synagogue," a man of considerable authority in the Jewish community – an "establishment" figure, to be sure. But, grasping at one last thread of hope to save his daughter, Jairus' love for her enables him to risk his standing in the community to approach this controversial rabbi. Through such complete and unconditional love – like the love of God our Father for us, his children – we can lift up the fallen, bring healing to the suffering and restore life to the dead.

The God of life and resurrection.

The sick woman in today's Gospel is so convinced that Jesus not only can help but *will* help her that she fights her way through the crowds just to touch his cloak. She realizes not only the power Jesus possesses but the depth of his compassion and love for her. Jesus reveals a God who seeks not judgment or vengeance but restoration and healing. Our God is present, not in death and destruction, but in life and resurrection (first reading). Faith compels us not to mourn God's absence where he is not but to seek God and realize God's presence in compassion, forgiveness and justice.

For reflection:

- Have you ever known a parent whose love for his/her child/children truly imitated the love of God?
- Have you ever feared someone or something only to find that fear totally unfounded?
- Have you ever been in a difficult or painful situation where you felt God was totally absent? In what ways did you eventually sense God's presence again?

14th Sunday of the Year

Readings:
Mark 6: 1-6
Ezekiel 2: 2-5
2 Corinthians 12: 7-10

Mark begins a new theme narrative with today's **Gospel:** the blindness of people to the power and authority of Jesus. The people of his own hometown reject his message. They consider Jesus too much "one of *them*" to be taken seriously. They are too obsessed with superficialities – occupation, ancestry, origins – to realize God present in their midst and to be affected by that presence.

Today's **first reading** is the story of another prophet who experienced trying times. Ezekiel is called by God to speak his word to his own people – Judean Jews who have been repatriated from their beloved Jerusalem to Babylon. They are a defeated, distrusting people who feel abandoned by God and suspicious of anyone who claims to speak of the God they, in fact, had themselves "rebelled" against.

In the final reading in this weekly series from his letters to the Corinthians **(second reading)**, Paul reflects on the difficult challenge of discipleship.

Themes:

The authority of inspiration.

There is the kind of authority that one possesses by virtue of an office or position, the authority that bestows the "power" to make decisions and set policy. But there is another kind of authority that one possesses by virtue of study, performance or commitment to a high set of moral and ethical standards, an authority that gives that individual the "power" to inspire. Such is the authority of Jesus. His authority is not derived from his ability to manipulate the fears, suspicions, apathy or ignorance of those around him but from the spirit of mercy, justice and compassion he is able to call forth from them. Those who speak not to our emotions and wants but to our consciences, who speak not in catchy slogans and buzz words but in the conviction of their actions possess the authority of Jesus that is deserving of our respect and attentiveness.

The presence of God in our very midst.

Like the people of Jesus' hometown, we often fail to realize the presence of God in our very midst: in the simplest acts of kindness, in the humblest efforts of compassion for others, in the singular attempts to secure the justice and peace of God in hidden and forgotten places. Christ has come to show his people the limitless possibilities of living and celebrating to the fullest the love and life of God in our own homes and hearts.

The faith of the disciple/prophet.

In embracing discipleship, we take on the role of *prophet* – "one who proclaims." For some, such proclamation leads to martyrdom; for others, prophecy takes the form of social activism for the sake of the poor and the victimized; but for many of us, the call to be a disciple/prophet means to proclaim in the simple struggle of our everyday lives the depth and totality of God's love for us. To be a prophet, to be a proclaimer of the Word we have heard, can result in our being ostracized, ridiculed, rejected and isolated. But genuine faith never falters in the conviction that the justice of God will triumph over injustice, that his mercy will triumph over hatred, that his light will triumph over the darkness of sin and death.

For reflection:

- Who have been the people who have inspired you in your life, who could rightly be said to "have authority over you"?
- Have you ever been amazed to encounter the Spirit of God in people you overlooked or in whom did not expect to find it?
- Have you ever known someone who possessed the courageous, unwavering faith of the "prophet"?

15th Sunday of the Year

Readings:

Mark 6: 7-13
Amos 7: 12-15
Ephesians 1: 3-14

In today's **Gospel**, the Twelve – each of whom has been called personally by Jesus – earn the title of "apostle" – "one who is sent." These unlikely candidates for such a task are carefully prepared and taught by Jesus for this moment. They undertake their first preaching and healing tour depending only on God for their inspiration and on the charity of others for their needs. Remember that hospitality was considered a sacred responsibility in the east – it was not up to the stranger to seek hospitality but up to the prospective host to offer it.

The **first reading** recounts the call of another unlikely candidate for the ministry of proclamation, Amos, the "shepherd and dresser of sycamores," sent by God to prophesy to Israel.

Today's **second reading** begins a series of passages from Paul's letter to the Ephesians, one of Paul's "captivity" letters. The apostle spent two years with the Christian community at Ephesus, but many scholars believe that this letter, given its strong theological bent and comparatively impersonal tone, is addressed to the larger Church. Today's reading is the opening of the letter, an epistle that is part prayer and part theological discourse on the nature of the Church under Christ its head.

Themes:

The disciple's journey.

Like the journey of the Twelve through the region of Galilee and Amos' journey to Judah, our lives are journeys to the reign of God. Each step of the journey can be a moment of grace, of encounter with the holy, of rebirth and transformation, of healing. God calls us, in every step of our journey, to proclaim his love and peace and to witness his justice and mercy.

To welcome one another as Christ.

In his rule for monasteries, St. Benedict exhorts his monks to welcome visitors, strangers, the lost and the poor with joyful generosity: "Let all be received as Christ" has been a watchword of Benedictine communities for centuries. In extending hospitality in that same spirit, we joyfully profess our faith in Christ, the Servant of God, and our hope to realize his vision of one human family under the loving providence of the Father.

Our call to be disciples and prophets.

God calls all of us to the vocation of prophet ("one who proclaims") and disciple ("one who follows, one who comprehends"). Like God's call to the Amoses, Ezekiels, Peters and Andrews of Scripture, ours is a call to proclaim our faith in our places of work, study and play, to follow Christ in his vision of justice, peace and reconciliation.

For reflection:

- Have you known prophets and disciples whose lives proclaimed the love of God, who followed Christ in their simple generosity and compassion for others?
- In what ways have you approached and experienced life as a journey, as a progression toward fulfillment?
- Consider the sacred character of hospitality, of welcoming those who come into our homes and churches. How is hospitality an act of faith and a ministry?

Readings:

Mark 6: 30-34
Jeremiah 23: 1-6
Ephesians 2: 13-18

The apostles return from their first mission of preaching and healing and report to Jesus. He gathers them in an "out-of-the-way" place, but the people find them and keep coming. Even their attempt to escape by boat to the other side of the lake is foiled once word gets out.

This incident recorded by Mark in today's **Gospel** (which precedes his account of the feeding of the multitude) offers two important insights into our Church's ministry:

- that the mission of the Church does not spring from mass marketing techniques or publicity strategies but from the Gospel of compassion we seek to live and share, from the authority of our commitment to forgiveness and reconciliation; and

- that leadership, inspired by the wisdom of God, means not dictating and ruling over others but inspiring, providing for and selflessly caring for those whom we are called to lead.

In his compassion for the crowd, Jesus becomes, for Mark, the wise and just "shepherd" of Jeremiah (today's **first reading**) and the psalmist (today's responsorial Psalm 23).

In today's **second reading**, Paul praises Christ "our peace" who reconciles us to God and to one another.

Themes:

The 'shepherds' we heed.

We seek affirmation, reassurance, support, comfort and approval in so many people and things that fail us: the latest, the newest, the hottest, the best-selling. We are sheep looking for a fail-safe, pop psychology, formula shepherd. But the lifestyles for which we sell our souls leave us all the poorer; the "shepherds" we herd after fail us. In Christ Jesus, God gives us a shepherd to guide us along the way of peace and justice, to seek not the empty riches of consumerism but the priceless treasure of compassion and reconciliation, to journey through our lives not in fear and self-interest but in the joy and certainty of what is right and just. Christ the Shepherd is also, for all "shepherds," a model of wisdom and selflessness.

Our need for 'out-of-the-way' places.

From the clamor of the marketplace and the demands of our calendars and "Things to do" lists, we need "out-of-the-way" places be alone with God, to listen to the quiet of our hearts to hear the voice of God. Jesus invites us to find and make quiet time in our days to re-center our lives in the life and love of God.

For reflection:

- Who are the "shepherds" in our culture today who lead us away from God? Who should be the voices we listen to on our search for God?

- As a church and parish family, what should we be ready to offer one another as a community of disciples?

- What attitudes, gifts and skills make for a good leader?

Readings:

John 6: 1-15
2 Kings 4: 42-44
Ephesians 4: 1-6

Today the Lectionary interrupts the semi-continuous reading of Mark's Gospel for a five-week reading of Chapter 6 from the **Gospel** of John – the "bread of life" discourse of Jesus.

The miracle of the feeding of the multitude with a few loaves and fish is the only miracle recorded in all four Gospels. This story was especially cherished by the first Christians for whom the Eucharist was becoming the center of their life together. Jesus' actions are indeed "Eucharistic": bread (and fish) are given, Jesus gives thanks (the word used in the Greek text of Mark's Gospel is *eucharisteo*), breaks the bread and share the gifts with those who have gathered.

John's account of this miracle introduces the bread of life discourse of Jesus by presenting the liturgical dynamics of the Eucharist. In coming together for the Eucharist, we become "one body (in the) one Spirit" (**second reading**). It may be that the real miracle in this Gospel is not the multiplication of the loaves and fishes but the transformation of a crowd of self-seeking men and women into a community of sharers.

Today's Gospel parallels a similar miracle performed by the prophet Elisha in today's **first reading** from the second book of Kings.

Themes:

Becoming a 'Eucharistic' community.

The real miracle in today's Gospel is Christ's transforming a multitude of people into a community of sharing – all begun by one boy's act of giving. Remember that, before feeding the crowds, Jesus first challenged his disciples *to do something*. The multiplication of the loaves and fish did not start with nothing; Jesus was able to feed the crowds because a little boy was willing to share all he had; from his gift, small though it was, Jesus worked a miracle – and a new community of faith was formed as a result. We are called by Christ to become the Eucharist we received at this altar: giving thanks for what we have received by sharing those gifts – our talents, our riches, ourselves – to work our own miracles of creating communities of joyful faith. As we pray in the second Eucharistic Prayer: "May all of us who share in the body and blood of Christ be brought together in unity by the Holy Spirit."

One bread, one cup, one body.

The *one* bread and *one* cup of the Eucharist transforms us into *one* family. The miracle of the loaves and fish did not start with nothing – Jesus was able to feeds the five thousand because someone was willing to give all that they had; from that gift, small though it was, Jesus worked a miracle. Eucharist is possible only when self defers to community, only when serving others is exalted over being served, only when differences dissolve and the common and shared are honored above all else. In the Eucharist of Christ, the humble Servant-Redeemer, we seek to become what we receive: *one* bread, *one* cup, *one* body, *one* family.

For reflection:

- We are part of many communities in our lives: families, parishes, classes, teams, businesses, etc. What have been some of your most joyful and enriching experiences of community and what made them so?
- What "small gifts" have you received that have made a big difference in your life?
- How can we take this Eucharist beyond the walls of your church? How can the Eucharist be given to others in places other than this church, in ways other than this liturgy?

18th Sunday of the Year

Readings:
John 6: 24-35
Exodus 16: 2-4, 12-15
Ephesians 4: 17, 20-24

Several scholars have suggested that Chapter 6 of John's **Gospel** may have originally been the text of a homily by an early Christian teacher on the Eucharistic action of Jesus.

Jesus is apparently speaking to two groups of people: those who witnessed the miracle of the loaves (last Sunday's Gospel) and those who did not see the miracle but have heard about it and want to see a similar sign. To the former, Jesus tells them that there is something much deeper in this event than "perishable food" being multiplied; the real "food" is the word of God proclaimed, its power and authority manifested in the miracle of the loaves.

To the latter group who seek a sign as the Israelites sought a sign from Moses, Jesus reminds them that it was not Moses himself but God working through Moses that provided their "grumbling" Exodus ancestors with bread in the desert (recalled in today's **first reading**). God has given his people a new bread for the new covenant – the Risen Christ.

There is a clear baptismal dimension to today's **second reading** from Ephesians. In Christ, former ways and old attitudes must be put aside and "put on" the justice and holiness of God.

Themes:

'Non-perishable' food for the journey.

There will come a time when the "perishables" of wealth, power and prestige leave us dissatisfied and hungering for the "food that remains for life eternal" – the spirit of compassion, justice, reconciliation and mercy of Christ. Jesus the Word is the "Bread of life" that is more life-giving and life-sustaining than the "perishable foods" of this fleeting world.

The gift of persevering, constant faith.

We often treat God and prayer as a kind of safety device to be kept separately from the rest of our lives in a glass case with the sign, *In case of emergency, break glass.* We "get religion" when times are bad, when the suffering becomes unbearable, when death is imminent; we experience "conversion" only when we want something and God delivers. The crowds in today's first reading from Exodus and Gospel reading from John are typical: the starving Israelites turn on Moses and demand that God do something; the crowds want to make Jesus the Miracle-worker their king but will later have nothing to do with Jesus the Crucified. Discipleship demands constancy and courage to stand with the suffering Jesus so that, one day, we might stand with the Risen Jesus.

Eucharist: vehicle for conversion.

All three of today's readings speak of conversion, of radically rethinking our approach to life and the values we hold dear. In today's Gospel, Jesus speaks not only of receiving the Eucharist but how the Eucharist should transform our lives completely: from ambition to servanthood, from asking to giving, from cynicism to thanksgiving. The Eucharist demands more than the opening of our hands to take and our mouths to consume; the Eucharist demands that we open our hearts and spirits, as well, so that we may become what we receive.

For reflection:

- Have you ever prayed for something that really wasn't worthy of God's attention?
- How is the Eucharist a vehicle for transformation, reconciliation and perceiving the presence of God in our midst?
- Have you ever worked hard to seek something that turned out to be among life's "perishables"?

19th Sunday of the Year

Readings:

John 6: 41-51
1 Kings 19: 4-8
Ephesians 4: 30 – 5: 2

From time immemorial bread has been the "staff of life," the basic and most important food in everyone's diet. To the "murmuring" Jews ("murmuring" as their ancestors did in the desert – last Sunday's first reading), Jesus tries to help them see the deeper meaning of his claim to be "bread come down from heaven." Christ is the "bread of heaven" that transcends this experience of life to the life of God. Christ the Bread is the love, justice and compassion of God incarnate; God, our "Father," is revealed in him.

The operative verbs in today's **Gospel** are "believe" and "trust": God provides for and sustains our faith in his gift of Jesus the Bread in the same way that First Testament wisdom nourished all who paid heed.

God as Provider and Sustainer is also revealed in today's **first reading** from the first Book of Kings. The discouraged Elijah, forced to flee for his life by Queen Jezebel, is restored to hope and strength with the bread and water provided by the angel. God does not demand Elijah – or us – to undertake the journey to his holy mountain without providing us with "food" for the journey.

In today's brief **second reading** from his letter to the Ephesians, Paul urges his readers to become "Eucharist," imitating God in their kindness, forgiveness and love for one another.

Themes:

To be 'consumed' by the Eucharist we receive.

To receive the Eucharist worthily, we must allow ourselves not only to consume but to be *consumed* by the life and love of God. In the sacrament of the "Bread of life" we become the one body of Christ; as that one body,

"imitating God" and "following the way of love" (second reading), we can bring the new life of God into our world.

God: the Creator as Father of his creation.

To his Jewish hearers, Jesus' most astounding and revolutionary teaching is that God, Creator and Lord of all life, is our Father. That revelation should affect every dimension of our lives: God is not a mysterious cosmic tyrant to be feared but the Loving Giver of life whom we can approach in confidence; the boundaries and differences that separate people are eclipsed by the ever new realization that every man and woman share the same humanity, becoming one human family under the "Fatherhood" of God.

To be 'bread' for one another.

As Jesus became bread for us, he calls us to be bread for one another. Jesus, the "bread of life," did not hesitate to give everything – including his life – that he might bring to the world the new life of his Resurrection. We who claim the name of Christian are challenged to give in that same spirit – to look beyond our own needs and security to the good of others, to give not from our treasure but from our poverty, to nourish one another in the love, compassion and selflessness of the Gospel.

For reflection:

- When and how have you found the Gospel to be a source of encouragement and sustenance on your life's journey?
- What does the Eucharist teach us about justice, selflessness and reconciliation?
- How can we be "Eucharist" to one another?
- How different would our relationships with God and with one another be if God did not seek to be our "Father"?

20th Sunday of the Year

Readings:

John 6: 51-58
Proverbs 9: 1-6
Ephesians 5: 15-20

Two dimensions of Jewish worship provide the context of today's **Gospel**, the fourth part of the "bread of life" discourse in John 6.

When an animal was sacrificed on the temple altar, part of the meat was given to worshipers for a feast with family and friends at which God was honored as the unseen "guest." It was even believed by some that God entered into the flesh of the sacrificed animal, so that when people rose from the feast they believed they were literally "God-filled."

In Jewish thought, blood was considered the vessel in which life was contained: as blood drained away from a body so did its life. The Jews, therefore, considered blood sacred, as belonging to God alone. In animal sacrifices, blood was ritually drained from the carcass and solemnly "sprinkled" upon the altar and the worshipers by the priest as a sign of being touched directly by the "life" of God.

With this understanding, then, John summarizes his theology of the Eucharist, the new Passover banquet (remember that John's Last Supper account will center around the "mandatum," the theology of servanthood, rather than the blessing and breaking of the bread and the sharing of the cup). To feast on Jesus the Bread is to feast on the very life of God – to consume the Eucharist is to be consumed by God.

Today's **first reading** imagines God's wisdom as a hostess giving a grand banquet to which she invites all who would forsake the conventions and ways of the world to seek the peace and justice of the Holy One.

Far less eloquent but more direct is Paul's exhortation in today's **second reading** to avoid "getting drunk on wine that leads to debauchery." Be careful of your conduct in these "evil days," the apostle warns, and seek "the will of the Lord" in all things.

Theme:

Eucharist: sustained in the life of God.

In inviting us to feed on his flesh and drink of his blood, Jesus invites us to embrace the life of his Father: the life that finds joy in humble servanthood to others, the life that is centered in unconditional, total, sacrificial love; the life that seeks fulfillment not in the standards of this world but in the treasures of the next. In the "bread" he gives us to eat, Christ shows us how to distinguish the values of God from the values of the marketplace; he instructs us on how to respond to the pressures and challenges of the world with justice and selflessness; he teaches us how to overcome our fears and doubts to become the people that God has created us to be – a people of compassion, reconciliation and hope.

For reflection:

- How would you define "wisdom"? What are the defining characteristic of the *wise* man or woman? Who is/was the wisest person you've ever known?
- How do you think your participation in the Eucharist has transformed your beliefs and attitudes?
- Today's readings' contain several images of preparing and sharing meals. What do these images mean to us who struggle to become a Eucharistic community?

21st Sunday of the Year

Cycle B

Readings:
John 6: 60-69
Joshua 24: 1-2, 15-17, 18
Ephesians 5: 21-32

Today's concluding section of the "bread of life" discourse from John's **Gospel** is a turning point for the disciples of Jesus. Will they join the ranks of the skeptics, who have dismissed Jesus and his talk of "eating his flesh" or commit themselves to Jesus – and the shadows of the cross that begin to fall? We can hear the pain in Jesus' question: "Do you want to leave me, too?" Peter's simple, plaintive answer is the confession of faith that disciples of every age who have come to realize the spirit of God acting in and re-creating their lives.

In today's **first reading**, from the conclusion of the Book of Joshua, the great military leader Joshua (Moses' successor) and the Israelites are at a turning point in their relationship with Yahweh. At Shechem, Joshua bids farewell to the people he has led to the land of Canaan by challenging them to either embrace the gods of the land in which they now dwell or reaffirm their covenant with the God who brought them out of Egyptian captivity to freedom in this new place. Like the disciples in the Gospel, Joshua and his people are called to embrace the spirit of the redeeming and loving God.

Today's **second reading** from Ephesians may sound sexist by our standards, but if read in the context of Paul's time, the apostle very beautifully equates the relationship of Christ to his Church to that of spouses' love for one another (a metaphor that is found frequently in both the writings of the prophets and the evangelists to explain the depth of God's love for his people). The obedience and fidelity that Paul speaks of is mutual and total: Husband and wife must give to each other totally, completely and willingly, just as Jesus the Crucified gave himself totally, completely and willingly for us.

Themes:

The 'words of eternal life': God's constant presence in all that is good.

Hopelessness can easily become a way of life; the sense that God has abandoned us or that God just doesn't exist in our lives can cripple us emotionally and spiritually. But the faithful disciple understands that God is the only constant source of anything and everything that is good. Despite our own doubts and misgivings about the Gospel, we know in the depths of our hearts that, in the end, the words of Jesus will triumph. We mourn God's absence in times of pain, change and despair, but we know we will rediscover God in acts of love, generosity, support and healing extended to us by others. Peter's simple, plaintive answer is that confession of faith: God is not present in the darkness of evil but in the light of goodness that seeks to shatter that darkness.

The challenging, discomforting Gospel.

The "good news" is not always easy news to hear and embrace. Many people cannot "endure this kind of talk" of Jesus not because they don't understand him but because they understand him all too well. While we are obsessed with maintaining our lifestyle, Christ speaks to us of *life* – its purpose, its meaning, its ultimate fulfillment. To be worthy of the name "Christian" demands the constant, focused faith articulated by Simon Peter: "You, Lord, have the words of eternal life."

For reflection:

- Consider the stories of those who have lived, in their courageous charity, the confession of Peter.
- When and how does the Spirit of God "speak life" to us in the midst of the seeming hopelessness and despair of the "flesh"?
- On what occasions, to what challenges, do we voice Peter's question/prayer: "Lord, to whom shall we go?"

126

Readings: *Mark 7: 1-8, 14-15, 21-23*
Deuteronomy 4: 1-2, 6-8
James 1: 17-18, 21-22, 27

Today's **Gospel** returns to Mark's story of the Christ event with a confrontation that Mark's first Christian readers knew all too well.

A contentious debate raged in the early Church as to whether or not Christians should also keep the practices of Judaism. Jesus challenges the scribes' insistence that faithfulness to ceremonial washings and other rituals constitutes complete faithfulness to the will of God. He scandalizes his hearers by proclaiming that "nothing that enters a man from outside can make him impure; that which comes out of him, and only that, constitutes impurity." It is the good that one does, motivated by the spirit of the heart, that is important in the eyes of God, not how scrupulously one keeps the laws and rituals mandated by tradition.

Through the centuries of Judaism, the scribes had constructed a rigid maze of definitions, admonitions, principles and laws to explain the Pentateuch (summarized in Moses' eloquent words to the nation of Israel in the **first reading**). As a result, the ethics of religion were often buried under a mountain of rules and taboos. Jesus' teachings re-focus the canons of Israel on the original covenant based on the wisdom and discernment of the human heart. Such a challenge widens the growing gulf between Jesus and the Jewish establishment.

The **second reading** for the next five Sundays is taken from the letter written under the name of James of Jerusalem, the "brother of the Lord" and leader of the Jerusalem community. The letter is a series of guidelines on the role of Christian faith and morals in everyday life. Many scholars believe the letter of James was originally an oral sermon committed to epistle form by a scribe. Today's passage exhorts us to be constantly open to the "gift" of God's word and act upon it by works of charity and selflessness.

Themes:

The good 'within' us.

It is not the prayer book or rosary or ten-dollar bill we drop into the offering that constitutes faith – it is the love and trust we have in our hearts that make those things expressions of that faith. Praising and serving God as men and women of faith begins within each individual heart listening and responding to the voice of God calling forth the good within each one of us.

Heart-felt reverence vs. empty tradition.

We can become more concerned about avoiding sin than about actually doing good; we can become so focused on the rituals and words of faith that we fail to grasp the spirit of that faith. In today's Gospel, Jesus challenges the Pharisees' insistence that faithfulness to ceremonial washings and other "human" traditions constitutes complete faithfulness to the will of God. It is the good that one does, the love and compassion that "come out" of a person that is exalted by God. Faith begins with encountering God in our hearts; our faith is expressed in the good that we do and the praise we offer in the depths of our hearts, not simply in words and rituals performed "outside" of ourselves.

For reflection:

- Recall experiences in your life when the spirit of the human heart triumphed over poorly-conceived and inadequate laws or stifling legalisms.
- Consider the many difficulties we encounter in trying to live the beliefs and values we say we hold dear.
- Why do people feel disaffected by faith that has become "institutionalized"? How can a parish/community respond to such disaffection?

Readings: *Mark 7: 31-37*
                     Isaiah 35: 4-7
                     James 2: 1-5

Ephphatha – "Be opened!"

Isaiah's vision of a Messiah who would come with hope and healing (**first reading**) is realized in this episode from Mark's **Gospel**: the deaf hear, the silent are given voice, the lame "leap like a stag." The exhortation *Ephphatha!* is not only addressed to the man born deaf but to his disciples both then and now who fail to hear and see and speak the presence of God in their very midst.

Jesus' curing of the deaf man with spittle (which, in Jesus' time, was considered curative) is an act of *re*-creation. God's reign is present in human history in the extraordinary ministry of Jesus. Throughout Mark's Gospel, Jesus insists that his healings be kept quiet in order that his full identity be revealed and understood only in the light of his cross and Resurrection.

In today's **second reading**, from the letter of James, the author warns the community not to show "favoritism" to those who impress us with their wealth or celebrity. The Gospel calls us to see all men and women as equals before God – with a preference given "to the poor in the eyes of the world" whom God has made "rich in faith."

Themes:

Ephphatha: the gift of listening.

Jesus restores the deaf man's hearing with the word *Ephphatha – Be opened!* We, too, can bring healing and life to those who need the support, the affirmation, the sense of loving and being loved that the simple act of listening can give. The pastor and theologian Dietrich Bonhoeffer observed that "the first service one owes to others [as Christians] consists in listening to them. Just as the love of God begins with listening to his Word, so the beginning of love is learning to listen to them. It is God's love for us that he not only gives his Word but also lends his ear. . . . Christians so often think they must always contribute something when they are in the company of others. . . . They forget that listening can be a greater service than speaking."

'Deaf' to the presence of God.

In times of grief, despair and failure, we can be "deaf" to the presence of God, isolating ourselves from God's presence in the love and compassion of others; or we can become so preoccupied with the noise and clamor of the marketplace that we are unable to hear the voices of those we love and who love us. For us who claim to be faithful disciples of Jesus, *Ephphatha* must become our prayer, as well: that we may be always "open" to the voice of God wherever and in whomever he speaks.

For reflection:

- How can listening be a valuable gift to another?
- In what ways are we "deaf" to the love of God?
- How can we create in our own community a place of welcome for the deaf, the blind, the lame and the poor among us?

Readings:

> *Mark 8: 27-35*
> *Isaiah 50: 4-9*
> *James 2: 14-18*

In today's **Gospel**, Peter is a model of vacillating faith, a model that typifies our own reaction to the call to discipleship.

Caesar Philippi was a bazaar of shrines and temples, with altars erected to every concept of the divinity from the gods of Greece to the godhead of Caesar. Amid this marketplace of gods, Jesus asks Peter and the Twelve, "Who do people say that I am? . . . Who do you say that I am?" This is a turning point in Mark's Gospel: until now, Mark's Jesus has been reluctant to have people believe in him only because of his miracles. Jesus talks, for the first time in Mark's Gospel, about dark things ahead: rejection, suffering, death and resurrection (a concept the disciples are unable to grasp).

In this incident (recorded by all three synoptics), Peter immediately confesses his faith in Jesus as the Messiah – the Messiah of victory and salvation. But when Jesus begins to speak of a Messiah who will suffer rejection and death, Peter objects. Peter's reaction is ours, as well: We prefer to follow the popular, happy Jesus, the healing and comforting Jesus – but we back away from the suffering, humble, unsettling Jesus of the cross.

The **first reading** is taken from the third "servant" song of the prophet Isaiah (a portion of this passage is also read on Palm Sunday). Isaiah portrays the suffering servant as one who is insulted, abused and rejected for the word God has called him to proclaim.

Today's reading from the letter of James (**second reading**) is the heart of this short epistle: the relationship of faith to good works. "Lifeless" faith results in no good works, inspires no loving response to the word we have heard, possesses no power to save. "Living" faith rejoices in God's word and celebrates that presence in acts of compassion and charity.

Themes:

'Who do you say that I am?'

The question Jesus asks Peter and his disciples is also asked of every would-be disciple of every place and time – it is a question that demands and deserves an unconditional and unequivocal answer. Every moment we live, every decision and choice we make, every good thing we do is our most revealing and meaningful response to the question, *Who do* you *say I am?* Our love for family and friends, our commitment to the highest moral and ethical standards, our willingness to take the first step toward reconciliation and forgiveness are our ultimate confession of faith in Jesus Christ as the Lord and Word of God incarnate.

The crosses we are called to take up.

Taking up our crosses often calls for us to "crucify" our own interests and self-centeredness for the sake of others. Following in the footsteps of Jesus means to be totally caring and unconditionally loving of others as was the Jesus of the Gospels. Taking up our crosses – whatever that cross may be – is difficult and often humiliating, but it can be liberating and life-giving, for both ourselves and those around us.

Following Jesus, the crucified and victorious Christ.

We cannot belong to the company of Jesus unless we embrace the Crucified One's spirit of selfless servanthood; we cannot stand with the Crucified Jesus unless we unconditionally and completely love and forgive others as he did; we cannot hope to share in the victory of the Risen Christ unless we "crucify" our fears, self-consciousness and prejudices that blind us from seeing him in the faces of every human being.

For reflection:

- How do our actions sometimes give different and conflicting answers to Jesus' question, *Who do you say that I am?*
- In what ways can we "crucify" our own interests for the sake of others?
- In whom have you recently seen the face of the Crucified Christ?
- When have you been confronted by the discomforting Jesus – as opposed to the comforting Jesus?

Readings:

Mark 9: 30-37
Wisdom 2: 12, 17-20
James 3: 16 – 4: 3

Different hopes and expectations of the long awaited "age of the Messiah" collide in today's **Gospel.**

A somber Jesus speaks cryptically of the death and resurrection awaiting him in Jerusalem, while those closest to him argue about their own greatness and status in the Messiah's reign (that must have been quite a conversation to elicit such a strong reaction from Jesus!). The disciples, long resigned to their people's humiliation and subjugation, dream of a kingdom of power and influence in which ambition is exalted; Jesus explains to them (yet again) that the Messiah's reign will be a kingdom of spirit and conversion in which humble service to others is exalted.

Jesus outlines here the great paradox of discipleship:

Do you wish to be first? Then become last.
Do you seek to attain greatness? Then become small.
Do you want to be masters? Then become the servants of those you wish to rule.

To emphasize the point, Jesus picks up a little child and places the child in the midst of these would-be rulers and influence-peddlers. A child has no influence in the affairs of society nor offers anything to adults in terms of career advancement or prestige enhancement; just the opposite is true: a child needs everything. To be "great" in the reign of God, Jesus says, one must become the "servant" of the "child" – the poor, the needy, the lost.

The Book of Wisdom, written less than 100 years before the birth of Jesus, is one of the last books, chronologically, of the First Testament (despite the claim to be "of Solomon"). Wisdom is addressed to the Jewish community of Alexandria, Egypt, a port city of sophisticated Greek culture. Influenced by the great value that culture placed on learning, the writer teaches that the ultimate goal of wisdom is life with God. The Book of Wisdom contains one of the First Testament's most extensive discussions of life after death.

Today's **first reading** from the Book of Wisdom foretells, with eerie accuracy, the evil machinations that led to Jesus' death. Wisdom portrays the wicked's attempt to suppress the truth spoken by the "just one" by destroying him and leaving his fate to the God he proclaims.

In today's **second reading**, the writer of James speaks to the theme of service by exhorting the Christian community to put one's own individual "cravings" last for the good of all, cultivating peace and "the harvest of justice."

Themes:

The 'servant' disciple.

To put another's hopes and dreams ahead of one's own, to seek to bring forth and affirm the gifts of others for no other reason than the common good, to seek reconciliation at all costs is to be the "servant" Christ speaks of in today's Gospel. Christ calls us to be "servant" disciples: to seek always "to rank first" among our families, friends and communities by taking on the spirit and role of servant to them. The cross demands that we put aside whatever reluctance and discomfort that inhibits us from embracing completely and unreservedly the Gospel spirit of humble, Christ-like servanthood.

The child: teacher of discipleship.

We both teach and are taught by our children. "To welcome a child for my sake" is a clear mandate to share with them the light of faith in the moral and ethical values we have learned. In their simple joy and wonder of the world they are constantly discovering, in their ready acceptance of our love, in their total dependence on us for their nurturing and growth, children are the ideal teachers of the Spirit of humble servanthood and constant thanksgiving that Jesus asks of those who would be his followers.

'Child-like' faith.

Christ calls us to the simple faith of a child: to love God and one another without condition or expectation, with honesty and faithfulness. "Child-like faith" is never dissuaded or discouraged, never becomes cynical or jaded, never ceases to be amazed and grateful for the many ways God reveals his presence in our lives. The power of such "simple faith" is its ability to overcome every rationalization, fear, complication and agenda in order to mirror the selflessness of Christ Jesus. Only in embracing the child's simple and straightforward kindness, compassion, generosity and forgiveness can we attain true greatness in the reign of God.

For reflection:

- Do you know of individuals whose humility has led them to accomplish great things for their people?
- What have children taught you about the Gospel values of servanthood, charity, compassion and justice?

Readings:
Mark 9: 38-43, 45, 47-48
Numbers 11: 25-29
James 5: 1-6

As we have seen throughout Mark's **Gospel**, the people of Jesus' time held great stock in the existence of demons: whatever mental illness or physical infirmity they could not understand was caused by some "demon." It was also the belief that a demon could be exorcised if one could invoke the name of a still more powerful spirit to order the evil and unclean spirit out of a person.

John tried to stop someone who seemed to be cashing in on Jesus' growing reputation as a healer by invoking Jesus' name to cast out a demon. John's concern, at first reading, appears to have some merit – but recall the ongoing battle going on among the disciples as to who is the greatest among them. Jesus responds, therefore, by condemning his followers' jealousy and intolerance, warning against an elitist view of discipleship that diminishes the good done by those we consider "outsiders."

Today's Gospel selection includes Jesus' exhortation that it is better lose one's limb if it leads one to sin. Two notes about these final verses:

- The "millstone" Jesus speaks of is the large piece of stone that is turned by a pack animal to grind grain. Drowning a criminal by tying him to one of these large heavy stones was a method of execution in Rome and Palestine.
- Gehenna was a vile place in Jewish history. The young King Ahaz (2 Chronicles 38: 3) practiced child immolation to the "fire god" at Gehenna. In Jesus' time, Gehenna, a ravine outside Jerusalem, served as the city's refuse site. Gehenna became synonymous with our concept of hell for the Jews.

In the **first reading** recounts a First Testament story similar to today's Gospel. Moses' young assistant, Joshua, takes the part of John in this story, expressing to Moses his concern that Eldad and Medad, who were not formerly confirmed as elders by Moses, were nonetheless "prophesying." Moses urges, instead, thanks to God for the gift he has bestowed on Israel through Eldad and Medad.

In the **second reading** is the final selection in this series of Sunday readings from the letter to James. In today's reading, the writer has hard words for his readers on the fate of the unjust rich. Their wealth will one day decay into nothing; but their exploitation of the poor for the sake of such wealth will lead to their permanent destruction at the hands of the God of justice.

Themes:

Acting in Jesus' name: tolerance and acceptance.

We may not think of ourselves as perfect, but we do (however unconsciously) consider our perspective of the world and our own belief and value systems to be the standards that others would be wise to embrace. To "act in Jesus' name," however, means to reach out to all without condition, without prejudice, without judgment. Thomas Merton put it this way: "As soon as you begin to take yourself seriously and imagine that your virtues are important because they are yours, you become the prisoner of your own vanity, and even your best works will blind and deceive you. And the more unreasonable importance you attach to yourself and to your works, the more you will tend to build up your own idea of yourself by condemning other people. Sometimes virtuous people are also bitter and unhappy because they unconsciously believe that their happiness depends on their being more virtuous than others."

Acting in Jesus' name: leading others to God.

The faith we have received is not a commodity for our private use alone. Sharing our faith with our children is both a great joy and great responsibility. Anyone and everyone in some kind of trouble or need has a claim on our compassion and charity because they are dear to Christ. Whether we are acting as parents, as citizens, as businessmen and women, we are still disciples, still called to follow Christ, still called to proclaim to others to Gospel of love, compassion and justice.

'Cutting off' that which cuts us off from God.

To be faithful to the call of discipleship means letting nothing – *nothing!* – dissuade us or derail us in our journey to God; authentic discipleship does not allow the pursuit of prestige, wealth, social status or instant gratification to desensitize us to the presence of God in our lives nor diminish the love of God we cherish in family and friends. The gift of faith demands that we let go of whatever makes us less than what God has created us to be – and that includes not only "cutting off" the sinful hand or "tearing out" the evil eye, but also letting go of our anger, prejudices, hatreds and demands for vengeance and retribution. In casting off the shackles that prevent us from living lives worthy of the title of "disciple," we re-create our world in the light and love of God.

For reflection:

- How and when does our faith become "elitist"?
- Consider ways in which we take something that is essentially good and use it destructively.
- Without teaching or preaching, how do we lead others to – or away from – God?

27th Sunday of the Year

Readings: *Mark 10: 2-16*
Genesis 2: 18-24
Hebrews 2: 9-11

The question of divorce was among the most divisive issues in Jewish society. The Book of Deuteronomy (24: 1) stipulated that a husband could divorce his wife for "some indecency." Interpretations of exactly what constituted "indecency" varied greatly, ranging from adultery to accidentally burning the evening meal. Further, the wife was regarded under the Law as a husband's chattel, with no legal right to protection and very little recourse to divorce herself. Divorce, then, was tragically common among the Jews of Jesus' time.

In today's **Gospel**, Jesus cites the Genesis account of the creation of man and woman (**first reading**) to emphasize that husband and wife are equal partners in the covenant of marriage ("the two become one body"). The language of Genesis indicates that the Creator intends for the marriage union to possess the same special covenantal nature as God's covenant with Israel. Jesus again appeals to the *spirit* of the Law rather than arguing legalities: It is the essence of their marriage covenant that husband and wife owe to one another total and complete love and mutual respect in sharing responsibility for making their marriage succeed.

Today's Gospel reading also includes the story of Jesus' welcoming the little children. Again, Jesus holds up the model of a child's simplicity and humility as the model for the servant-disciple.

Today begins a series of seven short excerpts from the "letter" to the Hebrews. Hebrews, which scholars have concluded was not written by Paul, is more of a sermon than a letter. Addressed most probably to a community of Jewish priests in Antioch who have embraced the new faith, Hebrews is really a theological treatise on Christ the high priest who fulfills and perfects the First Testament covenant. Hebrews illustrates the extent to which First Testament images and spirituality played in the development of early Christian thought.

The writer of Hebrews, in today's excerpt (**second reading**), writes that in order that Jesus' death might be a liberation from the slavery of sin and death, Jesus had to share our nature fully and become our "brother."

Themes:

The covenant of marriage.

In Jesus' time, there was little appreciation of love and commitment in marriage – marriages were always arranged in the husband's favor, the husband could divorce his wife for just about any reason, the woman was treated little better than property. But Jesus teaches that marriage is much more than a legal contract or arrangement – marriage that is *sacrament* is centered in the love of God, a love that knows neither condition nor limit in its ability to give and forgive. Marriage, as Jesus taught, is a total giving and sharing by each spouse as the line between "mine" and "yours" disappears into only "us." True love, as Jesus taught us in his life, death and Resurrection, seeks to overcome pain and hurt in order to be a constant source of life and hope.

The child: model of discipleship.

Children possess that marvelous sense of wonder, inquisitiveness and simplicity that deflate adult "logic" and the "conventional wisdom" and make us look at the essence of our actions and our beliefs. It is that sense of wonder at how remarkable our world is and that inquisitiveness as to why things cannot be right and good for everyone that Jesus calls his disciples to embrace for the sake of God's reign.

For reflection:

- How should the concept of marriage as a covenant and sacrament (rather than as a legal contract) affect our approach to marriage?
- In what ways do husbands and wives *live* the sacrament of their marriage?
- What do the wonder, inquisitiveness and simplicity of children teach us about the basic values of the Gospel?

Readings:

Mark 10: 17-30
Wisdom 7: 7-11
Hebrews 4: 12-13

The rich young man in today's **Gospel** is one of the most pitiable characters in the Jesus story. Clearly, Jesus' teachings and healings have touched something in him but his enthusiasm outdistances his commitment. Assuring Jesus that he has kept the "you shall nots..." of the Law, Jesus confronts the rich young man with the "you *shalls*" of the reign of God: "Go and sell what you have and give it to the poor."

And, as Mark describes it, the man's face fell as "he went away sadly." He can't bring himself to do it. His faith is not strong enough to give up the treasure he possesses for the "treasure in heaven." The young man walks away, sad certainly, perhaps feeling even somewhat disillusioned that his hero Jesus is not who he thought and hoped he would be.

Then Jesus, speaking to his disciples, turns another Jewish belief upside-down. Popular Jewish morality was simple: prosperity was a sign that one had found favor with God. There was a definite "respectability" to being perceived as wealthy and rich (how little things have changed!). Great wealth, Jesus points out, is actually a hindrance to heaven: Rich people tend to look at things in terms of price, of value, of the "bottom line." Jesus preaches detachment from things in order to become completely *attached* to the life and love of God.

Throughout the Gospel, Jesus points to the inadequacy of viewing religion as a series of codes and laws. The young man was no different than his contemporaries in seeing one's relationship with God as based on a series of negatives ("you shall not..."). Discipleship is not based on *not doing* and avoiding but on *doing* and acting in the love of God. Jesus calls us not to follow a code of conduct but, rather, to embrace the Spirit that gives meaning and purpose to the great commandment.

Today's **first reading**, again this week from the Book of Wisdom, praises wisdom – the search for God – as worth more than all the world's riches – an image that the young rich man in today's Gospel could not grasp.

The writer of Hebrews (today's **second reading**) picks up a related theme: The Word of God, "sharper than any two-edged sword," judges the things of the heart and spirit, for which we will be held accountable.

Themes:

A call to radical conversion.

The rich young man in today's Gospel exists in many of us: we gladly embrace the Jesus who comforts us and affirms us; we happily shout *Amen!* to his teachings about the meek inheriting the earth and loving one another as God loves us. But once we realize that Jesus is speaking directly to each one of us, asking you and me to change our lives radically in order to follow him, we begin to back away from Jesus: *It's a wonderful ideal, but I have too many responsibilities to just give up everything to follow you, Lord. After all, we can't all be like Mother Teresa and St. Francis. The world is a lot more complicated than that.* But it is exactly that "ideal" that Jesus demands from everyone who would be his disciple; it is that radical spirit of conversion that Jesus asks us to embrace in imitating his example selflessness and servanthood.

The curse of consumerism.

Throughout our lives, we collect and accumulate all kinds of things to help us make the journey from one milepost to the next; but too often the prosperity that should enable our journey becomes more important to us than the journey itself. Note that Jesus does not condemn wealth and possessions as evil in themselves; what is evil is when the pursuit of wealth and riches displaces God as the center of our lives. Given the choice between the life of God and the lifestyle of his possessions, the young man chooses his possessions. Wealth is seductive: what we consume can consume us. We can be swallowed up in our pursuit of wealth, prestige and power, becoming immune to the joy of the human experience. Whatever we possess that inhibits us from embracing the love of God to the fullest is a curse, not a blessing.

To do God's Work.

Discipleship is not a matter of avoiding what is bad, evil and unGodly; discipleship is a matter of *seeking* what is right, *working* for justice and peace, *doing* what is good. Jesus challenges the young rich man – and us – to move beyond a passive, fearful relationship with God based on "you shall nots" to an active, joyful relationship based on "you shalls."

For reflection:

- Has your possession of something of value ever turned out to be an unhappy, unsatisfying experience for you?
- Have you ever known anyone like the rich young man?
- How has our consumer society's values and attitudes diminished our humanity?

29th Sunday of the Year

Readings:

Mark 10: 35-45
Isaiah 53: 10-11
Hebrews 4: 14-16

In the **Gospel** reading a few weeks ago (just a chapter ago in Mark's Gospel), Jesus admonished his disciples for their pointless argument among themselves as to who was the most important. James and John apparently did not get the message. In today's Gospel account, the two sons of Zebedee – who, with Peter, made up Jesus' inner circle – ask for the places of honor and influence when Jesus begins his reign. James and John proclaim their willingness to "drink the cup" of suffering and share in the "bath" or "baptism" of pain Jesus will experience (the Greek word used is *baptizein*, meaning to immerse oneself in an event or situation). Jesus finally tells them that the assigning of such honors is the prerogative of God the Father.

Most readers share the other disciples' indignation at the incredible nerve of James and John to make such a request. (Matthew, in his Gospel, casts the two brothers in a little better light by having their mother make the request – Matthew 20: 20.) Jesus calls the disciples together to try again to make them understand that he calls them to greatness through service. His words "It cannot be that way with you" should haunt all of our ambitions and dealings with others.

Isaiah, in his fourth and last song of the "suffering servant" (**first reading**), sings of the ultimate exaltation of the servant, whose sacrifice reconciles God and his people. (These verses are also the conclusion of the first reading for Good Friday.)

Christ is praised by the author of Hebrews (**second reading**) as the "great high priest" who, in his death and resurrection, reveals to us a God of great mercy and compassion.

Themes:

The leader as servant.

Titles and honors, domains and influence, mean little in the Gospel scheme of things. As John and James learn in Jesus' gentle but firm rebuff of their self-serving request, Christianity is not a personal, compartmentalized, "Jesus-and-me-against-the-world" religion of rituals and laws but a deeply-felt, complete commitment to giving oneself totally and completely in the service of others. In God's eyes, greatness is not measured in reducing others to one's service but in reducing oneself to their service. In the reign of God, power and clout belong to those who take on Christ's role of the obedient servant; to them belong a share of the Suffering Servant's victory of the Resurrection.

'It cannot be like that with you': discipleship at odds with the world.

Jesus' admonition is almost a pleading: *If you really understand me and what I am about, if you really want to be my disciple, if you really seek to be worthy of my name, then you must see the world differently and respond to its challenges with a very different set of values.* The world may try to justify vengeance rather than forgiveness, to glorify self-preservation over selflessness, to insist on preserving the system and convention for the sake of compassion and justice – *but it cannot be that way with you.*

The cost of faithful discipleship

When James and John make their bold request of Jesus to sit at his right hand in his coming kingdom, Jesus tells them that they must be willing to "immerse" themselves in the suffering and pain Jesus will endure for the love of God. For the faithful disciple, greatness begins with giving oneself in service to others in imitation of Jesus the Servant-Redeemer; consequently, such service can begin only when we "empty" ourselves of our own self-centered needs, wants and interests in order to be "filled" with the Gospel spirit of loving servanthood, compassion and forgiveness. In the reign of God, greatness marks those who take on Christ's role of the obedient servant; to them will belong a share in the victory of his Resurrection.

For reflection:

- Do you know of people who have inspired others by their sense of service to those they led?
- How can humility triumph over the values of the world?
- When, in your life, was it most difficult to heed Jesus words, "It cannot be that way with you?"
- Have you ever experienced the satisfaction of "emptying" yourself for someone else?

Readings: *Mark 10: 46-52*
Jeremiah 31: 7-9
Hebrews 5: 1-6

Mark's story of the blind Bartimaeus (**Gospel**), which takes place just before Jesus' Palm Sunday entry into Jerusalem, is as much a "call" story as a healing story. For Mark, Bartimaeus is model of faith. The blind beggar calls out to Jesus using the Messianic title "Son of David." He is persistent and immediate in coming to Jesus. He asks first, not for his sight, but for compassion: He understands that this Jesus operates out of a spirit of love and compassion for humanity and places his faith in that spirit. Ironically, the blind Bartimaeus "sees" in Jesus the spirit of compassionate service that, until now, his "seeing" disciples have been unable to comprehend.

Bartimaeus is part of Jeremiah's "remnant" (**first reading**) of the humble and poor faithful – including the blind, the lame, the sick, mothers and their children – whom the Lord will restore as his holy people.

The writer of Hebrews (**second reading**) exalts the great love and forgiveness of God to raise up, for our sakes, Jesus Christ to be our eternal high priest.

Themes:

'Rabboni, I want to see.'

Bartimaeus' plaintiff cry to Jesus, "Rabboni, I want to see," should be our prayer: *Lord, I want to see the good in even the most trying and difficult people. I want to see the way to make things right again. I want to see reason for hope. I want to see your hand, Lord, at work in the events of my life.* The remarkable Helen Keller often spoke about blindness – not her own physical affliction, but the tragic "blindness" experienced by many seeing people: "I have walked with people whose eyes are full of light but who see nothing in sea or sky, nothing in city streets, nothing in books. It were far better to sail forever in the night of blindness with sense and feeling and mind than to be content with the mere act of seeing." Christ comes to heal our spiritual and moral blindness and open our eyes to the wonders and joys of God's reign. Note what Jesus says in Bartimaeus' request to see: "Your faith has healed you." As Bartimaeus experiences, faith enables us to recognize the Spirit of God in every person and to discern the way of God in all things.

'The faithful remnant.'

In the reign of God, no one is worthless, no one is marginal, no one is an outcast. As Jesus is about to enter Jerusalem to complete his mission as Redeemer, he meets one of the marginalized of his society – a blind man not even accorded a name of his own (he is simply called "Bartimaeus," the son of Timaeus). Today's Gospel challenges us to see all human beings with the eyes of faith, realizing that all are part of the "remnant" of Jeremiah's prophecy, all are sons and daughters of our compassionate Father in heaven.

For reflection:

- Have you ever experienced "blindness" of any kind – physical, intellectual, emotional, etc. How was that experience an "eye opening" experience for you?
- Who do you know who are among the faithful "remnant" like Bartimaeus who, despite their need and poverty, show us the light and riches of God?

Readings:

Mark 12: 28-34
Deuteronomy 6: 2-6
Hebrews 7: 23-28

In today's **Gospel**, Jesus "synthesizes" his message into the single "Great Commandment."

The Jews knew these two commandments well. To this day, observant Jews pray twice daily the *Shema*: to love God "with all your heart, and with all your soul and with all your strength." The word *shema* means "to hear," and comes from the first words of the prayer, "Hear, O Israel. . ." The text for the *Shema* is inscribed in the "Mezuzzah," a small container affixed to the door of every Jewish home. The *shema* is found in Deuteronomy 6: 4-6 (today's **first reading**). The Torah also outlined a Jew's moral and ethical responsibility to one's neighbors.

Jesus is the first to make of these two a single commandment: "There is no other commandment greater than these." The only way we can adequately celebrate our live for God is in extending that love to our neighbors.

In today's **second reading**, from the letter to the Hebrews, Christ's sacrifice is portrayed as the perfect and complete sacrifice to God, reconciling God and humanity once and for all. Because he lives on in his Resurrection, Christ continues as our high priest before God, rendering the "old covenant" priesthood obsolete.

Themes:

Love as the purpose of our lives.

In the very act of creating us, God invites us to participate in his act of creation by embracing his spirit of love. It is in love and compassion for one another that humanity most closely resembles God; it is in charity and selflessness that we participate in the work of creation. In the two "great commandments" we discover a purpose to our lives much greater than our prejudices, provincialism and parochialism; in them, we find the ultimate meaning and purpose of the gifts of faith and life.

Love as the center of faith.

Today's Gospel strikes at the heart of that safe, comfortable insularity from pain and distress that we often seek in the institutional nature of the Church. Christ's words are sobering: Our rituals and sanctuaries mean nothing before God if they are devoid of the love and compassion he reveals in them. Only in loving all of God's creatures can we even attempt to love God. The scribe in today's Gospel comes to understand that reality. Our faith is centered on the two great commandments of loving God and loving neighbor – everything we believe and do must be born of such love if we are truly to be the Church of the Risen Christ.

For reflection:

- In what ways can the "externals" of our faith distract us from the core of our faith?
- Have you ever been confronted with a situation in which love demanded more of you than you were prepared to give?
- How is love an act of creation? Of liberation?

Readings:

Mark 12: 38-44
1 Kings 17: 10-16
Hebrews 9: 24-28

Preaching in the Jerusalem temple days before the Last Supper and his crucifixion (**Gospel**), Jesus indicts the scribes for their lavish but empty show of faith. The scribes in their superior and haughty attitude are the antithesis of what Jesus wants his disciples to be.

In Jesus' time, a scribe, as the accepted expert the Law, could serve as trustee of a widow's estate. As his fee the scribe took a portion of the estate. Obviously, scribes with a reputation for piety were often entrusted with this role. With their abilities to manipulate the interpretations of the Law to their advantage, abuses of the system were common.

Throughout Scripture, widows were portrayed as the supreme examples of the destitute and powerless (today's **first reading** from the 1 Kings is an example). Jesus again makes a considerable impact on his hearers, then, by lifting up a widow who has nothing as an example of faithful generosity. Only that which is given from our own need and poverty – and given totally, completely, humbly and joyfully – is a gift fitting for God.

The author of Hebrews (**second reading**) continues his teaching to Jewish converts about the eternal priesthood of Christ as the completion of the Mosaic priesthood. In his death, Christ has won salvation for those who have died; he will return at the end of time to gather the surviving faithful before God.

Themes:

Giving from our poverty: 'reckless' generosity.

There is a recklessness in the widow's generosity: though a small amount, she certainly could have used the money for her own considerable needs, yet she gives it all for the love of God. She gives not from her surplus but from her substance, not from her treasure but from her poverty. Her sense of "reckless" giving challenges our concept of carefully-planned, tax deductible, convenient and painless giving. Jesus' concept of charity is centered in the kind of total and unconditional love that make such sacrificial giving a joy.

The 'measure' of the heart.

The widow's mite of the Gospel takes many forms. Be it time, money or enthusiasm, the widow's mite is "mighty" indeed, accomplishing great things not because of the size of the gift but because of the selfless and total love behind the gift. In the Gospel scheme of things, it is not the measure of the gift but the measure of the compassion and joyful spirit of giving that directs the gift that is great before God. Christ calls us not to seek greater things or talents to astound the world but for greater love and selflessness with which to enrich the world.

To honor the attitude of servanthood.

Jesus does not ask blind obsequiousness of us, but he does call us to embrace his spirit of servanthood that finds fulfillment and satisfaction in the love, compassion and kindness we can extend to others, the spirit that enables us to place the common good and the genuine needs of others above our own wants and narrows interests. The faithful disciple honors the dignity of the servant above the power of the rich, canonizes humility over celebrity and finds inspiration in the total generosity of the widow rather than the empty gestures of the scribe.

For reflection:

- Have you ever known or seen the "widow" of today's Gospel?
- Consider examples of how you have received the "widow's mite."
- How can the "gift" of money be meaningless?
- How is true giving "reckless"?

33rd Sunday of the Year

Readings:

Mark 13: 24-32
Daniel 12: 1-3
Hebrews 10: 11-14, 18

The first generation of Christians expected Christ to return in their lifetimes. When their world began to collapse around them under the Roman onslaught of Jerusalem, they wondered in their anguish, *When will Jesus return for us?*

With every experience of loss, with every sign of illness, with ever hint of age creeping upon us, we become more and more aware of our mortality. We live on the edge of eternity. Jesus does not deny the pain and anguish of the end (citing in today's **Gospel** reading graphic images of the prophet Daniel) nor that the earth will indeed pass away. But the important thing is not when Jesus will come (for we know he will), but our readiness to meet him.

As noted above, Mark's Jesus uses several images of the prophet Daniel to describe the final days. In today's **first reading**, Daniel tells of the archangel Michael, Israel's patron angel, raising up with him the souls of the faith "who [are] found written in the book." No other book in the First Testament portrays such a resurrection of the just.

On this next to last Sunday of the liturgical year, the final reading in this series from the "letter" to Hebrews (**second reading**) speaks of the Risen Christ, the eternal High Priest who now awaits at the "right hand of God" until his final victory at the end of time when "his enemies are placed beneath his feet."

Themes:

The 'signs' of the fig tree.

There are signs all around us – like the late autumn winds of November – that remind us that we live in the shadow of eternity. In everyone's life the "fig tree" grows and flowers and finally withers. But the signs should not frighten us or terrify us into submission before the horrible wrath of God. Jesus urges us to recognize such "signs" with eyes and spirits of faith: to realize that every changing world and passing stage, every pain and triumph, are opportunities for growth, maturity and understanding along the journey – "signs" that can guide us back and point us forward to the eternal life of God and the promise of the Resurrection.

The preciousness of time.

Today's readings speak of the preciousness of time: God has given us only so many days to complete our journey through this life to the forever of the next. Yet we often squander the limited time we have been given on the fleeting things of this world rather than on the treasures of the next. To attempt to hold on to the harvest of the withering "fig tree" will only lead to disappointment in the end. Cardinal Newman said: "Fear not that your life shall come to an end, but rather that it never had a beginning."

Our ever-changing journey through time.

Life is a journey through changing worlds and passing stages. Change – sometimes frightening, often painful, always difficult – is part of that journey for all of us. But when our "heavens and earths" pass away, the promise of the life of God and the values of the Gospel remain constant. With every change in direction, with every sign of age, with every new milestone, we remain heirs to the promise of the Resurrection.

For reflection:

- In what experiences have you become aware of the brevity of life?
- How do we cope, in the spirit of Jesus, with the traumatic changes we all undergo in our lives?
- This month of November is traditionally the month of the faithful departed. What does this month – the month of coming winter, the month of Thanksgiving, the month prior to Advent and Christmas – teach us about death and resurrection?

Solemnity of Christ the King

Readings:

John 18: 33-37
Daniel 7: 13-14
Revelation 1: 5-8

We celebrate the kingship of Jesus with John's **Gospel** account of what is perhaps Jesus' most humiliating moment: his appearance before Pilate. It is a strange exchange: Pilate has been blackmailed by the Jewish establishment into executing Jesus; it is the accused who dominates the meeting and takes on the role of inquisitor; Pilate has no idea what Jesus is talking about when he speaks about "the truth."

Pilate, a man of no great talent, was under a great deal of political pressure. He had needlessly alienated the Jews of Palestine by his cruelty, his insensitivity to their religious customs and his clumsy appropriation of funds from the temple treasury for public projects. Reports of his undistinguished performance had reached his superiors in Rome. Jesus proclaims himself ruler of a kingdom built of compassion, humility, love and truth – power that Pilate cannot comprehend in his small, narrow view of the world.

The prophet Daniel (**first reading**) envisions the heavenly court in which "One...coming on the clouds" (that is, coming from God) unites all the nations and peoples of the earth into an eternal dominion of peace. John, in the Book of Revelation (**second reading**) has a similar vision, but identifies Daniel's vision as Jesus, "the first-born of the dead" – that is, the first to experience the Resurrection.

Themes:

Acclaiming Jesus as our 'King.'

Today's solemnity challenges us to make an active, positive and unqualified declaration of faith: that Jesus is the Master, the Ruler, the Lord of our lives. Today's Solemnity of Christ the King confronts us with the beliefs that rule our hearts and minds and the values that govern our decisions. We cannot be Christians by default but only by a conscious, deliberate choice; we cannot respond passively to the call to discipleship, only actively can we embrace the spirit of the "kingdom" of God, a kingdom built on compassion, justice and truth. Being true to our identity as Christians demands making deliberate and conscientious choices that begin, not with legalisms and loopholes, but in the truth proclaimed by Christ, in the spirit of the unconditional and complete love of God.

Becoming disciples of the truth.

To be faithful disciples of Christ is to be servants of truth – truth that liberates and renews, truth that gives and sustains life and hope, truth that transcends the rationalizations, half-truths and delusions of our culture and society. The truth can be very difficult to accept; sometimes "testifying" to the truth can be costly. But once the truth about something is realized and accepted, then that truth can empower, change and renew. Jesus has come to reveal the truth about our relationship with God, the Author of love, and the impact of that truth on our relationships with one another. The Gospel of Jesus is centered in the truth that speaks of the great creative and life-sustaining love of God, truth that serves as a looking glass for seeing the world according to the intended design of God.

For reflection:

- Have you ever experienced the sense of freedom and empowerment that comes in realizing the truth about something?
- How does Jesus' response to Pilate crystallize what Jesus has said to us in the Gospel during this past year?
- How has the Gospel of truth affected choices you have had to make in your life?

139

Lectionary Cycle C
The Year of Luke

The Proper of the Seasons – Cycle C

Readings:
Luke 21: 25-28, 34-36
Jeremiah 33: 14-16
1 Thessalonians 3: 12 – 4: 2

Advent begins at the end – the promised return of Christ at the end of time (**Gospel**). For the faithful disciple, history is a moving forward, a journey to the fulfillment of God's reign, when Christ will return as Lord of all. We therefore live in a permanent state of Advent watchfulness, preparation and perseverance as we await the return of the Holy One who has already come.

Chaos reigns in the Israel of Jeremiah's time: Jerusalem has fallen (586 B.C.), the dynasty of David's royal line has been broken off. The prophet Jeremiah proclaims that God will again raise up "a just shoot" from the lineage of David to lead God's people (**first reading**).

The Thessalonians expected Christ's return in their lifetimes; that expectation resulted in divisions, rancor and complacency within the community. Paul calls on them to embrace a new attitude of constant vigilance in the ways of the Gospel in order to be worthy of welcoming the Lord whenever he returns (**second reading**).

Themes:

Advent: a call to 'be on guard . . . watch.'

Today we begin the four weeks of preparation for Christmas – but today's Gospel is hardly filled with Christmas cheer. In blunt and stark language, Jesus speaks of the end of time as we know it. And that is the real theme of Advent: the swiftly passing nature of the real world. The moments we are given in this experience of life are precious and few. God gives us this lifetime in order that we might come to discover him and know him in the love of others and the goodness of this world in anticipation of the next. Advent calls us to see beyond the finite time frame of this world to the eternity of the reign of God. The people of the First Testament looked forward to the coming of the Messiah to re-create the world; now, we await the return of the Messiah, the Risen Christ, to transform our world again.

The many seasons of Advent.

Our lives are a continuing series of Advent experiences: we are painfully aware that the world is not as just, not as loving, not as a whole as we know it can and should be; we are constantly waiting to become, to discover, to understand, to change, to complete, to fulfill. Hope, struggle, fear, expectation and fulfillment are all part of life's many Advents. Christ comes at a point in time to reveal to us the possibilities of God; Christ's promised return at the end of time challenges us to realize those possibilities. Christ's coming among us – as *one* of us – give us reason to hope in such possibilities: that light will shatter the darkness, that we can be liberated from our fears and prejudices, that we are never alone or abandoned by our God.

'An Advent people.'

The season of Advent confronts us with both the preciousness and precariousness of life, the inevitable – yet still always difficult – changes that we must contend with in the course of the time we are given. For men and women of faith, time is not static but progressive, constantly moving forward to the fulfillment of God's reign. We begin the liturgical season of Advent at the end: this first Sunday of Advent (and of a new liturgical year) focuses on the last day, when Christ returns to lead us into a new time – the eternity of God's reign. The theologian Karl Rahner said that we are an "Advent Church," a Church that lives always in hopeful anticipation of the Christ who comes in its faithfulness to the Gospel of justice and reconciliation.

For reflection:

- How do the traditions and myths surrounding Christmas help us understand the disciple's call to readiness for the Lord's coming?
- How can we make this Advent a time of transformation, of re-creation?
- Do you have any intense experience of *waiting*, of *watching*, of *readiness*? What did it teach you about the preciousness of life?
- How is Christmas an "adult" feast?

Second Sunday of Advent

Readings:
Luke 3: 1-6
Baruch 5: 1-9
Philippians 1: 4-6, 8-11

So important is the emergence of John the Baptizer in human history that Luke dates his appearance in six different ways. In his **Gospel**, Luke introduces John as prophets were introduced in the First Testament ("...the word of God was spoken to John son of Zechariah in the desert"). As does Matthew and Mark, Luke cites the famous passage from Isaiah regarding "a herald's voice in the desert" to describe the Baptizer's mission – but Luke quotes more of the Isaiah prophecy than his synoptic counterparts, including the promise of universal salvation that is so central to Luke's Gospel.

Forms of "baptism" were common in the Judaism of Gospel times – in some Jewish communities, it was through baptism rather than circumcision that a Gentile became a Jew. But John's baptism was distinctive. His baptism at the Jordan was a rite of repentance and *metanoia* – a conversion of heart and spirit. The Baptizer's ministry fulfilled the promise of Ezekiel (Ezekiel 36: 25-26): that, at the dawn of a new age, the God of Israel would purify his people from their sins with clear water and instill in them a new heart and spirit.

In today's **first reading**, the prophet Baruch portrays the post-exilic Jerusalem as the mother of a nation that God brings back together after many years of war and exile. For the re-created Israel, justice and peace will be its light; faithfulness to God will be its glory.

Paul begins his letter to the Church at Philippi (the **second reading**) with the prayer that they may come to the day of the Lord pure and blameless, fully transformed by the Gospel spirit of justice and love.

Themes:

Our call to be 'prophets' of the Lord.

Each one of us is called to be a prophet of Christ. The word *prophet* comes from the Greek word meaning "one who proclaims." Prophets call us to look beyond legalisms and the bottom line to see what is right, what is authentically good, what is truly of God; they echo the Baptizer's message that we find our ultimate purpose in God; they proclaim in their ministries, in their compassion and their kindness, in their courageous commitment to what is right that Jesus the Messiah has come.

'Clearing a straight path' to the Lord.

As men and women of faith, we believe that time is moving toward something, that human history is a journey to fulfillment and completion in the Lord. The Baptizer's Advent message challenges us to seek our life's ultimate fulfillment and completion in God. The many elements of our Christmas celebration mean little unless they point to the Christ who comes to reconcile us to God and to one another, the Christ who illuminates our spirits with the light of God's love and compassion, the Christ who teaches us the ways of God's justice and peace. Building that Christ-directed "road" is not easy – it often means leaving the conventional path in order to travel the values of the Gospel; it sometimes means being a "prophetic" trailblazer, creating new paths that are questioned or ridiculed by more cautious pilgrims. Advent calls us to build and re-build the roads we travel to Christ, the Word and Light of God who leads us to the Father.

'Filling in the valleys . . .'

There are so many wastelands and barren places into which we can bring life, so many roads and avenues we can transform into highways through our charity and forgiveness. In giving the needs of others priority over our own interests, in taking the first humbling steps toward reconciliation with another, in seeing in other people the face of Christ, we make a "highway" in our world for the Lord who comes.

For reflection:

- Who are the "prophets" among us now who proclaim the Messiah in our community and our world today?
- How is the Gospel both a message of hope and a warning?
- What are the "wastelands" of our community and society into which we can create a "highway" for the God of mercy, peace and justice?

Third Sunday of Advent

Readings:
Luke 3: 10-18
Zephaniah 3: 14-18
Philippians 4: 4-7

Today's **Gospel** is Luke's unique reporting of the themes of John's preaching.

The Baptizer is approached by two groups whose professions were scorned by the Pharisees: tax collectors, who usually made handsome profits by gouging their fellow Jews, and Jewish soldiers who belonged to the Roman peacekeeping force. John requires of them not a change of professions but a change of heart and attitude, that they perform their duties with honesty and integrity. John calls for selfless concern for one's disadvantaged brothers and sisters.

John assures his Jewish listeners that he is not the Messiah; in fact, John considers himself lower than the lowest slaves (only a non-Jewish slave could be required to loosen his master's sandal strap and John does not presume to do even that).

In proclaiming the Messiah's "baptism in the Holy Spirit and fire," John employs the image of a "winnowing-fan." A winnowing-fan was a flat, wooden, shovel-like tool, used to toss grain into the air. The heavier grain fell to the ground and the chaff blew away. In the same way, John says, the Messiah will come to gather the "remnant" of Israel and destroy the Godless.

The prophet Zephaniah, whose prophecies warn in horrific language and images of the coming "Day of the Lord," offers at the end of his relatively short book a song of hope that God, "who is in your midst," will forgive the faithless Israel and reconcile all men and women to himself (**first reading**). Several of Zephaniah's images were included by Luke in his Gospel account of the Annunciation to Mary.

The apostle Paul echoes Zephaniah's theme of joyful expectation in his letter to the Philippians (**second reading**). It is from the opening words of this epistle that this Third Sunday of Advent came to be known as *Gaudete* Sunday ("Rejoice!").

Themes:

Our call to be 'Christ bearers.'

Through baptism, we take on the role of "Christ bearers." Like John's proclamation at the River Jordan, we are called to be witnesses of God's love by the love we extend to others; precursors of his justice by our unfailing commitment to what is right and good; lamps reflecting the light of God's Christ in our forgiveness, mercy and compassion; harvesters of souls through our humble and dedicated servanthood.

'Joy to the world.'

The Christ event calls us to joy – to realize and celebrate the joy of God's presence that we are often too busy or too jaded or too overwhelmed to see. But such joy is not confined to happy and romantic notions of the Christmas season. Zephaniah calls his people to be glad and exult "with *all your heart*" for "the Lord is in your midst"; Paul writes that we should "rejoice *always*...for the Lord is near"; John preaches to the crowds that they should make ready for the Messiah by *everyday* acts of justice and charity. This is the season that we give at least a hearing to "joy to the world" and "peace on earth to all people of good will." The challenge of Christmas is to make such joy a living reality in every season of the year.

For reflection:

- How do we "sin" against the joy of faith?
- Who are the "Christ bearers" of our age – those whose lives preach the "good news" of Christ's presence?
- How is the Advent/Christmas season both a cause for celebration and a call to repentance?
- Where and when have you found unexpected, almost invisible signs that the Lord is indeed in our midst?

Fourth Sunday of Advent

Readings:

Luke 1: 39-45
Micah 5: 1-4
Hebrews 10: 5-10

The readings for the Fourth Sunday of Advent each year shift the focus from Advent's call to preparation for the Messiah to setting the stage for the Christmas event. In today's **Gospel**, Elizabeth proclaims her joy-filled faith in God's promise of salvation that will be accomplished through Mary's child and praises her young cousin for her "yes" to God's plan.

Bethlehem's only claim to fame was the fact that it was the birthplace of Israel's great king, David. Its historical significance long forgotten, Bethlehem had become a kind of "bus stop" or "train depot" for the great camel caravans that traversed the great roads of antiquity – a place where people met quickly to conduct business, change camels or spend a night during a long journey, and then continued on their lives. But Micah (writing 700 years before Jesus' birth) prophesies that the Messiah of God will dawn upon human history in "little" Bethlehem-Ephratha (Ephratha refers to the clan of Benjamin who settled there) (**first reading**).

Citing Psalm 40: 7-8, the author of the great theological treatise the Scripture canon has titled the Letter to the Hebrews interprets the psalm as a sign of the eventual displacement of the First Testament Law and Covenant with the sacrifice of the body of Christ (**second reading**).

Themes:

God's promised fulfilled.

The Spirit of God is the principal albeit unseen player in the events of Christmas. Jesus' birth is the work of the Holy Spirit – God has directly intervened in human history. God's Spirit, who inspired the prophets to preach, who enabled the nation of Israel to enter into the covenant with Yahweh, continues at work in the world in new and creative ways. Jesus Christ is the ultimate and perfect fulfillment of that covenant.

'O little town of Bethlehem . . .'

Despite the romantic theme of the carol, "O Little Town of Bethlehem," Bethlehem was among the last places the world expected the long-awaited Messiah to first appear; yet in little insignificant Bethlehem, a bus stop along the great eastern caravans, God chose to touch human history. Too often we let the busy "Bethlehems" of our lives distract us from letting the spirit of Christmas become a part of our lives. Sometimes God is too quiet, too silent, too simple for us to hear and see. Like the travelers who pass through Bethlehem, we fail to see God in our everyday world. Hope and grace can often be found in hidden and quiet places. The miracle of Christmas is beautifully expressed in the hopeful words of the Phillips Brooks' carol: "[Yet] in thy dark streets shineth/the everlasting light./The hopes and fears of all the years/Are met in thee tonight."

The 'mystery' of Christmas.

The "mystery" of the Incarnation is not that God could become one of us – the inexplicable part is how God could give his love away so freely to his people, without expectation or condition. We don't have the ability to comprehend the whys of love so deep and profound that God could condescend to become one of *us*. Mary and Elizabeth, in their exchange of greetings, are among the first to understand exactly what is to happen. As St. Ireneaus preached: "Because of his great love for us, Jesus, the Word of God, became what we are in order to make us what he is himself." All we can do to respond to such love is to share it, to make the Christ who comes a reality, a living light, in our lives and the lives of others.

For reflection:

- In what small and hidden "Bethlehems" among us are God's joy and hope present for all of us?
- Share stories of God's Spirit present and working in our world as it was in the events of the Incarnation.
- How do our Christmas customs and traditions express the "mystery" of the Incarnation?

Christmas

Readings:

Mass of the Vigil   *Matthew 1: 1-25*
Isaiah 62: 1-5
Acts 13: 16-17, 22-25

The readings for the Vigil Mass of Christmas celebrate Jesus' birth as the fulfillment of the First Covenant.

For Matthew, the story of Jesus begins with the promise to Abraham – that Jesus is the ultimate and perfect fulfillment of the Law and Prophets; so Matthew begins his **Gospel** with "a family record" of Jesus, tracing the infant's birth from Abraham (highlighting his Jewish identity) and David (his Messiahship).

Matthew's version of Jesus' birth at Bethlehem follows his detailed genealogy. This is not Luke's familiar story of a child born in a Bethlehem stable, but that of a young unmarried woman suddenly finding herself pregnant and her very hurt and confused husband wondering what to do. In Gospel times, marriage was agreed upon by the groom and the bride's parents, but the girl continued to live with her parents after the wedding until the husband was able to support her in his home or that of his parents. During that interim period, marital intercourse was not permissible.

Yet Mary is found to be with child. Joseph, an observant but compassionate Jew, does not wish to subject Mary to the full fury of Jewish law, so he plans to divorce her "quietly." But in images reminiscent of the First Testament "annunciations" of Isaac and Samuel, an angel appears to Joseph in a dream and reveals that this child is the fulfillment of Isaiah's prophecy. Because of his complete faith and trust in God's promise, Joseph acknowledges the child and names him *Jesus* ("Savior") and becomes, in the eyes of the Law, the legal father of Jesus. Thus, Jesus, through Joseph, is born a descendent of David.

Matthew's point in his infancy narrative is that Jesus is the Emmanuel promised of old – Isaiah's prophecy has finally been fulfilled in Jesus: the "virgin" has given birth to a son, one who is a descendent of David's house (through Joseph). Jesus is truly *Emmanuel* – God is with us.

The promise fulfilled is also the theme of Isaiah's insistence that God will fulfill his promises to the exiled Israelites returning home (**first reading**). Like the great love of a generous spouse, God not only forgives his people but entrusts to them the promise of the Messiah.

Paul's sermon to the Jews at Antioch Pisidia in the Acts of the Apostles (**second reading**) is a concise chronicle of the promise of Emmanuel fulfilled.

Mass at Midnight   *Luke 2: 1-14*
Isaiah 9: 1-6
Titus 2: 11-14

Centuries of hope in God's promise have come to fulfillment: the Messiah is born!

Luke's account of Jesus' birth (**Gospel**) begins by placing the event during the reign of Caesar Augustus. Augustus, who ruled from 27 B.C. - 14 A.D.), was honored as "savior" and "god" in ancient Greek inscriptions. His long reign was hailed as the *pax Augusta* – a period of peace throughout the vast Roman world. Luke very deliberately points out that it is during the rule of Augustus, the savior, god and peace-maker, that Jesus the Christ, the long-awaited Savior and Messiah, the Son of God and Prince of Peace, enters human history.

Throughout his Gospel, Luke shows how it is the poor, the lowly, the outcast and the sinner who immediately hear and embrace the preaching of Jesus. The announcement of the Messiah's birth to shepherds – who were among the most isolated and despised in the Jewish community – is in keeping with Luke's theme that the poor are especially blessed of God.

In his "Book of Emmanuel" (chapters 6-12), the prophet Isaiah describes Emmanuel as the new David, the ideal king who will free his enslaved people (**first reading**). The "day of Midian" refers to Gideon's decisive defeat of the Midianites, a nomadic nation of outlaws who ransacked the Israelites' farms and villages (Judges 6-8).

Paul's letter to his co-worker Titus articulates the heart of the mystery of the Incarnation: the grace of God himself has come to us in the person of Jesus Christ (**second reading**).

Mass at Dawn   *Luke 2: 15-20*
Isaiah 62: 11-12
Titus 3: 4-7

Typical of Luke's Gospel, it is the shepherds of Bethlehem – among the poorest and most disregarded of Jewish society – who become the first messengers of the **Gospel.**

As Israel rebuilds its city and nation, the prophet Isaiah calls his people to lift their hearts and spirits to behold the saving power of God (**first reading**).

In a letter to his co-worker Titus, Paul writes that our salvation comes as a result of the initiative of our merciful God (**second reading**).

Mass During the Day   *John 1: 1-18*
Isaiah 52: 7-10
Hebrews 1: 1-6

The **Gospel** for Christmas day is the beautiful Prologue hymn to John's Gospel. With echoes of Genesis 1 ("In the beginning . . . ," "the light shines on in darkness . . ."), the Prologue exalts Christ as the creative Word

of God who comes as the new light to illuminate God's re-creation.

In the original Greek text, the phrase "made his dwelling place among us" is more accurately translated as "pitched his tent or tabernacle." The image evokes the Exodus memory of the tent pitched by Israelites for the ark of the covenant. God sets up the tabernacle of the new covenant in the body of the Child of Bethlehem.

Israel has been brought to ruin by its incompetent, unfaithful rulers. But God himself leads his people back to Zion (site of the Jerusalem temple) from their long exile in Babylon. Again and again, the Lord restores and redeems Israel (**first reading**).

No prophet could imagine the length God would go to save and re-create humankind. But Christ, "the exact reflection of the Father's glory" and "heir of all things through whom he created the universe," comes as the complete and total manifestation of God's love, fulfilling the promises articulated so imperfectly and incompletely by the prophets (**second reading**).

Themes:

Christmas: a celebration for all of humanity.

From the Christmas story in Luke's Gospel, we have a romantic image of shepherds as gentle, peaceful figures. But that manger scene image is a far cry from the reality: The shepherds of Biblical times were tough, earthy characters who fearlessly used their clubs to defend their flocks from wolves and other wild animals. They had even less patience for the pompous scribes and Pharisees who treated them as second and third-class citizens, barring these ill-bred rustics from the synagogue and courts.

And yet it was to shepherds that God first revealed the birth of the Messiah. The shepherds' vision on the Bethlehem hillside proclaims to all people of every place and generation that Christ comes for the sake of all humankind.

Christmas: the beginning of the Christ event.

A favorite story of Martin Buber, the great Jewish philosopher, concerned a rabbi in Jerusalem to whom it was excitedly announced that the Messiah had come. The rabbi calmly looked out of the window, surveyed the scene carefully, and announced that, to him, nothing seemed to have changed, and then calmly returned to his study.

The Messiah *has* come – but what difference does that make in our lives? If the rabbi were to look out his window tonight, he would certainly see many different things: He would see the lights and decorations and illuminated trees and wreaths, he would hear the carolers sing their songs about "joy to the world" and "peace on earth," he would behold the smiles and joy of people extending greetings to one another.

But what would the rabbi see out of his window tomorrow? or next week? or a day in February? or April? or July?

The Messiah *has* come! What happened one Palestinian night when a son was born to a carpenter and his young bride was the beginning of a profound transformation of humanity. But has it made a difference? Has our world become a better place since the Son of God became incarnate here? Has anything changed? The theologian Martin Buber described the difference this way: "Men [and women] become what they are, sons [and daughters] of God, by *becoming* what they are, brothers of their brothers [and sisters of their sisters]."

'The Word made flesh'/'a life for the light of all.'

The miracle of Christmas is God's continuing to reach out to humankind, his continuing to call us to relationship with him despite out obstinacy, selfishness and rejection of him. In Jesus, the extraordinary love of God has taken our "flesh" and "made his dwelling among us." In his "Word made flesh," God touches us at the very core of our beings, perfectly expressing his constant and unchanging love. Christ is born – and human history is changed forever. In profound simplicity and stillness, the light of Christ has dawned and the darkness of hatred, intolerance and ignorance is shattered.

The 'Bethlehems' of our hearts.

In his acclaimed autobiography, *The Seven Story Mountain,* Thomas Merton wrote about his first Christmas as a monk at Gethsemani Abbey in Kentucky:

"Christ always seeks the straw of the most desolate cribs to make his Bethlehem. In all other Christmases of my life, I had got a lot of presents and a big dinner. This Christmas I was to get no presents, and not much of a dinner: but I would have indeed, Christ, God, the Savior of the world.

"You who live in the world: let me tell you that there is no comparing these two kinds of Christmas. . . . The emptiness that had opened up within me, that had been prepared during Advent and laid open by my own silence and darkness, now became filled. And suddenly I was in a new world."

The true miracle of Christmas continues to take place in the Bethlehems of our hearts. The trappings of Christmas, for the most part, do not begin to capture the full magnitude of the Christmas event. In the emptiness of our souls, God forgives us, reassures us, exalts us, elates us, loves us. In the coming of Jesus, God's love becomes real, touchable and approachable to us. The true meaning of Christmas is that simple – and that profound.

'O Holy Night.'

Christmas is a feast that appeals to our senses: the sights of glittering lights, the taste of the many delicacies of Yuletide feasting, the smell of freshly cut evergreen branches, the feel of the crisp winter air and newly-fallen snow, the sound of the magnificent music of Christmas.

But the first Christmas had none of those things. Consider the actual sights and sounds and feels and tastes – and smells! – of that night: the damp, aching cold of a

cave on the Bethlehem hillside; the burning in the eyes and throat from days of traveling along hard, dusty roads; the sudden panic of discovering there is no place to stay in a strange city, the paralyzing fear that robbers and wild animals could strike out of nowhere; the silence of the night, broken only by the cry of wolves and the bleating of sheep; the screaming of a young girl delivering her first child alone, with her carpenter husband offering what help he could; and the overwhelming stench of a cave used as a barn: the smell of animals, of manure, of perspiration.

That first Christmas night was human life at its dreariest, dirtiest and messiest, the human experience at its most painful, most exhausting, most terrifying. The first Christmas was dirty and grimy and, frankly, stunk to high heaven – but it was as holy as the highest heights of heaven. In our imperfections, in our sin, in our obtuse selfishness, God enters our human life and sanctifies it. The glorious sights and sounds, tastes and aromas of this holy night invite us to embrace the great love of God, the love that can transform our humanity from the hopelessness of a lonely birth in a cave to the hope and joy of redeeming grace.

For reflection:

- It has been a busy time, getting to this day. Was it all worth it?
- "We need a little Christmas . . ." so the song goes from the musical *Mame*. Why do we need Christmas *this* year?
- How is the first Christmas as described by Luke at odds with our Christmas celebration? How can we reconcile the difference in the simplicity of the first Christmas and the extravagance of our celebration?
- How can we make "shepherds" (outcasts, the poor and rejected) part of our Christmas?
- What one Christmas tradition, practice or story speaks to you most especially of the holiness of this night/day?
- Share your most memorable Christmas – a memory that even today affects your understanding of the mystery of the Incarnation.

Readings:

Luke 2: 41-52
Sirach 3: 2-6, 12-14, Colossians 3: 12-21

Today's **Gospel** was probably a later addition to Luke's Gospel, found in the rich oral tradition of stories told about Jesus. Like many childhood stories of famous people, this one is retold because it shows signs in Jesus' boyhood of the qualities that will emerge in his adulthood and mark his life forever in history. Luke clearly has the events of Holy Week in mind in the details he has included in the story: the journey to Jerusalem at Passover, the encounter with the teachers at the Temple, the three days Jesus is lost.

At the age of 12, a Jewish boy becomes a "son of the Law" – he becomes personally responsible for following the Torah. The faithful Jesus reveals himself as the perfect servant of his Father from the time of his first legal pilgrimage to Jerusalem.

It was the Jewish practice for teachers to conduct classes not in a lecture format but as an open discussion in which participants were encouraged to ask questions. It is inaccurate to suggest, as old paintings suggest, that Jesus dominated the scene, overwhelming the teachers with the depth of his insights. As Luke tells the story, Jesus was listening to the teachers and eagerly searching for knowledge in his questions like a highly motivated and interested student.

Luke reports that Mary "kept all these things in memory." Perhaps Mary confronted for the first time the reality that, although she was indeed his mother, her son did not belong to her.

The Book of Sirach is a collection of carefully-crafted maxims and commentaries based on the Law. The author ("Jesus, son of Eleazar, son of Sirach" – 50: 27), a wise and experienced observer of life, writes on a variety of topics in order to help his contemporaries understand the role of faith in everyday life.

Today's **first reading** is a beautiful reflection on the fourth commandment. To honor one's parents, Ben Sira writes, is to honor the Lord God himself.

Paul wrote his letter to the Colossians (one of Paul's "captivity epistles") at the urging of Epaphras, the leader of the church there. The young church was being torn apart by adherents of Gnosticism ("knowledge"), a philosophy that stressed the superiority of knowledge over faith. Paul writes that such Gnostic teachings are but "shadows"; Christ is "reality," the "image of the invisible God, the first-born of all creation" in whom we are redeemed. In today's **second reading** from Colossians, Paul presents a picture of real community, formed in the perfect, unconditional love of Christ.

Themes:

The family: 'the little church.'

Today's feast is a celebration of family – that unique nucleus of society that gives us life, nurture and support throughout our journey on earth. Families are the first and best places for the love of God to come alive. Within our families we experience the heights of joy and the depths of pain. The Fathers of Vatican II called the family "the first and vital cell of humanity . . . the domestic sanctuary of the Church." Families reflect the love of Christ: love that is totally selfless, limitless and unconditional, both in good times and (especially) in bad times. Today's Feast of the Holy Family calls us to re-discover and celebrate our own families as harbors of forgiveness and understanding and safe places of unconditional love, welcome and acceptance.

The cross and the crib.

It is easy to welcome Jesus the innocent child of Christmas; much more difficult is to welcome Jesus, the humble Crucified of Holy Week and Easter. Luke's Gospel of the Child Jesus reminds us that the crib is overshadowed by the cross, that this holy birth is the beginning of humankind's re-birth in the Resurrection. With Jesus, we must be about "the Father's house," bringing the justice, reconciliation and compassion won by the cross into our families and communities.

A model of holiness for all families.

In Matthew's and Luke's stories of Jesus' birth and childhood (which were later additions to those Gospels, drawn from the many stories about Jesus' life that were part of the early Christian oral tradition that had developed), life for the family of Joseph, Mary and Jesus is difficult and cruel: they are forced from their home; they are innocent victims of the political and social tensions of their time; they endure the suspicions of their own people when Mary's pregnancy is discovered; their child is born under the most difficult and terrifying of circumstances; Joseph and Mary endure the agony of losing their beloved child. And yet, through it all, their love and faithfulness to one another do not waver. The Holy Family is a model for our families as we confront the many tensions and crises that the threaten the stability, peace and unity that are the joys of being a family.

For reflection:

- What rituals and customs in your own family reflect the spiritual dimension of Christmas?
- What experiences has your family shared that have brought you closer together? Consider both the wonderful and the catastrophic; times of trial, tension and tragedy; times that demanded extraordinary efforts to forgive and reconcile.
- Can you, as a parent, identify with Joseph and Mary in today's Gospel?

Solemnity of Mary, Mother of God

Cycles A, B and C

Readings:

Luke 2: 16-21
Numbers 6: 22-27
Galatians 4: 4-7

Today's solemnity is the oldest feast of Mary in the Church, honoring her by her first and primary title, "Mother of God."

Jesus is given the name *Yeshua* – "The Lord saves." The rite of circumcision unites Mary's child with the chosen people and makes him an heir to the promises God made to Abraham – promises to be fulfilled in the Child himself (**Gospel**).

From the Book of Numbers (one of the five books of the Law) the Lord gives to Moses and Aaron the words of priestly blessing (**first reading**).

The Church of Galatia is facing defections because of Judaic preachers who insist that pagan converts submit to the Jewish rite of circumcision and the observance of the Law. Paul's letter maintains that salvation is through Christ alone, that Christ's followers are no longer under the yoke of the First Law. Paul puts the Christmas event in perspective: through Christ, born of Mary, we become sons and daughters of "Abba," meaning Father (**second reading**).

Themes:

'Theotokos' – 'God-bearer.'

Today we honor Mary under her most ancient title – "*Theotokos,* Bearer of God." Mary, the mother of the Child of Bethlehem, is the perfect symbol of our own salvation. In accepting her role as mother of the Messiah, she becomes the first disciple of her Son, the first to embrace his Gospel of hope, compassion and reconciliation. She is the promise of what the Church is called to be and will be and seeks to become; she is the hope and comfort of a pilgrim people walking the road of faith. Mary, the "bearer of God," is a genuine and fitting example for us of what it means to be a faithful disciple of the Servant Redeemer – "bearers of God" in our own time and place.

Mary: our mother and sister.

Her statues have always radiated sweetness. She is always young and pink-cheeked and slender, with hair cascading down to her waist.

But the Mary of the Gospels is neither a fairy tale princess nor the romanticized "lovely lady dressed in blue." The flesh-and-blood Mary was an altogether human woman:

- the pregnant adolescent who was painfully misunderstood by the man she loved;
- the young mother, virtually alone, is forced to give birth to her firstborn in a damp cave one night on the outskirts of a place unknown to her;
- the frantic parent searching for her lost child in Jerusalem;
- the caring woman who was not afraid to speak her mind or voice her questions;
- the anguished mother who stood by courageously while, in a travesty of justice, her son was executed.

The figure we venerate in mysterious icons was a woman with her feet firmly planted on earth. Mary of Nazareth knew the pain that only a mother could feel; she knew the joy that only a totally selfless and giving woman of faith could experience.

Luke's Gospel reveals an uneducated adolescent who, in a dusty village in a small backwater of a conquered country, said, *Be it done to me according to your word,* stuck by that decision and changed the course of history. If Mary, the young unmarried pregnant girl, can believe in the incredible thing that she is to be a part of, if she can trust herself and believe in her role in the great story, than the most ordinary of us can believe in our parts in the drama, too.

[Adapted from *The Fire in the Thornbush* by Bishop Matthew H. Clark.]

In the new year 'of our Lord.'

G.K. Chesterton made this observation about New Year's: "The object of a new year is not that we should have a new year. It is that we should have a new soul and a new nose, new feet, a new backbone, new ears and new eyes."

Today a new year lies before us like a blank page or canvas. So many possibilities – much more than just the simple resolutions we are lucky to keep beyond the kick-off of today's first football game. But a whole new year, a new entity of time, begins today. We Christians believe that God has sanctified all time in his work of creation and his loving re-creation of the world in the Risen One. The God who makes all things new in Christ enables us to make this truly a *new* year for each one of us – a time for renewal and re-creation in the love of God, a time for making this year a year of peace in our lives and homes, a time for making this new year truly a "year of our Lord."

For reflection:

- In what ways is the Mary of the Gospels a real companion to us on our journey through the New Year?
- What was your "favorite year"? What made it a special time for you? How can you resolve to bring those elements into the New Year before you?
- Share the hopes, the challenges, the promises that the new year presents. How can we make this new year *anno Domini* – a "year of our Lord"?

Second Sunday after Christmas

Readings:

John 1: 1-18
Sirach 24: 1-4, 8-12
Ephesians 1: 3-6, 15-18

Today's readings call us to pause before the Bethlehem scene and contemplate the great destiny of the Child of Bethlehem.

The **Gospel**, the beautiful Prologue hymn to John's Gospel, with its echoes of Genesis 1 ("In the beginning . . .," "the light shines on in darkness . . ."), exalts Christ as the creative Word of God that comes as the new light to illuminate God's re-creation. In the original Greek text, the phrase "made his dwelling place among is" is more accurately translated as "pitched his tent or tabernacle." The image is also evoked by the teacher Ben Sira in today's **first reading**. In Sirach's hymn to the wisdom of God, holy wisdom is described as present before the Lord at the very beginning of creation and now present within the holy city. The writer's vision foreshadows Christ, God's Wisdom incarnate who, raised by God from the dead, continues, as John describes in his Gospel, to "make his dwelling place (literally, "pitched his tent") among us."

In his introduction to his letter to the Ephesians (today's **second reading**), Paul prays that the Christian community at Ephesus may receive the "spirit of wisdom" in order to realize the "great hope" to which God has called them in Christ Jesus.

Themes:

The 'wisdom' of God incarnate.

In the Child born of Mary at Bethlehem, the wisdom of God becomes real to us. His very birth manifests the constant and inexplicable love of God for his people, present for all time; his ministry as Messiah will teach us how we can transform humanity's dark night of sin and emptiness into the eternal day of God's peace and wholeness; his embracing of the cross will be the ultimate victory of holy wisdom over the Godless wisdom of the world.

The God who 'pitches his tent' among us.

Our God is a God constantly present to us in so many ways. He is present in the gifts of holy creation; he is present to all humanity in the birth of Christ; he is present in the Spirit of wisdom and goodness inspiring us to do the work of the Gospel; he is present to us in prayer and sacrament. The Messiah Jesus is the light who illuminates for us the life and presence of God, who reveals to us the great and unconditional love of God, the Creator who loves us like a parent loves his/her very own sons and daughters.

For reflection:

- How has God's "holy wisdom" influenced or changed or life?
- In what ways have you discovered the preeminence of "holy wisdom" over conventional wisdom?
- Where, when and how is God's "tent" pitched in your midst?

Epiphany

Readings:
Matthew 2: 1-12
Isaiah 60: 1-6
Ephesians 3: 2-3, 5-6

Today's **Gospel**, the story of the astrologers and the star of Bethlehem, is unique to Matthew's Gospel. Note that Matthew does not call them kings or "magi" but "astrologers," nor does he give their names or report where they came from – in fact, Matthew never even specifies the number of astrologers (because three gifts are reported, it has been a tradition since the fifth century to picture "three wise men"). In stripping away the romantic layers that have been added to the story, Matthew's point can be better understood.

A great many First Testament ideas and images are presented in this story. The star, for example, is reminiscent of Balaam's prophecy that "a star shall advance from Jacob" (Numbers 24: 17). Many of the details in Matthew's story about the child Jesus parallel the story of the child Moses and the Exodus.

Matthew's story also provides a preview of what is to come. First, the reactions of the various parties to the birth of Jesus augur the effects Jesus' teaching will have on those who hear it. Herod reacts with anger and hostility to the Jesus of the poor who comes to overturn the powerful and rich. The chief priests and scribes greet the news with haughty indifference toward the Jesus who comes to give new life and meaning to the rituals and laws of the scribes. But the astrologers – non-believers in the eyes of Israel – possess the humility of faith and the openness of mind and heart to seek and welcome the Jesus who will institute the Second Covenant between God and the New Israel.

Secondly, the gifts of the astrologers indicate the principal dimensions of Jesus' mission:

- *gold* is a gift fitting for a king, a ruler, one with power and authority;
- *frankincense* is a gift fitting for a priest, one who offers sacrifice (frankincense was an aromatic perfume sprinkled on the animals sacrificed in the Temple);
- *myrrh* is a fitting "gift" for some one who is to die (myrrh was used in ancient times for embalming the bodies of the dead before burial).

Today's **first reading**, from Trito-Isaiah (chapters 56-66), is a song of encouragement to the exiled Jews who are returning to Jerusalem from Babylon to rebuild their nation and their way of life. But Isaiah envisions more for the city than just its rebuilding: Jerusalem will be a light for all nations, a gathering place not only for the scattered Jews but for the entire world, where God will once again dwell in the midst of his faithful people Israel.

The letter to the Ephesians is Paul's "synthesis" on the nature of the Church. In today's **second reading**, Paul writes that the Church transcends national and cultural identities: in Christ, Jew and Gentile form one body and share equally in the promise of the Resurrection.

Themes:

A Messiah for all nations.

In Matthew's Gospel, it is the "Gentile" astrologers who discover the newborn "King of the Jews," while the people of the covenant (Herod, the chief priests and scribes) remain oblivious to his presence in their midst. The prophet Isaiah describes the Messiah as a "light for all nations" (first reading). In Christ, God is present in all of human history – God is not the exclusive property of one nation or people; no religious group holds title to the wonderful things God has done. Epiphany calls us to a new vision of the world that sees beyond walls and borders we have created and to walk by the light which has dawned for all of humankind, a light by which we are able to recognize *all* men and women as our brothers and sisters under the loving providence of God, the Father of all.

The search for God in our lives.

Cardinal Newman said that "to be earnest in seeking the truth is an essential requisite in finding it." The astrologers' following of the star is a journey of faith, a journey that each one of us experiences in the course of our own life. Christ's presence is not confined to Scripture and churches; he is present in everyone and everything that is good. We find the true purpose of this life in our search for God, the great Shepherd of our souls.

The 'stars' we follow.

What we read and watch and listen to in search of wealth, fame and power are the "stars" we follow. The journey of the astrologers in Matthew's Gospel puts our own "stargazing" in perspective. The astrologers set their sights on a star that leads them to God. Where will the our "stars" lead us?

For reflection:

- *Epiphany* comes from the Greek word meaning appearance or manifestation. Think about the "epiphanies" around us – the many ways the Lord "appears" or "manifests" his presence among us.
- How is your particular parish called to be "universal"? In what ways does the Gospel challenge your community to abandon the "safety" of itself to reach out to those considered "outside" of it (new immigrants, the poor, etc.)?
- A popular bumper sticker seen during this time of year reads: "Wise men still seek him." Who are the "wise" men and women in our world who have dedicated themselves to seeking Christ? What are their stories?

Readings: *Luke 3: 5-16, 21-22*
                     Isaiah 42: 1-4, 6-7
                     Acts 10: 34-38

Today's **Gospel** is the final of the Epiphany event: Jesus' baptism at the Jordan River by John.

Luke presents Jesus as the last person to be baptized by John, bringing John's ministry to completion. Luke describes the scene with many images from the First Testament:

- the sky opens ("Oh, that you would rend the heavens and come down . . ." – Isaiah 63: 19);
- the Spirit "descended upon him like a dove" (many rabbis likened the wind above the waters at the dawn of Genesis to a dove hovering above its newborn; in employing this image, Luke suggests that, in this Jesus, a new Genesis is about to take place);
- the "voice from heaven" identifies and confirms Jesus ("Here is my servant . . . my chosen one with whom I am pleased" – Isaiah 42: 1, today's first reading; "The Lord said to me, 'You are my Son; this day I have begotten you'" – Psalm 2: 7).

Jesus' baptism at the Jordan becomes the moment of God's "anointing" of his Messiah (the word *Messiah* means "anointed") for the work he is about to do.

Today's **first reading** is the first of the "servant songs" in Deutero-Isaiah in which the prophet tells of the "Servant" of God who will come to redeem Israel. In this first song, Isaiah speaks of the servant as God's "chosen one with whom I am pleased" – words that will be heard at the River Jordan.

Cornelius was a Roman centurion, a good and kind man who deeply respected and observed the high moral code and noble style of Judaic worship. In a dream, Cornelius is told to send for Peter and listen to what he has to say. Cornelius invites Peter to address his household. Peter's sermon (today's **second reading**) typifies early Christian preaching to the Gentiles: while God revealed his plan to his chosen nation of Israel, the Lord invites all people and nations to enter into the new covenant of the Risen Christ.

Themes:

Baptism: to become 'servants.'

We tend to view Baptism as an isolated milestone in our lives; but baptism is more than just a "naming" ceremony – it is an ongoing process that continues in every moment of our lives. In baptism, we are "grasped by the hand" of God (Reading 1) and "called" to become the servants of God; we are formed into God's holy people, a people who rise from the waters of baptism and, with the Spirit upon us, travel his road of justice and mercy to the fulfillment of the Resurrection. In baptism, we claim the name of "Christian" and embrace all that that holy name means: to live for others rather than for ourselves, in imitation of Christ. Our baptism makes each one of us the "servant" of today's readings: to bring forth in our world the justice, reconciliation and enlightenment of Christ, the "beloved Son" and "favor" of God.

The Spirit of God 'like a dove' upon us.

In all four Gospel accounts of Jesus' baptism, the evangelists use a similar description of the scene at the Jordan when Jesus is baptized by John: The Spirit of God descended and rested upon him "like a dove" – in other words, the Spirit of God resided within Jesus; that peace, compassion and love of God was a constant presence within the Carpenter from Nazareth. In baptism, we embrace that same Spirit – that same Spirit descends upon us giving direction and meaning to every moment of our lives.

The 'work' of Christmas begins.

The Christmas season officially comes to an end today at the banks of the Jordan River with Jesus' baptism by John. The glad tidings and good cheer of the holiday season are long over, Christmas has been packed away for the next 11 months and we can (finally) move on with our lives for another year. But the Messiah remains. Jesus is no longer the child in a Bethlehem manger but the adult Redeemer making his way to Jerusalem. The good news spoken by the angels continues to unfold; the most wondrous part of the Christ story is yet to be revealed. Today, the same Spirit that "anoints" the Messiah for his mission calls us to be about the *work* of Christmas in this new year: to seek out and find the lost, to heal the hurting, to feed the hungry, to free the imprisoned, to rebuild nations, to bring peace to all peoples everywhere.

For reflection:

- In practical terms, what does it mean to be the "servant" of God?
- Share stories about people you know upon whom "rests" the the Spirit of God.
- What "work" of Christmas remains to be done in your parish community? How have things changed – for the better and for the worse – since we celebrated Christmas?

Readings:

Matthew 6: 1-6, 16-18
Joel 2: 12-18
2 Corinthians 5: 20 – 6: 2

The readings for this first day of the Lenten journey to Easter call us to *turn*.

In Hebrew, the word for repentance is to *turn,* like the turning of the earth to the sun at this time of year, like the turning of soil before spring planting. The Lenten journey that begins on this Ash Wednesday calls us to repentance – to turn away from those things that separate us from God and re-turn to the Lord.

In today's **Gospel**, Jesus, in his Sermon on the Mount, instructs his listeners on the Christian attitude and disposition toward prayer, fasting and almsgiving. Such acts are meaningful only if they are outward manifestations of the essential *turning* that has taken place within our hearts.

Around 400 B.C., a terrible invasion of locusts ravaged Judah. The prophet Joel visualized this catastrophe as a symbol of the coming "Day of the Lord." The prophet summoned the people to repent, to *turn* to the Lord with fasting, prayer and works of charity (**first reading**).

In his second letter to the Corinthians, Paul alternates between anger and compassion, between frustration and affection in defending his authority and mandate as an apostle in the face of attack by some members of the Corinthian community. In today's **second reading**, the apostle appeals for reconciliation among the members of the community, a *return* to the one faith shared by the entire Church.

Themes:

Lenten 'turning': springtime rebirth.

During the next few weeks, the world around us will change dramatically: the days will grow longer and warmer; the ice and snow will melt away and the first buds of spring will appear; the raw winter iciness will be replaced by the warmth of summer; the drab grayness of winter will be transformed into the color and promise of spring. Likewise, the symbols of ashes and somberness that mark today's liturgy will be eclipsed in six weeks by the light and flowers and *Alleluias* of the Easter celebra-

tion. In fact, the very word "Lent" has come down to us from the ancient Anglo-Saxon word, *lencten,* meaning *springtime.*

The change we see around us should also be experienced *within* us during these weeks of Lent. We tend to approach Lent as something to be endured rather than to be observed, a time for *not* doing, for avoiding instead of as a time for *doing,* for *becoming;* but, like springtime, Lent should be a time for transformation, for change, for becoming the people that God has called to be. It is a time, as the prophet Joel proclaims in the first reading, for "rending our hearts, not our garments."

The ashes we receive today should be quiet symbols of something much deeper, much more powerful, much more lasting going on within us. In accepting these ashes we acknowledge the fact that we are sinners, that we are less than faithful to our baptismal name of Christian. But in accepting these ashes we also accept the challenge to become, as Paul writes to the Corinthians, "the very holiness of God."

Lenten 'turning': our 'desert' retreat.

The season of Lent that we begin today is a time to stop in the "busy-ness" of our everyday lives, to consider the truly important things in our lives, to realize the many blessings we possess in this world and the promised blessings of the next. Unfortunately, we have been conditioned to see Lent as a time for giving up and not doing, instead of as a time for doing and becoming. As Jesus began his ministry with a 40-day "retreat" in the desert wilderness, Lent should be our own "desert experience," a time to peacefully and quietly renew and re-create our relationship with God, that he might become the center of our lives in every season.

For reflection:

- Can the case be made that we *need* Lent?
- How can we Lent be made a time for doing, for becoming?
- What is your parish doing to make this a meaningful Lent for the community?
- What does the natural cycle of springtime teach us about the seasons of Lent and Easter?

First Sunday of Lent

Readings:

Luke 4: 1-13
Deuteronomy 26: 4-10
Romans 10: 8-13

The **Gospel** for this First Sunday of Lent is Luke's account of Jesus' desert experience. The desert here is more accurately understood as a wilderness – a dangerous, uncharted place, inhabited by wild beasts and bandits and believed to be haunted by demons.

Jesus' wilderness "retreat" is a time for discerning and understanding his mission as the Messiah. These 40 days are marked by intense prayer and fasting – not out of a sense of penance but to focus totally on God and the Father's will for him. The three temptations all confront Jesus with very human choices:

- *"command this stone to turn into bread"*: Will Jesus use his power for his own gratification and acclaim or to accomplish the will of God?
- *"prostrate yourself in homage to me"*: Will Jesus compromise the values of God to accommodate the values of the world?
- *"throw yourself down from here"*: Will Jesus pray that God will do Jesus' will rather than Jesus seeking God's will? Will Jesus seek to make God into Jesus' image or seek to become what God calls him to be?

Jesus' encounter with the devil depicts the struggle he experienced during this lonely and difficult time of coming to terms with the life that lay before him. Jesus then follows the Spirit obediently on to Galilee to begin his teaching ministry.

In today's **first reading**, from the Book of Deuteronomy ("second law"), recounts Moses' instructions to the Israelites for the offering of their "first fruits" to Yahweh. The offering is to made with a confession of faith and a prayer of humble gratitude to the Lord who led them to freedom and on whom they depend for everything that is good.

In the **second reading**, Paul assures the Romans that the mercy and forgiveness of God are offered to all men and women "who confess with [their] lips that Jesus is Lord." Regardless of how the world sees them, God sees everyone as his sons and daughters and hears their humble prayers.

Themes:

Lent: our own time of discernment.

After being baptized by John in the River Jordan, Jesus went off alone in the wilderness where he spent 40 days asking himself exactly what it meant to be the Christ, the Messiah. The same Spirit that led Jesus into the desert leads us into this 40-day "wilderness experience" of Lent, to ask ourselves the same kind of questions, to begin to understand who we are and who we are becoming. Lent is a time for us to discern what God calls us to be that we may re-center our lives at Easter with new hope and a renewed vision as we continue our journey to the dwelling place of God.

Lent: a time for making choices.

As Jesus was "tempted," so, too, are we confronted with the many different choices and goals life presents us. Every moment of our lives demands that we make hard choices – the fame, wealth, sex and power in the material world or the love, compassion, justice and mercy of the reign of God. Lent challenges us to examine the decisions we make and the value systems we employ in making those decisions.

For reflection:

- Both Jesus and the devil quote Scripture to support their positions in their encounter. What does their encounter say to us about the role of Scripture in making life choices?
- What roles do fasting, acts of penance and sacrifice for the poor play in Lent's call to the "wilderness"?
- What are some of the issues and decisions that life confronts us with that ultimately come down to a choice between the ways of God and the ways of the "devil"?
- What values do your struggle with in your life advocated by the "devil"?

Readings:

Luke 9: 28-36
Genesis 15: 5-12, 17-18
Philippians 3: 17 – 4: 1

Luke's account of the transfiguration (**Gospel**), is filled with First Testament imagery (the voice heard in the cloud, for example) that echoes the Exodus event. In Luke's Gospel, the transfiguration takes place after Jesus' instructions to his followers on the cost of discipleship. To follow Jesus is an "exodus" through one's own desert to the promised land, through Jerusalem to the empty tomb, through death to life. In offering to build three booths (or shrines) to honor Jesus, Moses and Elijah, Peter and his sleepy confreres do not understand that Jesus' exodus does not end with the glorious vision they have witnessed. It is only the beginning.

The Book of Genesis (**first reading**) tells the story of a nomadic chieftain named Abram who has a transforming religious experience at the city of Haram. Abram encounters Yahweh, who calls him to be the first patriarch of a new nation that Yahweh will raise up from Abram's (now Abraham) descendants. The elderly, childless Abraham sets aside whatever doubts and anxieties he has and trusts Yahweh completely. The Lord and his patriarch solemnize their covenant by enacting the covenant ritual of the ancients: the parties pass between the pieces of cut-up animals signifying that they would rather be destroyed like these carcasses than break this covenant.

Paul speaks to the Philippians of the passage from death to life (**second reading**). To those who remain faithful to their call to discipleship, God will transform their lives in the glory of his Son's Resurrection.

Themes:

Becoming agents of transfiguration.

The season of Lent calls us to *transfiguration* – to transform the coldness, sadness and despair around us through the compassion and love of Christ Jesus. Archbishop Desmond Tutu said that "God places us in the world as God's fellow workers – agents of transfiguration. We work with God so that injustice is transfigured into justice, so that there will be more compassion and caring, that there will be more laughter and joy, that there will be more togetherness in God's world."

The beginning of Jesus' 'exodus' experience.

The transfiguration of Jesus is a turning point in the Gospel – from the mountaintop Jesus journeys to Jerusalem and the climactic events of Holy Week. It is the beginning of a new exodus, Jesus's difficult "Passover" from crucifixion to resurrection. As his disciples, we, too, are called to experience this 'exodus' of Jesus. It is a difficult passage, an exodus that confronts us with the impermanence of this world and our own sinfulness; but it is a journey we travel to the very life of God.

For reflection:

- In what ways can we be "agents of transfiguration"?
- How are our lives like the Exodus experience of the Israelites?
- Have you experienced times of great suffering or turmoil that enriched your life, enabling you to do greater things?

Third Sunday of Lent

Readings:

Luke 13: 1-9
Exodus 3: 1-8, 13-15
1 Corinthians 10: 1-6, 10-12

The belief prevailed in Jesus' time that disasters and catastrophes were signs of God's anger against sinful individuals or people – those massacred in the temple by Pilate's soldiers during what the Romans perceived as a "revolt" and the workers who were killed when the tower they were building collapsed must have been horrible sinners. Nonsense, Jesus says in today's **Gospel**. In this present age, neither good fortune nor calamity are indicators of one's favor or disfavor with God. In the age to come, God will judge the hearts of every soul, regardless of their situation in life.

The parable of the fig tree is a parable of crisis and compassion:

- The fig tree draws strength and sustenance from the soil but produces nothing in return. Its only value is as firewood. A similar fate awaits those who squander their lives in greedy, selfish pursuits.
- God is the ever patient gardener who gives every "fig tree" all the time, care and attention it needs to harvest.

On the scorched desert plain, it was not uncommon for a piece of dried sagebrush to catch fire and quickly burn itself out. But the burning bush Moses witnesses (today's **first reading**) is not reduced to ashes but continues to burn brilliantly. In the burning bush, God reveals himself as the Holy One who transcends time and space ("I AM") and calls Moses to lead the Israelites out of their bondage to a "land flowing with milk and honey."

In today's **second reading**, Paul invokes the memory of Israel's Exodus to admonish the new Israel, the Church, to remain faithful on their exodus to the reign of the Risen Christ.

Themes:

The fig tree: the Gospel of the 'second chance.'

The parable of the fig tree has been called the "Gospel of the second chance." The vinedresser pleads for the tree, asking that it be given another year to bear fruit. We always live in the hope and mercy of God who keeps giving us "second chances" to rise from the ashes of sin to rebuild and reform our lives. God's love knows neither limits nor conditions; since the calls of Abraham and Moses, God continues to call his people back to him, despite their – and our – unfaithfulness and obtuseness. The only adequate response we can make to such spendthrift forgiveness from our God is to be as forgiving of one another and as supportive as we can be of those struggling through their second, third and however of many chances.

The fig tree: faith that takes 'root' within us.

All too often we approach faith in terms of externals only: we put in our time on Sundays, we contribute our weekly offering, we say the specified prayers. But unless that faith takes root within us and becomes not just the rituals we perform but the values that inspire them, then we are like the barren fig tree in the vineyard: lifeless, giving nothing to others, good only for firewood. God speaks to us not in cold stone tablets but in fire; he calls out not just to our sense of reason and rationalism but to our hearts and spirits; he seeks not just our assent but our commitment.

For reflection:

- Have you ever known anyone who just never seems to be able to get his/her life together, whom you just had to keep rescuing, picking up, bailing out of trouble? What did that person teach you about the Gospel of the fig tree?
- What practice or expression of your faith is most meaningful to you?
- Where have you been most surprised to discover the forgiveness and reconciling love of God?
- Many organizations come together to do good works. How does the Church differ in its approach to charity, morality and philanthropy?

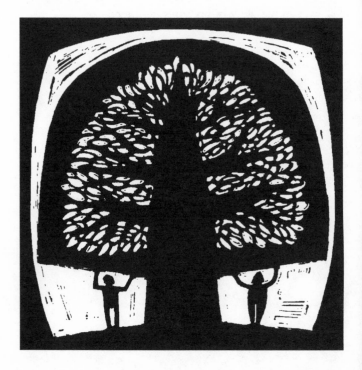

Fourth Sunday of Lent

Readings:
Luke 15: 1-3, 11-32
Joshua 5: 9, 10-12
2 Corinthians 5: 17-21

The parable of prodigal son, as today's **Gospel** is commonly known, is probably the most inaccurately titled story in all of literature. Jesus' tale tells us less about the boy's sin than about the abundant mercy of his father who forgives his son and joyfully welcomes him home even before the son can bring himself to ask. The father's joy stands in sharp contrast to the prodigal son's brother, who cannot even bring himself to call the prodigal his "brother" – in confronting his father, he angrily refers to the brother as "this son of yours." This parable of forgiveness and reconciliation (found only in Luke's Gospel) reveals a God of such great love that he cannot bear the loss of a single child. Jesus holds up the father – and *Father* – as models of the love and forgiveness we should seek in all relationships.

In today's **first reading**, the nomadic Israelites settle into the land of promise. They celebrate the Lord's eternal and endless love with their first Passover feast taken from the produce of their new homeland.

Paul praises Christ, in today's **second reading**, as the perfect agent of God's reconciliation of himself to us and to all of creation. The God who created everything out of nothing re-creates us anew, making of us, however unpromising and undeserving, sharers of his life. Christ calls us to this same "ministry of reconciliation."

Themes:

The prodigal: coming home.

The story of the prodigal son is a story about coming home. It is a parable about what makes our home special and unique places – places where we always belong, where we are always welcome, where we can always start over. God, before whom all of us are "prodigals," calls us to make our homes, parishes and communities places of patient, compassionate, unconditional love – places where the prodigals are always welcomed home with love and understanding.

The prodigal's father: the 'ministry of reconciliation.'

God calls us to the *work* of reconciliation: to actively seek the restoration of relationship and community with those whom we have hurt and with those who have hurt us. The father in today's Gospel parable is held up by Jesus as a model of the minister of reconciliation. Note that when he catches sight of his son in the distance, the father *runs* to greet and embrace him before the prodigal can even open his mouth to begin his carefully rehearsed speech. The father welcomes his son joyfully and completely, with no recriminations, no conditions, no rancor. Christ calls us to the "ministry of reconciliation" (second reading): to dedicate ourselves to seeking forgiveness and reconciliation with one another as God seeks with us.

The prodigal's brother: rejoicing in the return of the lost.

Jesus calls us not to condemn or gloat or belittle the prodigals among us but to enable their return, to keep picking them up no matter how many times they fall, to open our arms and welcome them back again and again and again. To forgive as God forgives – without rancor or recriminations, with joy and gratitude – is a radical act, an act of liberation. Dag Hammarskjold articulated this dimension of forgiveness when he wrote in what would become his book *Markings*: "Forgiveness breaks the chain of causality, because he who 'forgives' you – out of love – takes upon himself the consequences of what you have done. Forgiveness, therefore, always entails sacrifice. The price you must pay for your own liberation through another's sacrifice is that you, in turn, must be willing to liberate in the same way, irrespective of the consequences to yourself."

For reflection:

- Have you ever known someone who always readily offered you complete acceptance and forgiveness?
- Truth be told, most of us identify not with the prodigal son or the father in the parable, but with the older brother. Why?
- How can forgiveness be liberating? How can reconciliation be a beginning, a source of "new" life?
- What makes your home the unique, special place it is?

Fifth Sunday of Lent

Readings:

John 8: 1-11
Isaiah 43: 16-21
Philippians 3: 8-14

The story of the adulteress is a later addition to John's **Gospel.** A cherished tale from the then rich oral history of Jesus' life, it was added to John's text probably in the third century.

Once again, the scribes and Pharisees set up a trap to discredit Jesus. According to the Mosaic code, adultery was considered among the gravest of sins, punishable by death; but the law of the Roman occupiers forbade the Jewish authorities to impose and carry out the death sentence on anyone. The dilemma facing Jesus, then, is this: If Jesus condemns the woman, he undermines his own teachings on forgiveness and puts him in conflict with the Roman authority; if he does not condemn her, he breaks faith with the covenant Law.

Jesus' response to their hypocrisy challenges the Jews' understanding of judgment and authority:

- God reserves the role of judging others to himself; to us belongs the work of forgiveness and reconciliation. God's commandments are addressed to each one of us as individuals to keep. We are called to judge our own actions and pass sentence on our own lives.
- While the scribes and Pharisees view authority as a license to criticize, ensnare and condemn this woman, Jesus sees authority as a gift for transforming her life and reconciling her with God.

"Exodus" is not a single historical event but a pattern of history, a passage from death to life. In today's **first reading**, Isaiah proclaims a "new" exodus experience of forgiveness and reconciliation.

The apostle Paul recounts for his Philippian brothers and sisters (**second reading**) his joyful "forfeiting" of everything ("rubbish") in order to know the Risen Christ and how he continues to live in hope that the "prize" of life in Christ Jesus might be his.

Themes:

The spirit of the law 'written on our hearts.'

Jesus' confrontation with the woman's accusers challenges their (and our) belief that to be "law abiding" is enough. Jesus calls us not simply to follow the "Law" but to embrace the *spirit* of the Law: not to demand rigid adherence and conformity but to seek instead mutual understanding, forgiveness and reconciliation; not to be satisfied with condemning the sinful and fallen but to work to bring forth resurrection from the ashes of their sin through understanding and reconciliation.

Recognizing our own sinfulness.

The season of Lent calls us to recognize our own sinfulness, our own culpability for our actions, our own responsibility for our less than holy attitudes and values and our own need for redemption and resurrection. Confronting the demons of the world must begin with confronting the demons in our own hearts. We cannot change what is beyond us until we change what is within us; we cannot lift up the fallen until we realize that we, too, are fallen; we cannot raise others to health and hope until we seek our own healing; we cannot pass sentence on others until we judge our own lives.

For reflection:

- What issues have you confronted in your life that demanded more than a "legalistic" approach or answer?
- What are the practical applications of the proverb, "Hate the sin, love the sinner"?
- When have you been confronted with your own need to take responsibility for your own culpability in a situation?

Passion (Palm) Sunday

Readings: *Blessing and Procession of Palms:*
Luke 19: 28-40
Liturgy of the Word: Luke 22: 14 – 23: 56
Isaiah 50: 4-7
Philippians 2: 6-11

Typical of his **Gospel**, Luke's account of Jesus' entry into Jerusalem portrays the coming of a Messiah of peace. The kings of antiquity rode horses when they came in war, but entering Jerusalem on an ass indicates the "kingship" of peace and service that Jesus has come to exercise. The crowds who welcome Jesus into the city greet him with words similar to the song of the angels in Luke's nativity narrative: "Peace in heaven and glory in the highest!"

Another uniquely Lucan detail is the fact that the people do not wave palm branches as Jesus enters Jerusalem. Luke's crowds place their single most valuable piece of clothing – their cloaks – on the ground to honor Jesus. The holy poor of Luke's narrative place all that they have at the disposal of their Messiah-king.

Throughout his Gospel, Luke's Jesus has preached the joy of humble servanthood. In his final hours, Jesus exhibits that same great generosity, compassion and forgiving spirit: Only in Luke's account of the **Passion** does Jesus heal the severed ear of the high priest's servant. He does not rebuke his disciples for falling asleep during the garden watch. He urges the women of Jerusalem not to be concerned for him but for themselves: if such injustice can befall the innocent Jesus (the "green wood"), what horrors await an unrepentant ("dry") Jerusalem? At the Place of the Skull, Jesus' crucifixion becomes an occasion for divine forgiveness: he prays that God will forgive his executioners and promises paradise to the penitent thief crucified with him. Even Jesus' final words on the cross are not words of abandonment but of hope: Luke's Crucified does not cry out Psalm 22 (as he does in Matthew and Mark's narrative) but prays Psalm 31: 5-6: "Father, into your hands I commend my spirit." Luke's Jesus is the Suffering Servant whose death for the sake of humanity will be exalted in the Resurrection three days hence.

The **first reading** is taken from Deutero-Isaiah's "Servant songs," the prophet's foretelling of the "servant of God" who will come to redeem Israel. In this third song, Isaiah portrays the servant as a devoted teacher of God's Word who is ridiculed and abused by those who are threatened by his teaching.

In his letter to the Christian community at Philippi (in northeastern Greece), Paul quotes what many scholars believe is an early Christian hymn (**second reading**). As Christ totally and unselfishly "emptied himself" to accept crucifixion for our sakes, so we must "empty" ourselves for others.

Themes:

The faith we profess and the faith we live.

There is a certain incongruity about today's Palm Sunday Liturgy. We begin with a sense of celebration – we carry palm branches and echo the *Hosannas* (from the Hebrew for *God save [us]*) shouted by the people of Jerusalem as Jesus enters the city. But Luke's account of the Passion confronts us with the cruelty, injustice and selfishness that leads to the crucifixion of Jesus. We welcome the Christ of victory, the Christ of Palm Sunday; but we turn away from the Christ of suffering and of the poor, the Christ of Good Friday. These branches of palm are symbols of that incongruity that often exists between the faith we profess on our lips and the faith we profess in our lives.

To live for others as Christ died for us.

Luke portrays, in his account of Jesus' death, a Christ of extraordinary compassion and love, who forgives those who betray and destroy him, who consoles those who grieve for him, whose final breaths give comfort and hope to a condemned criminal who seeks reconciliation with God. The broken yet life-giving body of the Crucified Jesus calls us to embrace that same "attitude" of Christ: to move beyond our own brokenness and pain in order to bring healing, reconciliation and hope to all the broken members of his body.

The 'attitude' of Christ, the 'Suffering Servant.'

The Gospel calls us to take on the "attitude of Christ Jesus" in his passion and death: to "empty" ourselves of our own interests, fears and needs for the sake of others; to realize how our actions affect *them* and how our moral and ethical decisions impact the common good; to reach out to heal the hurt and comfort the despairing around us despite our own betrayal; to carry on, with joy and in hope, despite rejection, humiliation and suffering. The celebration of Holy Week calls us to embrace the attitude of Christ's compassion and total selflessness, becoming servants of God by being servants to one another.

For reflection:

- Have you known individuals who have exhibited great compassion and sensitivity to others despite their own suffering and pain?
- In what ways are we confronted today with the reality of the cross?
- How is Christ's "attitude," as articulated in Paul's hymn in Philippians, the antithesis to the "attitude" of today's world?
- Which character in Luke's Passion narrative do you identify with especially? What is it about their heroism – or failure – before the cross that strikes you?

Holy Thursday

Readings: *John 13: 1-15*
Exodus 12: 1-8, 11-14, 1 Corinthians 11: 23-26

The centerpiece of John's **Gospel** account of the Last Supper is the *mandatum* – from the Latin word for "commandment," from which comes our term for this evening, *Maundy* Thursday. At the Passover seder, the night before he died, Jesus established a new Passover to celebrate God's covenant with the new Israel. The special character of this second covenant is the *mandatum* of the washing of the feet – to love one another as we have been loved by Christ.

(John makes no mention of the establishment of the Eucharist in his account of the Last Supper. The Johannine theology of the Eucharist is detailed in the "bread of life" discourse following the multiplication of the loaves and fish at Passover, in chapter 6 of his Gospel.)

Tonight's **first reading** recounts the origin and ritual of the feast of Passover, the Jewish celebration of God breaking the chains of the Israelites' slavery in Egypt and leading them to their own land, establishing a covenant with them and making of them a people of his own.

The deep divisions in the Corinthian community have led to abuses and misunderstandings concerning the "breaking of the bread." In addressing these problems and articulating the proper spirit in which to approach the Lord's Supper, Paul provides us with the earliest written account of the institution of the Eucharist, the Passover of the new covenant (this evening's **second reading**). If we fail to embrace the spirit of love and servanthood in which the gift of the Eucharist is given to us, then "Eucharist" becomes a judgment against us.

Themes:

Becoming 'Eucharist' for one another.

Tonight's liturgy is like a song that is out of tune or a photograph out of focus. Things are "out of sync" tonight. Jesus' last Passover seder sinks into betrayal, denial and abandonment. The holy kiss of peace is desecrated. While his twelve closest friends carry on a petty squabble over who is the greatest among them, Jesus gives them the gift of perfect unity, the Eucharist. With his ultimate triumph at hand, Jesus stuns his disciples by washing their feet – a humiliating task usually relegated to the lowliest of slaves – as a model of the selfless love that should characterize the new community of the Resurrection.

True, this is the night on which the Lord Jesus gave us himself in the Eucharist and instituted the ministerial priesthood. But there are shadows: the joy of the Eucharist is shadowed by Christ's challenge to become Eucharist for one another; the authority and dignity of priesthood is shadowed by the stark command to "wash one another's feet" not as overseers but as servants.

As we gather to remember the night of the Last Supper, we confront how "out of sync," how shadowed our lives are in relation to the life to which God calls us. We partake of the Eucharist tonight vowing to become the body of Christ to our hurting world and renewing our baptismal promise to become the priestly people of the new Israel – to do for others as our Teacher and Lord has done for us.

The parable of the 'Mandatum.'

Tonight, the Rabbi who taught in parables teaches what is perhaps his most touching and dramatic parable.

In the middle of the meal, Jesus – the revered Teacher, the Worker of miracles and wonders, the Rabbi the crowds wanted to make a king just a few days before – suddenly rises from his place as presider, removes his robe, wraps a towel around his waist and – like the lowliest of slaves – begins to wash the feet of the Twelve. We can sense the shock that must have shot through that room. But, quietly, Jesus goes about the task. Jesus on his knees, washing the dirt and dust off the feet of the fisherman, then the tax collector, and so on. Despite Peter's embarrassment and inability to comprehend what is happening, Jesus continues the humiliating and degrading task.

The Teacher, who revealed the wonders of God in stories about mustard seeds, fishing nets and ungrateful children, on this last night of his life – as we know life – leaves his small band of disciples his most beautiful parable: As I, your Teacher and Lord, have done for you, so you must do for one another. As I have washed your feet like a slave, so you must wash the feet of each other and serve one another. As I have loved you without limit or condition, so you must love one another without limit or condition. As I am about to suffer and die for you, so you must suffer and, if necessary, die for one another.

Tonight's parable is so simple, but its lesson is so central to what being a real disciple of Christ is all about. When inspired by the love of Christ, the smallest act of service done for another takes on extraordinary dimensions.

For reflection:

- How can we be "Eucharist" to one another?
- In what ways can we "wash the feet" of others?
- Consider the ways our faith is "out of sync" with our human experience.
- Explore the range of emotions that are present both in the scene depicted in tonight's Gospel and in the elements of tonight's liturgy.

Good Friday

Readings:
John 18:1 – 19:42
Isaiah 52:13 – 53:12
Hebrews 4:14-16; 5:7-9

John's deeply theological **Passion** account portrays a Jesus who is very much aware of what is happening to him. His eloquent self-assurance unnerves the high priest and intimidates Pilate ("You have no power over me"), who shuttles back and forth among the various parties involved, desperately trying to avoid condemning this innocent holy man to death. Hanging on the cross, Jesus entrusts his mother to his beloved disciple, thus leaving behind the core of a believing community. He does not cry out the psalm of the abandoned (Psalm 22); rather, his final words are words of decision and completion: "It is finished." The crucifixion of Jesus, as narrated by John, is not a tragic end but the beginning of victory, the lifting up of the Perfect Lamb to God for the salvation of humankind.

Isaiah's fourth and final oracle of the "servant of God" (today's **first reading**) is a hauntingly accurate description of the sufferings that the innocent one will endure to atone for the sins of his people. Only in Jesus Christ is Isaiah's prophecy perfectly fulfilled.

The priesthood and sacrifice of Jesus are the themes of the letter to the Hebrews (scholars are unanimous in their belief that this letter, while reflecting Pauline Christology, was not written by Paul himself). The verses taken for today's **second reading** acclaim Jesus, Son of God and Son of Man, as the perfect mediator between God and humankind.

Themes:

The broken body of Christ.

The broken body of Jesus – humiliated, betrayed, scourged, abused, slain – is the central image of today's liturgy. Today, Jesus teaches us through his own broken body.

As a Church, as a community of faith, we are the body of Christ. But we are a broken body. We minister as broken people to broken people. The suffering, the alienated, the unaccepted, the rejected, the troubled, the confused are all part of this broken body of Christ.

This is the day to reflect on the reality of pain and suffering. This is the day to realize that the source of such brokenness – sin – is also a reality. But the "goodness" of "Good" Friday teaches us that there are other realities. For us who believe, the broken body of Christ is forever transformed into the full and perfect life of the Risen Christ. In conquering life's injustices and difficulties, we are healed and made whole in the reality of the Resurrection.

The cross: the tree of life.

Actually, it is a plank hoisted up on a pole anchored in the ground, but the wood of the cross is nevertheless a life-giving tree.

The tree of Good Friday repulses us, horrifies us and, possibly, shames us. The tree that is the center of today's liturgy confronts us with death and humiliation, with the injustice and betrayal of which we are all capable.

But through the tree of the cross we are reborn. The tree of defeat becomes the tree of victory. Where life was lost, there life will be restored. The tree of Good Friday will blossom anew, bringing life, not death; bringing light that shatters centuries of darkness; bringing Paradise, not destruction.

Crucifying the 'problem' Jesus.

This Jesus had become a problem. His ramblings about love and forgiveness and neighbor were fine, up to a point; but things were getting out of hand. To the highly sensitive leaders of Judaism his parable about "Good" Samaritans (!), his associating with prostitutes and tax collectors, his scorning of the intricate traditions of the cherished Law threatened the very foundation of their Jewish identity and society. So, very methodically and quite legally, a strategy developed. Even a fall-back plan – co-opting the Roman government – was set into motion. The result: The problem is "solved" on a cross on the outskirts of the town.

Two millennia later, Good Friday confronts us with the reality that the crucifixion of the "problem" Jesus takes place again and again in our own time and place:

- when people's lives and futures are cast aside for the sake of profit or political expediency, the problem Jesus is crucified again;
- when self-righteous anger stifles compassionate charity and strangles efforts at healing reconciliation, the problem Jesus is crucified again;
- when unjust laws and dehumanizing social systems are allowed to continue because "I've got mine," the problem Jesus is crucified again.

Good Friday calls us to follow the "problem" Jesus, "to die with him so that we may also rise with him."

For reflection:

- Have you experienced, in your own life, suffering that has been, somehow, life-giving?
- How is each one of us a member of the broken body of Christ?
- Where is the crucifixion of Jesus taking place now, in our own time and place?

Readings:

Gospel: Luke 24: 1-12
First Testament Readings: Genesis 1: 1 – 2:2
Genesis 22: 1-18
Exodus 14: 15 – 15: 1
Isaiah 54: 5-14
Isaiah 55: 1-11
Baruch 3: 9-15, 32 – 4: 4
Ezekiel 36: 16-28
Epistle: Romans 6: 3-11

Luke's Easter **Gospel** brings to completion the ancient prophecies foretold concerning the Messiah. The two men "in dazzling white garments" at the tomb invite the terrified women to "*remember* what he said to you."

Remember – not the mere recollection of a previous conversation but to understand with new and deepened insight the meaning of a past action and bringing its power and meaning into the present. It is in such creative and living "remembering" that the Church of the Resurrection is formed.

Typical of Luke, women – who possessed no true autonomy, whose testimony was considered of little value before a Jewish court – are the first proclaimers of the Easter Gospel. Sure enough, the disciples refuse to believe their wild story (in his original Greek text, the physician Luke describes the women's story as the excited babbling of a fevered and insane mind). Peter alone goes to investigate; Luke writes that Peter is "amazed" at what he sees, but still does not understand what has happened.

The **First Testament readings** all recount God's first creation and covenant with the people of Israel. In the passion, death and resurrection of his Son, the faithful God re-creates creation and vows a new covenant to his people.

Paul's **Epistle** to the Romans includes this brief catechesis on the Easter sacrament: in baptism, we die with Christ to our sinfulness and we rise with him to the life of God.

Themes:

The resurrection: a new creation.

Did the universe begin with a bang or a whimper? Is God the master firemaker who ignited a big bang that set creation on its journey through the cosmos? Or is God the meticulous craftsman who carefully formed one single cell – a thousandfold smaller than a single particle of dust – that contained within its microscopic walls the power to give birth to planets and stars and plants and animals – and us?

The scientists among us journey to the last frontiers of thought to discover how creation began. But the point is: it began. God set it all in motion. **The first Genesis.**

Nobody saw Jesus leave the tomb. Nobody saw life return to the crucified body. Nobody saw the massive stone roll away. Theories abound, scenarios have been devised to explain it away. Some say that the apostles stole the body – but could that band of hapless fishermen and peasants devise such a hoax? Maybe Jesus didn't die – maybe he revived three days later. But re-read the events of Good Friday. He didn't have a chance. Ponder the whys and hows, but you cannot escape the reality: the empty tomb, the eyewitness accounts of his appearances to Mary, Peter, the disciples traveling to Emmaus, the Eleven. Jesus is risen. **The second Genesis.**

On this night in early spring, we celebrate God's new creation. Death is no longer the ultimate finality but the ultimate beginning. The Christ who taught forgiveness, who pleaded for reconciliation, who handed himself over to his executioners for the sake of justice and mercy, has been raised up by God. We leave behind in the grave our sinfulness, our dark side, our selfishness, our pettiness – the evil that mars God's first creation.

Tonight, we join our renewed hearts and re-created voices in the "Alleluia!" of the new creation.

The presence of the 'Living One.'

The Risen Christ is present to us in the faithful witness of many good people who share the good news of the empty tomb by their day-to-day living of the Gospel of compassion and reconciliation. Like Mary Magdalene and her companions, we can bring into the darkness of our own time and place the joyful light of the Resurrection; into the cold, spiritless winter around us, we can bring the warmth and hope of the Easter promise.

For reflection:

- Who are the Mary Magdalenes, Johannas and Marys among us whose lives joyfully and excitedly proclaim today the good news of Easter's empty tomb?
- Tonight we celebrate with symbols: fire (light), story (Scripture), water (baptism) and bread (Eucharist). What do these symbols teach us about the Paschal mystery?
- How do we experience the presence of the "Living One" in our time and place?
- How would our lives be different if tonight had never happened?

Easter Sunday

Readings:
John 20: 1-9
Acts 10: 34, 37-43
Colossians 3: 1-4
or 1 Corinthians 5: 6-8

[NOTE: The Gospel for the Easter Vigil may be read in place of John 20: 1-9.]

John's Easter **Gospel** says nothing of earthquakes or angels. His account begins before daybreak. It was believed that the spirit of the deceased hovered around the tomb for three days after burial; Mary Magdalene was therefore following the Jewish custom of visiting the tomb during this three-day period. Discovering that the stone has been moved away, Mary Magdalene runs to tell Peter and the others. Peter and the "other disciple" race to get there and look inside.

Note the different reactions of the three: Mary Magdalene fears that someone has "taken" Jesus' body; Peter does not know what to make of the news; but the "other" disciple – the model of faithful discernment in John's Gospel – immediately understands what has taken place. So great are the disciple's love and depth of faith that all of the strange remarks and dark references of Jesus now become clear to him.

In this sermon recorded in Luke's Acts (**first reading**), Peter preaches the good news of the "Christ event" to the Gentile household of Cornelius. The resurrection of Jesus is the ultimate sign of God's love for all of humanity. The apostles' mandate to preach the Gospel is about to cross into the Gentile world beyond Jerusalem.

The imprisoned Paul writes (**second reading: Colossians**) that because we are baptized into Christ's death and resurrection, our lives should be re-centered in new values, in the things of heaven.

Paul's first letter to the Corinthians includes one of the earliest Easter homilies in Christian literature (**second reading: 1 Corinthians**). The custom in many Jewish households at Passover was to discard old yeast (leaven) and bake new unleavened bread for the feast. For Paul, this is a fitting symbol for the Christian community at Corinth: They must rid themselves of the self-centeredness and corruption which destroys their community and, together, share "the unleavened bread of sincerity and truth."

Themes:

The empty tomb: reason to hope.

While the Easter mystery does not deny the reality of suffering and pain, it does proclaim reason for hope in the human condition. The empty tomb of Christ trumpets the ultimate *Alleluia* – that love, compassion, generosity, humility and selflessness will ultimately triumph over hatred, bigotry, prejudice, despair, greed and death. The Easter miracle enables us, even in the most difficult and desperate of times, to live our lives in hopeful certainty of the fulfillment of the Resurrection at the end of our life's journey.

The empty tomb: the ultimate victory.

Today we stand, with Peter and John and Mary, at the entrance of the empty tomb; with them, we wonder what it means. The Christ who challenged us to love one another is risen and walks among us! All that he taught – compassion, love, forgiveness, reconciliation, sincerity, selflessness for the sake of others – is vindicated and affirmed in the Father raising him from the dead. The empty tomb should not only console us and elate us, it should challenge us to embrace the life of the Gospel. With Easter faith, we can awaken the promise of the empty tomb in every place and moment we encounter on our journey through this life.

The Church: the Resurrection community.

The Risen Christ is present to us in the faithful witness of every good person who shares the good news of the empty tomb by their living of the Gospel of selflessness and compassion. The empty tomb should inspire us to bring resurrection into this life of ours: to rise above life's sufferings and pain to give love and life to others, to renew and re-create our relationships with others, to proclaim the Gospel of *Christ who died, Christ who has risen, Christ who will come again!*

For reflection:

- Have any stories in the news this week struck you as examples of resurrection in our own time – of bringing hope, new life, new possibilities to once dark, hopeless places?
- Where is the Risen Lord present among us? How is the good news of the Risen Jesus proclaimed in the faithfulness and compassionate charity of people around you?
- How should our belief in the empty tomb affect our everyday outlook and attitudes?

Second Sunday of Easter

Readings:

John 20: 19-31
Acts 5: 12-16
Revelation 1: 9-11, 12-13, 17-19

The **Gospel** for the Second Sunday of Easter (for all three years of the Lectionary cycle) is Act 2 of John's Easter drama.

Scene 1 takes place on Easter night. The terrified disciples are huddled together, realizing that they are marked men because of their association with the criminal Jesus. The Risen Jesus appears in their midst with his greeting of "peace." John clearly has the Genesis story in mind when the evangelist describes Jesus as "breathing" the Holy Spirit on his disciples: Just as God created man and woman by breathing life into them (Genesis 2: 7), the Risen Christ re-creates humankind by breathing the new life of the Holy Spirit upon the eleven.

In scene 2, the disciples excitedly tell the just-returned Thomas of what they had seen. Thomas responds to the news with understandable skepticism. Thomas had expected the cross (see John 11: 16 and 14: 5) – and no more.

The climactic third scene takes place one week later, with Jesus' second appearance to the assembled community – this time with Thomas present. He invites Thomas to examine his wounds and to "believe." Christ's blessing in response to Thomas' profession of faith exalts the faith of every Christian of every age who "believes without seeing"; all Christians who embrace the Spirit of the Risen One possess a faith that is in no way different or inferior from that of the first disciples. The power of the resurrection transcends time and place.

The first readings for the Sundays of the Easter seasons are taken from Luke's Acts of the Apostles. Acts has been called the "Gospel of the Holy Spirit" because it recounts how the Spirit of God was at work forming this small group on the fringes of Judaism into the new Israel, the Church of the Risen Christ. Today's **first reading** is one of several brief "snapshots" Luke includes of the Jerusalem Church and the great works the apostles accomplished in the name of the Risen Jesus.

On the Sundays of this (Year C) Easter season, the second readings are taken from the mystical Book of Revelation. Tradition holds that the book was written around 95 A.D., in the wake of the great persecution of Christians during the reign of the emperor Domitian. Revelation is a collection of the visions and prophecies of "John" (not the evangelist), who introduces himself as a Christian exiled for his witness to the Risen One to the sparsely inhabited island of Patmos in the Aegean Sea.

In today's **second reading**, John writes of his Sunday vision of the triumphant "Son of Man" who has conquered death and now lives forever.

The Book of Revelation is filled with symbolism. The number "seven" (in today's reading: the seven lampstands of gold) is a biblical symbol of completeness and fullness. It has also been suggested that the writer of Revelation is appropriating the Romans' sacred portrait of the emperor holding seven stars, for the number of known planets. Christ is envisioned by "John" here as the triumphant Redeemer whom God has exalted as sovereign over the entire universe.

Themes:

Called to be Easter communion and community.

The Risen Christ calls us to communion with God through him and to community with one another. We trace our roots as parish and faith communities to Easter night when Jesus "breathed" his spirit of peace and reconciliation upon his frightened disciples, transforming them into the new Church; today's first reading from Acts is a snapshot of the ideal of the Church they became. Jesus' gift of peace and his entrusting to the disciples the work of forgiveness are what it means to be a church, a parish, a community of faith: to accept one another, to affirm one another, to support one another as God has done for us in the Risen Christ. What brought the apostles and first Christians together as a community – unity of heart, missionary witness, prayer, reconciliation and healing – no less powerfully binds us to one another as the Church of today.

Transforming skepticism into trust.

All of us, at one time or another, experience the doubt and skepticism of Thomas. While we have heard the good news of Jesus' empty tomb, all of our fears, problems and sorrows overwhelm us and prevent us from realizing it in our own lives. In raising his beloved Son from the dead, God also raises our spirits to the realization of the totality and limitlessness of his love for us. As Thomas experiences, Easter transforms our crippling sense of skepticism and cynicism into a sense of trust and hope in one providence of God.

For reflection:

- Have you ever known someone (or yourself) whose life was almost swallowed up in destructive skepticism, cynicism or despair? How was that skepticism transformed into hope and trust?
- In what ways is your parish community like – or can become like – the first Christian communities portrayed in today's readings?
- How can we "breathe" new life into situations and relationships?

Readings: *John 21: 1-19*
                       Acts 5: 27-32, 40-41
                       Revelation 5: 11-14

Chapter 21 is a kind of "appendix" to John's Gospel – John 20: 30-31 seems to be the original ending of the Gospel. The events recorded in Chapter 21 may have been included to challenge those who doubted the physical resurrection of Jesus, who believed that what the disciples saw were visions or hallucinations. Here the Risen Jesus is a very real and physical presence who points to the fish, lights the fire, cooks and serves the fish.

Today's **Gospel** records two events that take place at the Sea of Tiberias after the Resurrection. In a scene reminiscent of Luke 5: 1-11, Peter and a group of apostles have been fishing all night and have caught nothing. At daybreak Jesus appears on shore and tells them to try casting their net on the starboard side. The catch is a living parable of the Church's apostolic activity: the number 153 is probably intended as a universal number (some have suggested that it represents the number of known species of fish at the time), indicating the Church's mission to all men and women; the unbroken net may also be seen as a symbol of the new Church.

The miraculous catch includes two typical Johannine themes:

• the contrast of light and darkness, day (the Resurrection) and night (sin and evil), and
• the Eucharistic overtone of the meal, of Jesus taking bread and fish and giving it to Peter and the disciples.

After the meal, sitting by the fire he has made, Jesus invites Peter to atone for his triple denial of Jesus by the fire in the high priest's courtyard by declaring three times his complete love and unfailing devotion to him in the light of this Easter fire. Jesus the Good Shepherd (John 10) passes on the role of servant/shepherd to Peter and his brothers. It is a moment of re-creation and resurrection for Peter.

Peter's complete love and faithfulness to the Lord is recounted in today's **first reading** from Acts. The tension between the fledgling Christian community and the Jewish establishment grows. Peter declares the apostles' intention to continue to preach the good news of the Risen Christ in defiance of the Sanhedren's orders prohibiting their preaching.

Today's **second reading** from the Book of Revelation is the angels' hymn of praise acclaiming the universal reign of the "Lamb" (the visionary John speaks of the "Lamb" 28 times in Revelation).

Themes:

Called to proclaim the good news of Easter.

Christ calls us to bring the miracle of his Resurrection into our lives through our commitment to seeking justice, peace and reconciliation in all things. In looking beyond the failure of Peter and the disciples who abandoned him on Good Friday, the Risen Jesus renews his call to them to become "fishers" of humanity. As witnesses of the Resurrection, we, too, are called to bring the life of the Risen One to all things: to seek re-birth rather than condemnation and death, to rejoice in reconciliation rather than to moralize on the sins of the past, to accept one another as brothers and sisters rather than to isolate and dominate enemies, to work for what is best for all rather than for what is better for us alone.

Forgiveness: an experience of resurrection.

Today's Gospel is a beautiful story of forgiveness. Jesus asks Peter three times – just as Peter denied him three times – to profess his love for him. We can hear the pain and hurt in Peter's voice – but also the conviction – in his response after Jesus asks the third time: "Lord, you know everything. You know well that I love you." Jesus is not taunting Peter here; he is calling Peter to move beyond the past to take on the challenges of apostleship. In forgiving Peter as he does, in affecting reconciliation with Peter, Jesus transforms Peter's regrets and shame into understanding and conviction of the Gospel the fisherman has witnessed. Through forgiving one another and through constantly seeking reconciliation with those from whom we are separated, we enable such "resurrection" to take place in our own families, neighborhoods and communities.

For reflection:

• When have you found it most difficult to believe in the hope of Jesus' resurrection?
• Have you ever experienced forgiveness that could accurately be described as an experience of resurrection for the parties involved?
• Have you ever known someone or something you considered inconsequential, useless or of little proven worth who/that later proved to be of great value?

Fourth Sunday of Easter

Cycle C

Readings:

John 10: 27-30
Acts 13: 14, 43-52
Revelation 7: 9, 14-17

Today's brief **Gospel** is the conclusion of the Good Shepherd discourse in Chapter 10 of John's Gospel. Yahweh, the eternal shepherd of Israel (cf. Ezekiel 34), has raised up his own Son as the Good Shepherd to guide the new Israel of the Church to eternal life. In listening to the voice of Jesus the Good Shepherd, the "flock" finds its way to the Father.

Paul and Barnabas begin their first missionary journey at Antioch (**first reading**). At first, the Jews welcome their preaching about Jesus the Messiah; but Paul's acceptance of the Gentiles into the community without first demanding that they embrace Judaism angers the Jews who fear for their own traditions and cultures.

Today's vision from the Book of Revelation (**second reading**) is intended to encourage John's brother and sister Christians who are suffering great persecution at the hands of the Romans. John "sees" the triumphant faithful who have "survived the trial" and now dwell forever in the presence of God. John's vision echoes several Gospel images of Jesus the Redeemer: John the Baptizer's proclamation of "the Lamb of God," the "shepherding" of the faithful, the "springs of life-giving water."

Theme:

Hearing the 'voice' of the Good Shepherd.

A great deal is revealed in the voice that cannot readily be discerned in words alone: joy, compassion, consolation, sympathy, assurance. The Jesus of the Gospel "speaks" to us in a voice that reveals a spirit of compassion, invitation and acceptance. In our own time, the Risen One continues to speak to us in that same voice of hope, consolation and encouragement. The voice of Christ can still be heard amid the cacophony of voices – some very loud and discordant voices – that surround us and distract us from the things of God.

Becoming the 'voice' of the Good Shepherd.

For the man and woman of faith, life is centered in the Word of God – the Word spoken in the voice of Jesus, the Good Shepherd, the "Word made flesh" for us. The voice of the Shepherd echoes within our souls where the Spirit of God dwells, giving life to everything we say, do and believe. In our own acts of generosity, love and forgiveness, we speak the Word made flesh; we become the voice of the Risen Christ; we proclaim the good news of hope and grace that is the Easter miracle.

For reflection:

- How and where is the voice of the Good Shepherd heard amidst the noise and clamor of our society and world?
- In your life, when have you heard the voice of Christ speaking to you most strikingly in its hope, its consolation, its encouragement?
- What forces "snatch" us out of the hands of the Good Shepherd?

168

Readings:
John 13: 31-33, 34-35
Acts 14: 21-27
Revelation 21: 1-5

Today's **Gospel** takes place in the cenacle the night of the Last Supper. Jesus has just completed the dramatic washing of his disciples' feet and has further shocked his disciples with the warnings of Judas' role in the events to come. After Judas leaves, Jesus addresses his own, his dearest friends. He leaves them a "new" commandment of love – what is "new" is the model of selfless, sacrificial, forgiving love Jesus leaves them. This same "new" model of love is the indispensable sign of discipleship.

Paul and Barnabas return to Antioch where the Jews had previously tried to stone Paul for his attempts to create mixed communities of Jews and Gentiles (**first reading**). The two apostles persevere despite the obstacles and succeed in establishing a viable community in the city that had so violently expelled them.

Today's reading from the Book of Revelation is John's final vision of a new heaven and a new earth, the "passing away" of the old earth and the sea (a symbol of peril and evil) and the creation of a new city, the new and eternal Jerusalem (**second reading**). It is a vision of hope for the faithful of God's new covenant with humanity, a covenant sealed in the blood of the Son, the "Lamb" and "Bridegroom."

Themes:

Love: the distinguishing mark of discipleship.

To those who profess to follow him – from the Apostles to us to the very last generation who will inhabit this planet – Jesus gives a "new" commandment, a new standard for all human relationships: *as I have loved you, so must your love be for one another*. It is that concept of unconditional, sacrificial love that distinguishes us as men and women of faith, true disciples of the Risen One. Only in remaining selfless and caring in our dealings with others will our skeptical world come to understand the good news that Christ is risen.

Love: the spirit that binds us as Church.

As a Church, we come together at the "command" of Christ to accompany one another through our lives' journeys to the reign of God, to support one another in life's joys and sorrows, to "be Christ" to one another in love and compassion. Our identity as a Church, as disciples of the Risen Christ, is not in a building or in the mere act of identifying ourselves as Christian: our identity as Christians is centered in the joy and optimism of our love for others as God's children and as our brothers and sisters – the same love that unites the Father and Son and each of us to one another.

Love: creating a 'new heaven and earth.'

Jesus leaves his Church a "new" standard of love, a standard that transcends legalisms and measurements, a standard that renews and re-creates all human relationships, a standard that transforms the most Godless and secular world view. Jesus the Servant-Redeemer, is the incarnation of the love of the Father, a love that knows neither limit nor condition. In embracing the spirit and attitude of such love, we can create a "new earth" (second reading).

For reflection:

- In what ways does your local community "know" that your parish are "my disciples"?
- How can love be "new" or make a relationship "new"?
- How does the love taught and exemplified by Jesus differ from the popular concept of "love"?

Sixth Sunday of Easter

Readings:

John 14: 23-29
Acts 15: 1-2, 22-29
Revelation 21: 10-14, 22-23

In his Last Supper discourse, Jesus leaves his fledgling Church his gift of peace and the promise of the Spirit (**Gospel**).

Christ's gift of peace is not the absence of trouble and hostility ("as the world gives peace"); Christ's peace is the Scriptural concept of *shalom* – meaning the pursuit of everything which makes for the highest good. The peace of Christ finds its core in the Gospel principles of humble servanthood and holy justice.

The word *Paraclete* means advocate or consoler, one who intercedes and intervenes on behalf of good – it is the exact opposite of the "adversary," Satan. The Paraclete is that presence of God within us that opens our hearts and minds to the promptings of God's Word as proclaimed by Jesus.

Today's **first reading**, from Luke's Acts, is another watershed in the life of the young church. The question of whether or not Gentiles must first embrace Judaism before being admitted to the Christian community was the first major controversy the Church faced. The matter was dealt with at the first "council" of the Church, held at Jerusalem. The "Paraclete" guides the Church beyond its Jewish beginnings to embrace a mission that extends to all peoples and nations.

Today's **second reading** is John's final vision in the Book of Revelation of the new, eternal city of God, "built" on the Gospel proclamations of the Twelve, a city illuminated by the presence of God within it.

Themes:

Christ's peace: 'real' peace.

Peace that is of Christ is not just the absence of violence or conflict, but a deep sense of love, justice, truth and mercy, an understanding of our connectedness to one another as children of the same God that are the principal motivations of our actions, behavior and values. Gospel peace is not passive. It calls for an active response from us: to work to break through the barriers which divide us, to learn to understand one another and to pardon those who hurt us. "If we wish to have true peace," Pope Paul VI said, "we must give it a soul. The soul of peace is love. It is love that gives life to peace, more than victory or defeat, or weariness or need. The soul of peace is love, which for us believers comes from the love of God and expresses itself in love for each other."

Christ's 'dwelling among us' in his word.

Easter is a celebration of Christ's presence among us *now:* in sacrament, in Scripture, in community, in our living of the Gospel in our every day lives. The promise of the Resurrection is as much a reality for us as it was for the small band of disciples of the Gospel and the Acts of the Apostles. In even our smallest act of selfless kindness – prompted by the Paraclete instructing our open hearts and spirit's – we reveal the presence of the Easter Christ in our little piece of the world.

For reflection:

- In what ways do we work for the peace of Christ in our every day lives? How does such peace call us to *act* rather than to *stop?*
- Who have you known in your life who has been a true "giver" of Christ's peace?
- How did someone reveal to you – however unexpectedly – the presence of the Easter Christ?

Ascension of the Lord

Readings:
Luke 24: 46-53
Acts 1: 1-11
Ephesians 1: 17-23

Today's readings include two accounts of Jesus' return to the Father by the same writer:

The **first reading** is the beginning of the Acts of the Apostles, Luke's "Gospel of the Holy Spirit." Jesus' Ascension begins volume 2 of Luke's work. The words and images here recall the First Covenant accounts of the ascension of Elijah (2 Kings 2) and the forty years of the Exodus: Luke considers the time that the Risen Lord spent with his disciples a sacred time, a "desert experience" for the apostles to prepare them for their new ministry of preaching the Gospel of the resurrection. (Acts alone places the Ascension forty days after Easter; the synoptic Gospels – including, strangely, Luke's – specifically place the ascension on the day of Easter; John writes of the "ascension" not as an event but as a new existence with the Father.)

Responding to their question about the restoration of Israel, Jesus discourages his disciples from guessing what cannot be known. Greater things await them as his "witnesses." In the missionary work awaiting them, Christ will be with them in the presence of the promised Spirit.

Whereas in Acts Luke places Jesus' Ascension 40 days after Easter, in his **Gospel** the Ascension takes place on Easter night. Luke treats the same event from two points of view: in the Gospel, the Ascension is the completion of Jesus' Messianic work; in Acts, it is the prelude to the Church's mission.

Paul's letter to the Ephesians celebrates the union of all men and women in and with Christ, as members of his mystical body. In the opening chapter of his letter to the Ephesians (**second reading**), the apostle prays that the Christian community at Ephesus may be united by the great "hope" they share in the Risen Christ, whom the Father has made sovereign over all creatures and head of the Church.

Themes:

The Ascension: an ending and a beginning.

Jesus' Ascension is both an ending and a beginning. The physical appearances of Jesus are at an end; his revelation of the "good news" is complete; the promise of the Messiah is fulfilled. Now begins the work of the disciples to teach what they have learned and to share what they have witnessed. It is not a very promising start. Like any beginning or transition in life, it is a moment of great uncertainty, confusion and apprehension. Christ places his Church in the care of a rag-tag collection of fishermen, tax collector and peasants. And yet, what began with those eleven has grown and flourished through the centuries to the very walls of our own parish family. The Church Jesus leaves to them is rooted not in buildings or wealth or formulas of prayer or systems of theology but in faith nurtured in the human heart, a faith centered in joy and understanding that is empowering and liberating, a faith that gives us the strength and freedom to be authentic and effective witnesses of the Risen One, who is present among us always.

The commission to 'teach,' to 'witness,' to 'heal.'

Christ entrusts to his disciples of every time and place the sacred responsibility of teaching others everything he has taught and revealed about the Father: God's limitless love, his unconditional forgiveness and acceptance of every person as his own beloved child and our identity as God's sons and daughters and brothers and sisters to one another. Christ also calls us to be witnesses of God's presence in our lives. He also asks us to bring into the lives of others his healing forgiveness and reconciliation with God and one another. The words Jesus addresses to his disciples on the mountain of the Ascension are addressed to all of us two millennia later. We are called to teach, to witness and to heal in our own small corners of the world, to hand on to others the story that has been handed on to us about Jesus and his Gospel of love and compassion.

For reflection:

- What emotions and feelings do you think the eleven experienced as they walked down the mountain and returned to Jerusalem? Can you relate to such feelings?

- Who are the "apostles" to the small, hidden places on earth?

- What are the different ways we "teach" the good news? Two thousand years after it happened, how can we be effective "witnesses" of the resurrection? How do we bring "healing" as Christ did into the lives of others?

Readings:

John 17: 20-26
Acts 7: 55-60
Revelation 22: 12-14, 16-17, 20

In John's account of the Last Supper, after his final teachings to his disciples before the events of his passion begin, Jesus addresses his Father in heaven. He begins praying for himself, that he may obediently bring to completion the work of redemption entrusted to him by the Father. Next, he prays for his disciples, that they may faithfully proclaim the word he has taught them. Finally, Jesus prays for the future Church – us – that we may be united in the "complete" love that binds the Father to the Son and the Son to his Church, and that in our love for one another the world may come to know God (**Gospel**).

The stoning of the deacon Stephen was another defining moment for the new Church of Acts (**first reading**). His death parallels Jesus' own passion: Stephen's proclaiming the reign of God is angrily rejected by the Sanhedren and Jewish elders; as he is stoned, Stephen entrusts his soul to the Lord asking that his killers be forgiven. Luke points out that the witnesses piled their cloaks at the feet of a young man named Saul – a man who will play a critical role in the future "Acts" of the Church.

In this Sunday's final Easter reading from Revelation (**second reading**), John has a vision of Jesus himself, the "Alpha and Omega," who promises to return at the end of time to judge the living and dead. Several Scriptural and Gospel images of the Messiah are part of this vision: the tree and root of David, the light of God's Word, the bridegroom and the wedding feast, the promise of life-giving water.

Themes:

Our 'connectedness' and unity in the Father and Son.

In his "high priestly prayer," Jesus pleads with the Father that the extraordinary sense of "oneness" that exists between the Father and Son might be experienced by us. It is a unity of complete love embracing all: from Genesis to the Gospel of the empty tomb to our own parish family. Christ calls us to work for that sense of "oneness," that sense of "connectedness" within our own Church by recognizing and honoring the essential dignity that every one of us possesses as children of God and in seeking ways to tear down the barriers that divide and alienate us from one another.

The witness of the 'Stephens' among us.

Every generation of Christians – including our own – has known martyrs like Stephen who have suffered and died so that the Gospel might be handed on to the next generation of the faith community. In the anguish and suffering they endured for their witness to the truth, we realize our world's need for re-creation and resurrection; in their selfless struggle for what is right, we come to understand the love of God revealed in Jesus Christ; in their sacrifice for the sake of the persecuted and the oppressed, we discover humanity's unity in the life and love of God.

For reflection:

- Who have been the Stephens of our Church, whose proclaiming of the Easter Gospel and suffering on its behalf are a priceless gift to the Church?
- In what ways does your parish celebrate and live its "unity" in the Father and the Son? In what ways do we diminish or undermined that unity?
- In what ways do we realize and learn from those who came before us? How are we "connected" to the generations that have preceded us?

Pentecost

Readings:

John 20: 19-23
Acts 2: 1-11
1 Corinthians 12: 3-7, 12-13

Pentecost was the Jewish festival of the harvest (also called the Feast of Weeks), celebrated 50 days after Passover, when the first fruits of the corn harvest were offered to the Lord. A feast of pilgrimage (hence the presence in Jerusalem of so many "devout Jews of every nation"), Pentecost also commemorated Moses' receiving of the Law on Mount Sinai. For the new Israel, Pentecost becomes the celebration of the Spirit of God's compassion, peace and forgiveness – the Spirit that transcends the Law and becomes the point of departure for the young Church's universal mission (the planting of a new harvest?).

Today's **Gospel**, the first appearance of the Risen Jesus before his ten disciples (remember Thomas is not present), on Easter night is John's version of the Pentecost event. In "breathing" the Holy Spirit upon them, Jesus imitates God's act of creation in Genesis. In the Resurrection, the Spirit re-creates the band of disciples into the new Israel; the "peace" of understanding, enthusiasm and joy and shatters all barriers among them to make of them a community of hope and forgiveness. By Christ's sending them forth, the disciples become *apostles* – "those sent."

In his Acts of the Apostles (**first reading**), Luke invokes the First Testament images of wind and fire in his account of the new Church's Pentecost: God frequently revealed his presence in fire (the pillar of fire in the Sinai) and in wind (the wind that sweeps over the earth to make the waters of the Great Flood subside). The Hebrew word for spirit, *ruah*, and the Greek word *pneuma* also refer to the movement of air, not only as wind, but also of life-giving breath (as in God's creation of man in Genesis 2 and the revivification of the dry bones in Ezekiel 37). Through this life-giving "breath," the Lord begins the era of the new Israel on Pentecost.

Appealing for unity in the badly-splintered Corinthian community, Paul reminds the Corinthians of the presence of the Holy Spirit in their midst, which brings together the different charisms each possesses for the good of the whole community and the glory of God (**second reading**).

Themes:

The Spirit: the *ruah* of God.

The feast of Pentecost celebrates the unseen, immeasurable presence of God in our lives and in our church – the *ruah* that animates us to do the work of the Gospel of the Risen One, the *ruah* that makes God's will our will, the *ruah* of God living in us and transforming us so that we might bring his life and love to our broken world. God "breathes" his Spirit into our souls that we may live in his life and love; he ignites the "fire" of his Spirit within our hearts and minds that we may seek God in all things in order to realize the coming of his reign.

The Spirit: the powerful and enabling love of God.

Today we celebrate the Spirit – the great love that binds the Father to the Son and now binds us to God and to one another. It is a love that transcends words but embraces the heart and soul of each one of us; it gives voice to the things we believe but are too afraid to speak; it gives us the courage and grace to work for the dreams we are sometimes too cynical or fearful to hope for. The Spirit of God enables us to re-create our world in the love of God who loved us enough to become one of us, to die for us and to rise for us. The theologian and scientist Teilhard de Chardin noted that "love is the only force that can make things one without destroying them. . . . Some day, after mastering the winds, the waves, the tides and gravity, we shall harness for God the energies of love, and then, for the second time in the history of the world, man will have discovered fire."

The Spirit: the 'birth' of the Church.

Pentecost is a moment of profound realization and transformation for the community of disciples. The faith they had received, the wonders they had witnessed and the Word they had heard came together in a new understanding, clarity, unity and courage to begin the work Jesus had entrusted to them. In Jesus' "breathing" upon them the new life of the Spirit, the community of the Resurrection – the Church – takes flight. That same Spirit continues to "blow" through today's Church to give life and direction to our mission and ministry to preach the Gospel to every nation, to proclaim the forgiveness and reconciliation in God's name, to baptize all humanity into the life of Jesus' Resurrection.

For reflection:

- The Spirit of God reveals itself in today's readings in the forms of fire, wind and breath. What other images can help us understand the Spirit of God working within us?
- How does the presence of the Holy Spirit make your parish "different" from other groups and organizations of people?
- Share stories of God's Spirit alive around you. How would those stories be different if God's Spirit was not present there?

Trinity Sunday

Readings:

John 16: 12-15
Proverbs 8: 22-31
Romans 5: 1-5

As Ordinary Time resumes, two "solemnities of the Lord" are celebrated on the next two Sundays. Today's celebration of the Trinity originated in France in the eighth century and was adopted by the universal Church in 1334. The solemnity focuses on the essence of our faith: the revelation of God as Creator, the climax of his creation in Jesus the Redeemer, the fullness of the love of God poured out on us in the Sustainer Spirit.

In his final words to his disciples at the Last Supper, Jesus promises to send the "Spirit of truth [to] guide you to all truth" (**Gospel**). The Son has revealed the Father to the Church; the Spirit of truth and wisdom keeps that revelation alive in the Church.

The Book of Proverbs extols the wisdom of God – the creative force of God that brought all of creation into being, that became incarnated in the person of Jesus of Nazareth, that is present today in the Spirit of truth dwelling in our midst (**first reading**).

Paul assures the Church at Rome that we have been reconciled to God through Jesus Christ; in the midst of this world's sufferings and afflictions, the Spirit of God fills us with hope of the promised world to come (**second reading**).

Themes:

Trinity: the love of God revealed.

Many metaphors have been used to explain and depict the Trinity. St. John of Damascus, the great Eastern theologian of the eighth century, suggested that we think "of the Father as a root, of the Son as a branch, and of the Spirit as a fruit, for the substance of these three is one." Today we celebrate the essence of our faith manifested in our lives: the loving providence of the Creator who continually invites us back to him; the selfless servanthood of the Redeemer who "emptied" himself to become like us in order that we might become like him; the joyful love of the Spirit that is the unique unity of the Father and Son.

The 'why' of God.

Science gives us some insight into how the hand of God set our world into motion; faith challenges us to consider the mystery of *why* God set it all into motion. That is the core of faith: to encounter the Creator not only in his creation but in his love and care for that creation. Trinity Sunday is a celebration of the many dimensions in which we discover the *why* of God: God, the Creator and Sustainer of all that lives; God, the Christ who became one of us to show us the depth of God's love; the Spirit, the love of God living among us, the love that gives meaning and vision to us, God's beloved creation.

Discovering the truth of God.

Throughout our lives we seek hard and fast truths, truths written in stone that will last forever, permanent truths that will hold fast in every possible set of circumstances and challenge life throws at us. But truth is an ongoing process. God – Father, Son and Spirit – is a lasting reality; but God continues to reveal himself. He is not a silent God who ceases to reveal himself on the last page of Scripture. Through the Spirit dwelling within us and within the Church, God is still leading us into a greater realization of what Jesus taught in the Gospels.

For reflection:

- The shamrock, the triangle and the fruit tree (St. John of Damascus, cited above) have been all been used to depict the mystery of the Trinity. Are there any contemporary images that help you understand and appreciate the Triune God?

- How has God – Father, Son and Spirit – made his presence known to you? How would you explain this presence to a non-believer?

- What beliefs and attitudes of yours have changed over the years? How have those changes affected your understanding of God?

The Body and Blood of the Lord

Readings:

Luke 9: 11-17
Genesis 14: 18-20
1 Corinthians 11: 23-26

Today's celebration of the Body and Blood of the Lord originated in the Diocese of Liege in 1246 as the feast of Corpus Christi. In the reforms of Vatican II, the feast was joined with the feast of the Precious Blood (July 1) to become the Solemnity of the Body and Blood of the Lord. We celebrate today the Christ's gift of the Eucharist, the source and summit of our life together as the Church.

Today's **Gospel** is Luke's account of Jesus' feeding of the five thousand with five loaves of bread and two pieces of fish (the only one of Jesus' miracles recounted in all four Gospels). As he does throughout Luke's Gospel, Jesus performs a miracle out of his deep sense of compassion for the suffering and needy. But Jesus first asks the Twelve to gather up whatever they can from the community; with these few shared gifts Jesus creates a community of thanksgiving, a community of Eucharist.

Melchizedek is one of the more mysterious figures of the First Testament. He was the king of Salem, which later would become Jerusalem; he was also identified as a "priest" of "God, the Most High" – the first God of the Canaanite pantheon (**first reading**). His blessing of Abraham with bread and wine has been seen since the earliest days of the Church as a foreshadowing of the bread and wine of the Eucharist.

The deep divisions in the Corinthian community have led to abuses and misunderstandings concerning the "breaking of the bread." In addressing these problems and articulating the proper spirit in which to approach the Lord's Supper, Paul provides us with the earliest written account of the institution of the Eucharist, the Passover of the new covenant (**second reading**). If we fail to embrace the spirit of love and servanthood in which the gift of the Eucharist is given to us, then "Eucharist" becomes a judgment against us.

Themes:

Becoming a community of Eucharist.

Jesus was able to perform the miracle recounted in today's Gospel only because someone was willing to share the small amount he or she had. Today we celebrate Jesus' lasting gift to his Church – the bread and wine of the Eucharist, his own body blessed and broken for our sake. But that gift comes with an important "string" is attached: it must be shared. In *sharing* the body of Christ,

we *become* the body of Christ. If we partake of the one bread and cup, then we must be willing to become Eucharist for others – to make the love of Christ real for all. As St. Augustine preached to his North African Church, in *sharing* the body of Christ, we *become* the body of Christ.

The table of the Lord.

Christ calls us to his table, offering his peace, affirmation, support and love. We come to the Eucharist to celebrate our common identity as his disciples and to seek the sustaining grace to live the hard demands of such discipleship. We come to the Eucharist seeking the peace and hope of the Risen One in the compassion and support we offer and receive from one another. At Christ's table, we are always welcome. In celebrating the Eucharist, we make our parish family's table the Lord's own table, a place of reconciliation and compassion.

For reflection:

- How can we be "Eucharist" to one another? How can we bring the Eucharist from our church to our world?
- What do our own family rituals at dinner time and around the family table teach us about the Eucharist?
- In what ways do we do an injustice to our celebration of the Body and Blood of the Lord?
- The word *Eucharist* means "thanksgiving." How can our sharing of the Body and Blood of the Lord be an act of thanksgiving, even when we gather under the most painful of circumstances?

The Sundays of the Year – Cycle C

Second Sunday of the Year

Readings:
        John 2: 1-12
        Isaiah 62: 1-5
        1 Corinthians 12: 4-11

Today's **Gospel** is John's account of Jesus' first great "sign": the transformation of water into wine at the wedding feast at Cana. For the churches of the East, the miracle at Cana is the fourth great event of their celebration of the Lord's Epiphany or *manifestation* to the world (the first three: his birth at Bethlehem, the adoration of the magi and his baptism at the Jordan by John).

Cana invokes two important Scriptural symbols that point to the Messiahship of Jesus. First, wine in abundance was considered a sign for Israel of the Messianic age to come (one example is Isaiah 54: 5-14, Reading 4 for the Easter Vigil). The water in the six large stone jars used for the ritual washings mandated by the first covenant law is transformed by Jesus into Messianic wine, prefiguring the new covenant to be sealed in Jesus' blood (which we celebrate in the wine of the Eucharist).

Second, the limitless love of God for his people is described throughout Scripture in terms of marriage. Today's **first reading** from Isaiah is a beautiful example of this tradition. It is the strongest (yet still far from perfect) image we have to understand the depth of God's love for his holy people.

The evangelist John pulls together these two power Messianic symbols of wine and marriage to introduce the public ministry of Jesus, the promised Messiah and bridegroom.

A final note: In verse 4 of today's Gospel, Jesus is not as brusque toward his mother as he sounds to us in the English translation of the text. The address "Woman" was a common courteous form of address in Jesus' time. We do not have an equivalent in modern English for this idiomatic expression.

In the first eleven chapters of his first letter to the Corinthians, the apostle Paul confronts the Corinthian community with their divisions and moral failings. In the final four chapters (from which the **second reading** will be taken for the first seven Sundays of liturgical year "C"), Paul speaks eloquently and movingly of the unity in the Risen Christ they should seek and cherish above all else.

Today's selection from chapter 12 reminds the Corinthian church of the gifts each person is given by God to be used and accepted for the good of all and the glory of their Giver. No one gift is more important or valuable than another. All gifts work in harmony for the well-being of all.

Themes:

Signs of God's reign: the marriage covenant.

The love of God is manifested at its most powerful in the love between husband and wife, in marriages in which Christ is the always-present Wedding Guest. Throughout Scripture God speaks of his love for humankind in terms of espousal. Christ, who performed his first miracle at a wedding, called himself "the Bridegroom" who comes to bring his people to the wedding feast of the Father. As ministers of the marriage sacrament, husbands and wives, in their love for one another, help us all realize the great love of God the Father and Christ his Son, the Bridegroom.

Signs of God's reign: 'new wine.'

At Cana, Jesus offers for the first time the "new wine" of hope restored and reconcilation renewed. We, too, are invited to embrace this new vision in order to rebuild our world: that reconciliation may rise from the ruins of hurt and estrangement, that community may rise from the ruins of alienation and hatred.

For reflection:

- What have married couples taught you about the depth of God's love?
- What distinguishes a marriage "covenant" from a marriage "contract"?
- Sometimes when we look at a belief or situation from a different perspective, our thinking is transformed. Have you ever experienced such "new wine" in your life?
- Who do you know who have been or are stewards of the "new wine" of the Gospel?

Third Sunday of the Year

Readings:
      Luke 1: 1-4; 4: 14-21
      Nehemiah 8: 2-4, 5-6, 8-10
      1 Corinthians 12: 12-30

The writer of this year's cycle of **Gospel** readings, Luke, is a "second generation" Christian. Greek by birth and physician by profession, he was a traveling companion of Paul, through whom he met Mark and perhaps Peter himself. He writes his Gospel mainly for Gentiles like himself: for Luke, this Jesus fulfills not only Jewish dreams but every people's hopes for wholeness and holiness.

Luke's Gospel reflects a scientist's precision in locating dates, places and people; but Luke's Gospel also exhibits an interest in people rather than ideas. His account celebrates the compassion of Jesus for the outcasts and "second class citizens" of Jewish society, including women.

Luke begins his Gospel in the classic Greek historical style by personally (he is the only one of the four evangelists who ever refers to himself in the first person) assuring his readers (addressed in the singular "Theophilus," Greek for *friend of God*) the historical accuracy and theological authenticity of the research he has gathered to assemble this story.

According to Luke's account, Jesus begins his teaching ministry in Galilee. Galilee – a name which comes from the Hebrew word for *circle* – was a great agricultural region encircled by non-Jewish nations and cultures, thereby earning a reputation for being the most progressive and least conservative area of Palestine. A teacher with a "new" message such as this Rabbi Jesus would be expected to receive a favorable hearing in the openness of Galilean society.

Jesus returns to his hometown, the Galilean city of Nazareth. Nazareth was a city of great importance in Israel's history and economy, located on the major routes to Jerusalem, Alexandria and Damascus. In the Nazareth synagogue (the places where local Jewish communities outside of Jerusalem would gather for teaching and prayer), Jesus announces, using the words of the prophet Isaiah, the fulfillment of God's promise of a Messiah for Israel.

Jesus' proclamation of good news recalls an incident in Jewish history five hundred years before (**first reading**). The long Babylonian captivity was at an end and the Israelites had returned to Jerusalem. The temple was rebuilt and, under the dynamic leadership of Nehemiah, the city's walls were repaired. On the joyous day of rededication, the great priest and religious reformer Ezra assembled the faithful remnant of Jews to renew their ancient covenant with Yahweh.

Paul speaks to the Corinthian church as a pastor pleading to heal the wounds of division within his congregation (**second reading**). Borrowing an idea from the Stoic philosophy popular at the time, Paul invokes the image of the human body to portray the Church as a single community made up of individuals with diverse but indispensable gifts to offer.

Themes:

The 'good news': an approachable, loving God.

Today we hear in the opening words of Luke's Gospel his reason for compiling his Gospel. He writes for Theophilus – "friend of God" – "so that [you] may see how reliable the instruction you have received." Luke's story will recount the story of God becoming human in order to give humanity a new vision and insight into the fullness of God's live of peace, reconciliation and justice – a vision that can transform and re-create our very humanity. This story of Jesus who comes to "proclaim glad tidings to the poor . . . to announce a year of favor from the Lord" should make a profound difference in the lives of all who hear it. In his humanity, Jesus reveals a God who is approachable and present to us in all that is good and right and loving around us.

The 'good news': reconciliation, not condemnation.

The Jesus who begins his public ministry in the synagogue at Nazareth in today's Gospel is not the kind of Messiah Israel expected. While Israel longed for a Messiah who would lead them to victory and vindication, Jesus the Messiah comes with a much different message of humility, reconciliation, compassion and forgiveness. It was a difficult message for Israel to hear – and, often, difficult for us to grasp, as well. The "good news" of the Gospel calls us to become rather than to shun, to lift up rather than condemn, to seek the humble way of servanthood rather than the satisfaction of self-righteousness.

For reflection:

- Have you ever discovered the Spirit of the Gospel in some unexpected people and places?
- How and when do we as a Church embrace the Gospel with the openness of spirit of Galilee? With the narrow, fearful self-righteousness of Nazareth?
- What prophets do you know who have been rejected by their "native place"?
- In what ways do we become so bogged down with rigidity, sadness and judgment that we forget the true joyful meaning of the good news of the Gospel of Jesus?

Fourth Sunday of the Year

Readings:

Luke 4: 21-30
Jeremiah 1: 4-5, 17-19
1 Corinthians 12: 31 – 13: 13

There is a cost to being a prophet; to proclaim what is right, just and good can be a lonely, isolating experience.

Jesus and Jeremiah knew that all too well.

Today's **Gospel** continues last Sunday's account of Jesus' teaching in the synagogue at Nazareth. After proclaiming the fulfillment of Isaiah's vision of the Messiah, Jesus sits down – the posture assumed by one who is about to teach – and begins by explaining in no uncertain terms that he cannot perform any healings or miracles there because of their lack of faith. He teaches that the Messiah does not come for Nazareth alone but for every race, culture and nation of every place and age.

His explanation is met with indignation and anger. Many Jews of the time were so convinced that they were God's own people that they despised everyone else. They could not accept Jesus' idea that others – Gentiles! – were as loved by God as they were. Jesus is forced to leave his hometown.

Jeremiah was one of the great prophets during the restoration of Judah during the seventh century B.C. He was a deeply sensitive man who chose to forsake marriage and family life to give himself totally to his call to prophesy. Today's **first reading** recounts God's setting Jeremiah apart for the difficult, lonely mission of the prophet. Despite the persecution and scorn the prophet will endure, the God of mercy and justice assures his prophet that the Lord will triumph through him.

Of all the gifts God gives to his people for the good of the community, Paul reminds the faithful of Corinth in today's **second reading** that the greatest gift of all is love. Steeped in Greek philosophy and culture, the Corinthians deeply respect the things of the mind and honor the intellectual. But without the spirit of love dwelling in one's hearts, the gifts of the intellect are worthless.

Themes:

The loneliness and isolation of being a prophet.

Standing up for what is right, speaking out for such things as ethics and justice, are the call of the prophet. In today's Gospel, Jesus' words about his mission are met with such anger that he is driven out of his own town; Jeremiah and the prophets of the First Testament also endured persecution and ridicule for their faithfulness in proclaiming the word of God. To speak – and to listen – as prophets demands the courage and conviction to risk isolation, ridicule and persecution for sake of the justice and mercy of God.

Called to live the 'prophetic' call.

Jesus was perceived as a layman in everything but carpentry. Religion, politics, economics – he possessed no special credentials in any of those fields. Yet he dramatically altered them all because he was faithful to the spirit within him. He prayed, reflected, argued, searched constantly for the truth. And in his proclamation of the truth, Jesus paid the price for being a prophet. We are called to be prophets: both to listen with open hearts to the prophets among us and to speak the prophetic truth ourselves in our homes, work places, classrooms and marketplaces.

Prophetic 'listening.'

Both to *speak* as a prophet and to *listen* as a prophet demands the honesty and courage to confront exactly who we are and our need for change and re-creation in the love of God. In today's Gospel, Jesus (as the prophet also experienced) encounters a people who are unable to hear, accept and act on his call to conversion: to change the evil systems that dehumanize them, making them much less than the holy people God has called them to be. Discipleship calls us to be not only proclaimers but "prophetic" listeners to the Gospel, in order that we might transform our lives in the grace of God.

For reflection:

- Has pressure from associates, co-workers or classmates ever made it difficult for you to speak the "truth"?
- How are we discouraged – or how do *we* discourage – the "prophets" among us?
- Whose prophetic voice have you had a particularly hard time hearing and accepting?

Fifth Sunday of the Year

Readings:

Luke 5: 1-11
Isaiah 6: 1-2, 3-8
1 Corinthians 15: 1-11

Commercial fishing has always been a hard way to make a living. It requires a substantial investment of time and money for boat and gear and its maintenance; it entails considerable risk in leaving the safety of home port for the open sea; it is hard work, sometimes with little reward; it compels crews to work together to bring in the catch. The work of the prophet/disciple demands that same kind of risk, personal investment, patience, hard work and sense of community.

The best fishing, Peter and his brothers knew, was done at night; little is caught during the heat of the day. So Peter's agreeing to lower his nets at Jesus' urging was, for a fisherman of Peter's experience, an act of considerable faith. And as today's **Gospel** recounts, Peter's faith is rewarded abundantly. If the first disciples of Jesus had any special grace at all, it was an openness to Jesus' initial call and teaching.

In Luke's account, Peter's reaction is somewhat surprising. Upon realizing who Jesus is, he cowers away. In the light of Christ's revelation, Peter recognizes his own unworthiness and humbleness in the sight of God. But Jesus assures him he has not come to drive sinners from his presence but to bring them back to God – to catch them in the "net" of God's love.

The **first reading** is the story of another prophet's call. It was believed that to see God's face would lead to one's doom, and so Isaiah (like Peter) shrinks away in fear before his vision of the Holy One. But in his purifying love, God calls Isaiah to be his envoy.

Today's selection from Paul's first letter to the Corinthians (**second reading**) also speaks of a simple, sinful people inspired by the grace of God to proclaim their faith and hope in the Father's great love and mercy.

Themes:

Discipleship: catching others in the love of God.

Those who embrace the real spirit of discipleship are able to celebrate God's presence in their own lives and, with grace, humility and trust, help others realize that same love in their lives. In the ordinary events of every day we are presented with countless opportunities to "catch" others in the extraordinary love of God in our own time and place.

Good enough to be forgiven and loved by God.

Many of us suffer from an "inferiority complex" when it comes to God: We're not saintly enough nor good enough nor wise enough in church protocols to consider ourselves "religious." Like Peter, we shy away from God because we cannot imagine that God loves sinful wretches like us. But that is exactly the *mystery* of God. God works through men and women who are just like us, however imperfect; taking the "humble" way out of a relationship with God is too easy. Thomas Merton observed that "the root of Christian love is not the will to love but the faith that one *is loved by God*...irrespective of one's worth. In the true Christian vision of God's love, the idea of worthiness loses significance. The revelation of the mercy of God makes the whole problem of worthiness something almost laughable...no one could ever, alone, be strictly worthy to be loved with such a love – [such a realization] is a true liberation of spirit."

For reflection:

- In what ways can we "catch" others in the love and mercy of God?
- When have you felt especially unworthy of God? How were you able to overcome that sense of unworthiness?
- When has or does God's presence feel most real and accessible to you?

Readings:

Luke 6: 17, 20-26
Jeremiah 17: 5-8
1 Corinthians 15: 12, 16-20

Whereas in Matthew's Sermon on the Mount Jesus speaks of "Beatitudes," in Luke's Sermon on the Plain, Jesus drops a series of bombshells. He takes the accepted standards of the times and turns them upside down: To those who are considered the "haves" of society, Jesus warns "Woe to you!" – wealth and power are not the stuff of the kingdom of God; but to the "have nots," Jesus says, "Happy and blessed are you" – love, humble selflessness, compassion and generosity are the treasure of God's realm. Jesus promises his followers poverty, suffering, persecution and grief – but their hope in God will be rewarded with perfect and complete joy.

Using the images of the green tree and the barren bush, the prophet Jeremiah, in today's **first reading**, echoes Jesus' teaching of the reward awaiting those who trust in God alone, as well as the fate of those who allow themselves to be consumed by the things of this world.

The intellectually-oriented Corinthians could not fathom the concept of the resurrection of the body. In today's **second reading**, Paul bluntly reminds them that the Church's belief and hope are centered in the Resurrection of Christ.

Themes:

The poverty of spirit.

Both as a lesson in living and as a prophecy of the despair brought on by hard economic times, Jesus' teaching in today's Gospel is (pardon the pun) right on the money. We can become so absorbed in pursuing the good things of life that we devalue the riches we already possess: the love of family and friends, the gift of good health, that special sense of joy we experience when we give of ourselves to others. Mother Teresa of Calcutta has often said to Western Christians: "Your poverty is greater than ours...the spiritual poverty of the West is much greater than the physical poverty of the East. In the West, there are millions of people who suffer loneliness and emptiness, who feel unloved and unwanted. They are hungry in the physical sense; what is missing is a relationship with God and with each other."

The values of God's reign.

Luke's version of the Beatitudes challenges everything our consumer-oriented society holds dear. While wealth, power and celebrity are the sought-after prizes of our world, the treasures of God's reign are love, humble selflessness, compassion and generosity. In freeing ourselves from the pursuit of the things of this world, we liberate ourselves to seek the lasting things of God.

For reflection:

- How and when have you experienced the "poverty" of spirit?
- Many have suffered all kinds of abuse and pain for the sake of God's mercy and reconciliation. Who have been or are those saints who have especially inspired you?
- How can poverty and the giving up of things be liberating?
- What can the poor teach us about the love of God?

Seventh Sunday of the Year

Readings:

Luke 6: 27-38
1 Samuel 26: 2, 7-9, 12-13, 22-23
1 Corinthians 15: 45-49

Continuing his Sermon on the Plain (**Gospel**), Jesus again turns upside down another accepted standard of Jewish morality. The principle of "do to no one what you yourself dislike" (as articulated in Tobit 4: 15) was not enough for those who seek to be God's holy people. Jesus demands that his disciples "love your enemies."

The Greek word for love used in this text is *agape*, a sense of benevolence, kindness and charity towards others. In other words, no matter what a person does to us we will never allow ourselves to seek anything but the highest good for him or her. The radical love of God that is the mark of the Christian is presented clearly and emphatically here. In Luke's Gospel, Jesus calls us not just to passive adherence to the standard of the "Golden Rule," but to actively seek out the good in everyone, to risk being duped or hurt in our compassion and forgiveness of another. The completeness and limitlessness of God's own love and mercy for us should be the measure of our love and mercy for one another.

As the young David became more and more popular as a result of his military triumphs, King Saul became more and more jealous until David was forced to flee for his life. But trusting in God's providence, David spares Saul's life and forgives the king the harm Saul has done him (**first reading**).

Paul teaches his Corinthian brothers and sisters that in being baptized and living the Gospel of love, peace and forgiveness we become like the Risen Christ, "the last Adam" (**second reading**).

Themes:

Reconciliation: breaking the cycle of hatred.

Christ's teaching on loving one's enemies challenges us to break the cycle of fear, hatred and vengeance that often ensnares us and all of society. St. Augustine said that "there is no greater invitation to love than loving first." In every relationship, in every set of circumstances, the faithful disciple of Jesus seeks to break the cycle of hatred and distrust by taking that often formidable step to love first, to trust, to heal, to be reconciled with those from whom we are separated.

Loving your enemies: the cutting edge of the Gospel.

Seeing beyond hatreds and differences, borders and boundaries, flags and uniforms, languages and cultures, suspicions and unsettled scores is the cutting edge of the Gospel. The relationship we seek with God we must first seek with one another. "If we wish to have true peace," Pope Paul VI said, "we must give it a soul. The soul of peace is love. It is love that gives life to peace, more than victory or defeat, more than self-interest or fear or weariness or need. The soul of peace is love, which for us believers comes from the love of God and expresses itself in love for others."

For reflection:

- What was the hardest experience you have had in forgiving someone?
- Have you ever taken the first step in being reconciled with someone? How did the dynamics of relationship change as a result? Did you regret taking that first step?
- Is the "Golden Rule" still workable in today's more complex and pluralistic culture?

Readings:

Luke 6: 39-45
Sirach 27: 4-7
1 Corinthians 15: 54-58

In the conclusion of the "Sermon on the Plain" (**Gospel**), Jesus invokes a style of preaching known as *charaz* – "stringing beads."

Luke has edited several of Jesus' sayings into three "beads":

- First, becoming a disciple is a constant process of seeking and conversion. The disciple never "surpasses" his/her instruction; nor is the disciple ever "better" than those he/she brings to God.
- Second, Jesus calls his disciples not to judge or condemn, but to seek personal conversion and reconciliation with others.
- Third, we cannot speak sincerely or effectively of God with our lips unless God is present in our heart. It is the joy and humility of our lives that affirms the power of the Gospel, not mere words or articulated dogmas.

The **first reading** from the teacher Jesus Ben Sira (writing in the second century B.C.) also uses the example of the fruit tree (as well as husks left in a shaken sieve and newly fired pottery) to teach the importance of evaluating the sincerity and commitment in one's words as the test of faith.

In the **second reading**, Paul concludes his long discourse on the Resurrection by praising God for the "victory" over death and sin won in the resurrection of his Son.

Themes:

The personal responsibility of discipleship.

Jesus' parables today all speak of the personal commitment and responsibility God demands of each one of us in making the Gospel the center of our lives. Unless the Gospel becomes more than words, unless the hope and love revealed in the Gospel affects our outlook and attitudes, then our faith is empty.

The call to personal conversion.

Authentic discipleship begins with confronting both the good and the evil we are capable of and the values that compel us to think, speak and act as we do. Like trying to remove "the speck" in our brother's eye, targeting scapegoats and assigning blame do not solve problems; judging the motives of others remedies nothing. We will not be judged by the "fruit" we "almost" yielded nor by the fruit we "could have" yielded if it weren't for a lack of time, a tough boss, an unfair teacher, a childhood of poverty, etc.; we will be known before God by the "yield" we work for and dedicate ourselves to harvesting for the love of God.

The disciple's call to humility.

Our embrace of the Gospel does not make us any better in the eyes of God or the world; baptism does not induct us into some kind of exclusive club or make us one of the ruling elite. We are always students of Christ, the Teacher of humility and reconciliation. In imitating Christ's forgiveness, compassion and love, we do not become the superiors of others; we only live up to our call to be their brothers and sisters under the providence of God.

For reflection:

- How can we, both individually and collectively as a church, "lord" our identity as God's people over those we consider lesser lights?
- Who have you known in your life whose life quietly reflected a total, joyful commitment to discipleship?
- Which of today's three parables are especially meaningful – and perhaps troubling – to you?

Readings:

Luke 7: 1-10
1 Kings 8: 41-43
Galatians 1: 1-2, 6-10

The centurion is one of the heroes of Luke's **Gospel**. The equivalent of a sergeant in today's army (centurions were considered the "backbone" of the Roman Army), the centurion displays unusual compassion toward his slave and respect for the values and beliefs of the Jews – who considered him, as a foreign occupier, "unclean." Jesus is amazed at the faith of this foreigner in the midst of the unbelieving people of the covenant and exalts the "unclean" officer's humility and trust by curing his slave.

The inclusion of this episode in Luke's Gospel reflects the experience of the early Church that was unprepared for the overwhelming acceptance of their young faith among Gentiles. For Luke (a Gentile himself), the story of the centurion points to the universal mission of the Church to proclaim the Gospel beyond Israel to every place and people.

Today's **first reading** also celebrates the universality of God's love. At the dedication of the temple, Solomon prays for foreigners who come to worship the Lord, thus affirming that the love of God extends beyond the borders of Israel to include all men and women of every nation.

The Christian communities in Galatia (Asia Minor) were among the first founded by Paul during his first missionary journey. After Paul's departure, Jewish converts ("Judaizers") demanded that Gentile converts to the Gospel embrace the ancient customs of Judaism (circumcision, dietary laws, etc.). In response, Paul fired off an emotion-packed letter to the Galatians (most scholars believe that the letter to Galatians is among the earliest writings of Paul, sent perhaps just before or immediately after the Council of Jerusalem, 48-55 A.D.) The Torah, Paul writes, is no longer binding upon the new Israel, the Church of the new covenant; the Gospel brings salvation to all men and women of every age.

Today's **second reading** is the first of six weekly readings from Paul's letter to the Galatians. Today's reading, the beginning of the letter, introduces Paul's overall theme: that Jesus' death and Resurrection are the dawning of a new age, a new life of grace.

Themes:

The centurion: a model of leadership.

The centurion – whom we never actually meet in Luke's story – is a unique figure in Scripture. Although part of the Roman occupation force, he won the respect even of the Jews, who speak on his behalf to Jesus. In Rome's highly secular culture, he possessed a deep, personal awareness of the spiritual. Despite the class distinctions of his society, the centurion was clearly a man of great compassion, whose respect and care extended even to one of his slaves – someone who was considered, under the law, as property, not entitled to even the most basic human rights. The centurion is a model of greatness as Jesus defines greatness: a leader who embraces an attitude of service towards others, an authority who empowers others to realize their own lives' potentials.

Looking beyond demographics, labels and statistics.

Too often we forget that the people we meet and deal with are more than just numbers and statistics, more than just potential customers, more than just members of broadly-defined ethnic groups and nationalities, more than just workers or employees whose only worth is their productivity, more than just faceless, nameless demographics. Today's readings challenge us to look beyond labels and roles to see fellow human beings: in the first reading, Solomon, in his prayer at the dedication of the Temple, asks Yahweh to hear the prayers not only of Jews but also of foreigners and non-Jews who come to honor the Lord; in today's Gospel, the centurion, a man of deep faith and compassion, approaches Jesus to heal a lowly slave. The Gospel demands that we look upon one another as brothers and sisters if we are to even hope to look upon God as Father. As American humorist Will Rogers wryly observed, "The Lord so constituted everybody that no matter what color you are, you require the same amount of nourishment."

For reflection:

- Consider leaders you have known who have possessed both the management abilities and moral authority of the centurion.
- In what ways does our society reduce humanity to simple demographics? What price have we paid for such labeling?
- Do you know any non-Christians who might serve as models of faith to Christians?

Tenth Sunday of the Year

Readings:

Luke 7: 11-17
1 Kings 17: 17-24
Galatians 1: 11-19

Jesus' raising of the widow's son in the village of Naim appears only in Luke's **Gospel**. Luke refers to Jesus here as "Lord," the First Testament Greek title for the Holy One who is Master of life and death. This story underlines two key themes of Luke's Gospel: the extraordinary love and compassion of Jesus for the poor and destitute (throughout Scripture, widows are the epitome of need and despair) and Jesus as the great fulfillment of Israel's Messianic hope when "the eyes of the blind will be opened, the ears of the deaf unstopped, the lame shall leap like a deer, and the tongue of the speechless sing for joy" (Isaiah 35: 5-6).

Elijah's raising of a widow's son in the first book of Kings (**first reading**) parallels Jesus' miracle in today's Gospel.

When Paul speaks of the Gospel of reconciliation (**second reading**), he knows first hand the depth of God's mercy and forgiveness and recounts for the struggling Church at Galatia the story of his own conversion.

Themes:

The greatness of the powerless and vulnerable before God.

One of the continuing themes of Luke's Gospel is Jesus' extraordinary compassion and love for the powerless and vulnerable. Luke includes several such stories in his Gospel, stories which are not found in any of the other three Gospels. We, too, are called by Christ to recognize and reach out to the those whom the world consciously or unconsciously dismiss as unimportant and marginal and welcome them into our midst as God's own.

The disciple's call to compassion.

In today's readings, both Elijah and Jesus reach out to help a widow, who typified for Palestinian society the most powerless and poorest of society. Both the prophet and the Messiah were moved to act out of their deeply-felt sense of love and concern for these poor women, whose only hope for survival, their sons, had died. Today's readings challenge us to be moved by the same sense of compassion and forgiveness: to bring hope and healing to others, without condition or considering the cost, only because they are brothers and sisters of us in the same Father.

For reflection:

- What gifts do the poor and powerless bring to our common table?
- Share stories of individuals and groups who have done great things out of a sense of simple compassion.
- In Jesus' time, widows were considered the most helpless and vulnerable in society. How can we reach out and restore to dignity and wholeness those our society considers among the most helpless and vulnerable?

Readings:
Luke 7: 36 – 8: 3
2 Samuel 12: 7-10, 13
Galatians 2: 16, 19-21

The penitent woman's intrusion into Simon's dinner (**Gospel**) party was a risky thing to do. Her washing of Jesus' feet was embarrassing to the reserved household of the host; but it was an act of extraordinary faith and confidence in the compassion of Jesus to forgive her sins and make her whole again.

Her attitude stands in stark contrast to the calculated reserve of the proper Simon, who believes that Jesus has disgraced himself by acknowledging this pitiful display. But Simon fails to understand everyone's need – including his own need – for forgiveness and reconciliation with those we hurt and who hurt us. We all need "five hundred coins" worth of forgiveness, but we may be too blind to our sinfulness or too afraid or too proud to ask that our debt be written off. Only in acknowledging that need are we able to experience the loving forgiveness of God the penitent woman receives at the feet of Jesus.

Gentile society of Luke's time had little regard for women. Throughout his Gospel, Luke exalts the role and gifts of women in his story of Jesus. In the final verses of today's Gospel, Luke identifies two of the women who will be among the first witnesses of Jesus' resurrection. Mary the Magdalene was a poor, mentally ill woman cured by Jesus; Joanna, the wife of Herod's chief steward and manager, was a woman of considerable position and means. Both women, of very different backgrounds, find sisterhood and community in the presence of the compassionate Jesus.

Today's **first reading**, from the second book of Samuel, is another story of forgiveness. David had fallen in love with Bathsheba, the wife of Uriah, one of his commanders. David had arranged for Uriah to be part of a military expedition against the Ammonites, a venture that would mean certain death for Uriah. Confronted with his crimes by the prophet Nathan, David acknowledges his guilt and Nathan assures the king of the Lord's forgiveness.

In today's **second reading,** Paul assures the Galatian community that we find purpose and meaning not in religious legalities or empty rituals but in total dedication to the Gospel of Christ Jesus. Crucified with Christ and living for God in Christ, we experience salvation by faith, not by the Law.

Themes:

The liberating spirit of forgiveness.

Without forgiveness, life is governed by an endless cycle of resentment and retaliation. The Jesus of the Gospel challenges us to break out of that cycle. The woman in today's Gospel alone had the dignity to risk rejection and scorn in approaching Jesus in love and humility. Every one of us has a deep need both to forgive and be forgiven and to experience the much needed joy for healing and reconciliation.

The disciples' call to be reconcilers.

As disciples of Jesus, we are called to be reconcilers, not judges; we are called to forgive, not keep score; we are called to welcome back those who want to return and to enable them to put their lives back together, not to set up conditions or establish litmus tests to prove their worthiness and sincerity. To love as Jesus loves demands that we live, not in skepticism or distrust, but in the faithful optimism that God always welcomes us back to him.

For reflection:

- The penitent woman's washing of Jesus' feet was considered a breech of etiquette, a brazen flouting of social convention. Have you ever witnessed such a disregard of what is considered proper that yielded such a transforming result?
- When have you witnessed the courage to ask for forgiveness?
- To forgive completely as Jesus forgives, what is demanded of the *forgiver?* Of the *forgiven?*
- Consider the lives of women of heroic faith whose lives have inspired you.

12th Sunday of the Year

Readings:

Luke 9: 18-24
Zechariah 12: 10-11
Galatians 3: 26-29

Today's reading from Luke's **Gospel** is the first of three predictions Jesus makes regarding the cross awaiting him in Jerusalem. He prepares Peter and the disciples for the revelation of the horrifying passion he will endure by asking them who *they* believe he is. Jesus responds to Peter's proclamation of faith in him as "the Messiah" by confronting his followers with the cost of that faith: to cast aside an image of ourselves based on worldly illusions and find the meaning of life in the servanthood of the cross.

Zechariah's prophecy (**first reading**) of the "day of the Lord" and Jerusalem's mourning for "him whom they have thrust through" is a moment of grace for Israel. The evangelist John will cite this passage in his account of Jesus' death on the cross (John 19: 37).

Paul continues his teaching to the Galatians (**second reading**) that the Law of old is fulfilled and perfected in the messianic work of Christ. In the faith we share in the Risen One, we are stripped of all labels and identities – save that of child of God.

Themes:

The cross: the sign of God's love.

Why did Jesus have to die on the cross? The basic catechism answer is that he died to redeem us, to forgive our sins, to show his love for us. But why did he have to die on a cross as he did? Couldn't God simply have snapped his cosmic fingers and proclaim us forgiven and be done with it? Wouldn't we have been just as 'saved'?

Yes, but it would have meant little to us, because we humans need to see, to hear, to sense love. The point of the cross is that, through it, God showed how much he loves us – God loved us enough to become one of us and to die for us. In the crucified Jesus, God's love can be seen, felt and experienced.

Answering the question, 'Who do you say I am?'

Jesus confronts us with the same question he poses to his disciples. Every thing we say and do is our response to that question; every decision and choice we make proclaims exactly who we believe this Jesus is. Every moment of our lives declares our faith in Jesus, "the Messiah of God," who comes to restore us to hope and transform us in the justice and peace of God.

'Denying' ourselves for the things of God.

We tend to see ourselves, for the most part, as the center of our own little universe. But to become true followers of Jesus, we must place ourselves second – "deny" ourselves – for the sake of others, in imitation of Christ, the Servant-Redeemer.

For reflection:

- Why is it so difficult to answer the question Jesus asks Peter and his disciples: *Who do you say I am?*
- How do our lives parallel Jesus' journey to Jerusalem?
- In what signs have you seen and sensed the love of God?
- In what ways can we meaningfully and effectively "deny" ourselves for the love of God? How does such "self denial" differ from destructive self-hatred?

13th Sunday of the Year

Readings:

Luke 9: 51-62
1 Kings 19: 16, 19-21
Galatians 5: 1, 13-18

The journey to Jerusalem is the focus of today's **Gospel**. Jesus proceeds to Jerusalem to take up the cross that awaits him there.

The most direct route to Jerusalem took Jesus and his band through a Samaritan town. The Samaritans and Jews despised one another. Their hatred dated back to the eighth century B.C., when Assyria conquered northern Israel (Samaria). Those northerners who survived the disaster intermarried with foreigners resettled by the Assyrians. The Jews of Jerusalem considered such accommodation with their hated enemy treason and, worse, a betrayal of the holy faith. Jerusalem banned the Samaritans from the temple and synagogues, refused their religious contributions and denied their legal status in court proceedings.

The spurned Samaritans would do everything they could to hinder and even attack pilgrims to Jerusalem. Although it was the most direct route from Galilee, Jews avoided the territories of the Samaritans. Jesus, however, proceeds through Samaria, regardless of their inhospitality and responds to their bitterness with tolerance and reconciliation.

Along the way, three would-be disciples ask to join Jesus. To the first, Jesus asks that he clearly understand the cost of discipleship; Jesus urges the second not to find excuses or rationalizations for avoiding the call of God; and Jesus reminds the third that discipleship demands a total dedication and commitment to seeking God in all things.

The demand Jesus makes of his disciples to abandon everything is mirrored in the demand Elijah makes of his successor Elisha to leave home and family to take up the work of the prophet (**first reading**).

Paul speaks of freedom in Christ (**second reading**) not as license to seek one's own gratification but as a responsibility to live in the spirit rather than the "flesh." "To live in freedom" is to be liberated from the pressures and concerns of the world in order to imitate the selfless Jesus in all things.

Themes:

The hard work of discipleship.

In today's Gospel, Jesus demands a clear, unhesitant, unambiguous and uncompromising commitment from those who want to be his disciples. There can be no "but first . . .," no "in a minute . . .," no "on second thought. . . ." The Gospel of forgiveness, reconciliation, justice and peace is not a collection of pious words we commit to memory but a spirit to which we commit our lives. We cannot be disciples by simply being spectators of God's presence; authentic discipleship calls us to become fully engaged in the hard work of making the reign of God to reality.

The 'forward movement' of authentic faith.

To lay claim to the title of disciple is a defining moment in our lives, a moment of decision and resolution. In taking up the call to be a disciple, we face the condition of our lives with honesty and integrity; the excuses and rationalizations we concoct to justify our tentativeness to embrace the Gospel begin to dissolve.

Jesus calls those who would be his disciples to embrace the spirit of the Gospel with absolute courage and conviction, not to look back to the lives we leave behind but forward to the possibilities of making the reign of God a reality in our own time and place.

For reflection:

- If Jesus were to personally ask three prospective disciples today to "Come after me," what excuses might they give? And how would Jesus respond to each?
- In what ways does faith compel us to look *forward* rather than become obsessed with what has passed?
- When has your faith demanded that you "leave behind" some belief or attitude that you had always accepted and had become secure and comfortable with?

14th Sunday of the Year

Readings:
Luke 10: 1-12, 17-20
Isaiah 66: 10-14
Galatians 6: 14-18

Jesus commissions 72 messengers to go before him to prepare for his arrival in the towns along his route to Jerusalem. The number *72* symbolized for the Jews the number of world's Gentile nations. In keeping with Luke's use of symbolic numbers and his Gentile perspective, the 72 disciples represent the new Church's mission to every nation and people under heaven.

Jesus instructs the 72 disciples:

- keep focused on the ways and values of God – travel light, accept the simple hospitality of those you visit;
- be proclaimers of peace "amid wolves";
- offer hope and healing, not judgment and condemnation;
- find satisfaction not in what you have done in God's name but to rejoice in what God has done through you.

Jesus' vision of Satan's fall assures the disciples of every age that, despite the dangers of "serpent and scorpion" (First Testament symbols of evil), the good that they do out of faithfulness to their call will ultimately triumph.

As Jesus continues his journey to Jerusalem in today's Gospel, we hear in **first reading** (from the last chapter of the book of Isaiah) the prophet's vision of Jerusalem's ultimate salvation through the goodness of a loving God.

In the last in this series of readings from his letter to Galatians (**second reading**), Paul makes a final "boast" in the tree of the cross as the instrument of our salvation, the symbol of a new covenant and the promise of the life of the Risen Christ.

Themes:

Called to be a disciple: 'travel light.'

To be a true disciple of Jesus often means making the hard choices, resolving to proclaim the peace and justice of God despite the ridicule and hostility of those whose lifestyles and power bases are threatened by such an ideal. Jesus instructs his disciples to "travel light" – not to clutter up our lives with material things and material values, like the pursuit of wealth, status and power. We who claim to be disciples of Jesus are called to focus our lives on the certainty of the reign of God and to proclaim that hope throughout our life's journey.

Called to be a disciple: 'lambs in the midst of wolves.'

The Gospel challenges us to make the hard choice and the unpopular decision, to endure the raised eyebrows and suspicious stares of those whose lifestyles and power bases are challenged by the demanding teachings of Jesus. We are called to proclaim the peace and justice of God in whatever circumstances, places, experiences and relationships we find ourselves. The decisions we make, the courses of action we take, the values we hold as important in our lives must reflect the spirit of the Gospel we embrace as disciples of Jesus.

Called to be a disciple: proclaiming peace.

Like the seventy-two in today's Gospel, Jesus appoints every disciple of every time and place to go before him to bring "peace" into the lives of others, to be messengers of his compassion, reconciliation and hope to every life we touch. Such is the "work" of faith, the "labor" of discipleship.

For reflection:

- What things in your life do you find sometimes slowing you down on your pilgrimage to the reign of God?
- When have you felt like a "lamb in the midst of wolves" for the sake of the Gospel or witnessed someone living the Gospel in such circumstances? How did you/that person respond?
- How do Jesus' instructions to the 72 apply to us, as we go about the work of discipleship in our own place and time?

15th Sunday of the Year

Readings:
Luke 10: 25-37
Deuteronomy 30: 10-14
Colossians 1: 15-20

A lawyer's question about who is – and, by implication, who is *not* – one's neighbor sets the stage for one of Jesus' most beloved parables, the story of the Good Samaritan (a story found only in Luke's **Gospel**).

Jesus stuns his hearers by making a Samaritan the hero of the story – especially in light of the inhospitality of the Samaritans during their journey to Jerusalem (see notes for the 13th Sunday of Cycle C). Jesus' hearers would expect a Samaritan to be the villain of the story. While the two clerics do not help the man for fear of violating the Torah by being defiled by the dead, the compassionate Samaritan – a man presumably with little concern for Jewish belief or morality – is so moved by the plight of the poor man that he thinks nothing of stopping to help regardless of the cost of time or money.

The Samaritan and the traveler illustrate that Jesus' concept of "neighbor" is not limited to one's own clan or community. Christ-like compassion must be manifested in deeds of kindness; morality, in the light of the Gospel, cannot be guided by laws inscribed in stone but ultimately by the spirit of the heart.

Selfless compassion is the "command" Moses speaks of to Israel (**first reading**) that has already been placed by God "in your mouths and in your hearts." Such compassion for others is not some obtuse, rationalist system reserved only for the learned or religious elite, but it is a way of life open to all.

The **second reading** for the next four Sundays is taken from the letter to the Colossians. There is some question as to whether or not Paul himself actually wrote this epistle. One theory is that the teacher Epaphras, a leader of the church at Colossae, asked Paul (who did not establish the Colossian church) for his advice on a number of issues regarding the growing "spirit" cult.

Today's reading, the beginning of the letter, is a hymn of praise to Christ, "the image of the invisible God" and supreme reconciler of all of creation to God. The Risen Jesus is the wisdom of God incarnate.

Themes:

The Good Samaritan: prototype of Gospel charity.

The Good Samaritan is the Gospel prototype of Gospel charity, the embodiment of the Gospel vision of humanity as a community of men and women – past and present – sharing the same sacred dignity as sons and daughters of God. "Good Samaritans" are, quite simply, people who recognize every human being as their neighbor and then permit nothing – prejudices, stereotypes, complications, costs, expected returns – to prevent them from hearing a cry for help. There is nothing mysterious about such charity; it is not something remote or distant (as Moses teaches his people in today's first reading). The Gospel calls us to do extraordinary things for others with the ordinary that we possess, to give of the talents and means we have to be Good Samaritans in our own time and place.

The Gospel definition of 'neighbor.'

And who is my neighbor? is one of the most critical questions asked of Jesus in the Gospel. The Jews of Jesus' time defined "neighbor" exclusively as other Jews. But Jesus' parable of the Good Samaritan expands such a limited concept. One of the most radical dimensions of Christianity is the principle that all men and women are "neighbors": children of the same heavenly Father, brothers and sisters in Christ.

For reflection:

- Who are the "Good Samaritans" you have met in your life who have modeled the charity and compassion of the Gospel?
- How do we rationalize our responding as the priest and Levite do to the cries of those in need?
- Who are the most forgotten and ignored of our "neighbors"? How can we be better "neighbors" to those we would rather not have as "neighbors"?

Readings:

Luke 10: 38-42
Genesis 18: 1-10
Colossians 1: 24-28

The sisters Martha and Mary mirror the two expressions of the disciple's call: loving service to others (Martha) and prayer and contemplation (Mary). But as Martha comes to realize in today's **Gospel,** discipleship begins with hearing the Word of God, with opening our hearts and spirits to the presence of God.

The eastern world believed that hospitality was a sacred obligation: that the opportunity to be of service to and to welcome others was a blessing. Today's **first reading,** Abraham's welcoming of the three strangers, illustrates that belief. The spirit of such hospitality is contained in Jesus' instructions to his disciples that the greatest among them – and us – are those who serve the others.

Writing from prison, Paul speaks words of hope and conviction to the community of Colossae at this most difficult time in the his life (**second reading**).

Themes:

The 'better portion.'

Like Martha, we can become so obsessed with the business and "busy-ness" of life that we fail to grasp the joy that is the essence of life. We can become so caught up with agendas and schedules that we are soon anesthe-tized to feeling and experiencing the very real presence of God in our lives; our need for having everything – and everybody – perfect and in order drives the imperfect and rumpled among us away. Jesus invites each of us to choose the "better portion" of welcoming the joy and love of family and friends that enrich and give meaning to our lives – despite the "mess," the warts, the disappointments and disorder they bring with them.

Gospel hospitality: welcoming others like Christ.

It is a motto of Benedictine monasteries around the world: "Let all be received here as would Christ" (*The Rule of St. Benedict,* chapter 53). Like Abraham's welcome of the three strangers and the welcome Martha, Mary and Lazarus extend to Christ in Bethany, hospitality is not only a holy responsibility but also a joyful opportunity to welcome and serve Christ in the persons of others who come to our tables. Gospel hospitality demands a sense of joy at welcoming our guests and gratitude that we may share what we have with them.

For reflection:

- Can Martha's attitude and concerns be destructive? Can Mary's attitude be too narrow and empty?
- In what ways do we make our homes and churches places of Gospel hospitality?
- How can we reclaim the "better portion" in our own busy lives?

17th Sunday of the Year

Readings:

Luke 11: 1-13
Genesis 18: 20-32
Colossians 2: 12-14

In today's reading from Luke's **Gospel**, the disciples ask Jesus to teach them how to pray. What is important to grasp is not the words of the prayer (Luke's version of the Lord's Prayer is shorter and more concise than Matthew's version), but the *attitude* of prayer Jesus teaches. To pray is not to impose our will on God but to ask God to make us open to his will; in other words, we pray not to change God's mind but for God to change ours.

Authentic prayer, as taught by Jesus and contained in the Lord's Prayer, has three elements:

- *acknowledging the goodness and love of God:* Jesus teaches us to call God "Father." God is not the cosmic tyrant out of whom gifts have to unwillingly extracted; God is the loving eternal Parent who delights in providing for his children's needs.
- *asking that we may do God's will:* Prayer worthy of God asks for the grace to do the work he calls us to do (forgiveness, reconciliation, justice), to become the people he calls us to become (brothers and sisters under our heavenly Father).
- *voicing our hope in the providence of God:* We come before God knowing that, just as a friend will aid a friend and parents will provide for their children, God will hear our prayers and give us all and more than we need. Even if it seems as if our prayers are unanswered, we live with the confident faith that God is always present to us.

Today's **first reading** is a humorous and entertaining example of eastern bargaining at its best. The good and faithful Abraham barters with God to spare the innocent of Sodom and Gomorrah. In the end, God reveals himself to be a God of limitless forgiveness and mercy.

In today's brief **second reading**, Paul also speaks of the forgiveness of God and the promise of the resurrection won for us by Christ on the cross.

Themes:

Prayer: the awareness of God.

We have managed to confine God and religious "stuff" to a Saturday evening/Sunday morning time slot; we have jealously shielded the home, work and play dimensions of our lives from any intrusion of the spiritual; we have established socially acceptable vehicles and formulas for "acknowledging" God. Real prayer, however, transcends those boundaries we have set and those formulas we have committed to memory (but not necessarily to practice). Prayer is a constant state of awareness of God's presence in every moment, every challenge, every decision of our lives. The Jesus of the Gospel calls us to become men and women of prayer: to embrace the spirit and attitude of prayer that constantly discerns and celebrates God's presence in all things.

Prayer: an attitude rather than a formula.

In today's Gospel, Jesus gives us more than a prayer text – he teaches us the attitude necessary for authentic prayer. In many of our prayers we ask God to come around to doing our will; but true prayer is to discover God's will for us. We often approach prayer as if we are trying to wring gifts from an unwilling God; in fact, we come before a God who knows our needs better than we do ourselves. True prayer is to imitate the compassion of Christ in raising our hearts and voices in a cry for forgiveness, reconciliation, healing and mercy for our world. Prayer, as Teresa of Avila taught her sisters, "is the conformity of our will to the will of God."

For reflection:

- At what times in your life have you been most conscious of God's presence? How have those experiences affected your sense of prayer?
- How would our lives differ if we actually lived the prayer Jesus taught his disciples?
- What exactly should we pray for?
- Who have you known in your life who could most accurately be called a man or woman *of prayer?* What can their lives teach us about the attitude of prayer?

18th Sunday of the Year

Readings:

Luke 12: 13-21
Ecclesiastes 1: 2; 2: 21-23
Colossians 3: 1-5, 9-11

Rabbis were often asked to arbitrate conflicts within families and communities. In today's **Gospel**, Jesus has been approached to settle such an argument over an inheritance. Jesus responds not by taking sides but by addressing the greed that has brought both sides to near blows. He tells the parable of the rich man who, in the midst of his good fortune, loses his sense of what is really important. Possessions create the illusion that we can control our lives; the drive for gain makes us oblivious to the needs and dreams of others. The "foolish" rich man in today's Gospel sadly discovers that wealth in the reign of God has nothing to do with stock portfolios, bank accounts or the social register.

Both Qoheleth (**first reading**) and Paul (**second reading**) address the real issue at the root of the quarrel over the inheritance: the greed of gain, the love of money, the consuming desire for things, the suffocating attitude of "me, first!"

Themes:

'Set your heart on the higher things.'

All three of today's readings warn of the futility of the "vain" pursuit of wealth and celebrity. To assess the success of one's life in terms of things bought and sold is to waste that life; to mindlessly and indiscriminately crave what this world prizes ultimately condemns one to a state of profound emptiness and poverty. Any *thing* in our lives that displaces the wisdom and life of God is "vanity" and "misfortune" (Ecclesiastes); our portfolios and bank accounts will be meaningless dross the moment God "requires" our lives from us (Gospel). Just as we have "died with Christ" (as Paul writes to the Colossians), we must "put to death" whatever in our lives distracts us from or deprives us of the lasting treasures of God.

Time: our journey to God.

We tend to live our lives believing that there will always be enough time to right our wrongs and to atone for our negligence and insensitivities to others; but, as today's readings make clear, our days are numbered, death is an inevitability for all of us. We are often as short-sighted as the rich farmer in today's Gospel: we can become so self-centered and self-sufficient that we shut ourselves off from the seemingly simple aspects of life in which we find the love and presence of God. Faith is the constant awareness that life is not the destination itself but a journey to God and that death is the final passageway.

For reflection:

- When were you last aware of the preciousness of time?
- In what ways do you experience life as a journey?
- Share experiences when you have become so absorbed in an enterprise or project that (as does the rich man in today's Gospel) you lost sight of something important in your life or the life of a loved one.

Readings:

Luke 12: 32-48
Wisdom 18: 6-9
Hebrews 11: 1-2, 8-19

Three short parables about the treasures of the reign of God are the central images of today's **Gospel**.

Death comes to us like a "thief" in the night, Jesus tells his listeners; therefore, we must always be ready to meet the Lord and enter his "kingdom" with "belts tightened" and through works of charity. The first generations of Christians read this parable as an indication that Christ would return in their lifetimes, in the middle of great paschal night.

Jesus frequently speaks of the coming reign of his Father as a wedding feast to which all of the faithful are invited. Luke includes the image in his Gospel, as well, with an interesting twist. Those who have embraced the spirit of servanthood taught by Jesus the Master will be served by the Master himself at the banquet table to come. Jesus targets the parable to the leaders of the Jewish establishment who have used their positions to advance their own prestige and wealth at the expense of the people they were appointed to serve. While God casts out the exploiters from his kingdom, the faithful leader-servants will be served by the Messiah himself at the great banquet of heaven.

The third parable is Luke's version of Jesus' story of the watchful steward who faithfully conducts the responsibilities entrusted to him by his master. This life on earth is a time that has been entrusted to us by God be about the business of preparing for the life of the world to come.

The fastening of belts and the ever burning lamps recall Israel's great Exodus event from enslavement to freedom (**first reading**). In Christ, the new Israel, the Church, will experience the new exodus event from death to life.

The **second reading** is the first in a series of readings over the next four Sundays from the final chapters of the letter to the Hebrews, the theological treatise of unknown authorship on the new covenant mediated by Jesus Christ, its eternal high priest. Today's reading is a hymn to faith, exalting the trust our ancestors in the faith placed in the goodness and mercy of God.

Themes:

The brevity of this life, the eternity of the next.

While we pay little or no attention to the reality that one day we will die and carry on pretending that we will live forever, the fact is that life is fragile and fleeting. If we have truly embraced the spirit of the Gospel, we are always conscious of the brevity of this life and live our days in joyful anticipation of the next.

Stewards of God's blessings.

God has entrusted us with many gifts, talents and blessings: we may have the intellectual ability to probe the mysteries of the cosmos or we may possess the less vaulted but no less wondrous talent of being a good spouse or parent. Whatever aptitudes and abilities we possess, we are "stewards" of those gifts; our "mastery" over them is determined by how selflessly and lovingly we use them for the benefit of others. The Spirit calls us to share our blessings without counting the cost or setting conditions or demanding a return. The most spendthrift, liberal charity will be repaid by God in the world to come.

Leadership: serving those we are called to lead.

Jesus' parable in today's Gospel is targeted at the leaders of the Jewish establishment who have used their positions to advance their own prestige and wealth at the expense of those they were called to serve. Leadership is not a matter of exerting power to intimidate others or enrich one's own situation; leadership is the ability to inspire and enable others to do what is right, just and good. Jesus promises that those who lead by example, who honor those in their charge who view their role as leader not as honor well deserved but as a responsibility to serve, will be seated and served by the "Master" himself at the banquet of heaven.

For reflection:

- What events and experiences in your life have most effectively reminded you of the brevity and preciousness of this life?
- Who have you known whose "mastery" of the gifts God has "entrusted" to them exhibited extraordinary faith?
- Have you known any "leaders" who might be described as "leader-servants" in the spirit of the Gospel?

20th Sunday of the Year

Readings:
Luke 12: 49-53
Jeremiah 38: 4-6, 8-10
Hebrews 12: 1-4

When Luke wrote these few lines of his **Gospel**, Christians were living through difficult times and circumstances. In many places they were treated with ridicule, disdain and intolerance. Jesus' words are addressed to them and to all Christians who have paid dearly for living their faith in their time and place.

Fire was a Scriptural symbol of judgment. The Lord will judge the hearts of all men and women in the light of the Gospel's "blaze."

The word used in the original text that reads here as "baptism" actually means a "plunging," a total submersion. Jesus continues on to Jerusalem where he will be "plunged" into the Passover of the new covenant into which, through baptism, we will all be "plunged," as well.

The Gospel is not a soft, easy message to embrace. Jesus does not sugarcoat his message: families and households will be divided over the hard demands of the Gospel of reconciliation, justice and servanthood.

The prophet Jeremiah prophesied that Judah's unfaithfulness would lead the nation to internal crisis and war. In today's **first reading,** Jeremiah pays the price for his hard words.

The writer of Hebrews, in today's **second reading,** also offers words of encouragement to those who struggle with the demands of the Gospel. The writer praises the victory of Jesus who paid the price of the cross for "the sake of the joy which lay before him."

Themes:

The 'fire' of discipleship.

The "fire" Jesus ignited on earth has burned in the hearts of many Christians ever since. Despite ostracism and opposition, they carry on, their commitment inflamed by mercy, justice and compassion, knowing that the promise of the Resurrection is fulfilled only through the cross and the crucifixion of oppression, injustice and hatred. For the faithful disciple, the unwavering love of God, as revealed by Jesus, in the ultimate hope, the "fire" that illuminates hearts and warms a world that has become cold to the peace, forgiveness and justice of its Creator.

Risking the 'unpopularity' of faithful discipleship.

Today's readings confront us with the difficult role of being disciples and prophets of God's compassion and forgiveness. Our faith can, in fact, be a sad source of division, separating us from those who have embraced a very different set of values than those taught by Jesus. As Jesus warns us, to live the Gospel faithfully is to put ourselves at odds with the world's values. God calls us not to seek power or status or even acceptance but to "submerge" ourselves in the Gospel spirit of compassion and humility without compromise or second guessing. The faithfulness of those who stand up to greed and injustice for the sake of the Gospel will be richly rewarded in the reign of God.

For reflection:

- Have you ever found yourself at odds with someone you care deeply about over a moral or ethical issue? How did you deal with it?
- How do we live the reality of the cross without losing hope in the reality of the empty tomb?
- Have you or anyone you've known and admired risked ridicule or rejection for what you/they have believed?

Readings:

Luke 13: 22-30
Isaiah 66: 18-21
Hebrews 12: 5-7, 11-13

Faith is a journey on which we embark to seek the dwelling place of God. Like Jesus' journey to Jerusalem, our faith journey is difficult and painful; doubt, despair and ridicule are among the obstacles we must encounter.

Jesus uses three images in today's **Gospel** that speak of the disciple's faith journey:

- *the narrow door:* The major cities of Palestine were built with walls surrounding the perimeter. Throngs of people could enter the city only through the great doors at the city's entrance. Jesus, however, calls us to enter the city of God through the "narrow door" – through the lonely, humble entry way of the human heart.

- *the locked door:* Conversion is not an instantaneous transformation in which we go from Godlessness to holiness. Our lives are a constant process of conversion, of working to become the people God has called us to become.

- *the feast:* God's invitation to the banquet of heaven is extended to all men and women of good will, not just to those who presume themselves to be God's special elite.

Isaiah prophesied a similar vision of all nations and peoples – Jew and Gentile alike – coming to the holy mountain of the Lord (**first reading**).

The writer of Hebrews (**second reading**) urges us to approach the suffering and pain that are so much a part of the human condition as a "discipline" that God the Father uses as his "school" to teach us his ways of humility, peace and justice.

Themes:

The hope of the 'narrow door.'

The "narrow door" of the Gospel – limitless love, unconditional forgiveness, sacrificial selflessness – is difficult to pass through, but it is the only entry into the reign of God. Jesus promises that anyone willing to struggle through that "narrow door" will be welcomed into the dwelling place of God. The spirit of the "narrow door," Dorothy Day said, is "to take the lowest place, to wash the feet of others with that burning love, that passion which led to . . . the victory of the cross."

Seeking the key to the 'locked door.'

Faith is not a pre-ordained condition nor an all-purpose pass key nor a guaranteed reservation to the here-after. God demands of us a personal, committed response to the gift of faith as the key to the promise of the Resurrection. Today's Gospel reminds us that if we are to be authentic disciples, we have to do more than *say* we are disciples, we have to do more than *claim* to believe; we have to *embrace* the spirit of discipleship, we have to live the faith we believe. Only then will "the Master" know "where we are coming from" and recognize us as invited guests to the banquet of heaven.

The banquet of heaven.

Jesus' teachings about Yahweh as Father and God's kingdom as a feast for all men and women, Jew and Gentile alike, struck at the heart of Jewish thought at the time. Heaven does not belong to the powerful, the learned or the religious elite, but to the people of the Beatitudes – the poor in spirit, the just, the humble, the peacemakers. They will gain entry into the banquet of heaven – and the door will be locked behind them.

For reflection:

- What lasting lessons have you learned from your own experience of making your way through the "narrow door"?
- How can we "eat and drink in the company" of Jesus and still not know him?
- We tend to think of *conversion* as a single, climactic act; but how is conversion a continual promise of becoming God's own?
- How can our own churches and tables better reflect the promised banquet of heaven?

22nd Sunday of the Year

Readings:
Luke 14: 1, 7-14
Sirach 3: 17-18, 20, 28-29
Hebrews 12: 18-19, 22-24

Gospel humility (a key theme of Luke's Gospel) is not a religious sado-masochism motivated by self-hatred or obsequiousness. As taught by Christ, humility is an awareness of who we are before God, of our constant need for God and our dependence on God for everything, of the limitlessness and depth of God's love and forgiveness. The Jesus of the Gospel, "who, though in the form of God, humbled himself . . . accepting even death on the cross" is the perfect model of the humble servant of God.

In today's **Gospel**, Jesus calls us to embrace the attitude of seeking out the "lowest places" at table for the sake of others, promising that at the banquet of heaven God will exalt such humility. In teaching us to invite to our tables "those who cannot repay us," Jesus challenges us to imitate the love of God: doing what is right, good and just for the joy of doing so, not out of a sense of duty, self-interest or the need to feel superior or in control. "Nothing can so effectively humble us before God's mercy as the multitude of his benefits," wrote Francis de Sales, "and nothing can so deeply humble us before his justice as our countless offenses against him."

The great sage writing in the Book of Sirach teaches the Jewish community 200 years before Christ that through humility one "will find favor in the Lord" (**first reading**).

At the foot of Mount Sinai, the Israelites knew God's greatness in such powerful images of clouds, fire, storms, thunder, lightning and the blast of angels' trumpets. They were terrified by the grandeur of God. But the writer of Hebrews (**second reading**) teaches us that, in Christ Jesus, the God of mercy and love becomes approachable to us.

Themes:

Humility: seeking God in all things.

Humility is the virtue of suspending our own wants and needs in order to consciously seek God in all people and experiences. True humility is centered in the things of God – love, compassion, mercy, selflessness, tolerance and forgiveness. If we truly understand the depth of God's love, we realize that all the blessings we have received come as a result of that love and not as a result of anything we have done to deserve them. The only adequate response we can make to such profound love is to try and return that love to those around us, to share the bounty of our tables with the "beggars" among us.

Humility: our brother and sister 'beggars.'

We sometimes view others in terms of abstract labels or impersonal demographics; we tend to dismiss people, for a variety of reasons, as not worth any investment of care or attention on our part. The Gospel, however, challenges us to embrace Jesus' example of humility: to welcome others into our lives because they are children of the God who is Father of us all. Humility, as tuaght by Jesus, is not the mere diminishing of one's self but the realization that, because we share with every human the sacred dignity of being made in the image and likeness of God, all are worthy of our respect and acceptance. To be humble as the servant Christ models humility is to see everyone as God sees everyone: brothers and sisters invited by a compassionate God to share the blessings of the same table, "beggars" all.

For reflection:

- How can the obsessive pursuit and attainment of power be a destructive force for the one who is considered "powerful"?
- Who have you known in your life whom you consider to be a model of Gospel humility?
- Have you ever witnessed the fall of someone victimized by their self-promotion?

23rd Sunday of the Year

Readings:

Luke 14: 25-33
Wisdom 9: 13-18
Philemon 9-10, 12-17

Today's **Gospel** is the beginning of a treatise, unique to Luke's Gospel, on the nature and demands of discipleship.

Jesus' sobering words in today's Gospel are meant to make us fully aware of the cost of discipleship before we embrace something we are not prepared for. The gift of grace comes at the price of the same cross awaiting Jesus in Jerusalem.

Some translations of today's Gospel ascribe rather harsh words to Jesus: in some texts, Jesus speaks of "turning one's back" on family; in other translations, the verb "hate" is used. A more precise translation of the idiom here is whoever *prefers* the love of family or self to Christ cannot be his follower.

The images of the unfinished tower and the king poorly prepared for battle illustrate the frustration and ultimate failure of the disciple who does not give himself/herself totally to the Gospel. When a follower of Jesus begins to hold anything back in imitating Christ, discipleship becomes a charade.

Today's **first reading** from the Book of Wisdom poetically expresses the reality that the ways of God transcend human values and judgments. The wisdom of God reaches into the human soul, while mortal judgment can only guess at the depth of God's love and mercy.

Paul's brief letter (25 verses) to the wealthy Christian Philemon (today's **second reading**) is one of the most fascinating documents in the canon of Scripture. In what is clearly a private letter, the apostle personally intercedes on behalf of Onesimus (the name means "useful" in Greek), a slave of Philemon who has fled his master's service and has sought asylum with Paul at Rome. Both master and slave were converted to the Gospel by Paul in Colossae. In pleading for mercy for Onesimus, Paul appeals to Philemon to accept Onesimus not as a slave but as a brother in Christ.

Themes:

Living the vision of the cross.

We have become so tolerant or oblivious to the brokenness and pain around us that we do not show any of the audacity that Jesus demands from those who would be his disciples. Jesus calls us to seek reconciliation rather than dominance, to love and forgive without limit or condition, to give totally and completely regardless of the cost or sacrifice. Christ calls us to transform our lives and the world we live in by embracing the vision of the cross – courageously and soberly taking on the difficult and demanding "Good Fridays" that confront us in order to bring forth the lasting transformation of the Easter promise.

'Planning' for greater things.

The parables of the tower and the king preparing for battle illustrate how the values of the heart should be at the core of every moment we live and every choice we make. The instinctive quest for wealth, prestige and instant gratification can diminish our relationships with family and friends; every decision and choice we make affect others in ways we may never realize. Jesus challenges us to live every moment of our lives as a time for preparation and "planning" for much greater and lasting things than this world of ours offers.

For reflection:

- What have you found most difficult – if not impossible – to "renounce" for the love of Christ?
- Have you ever found yourself in the position of the tower builder or the king regarding your own experience of faith?
- In what ways have you found the values of God at odds with the standards of success prized by our society and culture?

Readings:

Luke 15: 1-32
Exodus 32: 7-11, 13-14
1 Timothy 1: 12-17

The three "parables of the lost" in chapter 15 are unique to Luke's Gospel. Luke wrote his Gospel at a time when the Christian community was embroiled in a great controversy: many Jewish Christians were indignant that Gentiles should be welcomed into the Church without first embracing the traditions and laws of Judaism.

In these three parables, we enter God's world: God communicates the depth of his love in his unconditional and complete forgiveness; his mercy breaks through and demolishes all human restrictions. The Pharisees could not imagine a God who actually sought men and women out, a God who is more merciful in his judgments than we are, a God who never gives up hope for a sinner.

Today's **Gospel** reading of chapter 15 includes three parables:

*   *The parable of the lost sheep:* Shepherding demanding toughness and courage – it was not a job for the weak and fearful. Responsible for every sheep in his charge, a shepherd was expected to fight off everything from wild animals to armed poachers. Shepherds often had to negotiate the rugged terrain of the wilderness to rescue a lost sheep. Like the shepherd, God does whatever is necessary to seek out and bring back to his loving providence every lost soul.
*   *The parable of the lost coin:* Finding a small silver coin in a dark, dusty, dirt-floored Judean house was very difficult, but so great was the value of any coin to the poor that a woman would turn her poor hovel inside out in search of a lost treasure. So great is the value of every soul in the sight of God that he, too, goes to whatever lengths necessary to find and bring back the lost.
*   *The parable of prodigal son:* This is probably the most inaccurately titled story in all of literature. Jesus' tale is really about the great love of the prodigal's father, who forgives his son and joyfully welcomes him home even before the son can bring himself to ask. The father's joy stands in sharp contrast to the prodigal son's brother, who cannot even bring himself to call the prodigal his "brother" – in confronting his father, he angrily refers to the brother as "this son of yours." But the father is a model of joyful reconciliation that Jesus calls his disciples to seek in all relationships.

In today's **first reading**, Moses intercedes on behalf [of] his people who have disobeyed the Lord by repre[se]nting him in the form of gold calf). Moses pleads with [th]e Lord to "remember" his constant compassion and [m]ercy to his people and relent in his anger.

Today begins a series of readings from Paul's letters [to] his friend and co-worker Timothy. These letters, along [wi]th the letter to Titus, are known as the "pastoral epis[tle]s" of Paul because they outline codes of conduct and [au]thority for those who minister to the Christian commu-

nity. Today's **second reading**, from Paul's first letter to Timothy, is a hymn of thanksgiving: Paul praises the mercy and forgiveness of God who has raised Paul up as an apostle despite his many sins and "unbelief."

Themes:

The God of new beginnings.

The forgiveness parables taught by Jesus in today's Gospel reveals a God of beginnings: a God who is never satisfied with rejections and terminations and endings but who constantly seeks and offers second chances, clean slates and the opportunity to begin again and again and again. As Moses and the Israelites discover, as the apostle Paul recounts to his brother Timothy, as Jesus' stories of the lost sheep, the lost coin and the lost son illustrate, so great is the mysterious love of God that we are never written off as lost or dead or hopelessly irredeemable. The love of God is there for us even in our darkest moments, when our despair and feeling of alienation from God, family and friends are at their worst, when we are angriest at God and the things of God.

The inclusive love of God.

Our God is a God of reconciliation, a God who continually seeks us out despite our rejection of him. Our God is a God of inclusion – yet we sometimes make him a God of *exclusion*, excluding from our own presence those we deem as unworthy or unfaithful to be included among "God's people." As disciples we are called to embrace the spirit of the Christ who searched out the lost, who welcomed the unwanted and the unloved into his circle, who willingly suffered with and for them.

Rejoicing in the joy and rebirth of others.

Sometimes we find it difficult to accept success or good things happening to others: we demean their accomplishment, we belittle their achievement, we question their sincerity, we assign sinister motives to their intentions. But the Gospel calls us to rejoice for and with those who conquer adversity, who struggle to rebuild their lives, who manage to rise from the depth of despair and death to fulfillment and hope. Discipleship calls us neither to judge the lost nor condemn the fallen but to offer them the love we ourselves have received from God and to support them in rebuilding their lives in that same love.

For reflection:

*   Have you ever sought out someone or something with the zeal of the shepherd or widow?
*   Truth be told, most of us identify neither with the prodigal son or the father in the parable, but with the older brother. Why?
*   What are the danger signals that we are making God too exclusively ours?

25th Sunday of the Year

Readings:
Luke 16: 1-13
Amos 8: 4-7
1 Timothy 2: 1-8

The parable of the shrewd business manager (**Gospel**) is one of the most difficult parables of Jesus to understand. At first reading, it appears that Jesus is condoning extortion. But Jesus admires not the manager's lack of scruples but his decisiveness and ingenuity in taking control of his situation. We admire those who use their intelligence, charm and pluck to get ahead in this world — Jesus' parable challenges us to be as eager and as ingenious for the sake of God's reign, to be as ready and willing to use our time and money to accomplish great things in terms of the Gospel as we are to secure our own security and enjoyment. Jesus appeals to the "children of light" to be as enterprising and resourceful in pursuit of the reign of God as this steward is in making a place for himself in this world. We must restore money as the means to an end and not as the end itself; we are only stewards of our Master's property.

Amos is the reluctant shepherd turned prophet who spoke bravely against society's unconscionable exploitation of the poor, especially King Jeroboam II's military exploits to extend Israel's international commerce — trade that greatly benefited the wealthy — but financed by the taxes squeezed from the poor. The prophet warns that the Lord will not forget how the poor were destroyed for the sake of profit (**first reading**).

In his letter to Timothy (**second reading**), Paul urges prayers for all in authority. Such is our duty as both faithful Christians and as responsible citizens.

Themes:

To be resourceful in the ways of God.

The Gospel of the shrewd manager is not an endorsement of larceny but a lesson in using one's ingenuity to get things done. We must be as skilled and resourceful in the ways of God as we try to be in the ways of commerce and politics. Jesus' parable challenges us to be as eager and as ingenious for the sake of justice, mercy and reconciliation, to be ready and willing to use our time, skills and resources to accomplish great things in terms of the Gospel as we are to secure our own security and happiness. The cleverness, skill and plain nerve that the manager uses to save his position we must use, as well, to bring the reign of God to fruition in our time and place.

Being 'possessed' by our possessions.

Jesus constantly warned his followers of the dangers of money and possessions, of permitting the things we possess to *possess* us. Like the shrewd manager and his demanding master, we can become so obsessed with the pursuit of wealth and the manipulation of power that we seem to give us a piece of our humanity in the process: as computer printouts and balance sheets become the center of our existence, we unconsciously push the people and relationships dearest to us to the margins of our lives. The danger of owning things is forgetting that a thing's value is not the thing itself; a thing's true value is its use in helping us discover and cherish the more valuable and lasting treasures that God's gift of life offers us.

For reflection:

- Have you known someone who has used his or her "business savvy" and "street smarts" to accomplish great things in the ways of the Gospel?
- How can money and wealth be dehumanizing?
- Have you ever felt that something valuable you owned actually *owned* you?

26th Sunday of the Year

Readings:
Luke 16: 19-31
Amos 6: 1, 4-7
1 Timothy 6: 11-16

The rich man (sometimes known as "Dives" – "the rich") in the parable of Lazarus (a name which means "God's help") and the rich man (**Gospel**) is not really a bad man, but a self-centered, complacent one. Dives' sin is his remaining oblivious to the plight of the beggar at his gate and his blind acceptance of the poverty of so many and wealth in the hands of so few like himself as the natural, inevitable order of things. It was not his wealth that kept him from "Abraham's bosom," but his untrustworthy stewardship of what he had.

In today's **first reading**, the prophet Amos condemns the complacency of the rich of his own time and place.

Paul urges his friend Timothy (in the **second reading**) to carry on his ministry as teacher and leader of the Church, always "taking firm hold" of the life and spirit embraced in baptism.

Themes:

The 'Lazaruses' at our own gates.

Jesus' story about Lazarus and the rich man seems to belong to a time long ago and a place far away; but the fact is that there are many Lazaruses at our own gates. While we rejoice for Lazarus and applaud Dives' fate, our own self-centeredness and self-righteousness anesthetize our consciences from realizing the plight of the beggars around us. It is that lack of awareness that condemns the "worthless rich" (first reading). Christ calls us to see the plight and hear the cries of the poor and needy at our own gates and open our hearts to welcome them to our tables with compassion and honor.

The measure of discipleship: how we use what we have been given.

To possess money and things is not, in itself, wrong – the moral question is how we *use* our wealth, whether we are rich in money or talent. In Jesus' parable, the rich man is condemned not because he is wealthy but because he remains unmoved and unaffected by the suffering at his very door. Dives of the Gospel and the "worthless rich" of the prophet Amos do not understand that the many blessings we have received from God are given for us to share – to share not out of a sense of obligation but as a joyful opportunity to give thanks to God for his many blessings to us.

For reflection:

- Share stories of individuals who have used their wealth to accomplish great works for humankind.
- Who are the Lazaruses at our gates whose plight often goes unseen?
- In what ways do we view the world with the complacency and obtuseness of the rich man in the Lazarus parable?

Readings:

Luke 17: 5-10
Habakkuk 1: 2-3; 2: 2-4
2 Timothy 1: 6-8, 13-14

Faith is not something that is won, bought or earned. Faith only becomes real and genuine in our lives when we realize in all humility that faith is a gift freely given by God. The two images in today's **Gospel** point to this mystery of faith:

• The gift of faith is like the mustard seed, among the tiniest of seeds. The seed of faith needs to be nurtured or else it will wither and die; but allowed to grow, it yields the greatest of harvests.

• In the light of real faith, we realize our total dependence on the providence of God. To God's graciousness we owe everything. We recognize ourselves as God's "useless servants," deserving nothing by our own account. The only adequate response we can make to God's unfathomable and immeasurable goodness is to live lives of joyful gratitude and humble servanthood.

The prophet Habakkuk (**first reading**) proclaimed hope to a desperate Jerusalem, besieged by the warring Babylonians (600 B.C.). The book of Habakkuk begins with the prophet openly questioning the ways of God and demanding an account for God's governing of the world. God replies that "the vision still has its time," that the faithful will not only survive but triumph.

Paul's second letter to Timothy is more personal and revealing than his first. Writing from prison and aware that his own end is near, Paul offers words of encouragement to his friend in Timothy's own ministry as teacher and leader of the Christian community at Ephesus (**second reading**).

Themes:

The 'vision' of faith.

Faith is a prism through which we see the world as God sees it – the "vision" that "always has its time, presses on to fulfillment and will not disappoint" (first reading).

The gift of faith compels us to approach every challenge and experience we encounter with the vision and wisdom of God, to embrace the role of the Gospel "servant" dedicated to bringing hope, compassion and community out of the ashes of despair, selfishness and division.

The great harvest of 'mustard seed' faith.

It is the mustard seeds that each one of us plants that will reap not only the greatest yield but the most enduring and rooted harvest. With committed, persevering faith, we can "uproot" those things that strangle love, peace, justice and reconciliation in our lives; we can bring forth life and reconciliation in our lives; we can bring forth life and resurrection where there are only despair and alienation. Christ calls to embrace "mustard seed" faith – to believe that even the slighest act of goodness, done in faith and trust in God's presence, has meaning in the reign of God. The mustard seed challenges us to take hold of the opportunities we have for planting and reaping a harvest of justice, compassion and reconciliation in our own piece of the earth.

Our 'duty' to embrace the spirit of the Gospel.

Christ challenges the attitude that to fulfill the letter of the law is enough. The spirit of the Gospel is not just to give something to the poor but to *feel* for the poor and suffering and give from our all, to *love* them enough to grieve and suffer with them. In embracing the spirit of the Gospel, we do not exalt our own sense of charity but we recognize that such charity is the only adequate, fulfilling response we can make to God, for the many blessings we have received.

For reflection:

• Do you know of great things that have begun with small, simple "seeds" of faith and hope?

• Do you know of someone who, despite great obstacles, maintained the vision of faith and saw it to its "time"?

• Who have you known whose humility and dedication to charity models Luke's vision of the "servant"?

Readings:

Luke 17: 11-19
2 Kings 5: 14-17
2 Timothy 2: 8-13

The grateful Samaritan leper is another of the great saints of Luke's **Gospel**. Terrified communities cast out lepers from their midsts, leaving them to fend for themselves usually outside the gates of cities. This group of lepers included both Jews (Galileans) and Samaritans – they are so desperate in their plight that the bitter animosity between Jew and Samaritan evaporates in their need to depend on one another.

In sending the lepers off to those who can legally verify a cure rather than curing them outright, Jesus puts the lepers' faith to the test. Only one – one of those despised Samaritans! – realizes not only that he has been made clean but that he has been touched by God. His return to Jesus to give thanks reflects the healing that has taken place within the leper's soul. Faith is the recognition of the great love and compassion of God, a recognition that moves us to praise and acts of thanksgiving.

Jesus's healing of the Samaritan leper parallels Elisha's healing of the leper Naaman, commander of the armies of the king of Aram (today's **first reading**). The two "mule loads of earth" Naaman requests will be taken back to Aram so that Naaman may erect an altar to Israel's God on the soil of the Lord's holy place.

In today's **second reading**, Paul continues his exhortation to Timothy, the leader of the Ephesian community, to persevere, despite whatever difficulties, to preach the "un-chainable" word of God. The text includes what are perhaps verses of an ancient baptismal hymn sung in Timothy's church.

Themes:

Holy gratitude.

For men and women of faith, gratitude is a constant realization of God's imponderable love in breathing into each one of us the gift of life. Holy gratitude is to stand humbly before God, realizing that, in Christ, we have been "made whole," "made clean," "restored" to completeness in his hope and love. Like the Samaritan leper in today's Gospel, we come to understand that we have been cured despite our sufferings, that our blessings far outweigh our struggles, that we have reason to rejoice and hope despite the sadness and anxieties we must cope with. To realize and rejoice in the Father's love for us can transform cynicism and despair into optimism and hope and make whatever good we do experiences of grace.

The 'lepers' among us.

There are still lepers among us, people we have consciously or unconsciously cast out of society's gates by fear, mistrust and self-interest. They are the lepers – but we suffer the disease. The always reconciling, forgiving, welcoming love of Christ we extend to the "lepers" of our time and place makes us whole, as well.

For reflection:

- Have you ever had the experience of the leper in today's Gospel: in the midst of despair or hopelessness, realizing that you have, in fact, much to be grateful for?
- Who are the "lepers" on the outskirts of our city gates?
- How can an attitude of constant gratitude transform even the most mundane dimensions of everyday life?
- Have you known groups or communities who have been brought together by suffering or adversity and, together, have been able to accomplish powerful things?

29th Sunday of the Year

Readings:

Luke 18: 1-8
Exodus 17: 8-13
2 Timothy 3: 14 – 4: 2

The focus of today's **Gospel** parable is not the evil judge but the persistent widow. The judge here is not one of the Jewish elders but a paid magistrate appointed by the Roman governors. These magistrates were notoriously corrupt, extorting money from plaintiffs to secure favorable verdicts. The widow, typically defenseless in such dealings, persists until the judge just wants to be rid of her.

Jesus does not *liken* God to the unfeeling, insensitive judge but *contrasts* God to him: if such persistence will finally move such a corrupt figure will not the God of mercy and love be moved by the cries of his own beloved people? The parable of the widow and the unjust judge (found only in Luke's Gospel) calls us to perseverance in prayer – prayer that seeks not to force God's hand but prayer that opens our hearts and minds to his always available grace.

Today's **first reading** is another story of perseverance in prayer before God. Amalek and his tribe attacked the Israelites as they made their way to the promised land. During the conflict, Moses stood on the top of a hill and, as a sign of faith in God's continued providence, held high the sacred "staff of God." Moses' tenacious and steadfast faith in God wins the day for Israel.

In today's **second reading**, Paul exhorts Timothy to perseverance in his charge to preach God's word, "whether convenient or inconvenient."

Themes:

Prayer: bringing God's presence into our world.

The great Jewish theologian Rabbi Abraham Joshua Heschel said that "to pray is to bring God back into the world . . . to expand his presence." Prayer is not an act seeking to move God's heart for what we want but one which opens our hearts to what God wants for us. Trap-

pist Father Thomas Keating, the renowned spiritual director and retreat master, explains that "prayer is the fundamental way we relate to God. Like any relationship, it goes through stages, from acquaintance to friendliness, then on to friendship, love and finally union." To become men and women of prayer is to realize God's presence in our lives and trust in that presence and love for us.

Persevering faith.

The widow never loses hope that what is right and just will be hers. She is a model, for all of us, of persevering faith – that, when we feel most lost, abandoned, rejected and without hope, God can and will make his presence known to us in the love, compassion, kindness, understanding and support of others; that, despite the long frustration, struggle and acrimony we might endure, the light of God's justice, peace and goodness will ultimately triumph over the darkness of greed, injustice and hatred.

Faithfully persevering in what is just and right.

The widow in today's Gospel possesses a profound conviction of what is right that empowers her to carry on her search for justice despite being put off so many times by the judge. We possess a faith that empowers us with hope and discernment, enabling us to persevere despite the indignities and injustices that are so much a part of life. Jesus assures us that the integrity, commitment to justice and humility we maintain in the face of skepticism, rationalizations and the amoral "conventional wisdom" will, one day, be exalted by God.

For reflection:

- How has your prayer life changed and matured since you first learned the words to the "Our Father" and the "Hail, Mary"?
- Who have you known in your life who could trust in what was right and just overcame frustration, ridicule and persecution?
- When has the perseverance of the poor widow been rewarded in your life?

Readings:

Luke 18: 9-14
Sirach 35: 12-14, 16-18
2 Timothy 4: 6-8, 16-18

The Pharisee and the tax collector (or "publican") in Jesus' Lucan parable are caricatures of two extreme religious attitudes (**Gospel**).

Pharisees were the "separated ones" who positioned themselves in society as the great keepers of the holy law. They were held in great esteem by the Jewish masses, despite the Pharisees' haughty condemnation of those they viewed as less than faithful.

Tax collectors were Jews who worked for Rome. To become a tax collector, one would bid for a certain territory by paying a sum the government decided that area should yield in taxes. The tax collector then won the right to collect taxes from the people in that locale in order to recoup his investment and make a profit. The tax collectors could also count on Roman cooperation to enforce their outrageous charges. It was a system that was rife with extortion, with little accountability demanded of the tax collectors and no avenues of recourse for the poor they preyed upon. Tax collectors were despised by Jewish society as thieves and collaborators.

The parable contrasts two very different attitudes of prayer. The Pharisee approaches God seeking the reward he feels he deserves. His prayer is really a testimonial to himself for all the good things the *Pharisee* has done to merit God's grace. The tax collector, on the other hand, realizes his nothingness before God. He comes before God seeking his mercy because of the good things *God* has done for undeserving sinners like himself. It is the prayer of the humble, who come before God with an attitude of thanks and wonder for God's unconditional and limitless mercy that is heard and "exalted" before God.

The great Jewish sage Jesus Ben Sirach eloquently praises the justice and mercy of the Lord who hears the cries of the poorest and most helpless (**first reading**).

In Paul's farewell to Timothy (**second reading**), the imprisoned apostle, awaiting a second trial at Rome, expresses hope in the God of mercy whom he has faithfully preached.

Themes:

Making God into our image.

Like the Pharisee in today's Gospel, we can "use" God to justify our own belief systems and to advance our own idea of what the world should be. The Christ of compassion and reconciliation calls us to see ourselves as made in God's image, not to recast God in our image. To be men and woman of faith is to listen to God speaking in the depths of our hearts and to respond to God's invitation to become his holy people, to fulfill his will and hope for us.

Humility before one another.

In our own time and place, the parable of the Pharisee and the tax collector is played out not so much as a lack of humility before God but as a lack of awareness of the needs, the hopes, the cries for help of those around us. In our eagerness to do things for others, we begin to see them as objects of charity, vehicles for making ourselves feel good about ourselves; we fail to realize that they are our brothers and sisters who deserve our help for no other reason than they are, like us, children of God. Humility before God demands humility before one another, seeing them as God sees us.

To pray the humble prayer of the tax collector.

"Humility is absolutely necessary," Thomas Merton wrote, "if one is to avoid acting like a baby all one's life. To grow up, in fact, means to become humble, to throw away the illusion that I am the center of everything and that other people exist to provide me with comfort and pleasure." The Gospel of Jesus challenges us to embrace the humble, God-centered faith of the tax collector. Attitude and action are the essence of authentic discipleship, not just words and rituals empty of feeling or conviction. We manifest our love for God not through self-righteous acts of piety but through our love and care for the poor, the needy, the defenseless, the alienated and the rejected.

For reflection:

- In what ways have groups and causes re-shaped God into something that the Gospel teaches God is *not?*
- In what ways do we become more humble with age?
- How can our best intended prayers and acts of charity deteriorate into the prayers of the Pharisee?

Readings:

Luke 19: 1-10
Wisdom 11: 22 – 12: 1
2 Thessalonians 1: 11 – 2: 2

As the chief tax collector of Jericho, a very prosperous trade and agricultural village just northwest of Jerusalem, Zacchaeus was a very unpopular man with his fellow Jews (see last Sunday's notes on tax collectors). Though very wealthy, Zacchaeus (the name, ironically, means "clean") was a very unhappy and lonely man who desperately sought the peace of God taught by this rabbi named Jesus. But it is Jesus who takes the initiative and seeks out Zacchaeus, calling Zacchaeus down from the sycamore tree and inviting himself to Zacchaeus' house. In seeking out Zacchaeus, Jesus calls forth the good will of Zacchaeus that his neighbors fail to see (**Gospel**). The Messiah has come explicitly for the Zacchaeuses of the world: to lift up the fallen, to seek out the lost, to give hope to the poor and the forgotten.

The writer of the Book of Wisdom (**first reading**) speaks, in very poetic imagery, of the basic goodness of all creation in the eyes of God and God's unlimited capacity for forgiving and restoring to wholeness the creation he so loves.

Paul's second letter to the Christian community at Thessalonica (**second reading**) was prompted by the alarm and fear over certain rumors, falsely attributed to Paul, that the second coming of Jesus was imminent. Paul prays that the Thessalonians may live their lives "worthy of God's call" so as to be ready to receive Jesus, whenever he comes.

Themes:

Calling forth the good each person possesses.

Being a tax collector, Zacchaeus is despised and shunned by his neighbors. But Jesus recognizes the good Zacchaeus possess that his neighbors do not see. Zacchaeus' life is transformed by Jesus' acceptance of him. Today's readings speak of God's acceptance of all men and women, whether Jew or Gentile, good or bad, rich or poor ("You spare all things because they are yours, O Lord and lover of souls" – first reading). Jesus calls us to reach out and accept one another in the same way. Loved by God, our Creator and Father, and redeemed by Jesus, every human being has much to give, if we enable them to give and their gifts to be accepted.

The 'imperishable spirit' within each one of us.

Every man, woman and child possesses a sacredness and dignity by virtue of being created by God. Today's readings speak of God's love for all ("You spare all things, because they are yours, O Lord and lover of souls, for your imperishable spirit is in all things") and God's unwavering determination to be reconciled with the creation God so lovingly fashioned ("The Son of Man has come to search out and save what was lost"). As Jesus affirms the honest Zacchaeus in the eyes of his distrusting neighbors, so we are called to affirm, in our own commitment to the Gospel to reconciliation and justice, that "imperishable spirit" alive within everyone as a son or daughter of God.

For reflection:

- Who are the Zacchaeuses who are shunned and hated by our world?
- Have you ever discovered a talent or ability in someone you never dreamed that person possessed? How did you bring it out? How did that person respond and change as a result?
- For centuries, philosophers have argued whether humanity is basically good or bad. What do you think?

32nd Sunday of the Year

Readings:
Luke 20: 27-38
2 Maccabees 7: 1-2, 9-14
2 Thessalonians 2: 16 – 3: 5

The Sadducees – the priests and governing class of Judaism at the time of Jesus – were very conservative in matters of religion. Unlike the Pharisees, they dismissed the oral tradition and any doctrinal developments not specified in the Pentateuch. They put no credence in the thousands of detailed regulations and ritualistic practices that the Pharisees embraced. They rejected the notion of angels or spirits, the belief in an afterlife and the idea of a messiah.

The hypothetical case that the Sadducees concoct, based on Moses' teaching on marriage, and pose to Jesus in today's **Gospel** is designed to ridicule the so-called "Messiah's" ludicrous teaching on the resurrection. Jesus, first, dismisses their attempt to understand the reign of God in human, worldly terms: the life of God transcends our understanding of human relationships and values. And second, using the Sadducees' own cherished Mosaic writings, Jesus reminds them that God spoke to Moses of Abraham, Isaac and Jacob in the present tense, as still being alive before him and not as long-dead memories. God is not the God of the dead but the God of the living; Christ comes with the promise of always living in God and with God.

Two hundred years before Jesus, the Syrians conquered Judah. Antichus IV, who assumed the Syrian throne around 167 B.C., was a great admirer of Greek culture and philosophy. Antichus embarked on the Hellenization of all his Jewish subjects, ordering the destruction of Jewish sanctuaries and scrolls, outlawing their sacrifices and rituals and establishing pagan altars and shrines to the god Zeus. Under the leadership of the Maccabees, the Jews revolted. The first book of Maccabees chronicles the persecution that took place; the second book is a theological reflection on the tragedy that resulted.

Today's **first reading** from the second book of Maccabees recounts the martyrdom of seven brothers who willingly accepted death rather than renounce the God of Israel. Their profession of faith is one of the first expressions of hope in individual resurrection and new life after death found in the First Testament.

Today's **second reading** is the second of three weekly readings on these final Sundays of the liturgical year from Paul's second letter to the Thessalonians. In today's passage, Paul offers a prayer that the fledgling church may persevere in hope, faithfulness and unity as they await the fulfillment of that hope in the Risen Christ.

Themes:

The God of life.

Our God is not a God of *death* – remoteness, vengeance, destruction – but a God of *life* – joy, hope, re-creation. The hypothetical situation that the Sadducees present to Jesus reflects a very limited understanding of God and his love for humanity. Such a narrow perspective attests to our tendency to see God as the end rather than the *beginning* of life, to squeeze and pry God into our image rather than to see ourselves as being made into God's image. To become "sons and daughters of the resurrection" we must embrace a vision of humankind that transcends social convention and spiritless legalities – the Gospel vision of love of neighbor as brothers and sisters in Christ, all of us children of God.

The ways of God versus the ways of the world.

We often try to gauge God by our standards, to measure God by our yardstick, to define God by our systems of reasoning and understanding; we have become so intent on controlling everything that God, the Giver of life itself, is exiled from our lives, called back only when things go wrong or we need some kind of divine endorsement or affirmation. But the God revealed by Jesus defies our explanations and designs. We are "alive for God" – not God for us. Our response to Jesus' call to be his disciples begins with opening our minds and spirits to become what God intends us to be. In calling us to be "sons and daughters of the resurrection," Jesus expands our narrow vision of God beyond the limits of our imagination, to realize the possibilities for forgiveness, reconciliation and compassion that are the life and love of the living God.

For reflection:

- In what ways does the God of "life" differ from our concept of the God of "death"?
- How has your idea of God changed over the years?
- How does our understanding of being "sons and daughters of the resurrection" affect our approach to the choices we make in life?

33rd Sunday of the Year

Readings:

Luke 21: 5-19
2 Thessalonians 3: 7-12
Malachi 3: 19-20

Many Jews believed that the end of the world would be signaled by the destruction of the great temple at Jerusalem. That is exactly what happened in the year 70 A.D., when, in a desperate siege of Jerusalem by the Romans, more than a million Jews were killed. It is against the background of these events that Luke writes his life of Jesus.

In today's **Gospel** reading, Jesus predicts the destruction of the temple and a chronicle of catastrophes. But Jesus does not teach dread here but hope. Trying to calculate the end of time is a waste of time; the signs of the apocalypse – war, plague, earthquakes – will appear in every age and there always will be self-proclaimed "messiahs" who will manipulate such events for their own power. Jesus assures his followers that those who remain faithful to the vocation of discipleship will have nothing to fear when the end comes.

The prophet Malachi ("my messenger") prophesies, in today's **first reading**, that the Day of the Lord will be a day of destruction for the evil but a day of victory for the poor, humble and just.

The church at Thessalonica has been thrown into disarray by rumors, falsely ascribed to Paul, that the Parousia is imminent. Some, as a result, have taken the attitude that, since the end of the world is so near, hard work is useless exertion. In today's **second reading**, the apostle implores the community to maintain its life of prayer and work together, for it is in such prayer and work for the common good that we fittingly prepare for Jesus' return – whenever that might be.

Themes:

The transcendence of time: 'It will all be torn down.'

Today's readings confront us with the sobering reality that God's Spirit of unconditional forgiveness and limitless love is often at odds with the values of the "real" world; the demands of discipleship frequently collide with the things we value, the dreams we hope for, the fears that intimidate us. The things we seek and value are, at best, temporary: there will come a day when "not one stone will be left upon another, but it will all be torn down." Jesus challenges us to make our life's choices based on a vision of the life of God that is to come.

God's presence in time of turmoil.

In life's most difficult crises and in the fear and despair of responding to those crises, God remains present to us in the goodness within ourselves and in the caring compassion offered by others. The "words" and "wisdom" of the Gospel – justice, humility, compassion, forgiveness – possess the timeless qualities of transformation and renewal. God assures us of his presence and healing if we do not allow ourselves to be walled up by hopelessness but, through "patient endurance," we remain open to the possibility of bringing forth justice, reconciliation and resurrection in every moment of life he gives us.

For reflection:

- Have you ever been overwhelmed by the hopelessness of a situation? How did you get through it?
- Has the Gospel of justice and humility ever put you in direct confrontation to a belief or attitude you had held for some time or a social convention you had always taken for granted?
- Have any recent experiences in your life made you especially aware that one day "it will all be torn down"?

Solemnity of Christ the King

Readings:

Luke 23: 35-43
2 Samuel 5: 1-3
Colossians 1: 12-20

Throughout his **Gospel**, Luke has portrayed Jesus as the humble, obedient servant of God. In the Resurrection, the poverty of such humility and selflessness will be exalted by God.

In Luke's account, Jesus steadfastly refused any demonstration of power for himself but manifested the power of God only for the faith and healing of the poor, the troubled, the lost and the rejected. Even while hanging on the cross (in an incident recorded only by Luke), Jesus only claims power to save the "good thief" who places his trust in him.

For Israel, David is the epitome of the true king, who unites the tribes of Israel and Judah under the providence of Yahweh (**first reading**).

For the new Israel, Christ is the perfect King and Mediator who reconciles "through the blood of his cross" all of creation to its Creator (**second reading**).

Themes:

Christ the King: Lord of our lives.

Our baptism into the life of Christ is a bold statement to the world: that the Jesus of the Gospel is our Master, our Ruler, the Lord of our lives, that we share his vision of the world and seek to fulfill the hope of his kingdom. To be a disciple of Christ demands a clear, conscious decision, not passive, rote compliance. To claim Christ as King means to make his vision of compassion and justice the measure of our integrity and the compass for our journey through this life to the life of the world to come.

Christ the King: the triumph of hope.

Luke's account of Jesus' crucifixion is a rather hopeless depiction: Jesus, the generous teacher and the loving healer, is hung on a tree like a common criminal; he is the object of scorn and derision by the very people he came to serve and save. Only one of the two criminals, condemned to hang with Jesus, realizes the injustice of this tragedy. The criminal comes to terms with his own guilt and seeks reconciliation with God. In his last breaths, Jesus welcomes him into eternity. The way of the cross begins with confronting our own sinfulness and accepting responsibility for the wrong we do; God enters upon his reign when we begin to transform our lives from injustice to justice, from estrangement to forgiveness, from bigotry to community, from hatred to love.

For reflection:

- Have you ever realized your own need for conversion in recognizing the goodness of another?
- Throughout this past liturgical year, we have heard the Jesus of Luke's Gospel call us to be "servant-disciples" of humility and compassion. How does Luke's account of the crucifixion bring that theme to a climax?
- In what ways is the title of this Sunday's solemnity a statement of faith?
- This Sunday and next Sunday (the First Sunday of Advent) speak of "last things." What do Christians mean by "last things"?